Dancing Śiva has become a popular symbol in the West for Hinduism and Eastern mysticism. This book gives a detailed account of Śiva's Dance of Bliss by explicating a Sanskrit poem written in the fourteenth century by Umāpati Śivācārya, Śaiva theologian and temple priest. The bronze image of the King of Dancers, the God's temple in Cidambaram, South India, and its priests are all viewed in the light of the poem. Umāpati's Śaiva theology is discussed in relation to his life, and also in relation to Vedānta and yoga. The iconography and mythology of the Goddess and of other forms of Śiva provide necessary perspective. Art from Cidambaram and neighbouring sites illuminates the text.

CAMBRIDGE STUDIES IN RELIGIOUS TRADITIONS 7

THE DANCE OF ŚIVA

CAMBRIDGE STUDIES IN RELIGIOUS TRADITIONS

Edited by John Clayton (University of Lancaster), Steven Collins (University of Chicago) and Nicholas de Lange (University of Cambridge)

1. *Religion and the individual: A Jewish perspective*
   Louis Jacobs
2. *The body divine: The symbol of the body in the works of Teilhard de Chardin and Rāmānuja*
   Anne-Hunt Overzee
3. *The feminine principle in the Sikh vision of the Transcendent*
   Nikky-Guninder Kaur Singh
4. *The religious culture of India: Power, love and wisdom*
   Friedhelm Hardy
5. *Women under the Bō tree: Buddhist nuns in Sri Lanka*
   Tessa Bartholomeusz
6. *Evil and suffering in Jewish philosophy*
   Oliver Leaman
7. *The dance of Śiva: Religion, art and poetry in South India*
   David Smith

THE DANCE OF ŚIVA

Religion, art and poetry in South India

DAVID SMITH

Department of Religious Studies, Lancaster University

CAMBRIDGE
UNIVERSITY PRESS

Published by the Press Syndicate of the University of Cambridge
The Pitt Building, Trumpington Street, Cambridge CB2 1RP
40 West 20th Street, New York, NY 10011-4211, USA
10 Stamford Road, Oakleigh, Melbourne 3166, Australia

First published 1996

Printed in Great Britain at
Woolnough Bookbinders Ltd, Irthlingborough, Northants

A catalogue record for this book is available from the British Library

Library of Congress cataloguing in publication data

Smith, David James, 1944–
The Dance of Śiva: Religion, art and poetry in South India/David Smith.
p. cm. – (Cambridge studies in religious traditions; 7)
Includes bibliographical references and index.
ISBN 0 521 48234 8 (hardback)
1. Śiva (Hindu deity) 2. Umāpati Civācāriyār, 14th cent.
3. Nataraja Temple. I. Title. II. Series.
BL1218.S62 1996
294.5'513'095482–dc20 95–35644 CIP

ISBN 0 521 48234 8 hardback

namo gurubhyaḥ

For my parents

Contents

Illustrations

PLATES

FIGURE

Acknowledgements

I am grateful to Steve Collins, Friedhelm Hardy, Don Heald, Françoise L'Hernault, Alexis Sanderson, and David Shulman for reading part or all of the book, and for their valuable comments (the errors that remain being entirely my own); to the Lancaster University Research Committee for two grants for research trips to Cidambaram; to my colleagues in the Department of Religious Studies and the Centre for the Study of Cultural Values at Lancaster for stimulating environments; to my students at Lancaster for their enthusiasm; to John Loud, for permission to quote from his unpublished translation of the *Kōyil Purāṇam*, and for sending otherwise unobtainable texts; to Vivek Nanda, for many enjoyable discussions about Cidambaram; to S. R. Balasubramania Chethiar for the gift of books and encouragement; to C. N. Singaravelu for an illuminating discussion on the Tamil Śaiva Siddhānta; to S. Srinavasa Sarma for transcription of texts; to R. Nagaswamy for permission to use his photographs; to the French Institute of Pondicherry/École Française d'Extrême-Orient for permission to use photographs from its collection; to James Harle for permission to use his photograph of Bhadrakālī on the West *gopura*, an image currently guarded by a large cobra; to Anna Dallapiccola for the loan of journals; to Hermann Kulke for sending me a transcript of part of the *Dakṣa Khaṇḍa*; to Paul and Anna-Marie Heelas for hospitality in Madras; to Friedhelm Hardy for translating passages from the Tamil, and for many years of encouragement; to several learned Dīkṣitas in Cidambaram, for advice, gifts of books, and inspiration.

Introduction

NAṬARĀJA, THE KING OF DANCERS

Dancing Śiva is the form of the Hindu god Śiva best known in the West, and indeed seems to be the most popular visual representation of Hinduism for the modern world. Although there is a wide variety of Dancing Śivas, dating back to at least the fifth century AD, what has become so familiar to us is one particular form, known as Naṭarāja, 'King of Dancers'. This image achieved canonical form in Cōḻa bronzes of the tenth century AD and then continued to be reproduced in metal, stone, and other substances up to the present. The Cōḻa Naṭarāja is often said to be the supreme statement of Hindu art.

Naṭarāja dances, his right foot supported by a crouching figure, his left foot elegantly raised. Of his four arms, one swings downwards, pointing to the raised foot; another with palm held up signals, 'Do not fear!' In his other hands he holds aloft a drum and a flame. The river Gaṅgā sits in his hair. A cobra uncoils from his lower right forearm, and the crescent moon and a skull are on his crest. He dances within an arch of flames. This dance is called the Dance of Bliss (*ānandatāṇḍava*).[1]

This dance is said to have been first performed in Cidambaram, 244 km south of Madras, on the east coast of India. Historically, Cidambaram has been a centre for the worship of Dancing Śiva since the seventh century, and for the worship of the Dance of Bliss since its origination 300 years later. For worshippers of Śiva (*Śaivas*) the Dance of Bliss is eternal, having neither beginning nor end; and for many of them the Cidambaram temple is the most important of all Śiva temples. For Southern Śaivas, it is simply *kōyil – the* temple. All other Śiva temples have a Naṭarāja shrine, or at least a Naṭarāja image, beside the main *liṅga* shrine.

The theology of Naṭarāja is as follows. Naṭarāja is Lord of the Universe. His dance expresses the state of bliss which he enjoys and embodies. He dwells in the heart of every person, and though he is to be found throughout the universe his complete form is uniquely present in Cidambaram. Cidambaram is the heart of the world. Naṭarāja is always accompanied by his consort, whose name in Cidambaram is Śivakāmasundarī. She herself is his knowledge, his desire, his action. She embodies the compassion he feels for the world. Naṭarāja's left foot is raised in dance so that worshippers may bow down before it. He grants all wishes. The sight of Naṭarāja in Cidambaram is a great blessing, and worship of him frees one from rebirth.

Naṭarāja, Śiva as the king of dancers, did not become known in the West until the beginning of the twentieth century. In 1912 this form of Śiva received detailed treatment in an eloquent essay by A. K. Coomaraswamy entitled 'The Dance of Śiva'. The essay has been constantly cited, often in its entirety, in treatments of the Dance of Śiva. Its conclusion is quoted most frequently:

> How supremely great in power and grace this dancing image must appear to all those who have striven in plastic forms to give expression to their intuition of Life! . . . No artist of today, however great, could more exactly or more wisely create an image of that Energy which science must postulate behind all phenomena . . . Nature is inert, and cannot dance until Śiva wills it. He rises from His rapture, and dancing sends through inert matter pulsing waves of awakening sound, and lo! matter also dances appearing as a glory round about Him. Dancing, He sustains its manifold phenomena. In the fullness of time, still dancing, he destroys all forms and names by fire and gives new rest. This is poetry; but none the less, science.[2]

Coomaraswamy's training as a scientist along with his scholarly attainments enabled him to make a statement that has reverberated through the twentieth century. In 1976 Fritjof Capra in a popular combination of modern physics and Eastern mysticism gave a boost to Coomaraswamy's view.

> The dance of Siva *is the dancing universe*; the ceaseless flow of energy going through an infinite variety of patterns that melt into one another.
>
> Modern physics has . . . revealed that every subatomic particle not only performs an energy dance but also is an energy dance; a pulsating process of creation and destruction . . . For the modern physicists, then, Siva's dance is the dance of subatomic matter. As in Hindu mythology, it is a continual dance of creation and destruction involving the whole cosmos; the basis of all existence and of all natural phenomena. Hundreds of years ago, Indian artists created visual images of dancing Sivas in a beautiful series of bronzes. In our time, physicists have used the most advanced technology to portray the patterns of the cosmic dance. The bubble-chamber photographs of interacting particles, which bear testimony to the continual rhythm of creation and destruction in the

universe, are visual images of the dance of Siva equalling those of the Indian artists in beauty and profound significance.

The metaphor of the cosmic dance thus unifies ancient mythology, religious art, and modern physics.[3]

While Naṭarāja appeals to the modern world through the dynamic harmony of his image, he is at the same time redolent of an elemental primitivism with his skull, snake, and the tigerskin that is usually draped around his waist. The Sanskrit scholar Ingalls remarked,

More than one element of Śiva's iconography shows traces of a primitive and probably non-Aryan origin. The matted . . . hair, . . . the ornaments of skulls and snakes, as also the wild dance in which the god is often pictured, recall the costume and practice of a tribal shaman.[4]

One notable writer on dance, Beryl de Zoete, felt unable to explain this transformation of Śiva. In her study of dance in South India, *The Other Mind*, she wrote,

How and when Śiva, the pre-Aryan deity who is associated with such savage rites and sacrifices among the primitive tribes and devil-fearing castes of South India, became the mystic dancer, the ultimate embodiment of rhythm in the visible universe of created things and in the invisible universe of the human soul, we have no means of knowing.[5]

The present book deals neither with possible scientific connotations for Naṭarāja, nor with the early development of the image, though these topics are each worthy of a book in their own right. With regard to origins, however, it is surely true that the final image gains power from the obvious presence of primitive elements. The wild shaman dressed in skins goes back a very long way in human history. In Naṭarāja the state of possession enjoyed by such figures is transmuted into the inwardly concentrated, enstatic, bliss of the Upaniṣads, though the creature beneath his feet often writhes like a subhuman ecstatic.[6] Again, in Naṭarāja the uncoordinated prancing of the possessed shaman is transmuted into the perfect mastery of movement formulated in classical dance over a long period, and defined in a very extensive literature.

For hundreds of years prior to the Cōḻa bronzes Śiva was famous as a dancer, referred to as such in the *Mahābhārata*; and a wide variety of images so portrayed him. No attempt will be made here to chart the line of development of sculpture that led up to Naṭarāja, for those experimental variants were not continued once the perfect form had been achieved. The history of the literature of Dancing Śiva is more significant, in that the Tamil poets who worshipped earlier forms of dancing Śiva remain of great importance, their songs available today all over Tamilnadu on audio cassettes, and sung daily in the temples of Śiva. They will be referred to, but are not the substance of this study.

Our subject is Naṭarāja's Dance of Bliss in Cidambaram, and this comprises three elements, which all appear in place at the same time: the Naṭarāja bronze, the Ānanda Tāṇḍava, and the historical buildings of the Cidambaram temple. The earlier Tamil poets just mentioned often sang of Śiva dancing in Cidambaram, but this was an eight-armed Śiva dancing in the burning ground. No buildings in Cidambaram are earlier than the tenth or eleventh centuries; nor are there any pre-Cōḻa inscriptions. The Dance of Bliss, the Ānanda Tāṇḍava, is not mentioned before the *Cidambara Māhātmya.*

What follows is an attempt to present the essentials of that Dance by concentrating on the perspective of one uniquely placed individual, Umāpati Śivācārya of Cidambaram, who flourished at the beginning of the fourteenth century. Umāpati wrote a poem in Sanskrit dedicated to the foot that Dancing Śiva lifts up for the adoration of his devotees. This poem describes the temple of Cidambaram, and gives a picture of the Śaiva universe, of the Naṭarāja universe. Umāpati was both a priest in the temple and a major figure in the history of Śaiva Siddhānta. The poetic idiom he uses is difficult for the modern reader, and requires explanation; but at the same time it is a natural, if not *the* natural, language for Hinduism. The use of this very rich and important poem, virtually unknown outside Cidambaram, provides authenticity for the present study. In addition, constant reference is made both to other relevant texts, Sanskrit and Tamil, and to sculpture and painting, all from roughly the same period. While centring on Umāpati's poem in a manner that is analogous to Umāpati's centring on Naṭarāja's raised foot, each chapter considers a different angle of the topic, often using new and unpublished material.

Chapter 1 of this book discusses the Naṭarāja bronze itself, and the following chapter analyses the myths and legends of Cidambaram. Of key importance is the great temple of Cidambaram. It is in this temple that the bronze image of Naṭarāja takes pride of place, displacing from central importance the *liṅga* that is the holy of holies in every other Śiva temple. Here in the Hall of Consciousness, the Cit Sabhā, is installed the holiest of Naṭarājas.

The temple of the Lord of the Hall, Sabhānāyaka temple, which is its official title, covers a vast area, some 16 hectares, where three rectangular courtyards within a walled garden area, one inside the other, surround the centre. Four mighty gateways, *gopuras*, guard the outer entrances.

Although the temple was referred to and visited by the saint-singers of the seventh to the ninth centuries, no building in the temple goes back beyond the eleventh century. The *gopuras* belong to the twelfth and thirteenth centuries.

The Cidambaram temple is discussed in detail in chapters 3 and 4, but it would be helpful for its basic structure to be grasped from the outset. In the innermost courtyard stands the Cit Sabhā ('Hall of Consciousness') where Naṭarāja is housed. Immediately in front of this hall is another hall, the Kanaka Sabhā ('Golden Hall'), where rituals of worship are performed. A shrine to Viṣṇu is also present in this courtyard. This innermost courtyard is contained within another, where is found the temple's *liṅga* shrine. The third courtyard within which this second one is placed is gigantic, and has the immense *gopuras* as its gateways; it contains a variety of shrines and halls, and the temple tank. All this area is within a yet larger walled area taken up by gardens. The four roads beyond the temple are called Car Streets, North Car Street, East Car Street, and so on, their title coming from the fact that the festival cars progress through them. In the subsequent chapter on the Hall of Consciousness, the Cit Sabhā, central in the book just as it is in the temple, there is given what perhaps is the most detailed account yet published of this shrine.

The priests of Cidambaram, members of a hereditary group, devote themselves to the service of Naṭarāja and act as intermediaries between the God and his worshippers. Claiming a Northern origin, and different in feature from Tamilians, the priests in their gleaming white dhotis and long hair swept to one side are prominent in the centre of the city. Their historical role is discussed in chapter 3 and also in chapter 5, where Umāpati's career is considered.

Just as the inherent coherence of the image of Naṭarāja later led Coomaraswamy to attribute a scientific comprehension to its creators, so too it had earlier led the philosophers of the Śaiva Siddhānta school to connect their thought with it. The five actions (*pañcakṛtya*) of Śiva discerned by this system – creation, preservation, destruction, concealment, and grace – all came in time to be seen as expressed by Naṭarāja. Much work has been done on this school of philosophy briefly referred to by Coomaraswamy in his essay on the Dance of Śiva, though there remains a gulf between scholars working on Tamil texts, and those working on Sanskrit sources. It is now clear that the Śaiva Siddhānta school, often assumed by South Indians to be entirely South Indian in origin, was prevalent throughout much of India in the eighth to the tenth centuries, was refined and developed in Kashmir during the same period; and was

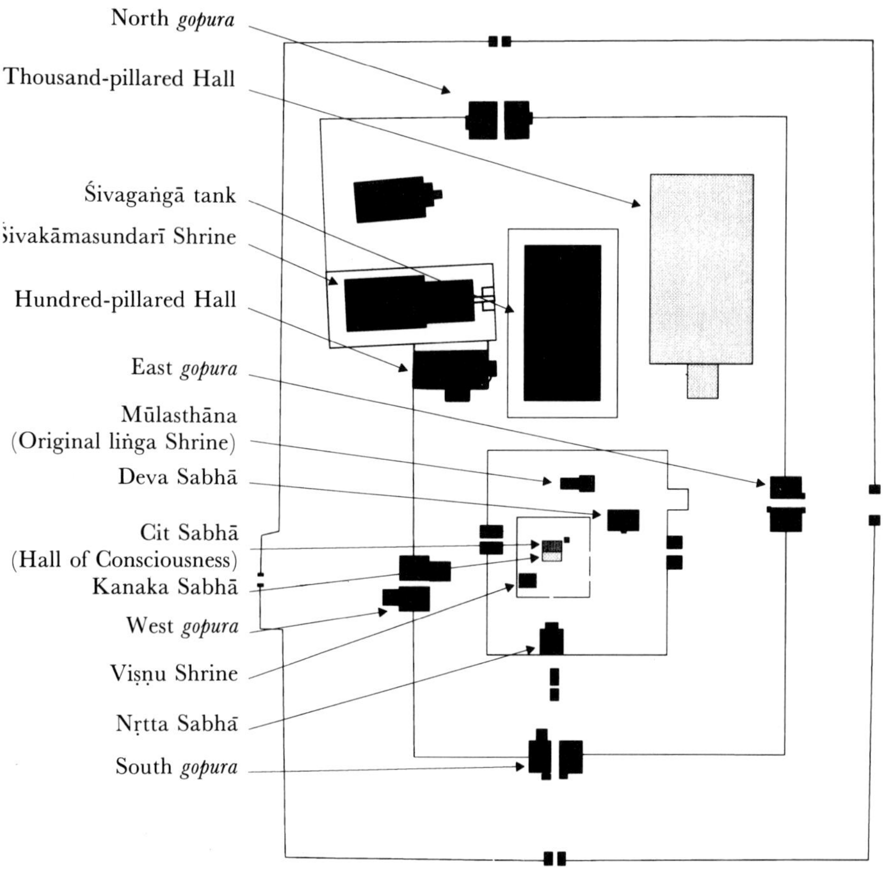

Fig. 1. Plan of Sabhānāyaka temple, Cidambaram. Principal features.

preserved and then altered in Tamilnadu. Chapter 5 considers the connections of Śaiva Siddhānta with the Dance, and also the growing influence of Vedānta.

Perhaps now outweighing Naṭarāja in the current Western appreciation of Hinduism is the Goddess, widely known in the form of Kālī. Both the mild and the fierce forms of the Goddess are of great importance in the worship of Naṭarāja in Cidambaram. Pārvatī, or, as she is called in Cidambaram, Śivakāmasundarī, 'Śiva's lovely beloved', stands beside Śiva as a bronze image in the Hall of Consciousness; she also has her own shrine within the temple precincts. As Kālī, she has her temple on the northern outskirts of the town, where pilgrims to Cidambaram complete their visit by worshipping her. Every Naṭarāja bronze should be complemented by a Śivakāmasundarī, and each pair is usually made by the same craftsman. Chapter 6 is devoted to the Goddess.

While Naṭarāja is, in the words of Coomaraswamy 'the clearest representation in any religion of the activity of God', he is of course only one aspect of the history of Mahādeva, the great God Śiva. Closely related to Naṭarāja are two other forms of Śiva, Śiva the wandering beggar, and Śiva the Terrible, Bhairava. Appreciation of these two forms is vital to a proper understanding of Naṭarāja. In the Southern version of Śaiva myth, it is the handsome wandering beggar who turns into the dancer, while in the North the terrifying Bhairava performs the dance, which is there always destructive. The other great Hindu God, Viṣṇu, is a kingly figure, modelled on a human king. The manifold nature of this God is expressed by his *avatāras*, themselves each essentially royal. This is true even of the cowherd Kṛṣṇa. In contrast to Viṣṇu, Śiva achieves multiplicity by the variety of roles he undertakes while maintaining the appearance of a wandering holy man.

While Hinduism now has to do without the king who is called for in so much of its ritual, the wandering ascetic remains a striking feature of the landscape, and scantily clad or naked figures with only a begging bowl and a staff or trident to their name are to be found in their thousands attending major religious events. Some men continue to make their home in the burning grounds, and maintain the tantric rituals which often verge on black magic. All the varieties of homeless wanderers have their apotheosis in Śiva, who always bears the long matted locks that are the badge of the free spirit. What must be stressed is the power of the wandering religious specialist to inspire fear and even terror, qualities to be found in the highest degree in his exemplar, Śiva. A characteristic of Cōḻa art, however, is its modification of the wandering beggar to bring out a compassionate beauty in this form of Śiva. Chapters 7 and 8 deal with Śiva as the Beggar and the Terrible.

There remains the human element. The Śaiva saints cannot be omitted: several are associated with Cidambaram, and the worship of all their images forms an integral part of the life of every Śiva temple in Tamilnadu. The most prominent human figures in the iconography of Cidambaram, as in many temples, are the stone carvings of dancing girls, who until this century were in the flesh key figures in the worship of the deity. The role of the male dancer seems to have been that of teacher of the dancing girls, and it might be thought that there is something essentially feminine about the dance for Hinduism. After all, another major form of Śiva is that of the half man, half woman, Ardhanārīśvara.

Śiva is inherently ambiguous. Half human, half divine are the *gaṇas* who accompany Śiva and often dance with him. Chapter 9 concludes with a consideration of Apasmāra and trance.

The final chapter considers the form of Umāpati's poem and his own understanding of that form. The reading of Śaivism that is made in this book is centred on Umāpati's view of Śiva, and the last words are Umāpati's.

PRINCIPAL TEXTUAL SOURCES

The primary source is *The Hymn of Praise to [Naṭarāja's] Curved Foot*, the *Kuñcitāṅghristava* of Umāpati Śivācārya. Written around 1300 AD, this Sanskrit poem of 313 verses is particularly wide ranging. The poem was known only to the priests of Cidambaram until it was printed for the first time in 1958. It was edited with a Tamil translation and notes by K. M. Rājagaṇeśa Dīkṣita. I am preparing for publication an edition of the text, with English translation and notes. The present study includes everything from the poem relevant to the Dance of Śiva.

Centred on Naṭarāja's upraised foot that grants salvation, the poem is an amalgam of philosophy, mythology, art, architecture, and ritual from a Śaiva viewpoint. Embedded in a particular place, Cidambaram in South India, and time, the fourteenth century, the poem describes the eternal dance in the heart of the world.

The best analogy for the form of Umāpati's poem is the necklace, for each verse is an individual jewel, designedly separate from those on either side. The deliberate avoidance of logical order makes the poem difficult to read for those not versed in its subject-matter.

The refrain of the poem, the conclusion to each verse, is

> *kuñcitāṅghriṃ bhaje*
> I worship Him Whose foot is curved.

The word *kuñcita*, 'curved' is a technical term for the dance step wherein the heel is raised, the toes bent down, and the middle of the foot curved.[7]

The oldest sources for the life of Umāpati are the two Sanskrit texts published in the preface to his *Bhāṣya* on the *Pauṣkarāgama*. One is the *Pārthavana Māhātmya*, in 240 *śloka*s, which claims to be the fortieth conversation between a certain Brahmānanda and his pupil Śaṅkara, in a work otherwise unknown called the *Cidambarasāra*. The site of Umāpati's *āśrama* was where Śiva, satisfied by Arjuna's penance, is said to have given him the Pāśupata weapon – the grove of Pārtha, Pārtha being a patronym of Arjuna. The other work is the *Rājendrapura Māhātmya*, by Śivānandanātha Dīkṣita, in 108 verses. Rājendrapura, 'Emperor Town', is another name for the site of Umāpati's *āśrama*, so called presumably because Vīra Cōḻa built a *maṭha* there.[8]

The earliest Sanskrit text to refer to the dance of Śiva in Cidambaram is the tenth-century *Sūta Saṃhitā*, but the first and fullest account of the Dance of Bliss is given in the twelfth-century *Cidambara Māhātyma*, the subject of a detailed study by Hermann Kulke.[9]

Clearly later than the *Cidambara Māhātmya*, but otherwise indeterminate in date, are four other Sanskrit *sthalapurāṇas*: *Vyāghrapura Māhātmya*, *Hemasabhānātha Māhātmya*, *Tilvavana Māhātmya*, and *Puṇḍarīkapura Māhātmya*. Of these, only the *Puṇḍarīkapura Māhātmya* has been published. Much of the *Vyāghrapura Māhātmya* derives from the *Sūta Saṃhitā*, but it also devotes a chapter to the dance competition between Śiva and Kālī.

A Tamil version of the *Cidambara Māhātmya*, the *Kōyil Purāṇam*, is attributed to Umāpati Śivācārya. Apart from omissions, it follows the Sanskrit very closely. It has been translated into English by John Loud.

Two other Sanskrit texts are often referred to in this book. These are the priests' manual for daily worship, the *Patañjalipūjāsūtra*, and their Festival Ritual manual, the *Citsabheśvarotsavasūtra*; both these texts are attributed to Patañjali.

CHAPTER I

The Naṭarāja bronze

The metal image, the Dancing God defined in iconography and expressed in bronze, is at the heart of the poem. The image in the temple was seen every day by the poet and his readers, and was meditated on every day by them in their homes. Not only does the bronze illustrate the iconography, it is the visual and literal embodiment of the highest divinity.

The essential feature of bronze and other metal images in the Hindu temple is that they are mobile images, made specifically as processional images. The base of such an image has holes for passing through carrying poles, or lugs so that restraining ropes can be attached. Yet most of the time a mobile image is stationary, waiting near or beside the fixed stone images in the sanctum, the *garbhagṛha.* Only in Cidambaram is the *mūlamūrti*, the holy of holies, mobile, carried out in festivals, and moved from one part of the sanctum to another, from the Cit Sabhā to the Kanaka Sabhā. Within the poem this image is constantly present, for Naṭarāja's upraised foot is referred to in every verse. Each verse refers also to Naṭarāja or other forms of Śiva, or other gods in relation to Śiva, so that each verse enshrines images, is a shrine, the reader moving from shrine to shrine as verse follows verse. The reader proceeds through the temple of the poem, and Naṭarāja is present at every step.

Naṭarāja imaged in bronze and housed in the Cit Sabhā in Cidambaram was the centre of the world of Umāpati the poet. Its holiness forbids it being photographed. Plate 1 is from a painting of the Cit Sabhā by one of the Dīkṣitas. According to the late Douglas Barrett, the foremost Western expert on Cōḻa bronzes, the present bronze is, 'to judge from available information, not earlier than the thirteenth century AD'.[1] The present bronze was taken by Sivaramamurti as the representative of a type, 'the Chidambaram', wherein only two or three locks are slightly raised above the shoulders; the remainder still hanging down, since the dance is in its earlier stages.

Valuable information concerning this bronze's predecessor is provided

1. Naṭarāja in the Cit Sabhā. Detail from painting by G. Parameśvara Dīkṣita. Courtesy: G. Parameśvara Dīkṣita.

by the Cōḻa paintings in the circumambulatory of the *garbhagṛha* in the great temple of Rājareśvara at Tanjavur. One painting shows the Cōḻa emperor worshipping at the Cit Sabhā.[2] Barrett distinguishes three basic types of Naṭarāja, and takes the view that the type shown in the Cōḻa painting is different from that of the present bronze:

> the one piece of evidence which might be expected to establish the type of the image in the early eleventh century AD, the paintings in the Rājarājeśvara temple at Tanjavur showing the Naṭarāja in the Kanakasabhā [the Cit Sabhā] – seems to depict an image closer to Type II [with outward streaming locks] than Type III [with the gentle undulation of one to four fairly short braids on or above the shoulders], with very long locks flying high above the shoulders.[3]

Photographs of the painting, however, do not seem to fit Barrett's description: two strands rise above each shoulder, but the majority of strands are lower, with three or four visible beneath the upper arms.[4]

There is no direct and unique connection between the Naṭarāja of the poem and the Naṭarāja (or type of Naṭarāja) now in the Cit Sabhā other than the presence of two musicians on the bronze and the number of flames on the encircling arch, the *prabhāvali* – twenty-one.[5] The references to the form alone of Naṭarāja are relatively few; seen several times a day by the poet and the readers he wrote for, and meditated upon by them, the form was more than sufficiently vivid for them.

Let us begin our examination of Umāpati's presentation with this most striking aspect, the streaming matted locks.

> When He playfully began His dance
> there proceeded from His twisted locks of hair
> as they beat against each other with increasing speed
> the water of the Heavenly River breaking into spray;
>
> wherever the spray drops fell
> became an eminent place of pilgrimage
> and they turned into selfborn *liṅga*s;
>
> that God who is surrounded
> by Nandikeśa and other Pramathas and Gaṇas,
> Whose foot is bent, I worship. (111)[6]

Centring on the dance of Lord Śiva, the poet divagates widely, his imagination flying out in many directions like the strands of Śiva's hair. The structure of the poem itself is analogous to the scene. As is well expressed in this verse, Naṭarāja is the centre and cause of all other religious phenomena as far as the whole poem is concerned. Śiva is at the

2. Detail of Naṭarāja. Vedaranyam, *c.* 1200.

centre of a universe modulated by and around Naṭarāja, and the poetry moves discursively from theme to theme, pivoting on the foot with which each verse concludes.

At all other Śiva temples the *liṅga* is the central shrine.[7] The Naṭarāja image in the Cit Sabhā is unique in its centrality. There are many *liṅgas*, and for the Śaiva the map of India is a map of *liṅgas*. Those that occur naturally are called 'selfborn' (*svayaṃbhū*).

Each drop of water when it lands becomes a *liṅga*. Thus are explained the multiplicity of *liṅgas* and their divine origin, but above all the centrality and priority of Naṭarāja are established.

A watery origin for *liṅgas* is less surprising than might be thought. Not all *liṅgas* in temples are of stone. Umāpati refers elsewhere to the famous five *liṅgas* in each of the five elements, a group which goes back at least to the *Sūta Saṃhitā*; and of these one is said to be formed of water, that at the Jambukeśvara temple outside Trichy.[8]

There is considerable variation in the portrayal of Naṭarāja's hair in the case of bronzes, for this most noticeable feature is where the individual artist is most free to improvise. Barrett's basic threefold division of types could be greatly extended. But within the creative profusion of hairstyles, a certain order is always maintained. In art, the strands of hair are invariably separated, and the divisions often marked and maintained by flowers. The frenzy of the human dancer, the gyrations which throw the hair first to one side of the face and then to the other, are entirely avoided. The rhythmic order of the hair forms frozen waves which are a safe haven for Gaṅgā, who is usually a mermaid on Śiva's right, gazing at the God with hands clasped in *añjali*.

> the hoods of the snakes that form His ear-rings
> are spread wide to kindly catch
> the moon in His crest
>
> while the excellent forest of His hair
> is parting to allow passage
> for the surging Gaṅgā;
>
> Him Whose foot is curved
> I worship. (163)[9]

A few verses spell out the form of Naṭarāja, such as verse 108:

> He bears the fire and the drum in two hands.
> The other two hands
> make the 'swinging' and the 'fear not' gestures.

Placing His right foot ever on Apasmāra,
with His left foot slightly bending
He ever gives everything to those who bow down –

He performs His dance in the Hall accompanied by Devī.
Him, Whose foot is curved,
I worship. (108)[10]

Here are the essential features of the classic form, every limb of significance. However, the opening phrase was left out from the translation – 'His form is sung in the Vedānta' (*vedāntodgītarūpaṃ*). These same limbs are identified with the formless Brahman of the *Upaniṣads*. One of Umāpati's notable theological positions is the conflation of the Vedānta and the Śaiva Siddhānta; this will be discussed in chapter 5 which reviews his thought in detail. Here we shall restrict ourselves to marvelling at the boldness of the poet's claim, for Naṭarāja's form is nowhere sung of in the *Upaniṣads*.

Apasmāra is generally said to be the demon of ignorance. However, he is referred to only a few times in the *Tēvāram*, and it is likely that he was in origin simply a pedestal figure, such as is found under the foot of other images of Śiva.[11] To be under Śiva's foot was a highly desirable condition. The very name for a Śaiva devotee in Tamil, *aṭiyāṉ*, 'servant', means literally 'one who is at the feet'.

Putting the three lines of ash on His forehead,
the hooded snake on His throat,
and the demon as the pedestal for His foot,
and holding fire and the *ḍhakkā* drum in His hands,
and sun, moon, and fire on His lotus face,

the host of gods and worlds
in the radiance called OṂ,
with the musician on each side,

He performs the Dance of Bliss in His own hall,
Him Whose foot is curved, I worship. (93)[12]

He gives Dharma to people
by the beat of His *ḍamaruka* drum,
Wealth by the fire He holds,
Love with the gesture of freedom from fear,
and the goal of man that is Mokṣa
with His lotus foot.

In so doing He, the Lord of Dancers,
the performer in the Hall of Consciousness,
looks after all people.

3. Naṭarāja. Vikrama Kulottuṅga period, *c.* 1150.
Courtesy: Dr R. Nagaswamy.

That God – embodied in dance,
His actions like no one else's –
Whose foot is curved,
I worship. (104)[13]

This connection of the four goals of man with the form of Naṭarāja is not found elsewhere, so far as I know. The role of the drum and the upraised foot are as usual, but the other two verge on the adventitious. One might have supposed the fire to represent Love (*kāma*), and the 'Do not fear' hand to assure the general stability necessary for wealth creation (*artha*). However, Love (*kāma*) in the Hindu tradition means above all sexual pleasure, and though of course fire is a very apt symbol for this, yet with the multiple mirroring of the hand's flame in the circle within which Śiva stands an inappropriate sensuality would have been suggested.

Umāpati does not refer to the now well-known correlation between Naṭarāja and the fivefold activities of God according to the Śaiva Siddhānta. This correlation is clearly set out by Coomaraswamy:

The dance, in fact, represents His five activities (*pañcakṛtya*), viz., *sṛṣṭi* (overlooking, creation, evolution), *sthiti* (preservation, support), *saṃhāra* (destruction, evolution), *tirobhāva* (veiling, embodiment, illusion, and also, giving rest), *anugraha* (release, salvation, grace). These, separately considered, are the activities of the deities Brahmā, Viṣṇu, Rudra, Maheśvara and Sadāśiva. This cosmic activity is the central motif of the dance.[14]

Coomaraswamy then quotes from three Tamil sources – the *Uṇmaiviḷakkam*, the *Citampara Mummaṇi Kōvai*, and the *Tirumantiram*. The earliest, and most important of these, is the *Tirumantiram*. The *Uṇmaiviḷakkam*, 'The Explanation of Truth', is a manual for the instruction of young Śaivas,[15] written by Maṉavācakam Kaṭantār, like Umāpati's teacher Maṟaiñāṉa a disciple of Meykaṇṭar, in 1255/6. The *Citampara Mummaṇi Kōvai* of Kumarakuruparar is a late (seventeenth century) hymn of praise that need not concern us. Tirumūlar's *Tirumantiram* is a work of the very greatest importance, on which very little has been written, and whose dating is uncertain, though it is clearly earlier than Umāpati.[16]

Coomaraswamy does not quote the apposite and earliest statement of identity between the five acts (*pañcakṛtya*) of Śiva and the limbs of Naṭarāja, which is *Tirumantiram* 2799:

Hara's drum is creation,
Hara's hand gesturing protection is preservation;
Hara's fire is dissolution;
Hara's foot planted down is concealment
Hara's foot, raised in dance, is grace abiding.[17]

Umāpati does refer to the five acts and relates them to the dance without connecting them to the pose:

> In the beginning He Whose form is the self
> created Brahmā for the creation of the worlds,
> Hari for their protection,
> and the form of Rudra for their destruction,
>
> and then Maheśa for concealing everything,
> the form of Sadāśiva with Pārvatī beside Him
>
> to show favour to those worlds.
> He performs the Dance of Bliss in the Hall.
> Him, His foot curved,
> I worship. (102)[18]

Whether or not Umāpati's failure to refer to this identification is surprising is not easy to say. I do not know of other early (pre-Umāpati) texts that make the identification, and it may be that Coomaraswamy's reference to it has given it undue prominence for modern writers.

Umāpati again identifies the goals of man with the limbs:

> Placing one lotus foot, the right one,
> on the demon (*bhūta*),
>
> raising up a little and bending sideways
> His left foot, shining with its tinkling anklet,
> with the letters *dha* and *na* written on it,
> worshipped by the celestials
> with Brahmā the Ordainer at their head,
>
> to give His worshippers what they desire –
> Dharma and the other ends of man –
>
> He performs the Dance of Bliss.
> Him Who grants boons,
> Whose foot is curved,
> I worship. (70)[19]

At first sight the compound *dhanalipi* looks like 'money writing' and hence 'postal order' or 'cheque'; such documents from devotees home or abroad play an important part in the economy of the Dīkṣitas. In fact *dhanalipi* means 'the writing of *dha* and *na*', and refers to the mental creation of the image of Śiva in the Ātmārthapūjā, where the worshipper, holding a piece of *darbha* grass, writes particular letters on the imagined form of the God.[20] This raises the whole question of the relation of such poetry's visualizations and those of the ritual texts. The mind of a person versed in ritual, as were Umāpati and many of his readers, was powerfully exercised in the calling up of images in strictly defined order, and in considerable numbers. The reading of the verses of a poem such as the *Kuñcitāṅghristava* is partly an analogous procedure, but one freed from the determinism of ritual, the iron logic of repeated variations of formula mantras. There is indeed what can only be described as a holiday atmosphere about *kāvya* that is very hard for the Western reader to sense. The poet devotes several verses to ritual because he wants to paint a complete picture, but here the reference to the ritual which, while a temple priest, he would have performed every day in his own home before setting out for the Cit Sabhā, slips in inadvertently, it seems to me.

The two musicians referred to above in verse 93 are named in two other verses. They are accretions to the form of the bronze. Although such figures are readily shown in attendance in sculpture, the Cōḻa bronze is essentially a single figure in isolation, closely modelled on the human individual, although a divinity.[21] But Naṭarāja is a special case, and the additional figures on the base fit easily into the perfect articulation of the dance.

While He Who has no beginning
dances, close beside Him
Bāṇa and the one called Bhānukampa
surpass the ocean's roar
with the sounds of their conch and drum.

And from OṂ, the surrounding arch,
twenty-one rays can be seen,
accompanied by the Dhvani mantra.

I worship Him, the Lord of the Hall,
before Whom the multitude of the gods bows down,
Whose foot is curved. (9)[22]

I praise the Lord Who is dancing
following the sound of *dhi mi dhi mi tak*
from the drums rapidly struck
by the bristling throng of arms
of the excellent *gaṇa* Bāṇa the Daitya;

His snakes, the ornaments of His arms,
lifting up their necks in joy
at the sound of the thousand-stringed veena
playing *tā nā tā nā ta na.*

Him, who grants freedom from fear,
Whose foot is curved,
I worship. (150)[23]

As the Lord dances Bhānukampa plays
great accompanying music with excellent instruments
including conch and horn filled with the mighty wind
from his thousand fierce faces:
huṃ, huṃ, bha, bhaṃ, bhaṃ, jhaṃ, jhī,

and His dancing hall is filled with the shaken hosts of gods
crying out, '*Hā hā ha ha,*' and being calmed by His attendants.
. . . (151)[24]

Verses 150 and 151 coming at an obvious approximation of the halfway point of the poem perhaps constitute a kind of musical interlude. These two musicians seem to be specific to Cidambaram.[25]

Śiva's drum (*ḍhakkā, ḍamaru*) is often referred to. The Gandharva Citrasena learned the complete science of music (*adhītasaṃgītavidyāsiddhānto*) from the sound of the drum in Naṭarāja's hand (118).[26] The drum reverberates throughout the universe (172), and denying that the contingent self is other than the true self loudly proclaims to the world the Truth (248). We may note that the drum now plays no place in the essential music of worship, though of course its beat is essential for dance performance, and would have accompanied dancing girls. A drum is included in the music that accompanies processions round the temple, but the daily ceremonies of pouring water over the Crystal Liṅga and the ruby Naṭarāja are accompanied by bells – a row of little bells on the East side of the front of the Cit Sabhā and the two great temple bells in the Eastern corner of the first enclosure. An eight-armed drummer, said to be Śiva, with a large five-headed drum, faces the Cit Sabhā at the base of the Nṛtta Sabhā.[27]

Viṣṇu too is credited with playing the drum; there is in the Śaiva legend referred to here an undercurrent of deliberate diminution of the severe orthodoxy of both the god and his worshippers, for drummers are of low caste, as is shown by the caste connotations of the common Tamil word for drummer, namely *paṟaiyaṉ*. Viṣṇu addresses his two wives.

'O Lotus Lakṣmī, don't let's play today
'I don't want my Snake-lord couch,
'nor Garuḍa.

'O Earth, come at once,
'for I am going to beat the drum
'in Tillavana with great skill
'to accompany the dance of the Foe of the Cities.'

So saying, in the beginning
Hari went to His stage,

Him who is unborn,
Whose foot is curved,
I worship. (230)[28]

This verse alludes to an episode in the Śaiva *sthalapurāṇam* of Kāñcīpuram, which begins, in Filliozat's paraphrase,

One day as Viṣṇu was practising yoga, he noticed in his heart a flame in the middle of which Sadāśiva was dancing . . . Questioned by his wife, he told her that he had seen the Supreme Being Śiva dance in his heart and that his dance had fascinated him.[29] [Viṣṇu, as required by Śiva, installs a *liṅga* in Kāñcīpuram (the Ekāmbara temple), and then he and all his entourage make their way to Cidambaram.] Śiva then began to dance. Śrī, the king of birds (Garuḍa) and the king of serpents (Ādiśeṣa) saw him and meditated on him. The Gaṇas performed on musical instruments while he danced. Viṣṇu wished to do so too and played the kettledrum. Afterwards he asked the God of the Vedas (Śiva) to grant him the boon of playing this instrument in all his dances.[30]

Viṣṇu playing the drum is incorporated into the statue of Ūrdhvatāṇḍava Śiva in the Nṛtta Sabhā, rising at an angle from the base of the sculpture, counterbalancing Kālī on the right-hand side.

Śiva dances in Viṣṇu's heart because as Supreme Being he is the consciousness present in every individual. This brings us to a major feature of Umāpati's Naṭarāja – that the Dancer is Himself *saccidānanda*, 'Being, Consciousness and Bliss'.

Brahman alone is true,
not this world, nor anything else.

Reflecting on this statement of the *Upaniṣad*s
the leaders of the wise
constantly look upon Him in their hearts,
He the mass of consciousness which cannot be seen,
His Dance of Bliss constantly repeated
like the flickering flame of a lamp,

illusion-free, shining white,
He is what is meant by Tat Sat,
. . . (261)[31]

He is 'that God Whose dance is manifest in the sportive manifestation of consciousness' (*cidvilāsaprakaṭitanaṭanam* 293).

Putting the three lines of ash on His forehead,
the hooded snake on His throat,
and the demon as the pedestal for His foot,
and holding fire and the *ḍhakkā* drum in His hands,
and sun, moon, and fire on His lotus face,

the host of gods and worlds in the radiance called OṂ,
the musician on each side,

He performs the Dance of Bliss in His own hall,
Him Whose foot is curved,
I worship. (93)[32]

A clear statement of the classic pose, omitting to mention only the *abhaya* gesture. By beginning with the putting on of ash, the poet links the Dancer to his devotees, who share with Śiva the performance of this action. The ash of the burning ground contrasts with the opulence of the next verse cited.

He is the Lord. He always wears
necklaces of perfect pearls
on His feet and round His neck,
on His body a golden breastplate
and ornaments studded with diamonds,
and heavenly garments.

As He performs His dance
He gives Dharma and the other ends of man
to all who come to Him
and protects them.

He has no beginning.
It is to Him that sages direct their sacrifice.
Him Whose foot is curved
I worship. (106)[33]

Whereas the Pallava poet-saints made their tireless pilgrimages across Tamilnadu to see Śiva in small brick-built shrines, the Śiva of our poet is now loaded with ornaments in his vast temple-palace. Not only is the roof of the shrine covered in gold, so too is the God himself. All human purposes have their source here; rich ornamentation is synonymous with the ethical ultimate. The traditional saying has it that Śiva likes *abhiṣeka*, anointing, and Viṣṇu ornamentation, but the naked beggar and wild dancer cannot escape the dynamic of the temple to attract wealth.

BHṚNGIN THE DEVOTEE

In addition to the Goddess standing beside him, representations of Naṭarāja commonly show other figures at his feet. We have already seen the two Gaṇa musicians. A figure found almost as early as Naṭarāja himself is Bhṛṅgin.

The blessed Bhṛṅgin, chief of munis,
bowed solely to the Lord, to the God alone
Who has the deer and the axe in His hands;

and at the decree of Caṇḍikā at His side,
angry that he did not look at her,
he lost from his fine body
the flesh and other 'feminine' parts.

By His grace,
he obtained three long legs and
residence in His place of honour.
Him Whose foot is curved
I worship. (154)[34]

Bhṛṅgin angered the Goddess by neglecting her in his exclusive devotion to Śiva; and after she had cursed him to lose his flesh (the soft, 'feminine', part of his body) he became so weak that he could not move. Śiva made him mobile by granting a third leg, whereupon he danced for joy. Bhṛṅgin has no special connection with Cidambaram, but is often found in Cōḻa stone sculptures of Naṭarāja at his feet. An image of Bhṛṅgīśa was donated to the Bṛhadīśvara temple by a courtier, Kōvan Aṇṇāmalai, of Rājarāja I in the eleventh century.[35] The image is almost as old as that of dancing Śiva, going back to the Sirpur Gupta image.[36] It is not impossible that the origins of the figure lie in the attempt to represent a dancer's leg movements – perhaps those of Taṇḍu, the eponymous teacher of the Tāṇḍava dance – an attempt which proved to have no appeal but gave rise to the story of the determined but initially disadvantaged devotee.

Like the Apasmāra demon, Bhṛṅgin is a foil for Naṭarāja. The angular figure, a pin man, contrasts with the wholly natural movements of Śiva and the smoothness of his flesh and muscles. Later paintings often show Bhṛṅgin accompanying Vyāghrapāda and Patañjali as audience for Śiva dancing in Cidambaram. A motley crew, it might be said, maintaining the standard of *bizarrerie* set by Śiva's sons, elephant-headed Gaṇeśa and six-headed Skanda; and contrasting with the straightforwardly royal qualities of Viṣṇu and his consorts. And yet the strangeness of these figures is a pale reflection of Śiva's strangeness; the difference is that Śiva's strangeness has been transmuted by centuries of aesthetic development, whereas Vyāghrapāda and Patañjali remain, as it might be said, raw in their figural condition.

At the royal centre of Gangaikondacolapuram, some 54 km by road from Cidambaram, both Kālī and Bhṛṅgin feature in the Naṭarāja sculpture on the outside of the *garbhagṛha*. Kālī there is a diminutive figure like Bhṛṅgin, dancing at Śiva's feet. Such a dancing Kālī features in approximately half of the published Cōḻa stone sculptures of Naṭarāja; Bhṛṅgin is less common.[37]

KĀLĪ

Another small figure often found by the feet of Naṭarāja is Kālī. Her diminutive form dances near Naṭarāja's feet at Gangaikondacolapuram. However, in Cidambaram she is found only beside that form of Śiva which has one leg kicked up, the 'High Tāṇḍava pose' (*ūrdhvatāṇḍava*) with which the God defeated the Goddess in their dance competition. There is a small statue of a dancing Kālī at the feet of Ūrdhvatāṇḍava Śiva in the hall south of the Cit Sabhā, the Nṛtta Sabhā, which is understood to be on the very site where the dance competition took place between Śiva and Kālī. Umāpati mentions the contest three or four times; but in general, except for the Nṛtta Sabhā, Kālī has no place in the temple; and in the Nṛtta Sabhā she is not conspicuous. Kālī, however, is also present in two of the representations of the Ūrdhvatāṇḍava, one of which is present on each *gopura*. In both the South and North *gopuras* she stands erect, four-armed, the two lower arms hanging straight down, the upper two holding indeterminate emblems. Her flaming hair is erect. On the East *gopura* she stands to Śiva's left; on the Southern, 'Pāṇḍyan' *gopura*, to his right. The left-hand position belongs to the consort, and the right-hand position is therefore more appropriate for an opponent. The important point is that she does not dance: elsewhere she may dance, as at Tiruvalangadu, where there is a magnificent bronze of her dancing complementing the no less magnificent bronze of Śiva in Ūrdhvatāṇḍava; but at Cidambaram, the *ānandatāṇḍava* is supreme. Umāpati does refer once to the Ūrdhvatāṇḍava:

> Paśupati in ancient days once danced with Kālī.
> In the assembly of gods and sages,
> raising up His foot
> and performing the elevated dance
>
> He defeated Kālī then
> as prelude to her expulsion.
>
> And all the gods and chief sages call Him Lord,
> and the sinless ones worship Him every day,
> Lord of the High Dance.
>
> . . . (46)[38]

4. Kālī dancing near Naṭarāja's feet (Bhṛṅgin partly visible to left). Bṛhadīśvara temple, Gangaikondacolapuram, *c.* 1025.

The stylistic development of the sculpture of the *gopuras* is clearly shown in the two Ūrdhvatāṇḍavas in plate 5. The East *gopura* shows a considerable development beyond the West; this image on the South *gopura* (not shown here), third in point of time, is only a poor copy of that of the East. In the West image (plate 5a), the Apasmāra faces right, and is not able to look up at Śiva's foot. Much more is present in the East image (plate 5b), and everything is beautifully executed. The upward leg though straight is not entirely vertical, and every other limb is subtly curved.

It is instructive to compare the Ūrdhvatāṇḍava in general with the Ānanda Tāṇḍava, to better appreciate the qualities of the latter. In the former mere athleticism, though majestic; and perhaps also a suggestion of the impassivity of the *liṅga*; of the immobility of the ultimate phallic column; of the triumph of the male force that sees off the dangerous female. In the Ānanda Tāṇḍava, there is perhaps above all the sense of grace: Śiva's movements are graceful; Śiva is the source of grace; and his curved foot is the channel for his grace.

The great success that the Naṭarāja image has in achieving its effect

5. Ūrdhvatāṇḍavamūrti. West *gopura* and East *gopura*, Cidambaram.

may be demonstrated by contrasting the front and rear views of a bronze. Athleticism is often brilliantly achieved from behind, where energetic movement is to be seen in the muscles of the back and thighs. But from the front this energy is only part of the highly structured expression of the whole image.

Other forms of dance are referred to in passing. Indeed, not much reference is explicitly made to the Ānanda Tāṇḍava form by Umāpati, but this is because it is constantly before him and in his heart. Of the other forms of dance, the following refers to Śiva as light so bright that the heavenly bodies appear dim, and also as eight-armed. The poets of

6. Naṭarāja. Vedaranyam, *c.* 1200.

the *Tēvāram* refer to dancing Śiva as eight-armed, and may therefore be understood as living prior to the classical Cōḻa formulation of the Ānanda Tāṇḍava of four-armed Naṭarāja.

> Before Whom the sun, moon,
> and fire do not shine at all,
> nor the stars nor lightning;
> from fear of Whom Indra, Vāyu,
> and Death the Restrainer,
> son of the sun's ray,
> ever keep far away;
>
> on Whose form the best of yogis
> constantly meditate in their heart-lotuses;
> the Blessed One of wonderful form,
>
> Who has eight hand-lotuses,
> Whose foot is curved,
> Him I worship. (73)[39]

On a cosmic plane he has multiple hands, and this cosmic form is coupled with Umāpati's one reference to the cremation ground, so frequently mentioned by the poets of the *Tēvāram* and Kāraikāl Ammaiyār as the scene of Śiva's dance.

> His eyes are sun, moon and fire
> His feet reach down to the subterranean world of snakes,
> His hair is in the sky,
> the eight directions are His clothes,
> His hands reach out to all worlds,
> He is unparalleled,
>
> His stomach is all the oceans,
> and the cemetery, Rudra's ground,
> is the auspicious spot for His dance,
>
> That God, eternal, Lord of the Cit Sabhā,
> Whose praises are sung by the throng of *śruti*,
> Whose foot is curved,
> I worship. (67)[40]

Here the dancer is the cosmos, his vast extension seeming to leave no room for the description of artistic movement; though another verse gives the dance on a grand scale – a rare instance in Umāpati Śivācārya of the standard Kāvya style:

7. Śiva dancing on Apasmāra with a cobra bending its hood beneath his raised foot. Pillar in the western entrance of the Śivagaṅgā tank, Cidambaram. Seventeenth century or later.

Manifestly with the fresh rays of his smiling face
and the shooting radiance from
the palms of his hand lotuses,
He forms a network of suns in the sky;
with the radiance of Śivā by His side
a novel garland of clouds on earth;

Who thus dances intensely a wonderful [dance],
He who performs the dance of a bee:
Him Whose foot is curved
I worship. (220)[41]

In the court style, the poet describes an artificial seeming universe, a world of illusion. Śiva is made to fill the sky with semblances of suns, and the Goddess, beside him, dark in colour, is low-lying cloud. The poet then, with a further degree of playfulness, abandons this extensive scene for the small-scale movement of the bee. In court poetry the buzzing from flower to flower can represent the courtier likewise taking his pleasure here and there. Normally, however, Umāpati eschews this style.

Another form of Śiva's dance is first found around the time of Umāpati. In this, the Vaiṣṇava form of Kṛṣṇa dancing on Kāliya, a popular form of Cōḻa bronze clearly inspired by Naṭarāja, is used or referred to by Śaiva artists by allowing the snake that Apasmāra plays with to rear up almost in the proportions of Kāliya beneath Śiva's uplifted foot.

While the full life span of Viṣṇu,
Kaiṭabha's foe,
is supposed to comprise an aeon,
an aeon goes by in half a second for Him,
virtually instantaneously.
Thus declare the Vedas.

What can be said of the lifetimes of Indra
and the world protectors?

Him Who is Time,
Who devours Time,
Who is the dancer on the hood of the snake,
Whose foot is curved,
I worship. (282)[42]

Śiva's dance is beyond time, and subsumes all other dances.

CHAPTER 2

The Cidambaram myth

Every major South India temple has its own legend, its local version of mythology. That of Cidambaram is found principally in the Sanskrit *Cidambara Māhātmya*[1] and in the Tamil version of the *Cidambara Māhātmya*, the *Kōyil Purāṇam*, one of the earliest Tamil *sthalapurāṇa*s.[2] The *sthalapurāṇa* forms the subject of the ceiling paintings on the north side of the *maṇḍapa* of the Śivakāmasundarī shrine in the temple, paintings which like the *maṇḍapa* itself probably date from the late seventeenth century. The story is also told in paintings on the ceiling of the veranda round the Cit Sabhā, which like the veranda probably date from the late nineteenth century. It is highly probable that the *sthalapurāṇa* was portrayed in paintings in Umāpati's day. Nothing can be said of these paintings, but it is likely that his imagination would have had visual prompting and affirmation of the reality of events.

The Cidambaram myth is at the same time the myth of the *ānandatāṇḍava*, and is essentially a reworking of the well-known Pine Forest myth but, unlike its model which is found in several Sanskrit Purāṇas, does not seem to be known outside Cidambaram until modern times.[3] The central episode concerns Śiva's visit as wandering beggar to the sages in the Pine Forest. He is accompanied by Viṣṇu in the form of a beautiful woman. Together they arouse the lusts of the sages and their wives. When attacked by entities from the sages' sacrificial fire, Śiva takes them as his attributes. He then dances the Ānanda Tāṇḍava for the first time. The repeat performance of this dance is awaited in Cidambaram by two sages, one of them Patañjali, an incarnation of Śeṣa, Viṣṇu's serpent, the second, Vyāghrapāda, otherwise unknown. They worship the *liṅga* while they wait. Finally, there is an account of a mythical king from the north, who, gaining a golden skin, moves to Cidambaram, rebuilds the temple, and institutes rituals and festivals.

The story begins with an account of Vyāghrapāda, 'Tigerfoot', who worships the original *liṅga* of the Mūlasthāna ('The Original Place'), while awaiting the performance in this world age of the Tāṇḍava Dance. His name, which has the prestige of Vedic occurrence,[4] is probably to be explained by the original, or at least alternative, name of Cidambaram, Vyāghrapura, 'Tigertown'.

> Once Madhyandana's son,
> worshipping Śiva's excellent *liṅga*
> obtained by His grace the paws of a tiger.
> Through His compassion
> he was able to bring to his son
> the Ocean of Milk and feed him on it;
>
> and he beheld in the Hall
> His supreme dance.
>
> I worship the God
> Who is the Lord of the Hall of Consciousness,
> Whose qualities are praised in the scriptures,
> Whose foot is curved. (10)[5]

The sage worships the original *liṅga* in the Tillai forest of Cidambaram every day with offerings of flowers, but the bees spoil them, and he seeks and gains the boon of having tigerpaws instead of hands and feet, and also an eye on each paw, so that he can climb trees for the best flowers. He marries the sister of the famous Vedic *ṛṣi* Vasiṣṭha, and begets Upamanyu, who is widely known in the Purāṇas as a teacher of Śaivism, but figures here only in receiving milk directly from Śiva. The gift is lavish, for it is no less than the Milk Ocean.

The other half of the dual act of principal devotees in the *sthalapurāṇa* is taken up by Patañjali, said to be the human form of Viṣṇu's supporting snake, Śeṣa. The form of Viṣṇu at Cidambaram, as in the great Viṣṇu temple of Śrīraṅgam, is that of Śeṣaśayana, Viṣṇu outstretched on the coils of the snake 'Remainder'. It is thus that the god floats on the waters of undifferentiated matter during the period between destruction and creation of the universe.

> Once, meditating on His dance
> Viṣṇu's body doubled in weight
> and Śeṣa, his support, had his body squeezed.
> Śeṣa drank the wine of what had happened
> from the lotus of Viṣṇu's mouth,
>
> and practising very severe penance
>
> reached His Holy Place
> via the tunnel mouth of the Silver mountain
> and witnessed the dance in the Sabhā.
>
> . . . (11)[6]

Because of the bliss of meditating on Śiva, Viṣṇu's body becomes heavier. When Viṣṇu wakes up, he tells his two queens, Śrī and Bhūmi (Prosperity and the Earth), and also Śeṣa, what happened on the preceding day. When he went to pay his daily respects to Śiva, Śiva told him that they were going to test the married ascetics in the Pine Forest. Viṣṇu is told to assume the form of an entrancing woman and Śiva goes as a handsome beggar. The sages are enamoured of Mohinī, Viṣṇu as the Enchantress, and their wives enamoured of Bhikṣāṭana, the Wandering Beggar. The older sages, angered at the intrusion and disruption, produce means of attack from their sacrificial fire: tiger, deer, axe, mantras, dwarf. All are of no avail, and Śiva takes them for himself, and an explanation is thus given for details of his iconography. He then performs the wonderful Ānanda Tāṇḍava dance. Śeṣa is very anxious to see this for himself, and, following Viṣṇu's instructions, leaves his son as his deputy and takes human form as Patañjali. He descends into the subterranean world of the Nāgas and enters a tunnel which leads up into Cidambaram. By this manoeuvre of the narrative Cidambaram is shown to be atop the cosmic mountain, although in fact it lies on a coastal plain. On arriving at Cidambaram, he meets Vyāghrapāda, and the pair wait for the performance of the Dance. Specific temples in Cidambaram house the *liṅgas* they set up and worshipped while waiting for the Dance.[7]

Umāpati chooses not to refer to the ṛṣis' attack on Śiva in the *Kuñcitāṅghristava*. The very idea of an attack on Śiva is not in consonance with the poem. It is also a material factor that there is no iconography of this event; it is only rarely represented in art,[8] being a transition between the two key iconographies of Southern Śaivism, Naṭarāja and Bhikṣāṭana.

Umāpati's next reference to the *sthalapurāṇa* is this:

> In the beginning
> on a full-moon Thursday in the month of the Deer,
> under the Puṣya lunar asterism,
> to fulfil the promise
> won by those excellent sages' asceticism,
>
> He summoned Snake-bodied Patañjali
> and the great sage, Tiger-footed Vyāghrapāda,
>
> and performed His dance
> against the wall
> in the blessed Hall of Consciousness.
>
> After it was over,
> He granted them permanent residence.
> . . . (8)[9]

8. Patañjali. East *gopura*, Cidambaram.

Thus ends the first half of the *sthalapurāṇa*. Śiva's performance for the two sages is represented by a majestic panel on the ceiling of the Śivakāmasundarī shrine, unfortunately now greatly damaged.

The last major part of the *sthalapurāṇa* is the story of Hiraṇyavarman, the King from the North, perhaps from Bengal, as the region is called Gauḍa. An important event in that story is the King bringing priests from the North to Cidambaram. Within the story they are the original priests, who left Cidambaram at Brahmā's request to attend his sacrifice. It is with Brahmā's decision to perform a sacrifice that the second half of the text begins.

> When Indra was summoned
> to Self-born Brahmā's sacrifice in Antarvedi
> where the hymns of the Sāma Veda were loudly sung,
> he did not come.

As soon as Brahmā learned that the lord of the gods
was watching His pure dance
Brahmā went himself in great haste to Indra

and by His overruling command
brought him back along with the Brahmans
and performed his sacrifice
amid the praises of the gods.
. . . (47)[10]

Antarvedi, literally '[the area] within the sacrificial ground', is the Doab, the district between the Gaṅgā and the Yamunā, a region of North India of particular sanctity, especially perhaps from the perspective of South India.

Clearly, one aim of the story can be seen to justify the presence of priests in Cidambaram who hail from the Gauḍa region. Indeed, a high status is claimed for them, since Brahmā intended to invite the gods, but they all refused to leave Cidambaram where they were watching the dance of Śiva; and at Vyāghrapāda's suggestion the priests are sent in their stead. The story would seem to confuse officiating priests with the recipients of the sacrifice.

Brahmā of a Hundred Sacrifices
performed a sacrifice in great Antarvedi,
a sacrifice that took a thousand years to complete.
In that assembly at Vyāghrapāda's behest
the chief ascetics were present.

So that they could continue to worship Him
He gladly sent a Dancer made of precious stone
arisen from the best of fires.

He is the source of that image,
His crown is of nine jewels.
His foot is curved.
I worship Him. (16)[11]

The second part of the verse adds information not found in the *Cidambara Māhātmya* or *Kōyil Purāṇam*. Śiva, to compensate the Dīkṣitas for their absence from his temple, gives them the Ruby Naṭarāja, Ratnasabhāpati, that features in the daily ritual today. At about 10.45 a.m., after the second *abhiṣeka* of the Crystal Liṅga, there is *abhiṣeka* of the Ratnasabhāpati, and most notably, a camphor lamp is moved five times behind this 10 cm high ruby image, to shine through it, so that it glows red with all the details of its form made manifest. This takes place on the east side of the Sabhā, and in modern times a special roof has been built on pillars in this part of the courtyard solely for this event. My friend Parameśvara Dīkṣita took pride in his 4-year-old son performing this lamp action with a small Naṭarāja in his home, and stressed to me that his son's skill was untaught and innate.

The next verse to be cited contains all the essential details concerning Hiraṇyavarman.

> Siṃhavarman, Lord of Gauḍa,
> distressed by his diseased body,
> came from his own land
> to be freed from affliction
>
> by bathing in the excellent water
> with its clumps of golden lotuses –
> thereupon becoming
> the blessed Hemavarman,
>
> witnessing, in company of the best ascetics,
> the dance of Śambhu, Śiva the mild,
> for Whom he built
> a wonderful jewelled temple.
>
> . . . . . (13)[12]

Brahmā's sacrifice formed the introduction to the last part of the *sthalapurāṇa*. Mention of the king himself is delayed by an account of the creation of the world. The fifth king of the Sun dynasty is the mighty Lokeśavikrama. His eldest son Siṃhavarman (Lion-prowess) is a leper and does not feel fit to succeed to the throne.[13] Instead, he devotes himself to asceticism, with the unspoken aim of finding a cure. In due course he makes his way south and meets a seated sage of awesome aspect who proves to be Vyāghrapāda, in *samādhi* from the last world age. The sage takes the prince to Cidambaram, and on Śiva's advice the prince bathes in the Śiva-Gaṅgā tank. He comes out of the water shining like gold, and is henceforth Hiraṇya- or Hema-varman, 'Golden Prowess'. Vyāghrapāda and his wife adopt the prince as their son. Then as a mass of radiance from the sky Vasiṣṭha, family priest of Hiraṇyavarman's father, arrives. He tells him his father is too old to rule, and he must return to rule the kingdom. The prince does not wish to, but Vyāghrapāda tells him to transfer his army and his subjects to Cidambaram, and to bring back the priests from Antarvedi. He does so and then rebuilds the temple. Patañjali writes his textbook on the ritual of the temple and the *sthalapurāṇa* ends with an account of the temple festival. As with the end of the first half, this conclusion is grandly portrayed in the seventeenth-century ceiling painting; unlike the former. it is undamaged but is in the darkest corner of the *maṇḍapa*.

All but one of the verses so far considered come from a small block near the beginning of the poem (verses 8–16). Consideration of this group will show the poem's handling and distortion of exterior narrative order.

In verse 8, the promise is made to Śeṣa that he will see the dance. In verse 9 we have the description of the performance of the promised dance (quoted chapter 1, p. 19). Verse 10 reverts to the opening episode of the *Cidambara Māhātmya*, referring to Vyāghrapāda gaining his tiger's feet and his son feeding on the milk sent by Śiva, before again mentioning the dance performance of verse 9. Verse 11 gives the antecedents likewise of Patañjali prior to the performance. Verse 12 concerns Jaimini, another sage who witnesses the dance, making the duo of Vyāghrapāda and Patañjali into a trio; referred to only incidentally in the *sthalapurāṇa*, when Vyāghrapāda gives his own mini *sthalapurāṇa* to the prince. Verse 13 summarizes the final section of the *Cidambara Māhātmya*. All these verses refer to the witnessing of particular performances of the Ānanda Tāṇḍava. Verse 14 tells of Patañjali writing the ritual manual for the Dīkṣitas; verse 15 the daily *pūjā*; verse 16 Brahmā's sacrifice. The last three form a transition into the next block (17–27) which gives a coherent account of the temple's ritual.

> In the beginning the blessed Lord of Serpents,
> Patañjali, taking precepts
> from varied places in the endless scriptures
> in a way that none could emulate,
> composed that Sūtra for
> the worship, festivals and aspersions
> of the Dancer,
>
> so that in the way that he has stated
> the three thousand Brahmans forever
> honour the Lord of Dancers.
> . . . (14)[14]

The *sthalapurāṇa* says that Hiraṇyavarman had the book when completed carried round the city to the sound of trumpets before installing it in the Sabhā (25.51–2). It may well be that the two texts were composed at the same time.

Verse 12 is another literary reference:

The yogi named Jaimini who first attained fame
through his commentary on the ritual section of the Vedas,
at Vyāsa's behest
prostrated himself
before the excellent Lord, the Lord of the Hall,

entered into the Hall
and composed the excellent hymn of praise
wherein every verse ends with a quote from the Veda.

Even today he dwells in the Hall
beholding the God
Who gave him his good fortune,
Whose foot is curved,
Whom I worship. (12)[15]

Association with Jaimini brings a vicarious authenticity. The ultra-orthodox Pūrva Mīmāṃsā stands behind the temple which practices 'Vedic' rituals; and his poem of praise is steeped in the Vedas. Our poet is deeply interested in other poets, he follows their example, and their example adds significance to his own work. Jaimini is mentioned again in the company of several other devotees:

The God swayed by devotion to Himself,
Who gave salvation to Pulkasa and the Brahman,
to the son of Valkala, to the man called Nanda,
and to the wise man who thought his own eye mere grass,

and Who gave eternal presence in Cidambaram
to Vyāghrapāda,
to the famous serpent-lord Patañjali,
and to Jaimini author of the hymn,

and thus fulfilled all their desires,
Him, ageless and immortal,
Whose foot is curved
I worship. (29)[16]

In addition to the trio of sages already considered, Umāpati refers here to two specific episodes of the *sthalapurāṇa*, namely that of Pulkasa and that of Vālkali. The two saints, Nanda (Tamil form, Nantaṉār) and Kaṇṇappār who gave his eye to the *liṅga*, are among the sixty-three saints (Nāyaṉārs) celebrated in the *Periya Purāṇam*. (Nantaṉār is discussed below, and Kaṇṇappār in chapter 9.) Pulkasa and Vālkali are of little moment in themselves, but belong to significant strata of the *sthalapurāṇa*. The *Cidambara Māhātmya* gives the following account of Pulkasa. Pulkasa is the name of an evil man who kills a family of Brahmans and then robs travellers. He makes friends with a Brahman and gives him half his money. The Brahman is pleased to get the money, but admonishes Pulkasa for his wickedness. Pulkasa then sees the error of his ways, and becomes depressed. The Brahman advises him to go to Cidambaram, the best of holy places, where the Lord of Ambikā dances. As soon as he sees the Little Hall in the distance he is to prostrate himself on the ground. He is to give away his wealth to both yogins and men in the world, and to strenuously protect the place from danger.

Full of faith Pulkasa goes to Cidambaram, accompanied by the Brahman despite their difference in caste. Pulkasa gives away all his wealth to yogins and others. When he sees in the distance the heavenly Little Hall (*dabhrasabhā*) of wonderful glory, he pays homage at a distance of 5 *krośa*s, and remains there continuing to do homage, full of joy, and protecting that place. In the course of time he dies, and after enjoying the delights of heaven attains supreme salvation. So too does the Brahman, it is briefly added.

Kulke, in his painstaking analysis of the *Cidambara Māhātmya*, which will shortly be referred to in detail, overlooks the fact that the story of Pulkasa is taken from the *Sūta Saṃhitā* (1.4.17-39), and tries to argue that it is based on another story from that text, namely the story of Durghaṭa. The version in the *Cidambara Māhātmya* differs from its source only in that Sūta's references to his audience, 'O Brahmans!' and so on, are removed and the phrasing altered to preserve the metre; and the interesting detail is lost that the Brahman who befriends Pulkasa is a brothel-keeper (*gaṇikāpati*). Two other sinners with interesting specific details are mentioned in the *Puṇḍarīkapura Māhātyma*, though they too have generic nomenclature – Durmata and Duḥsaha. The real interest, however, in the story of Pulkasa is in its contrast with that of Nanda, although both were of low caste. Nanda's story is here given according to the *Hemasabhānātha Māhātyma*, which devotes its ninth chapter to this Nāyaṉār. Nanda was renowned for saying that he would visit Cidambaram 'tomorrow', but his constant toil as a labourer did not allow time. Even when at last he goes, his family seek to restrain him since such a holy place is not for the likes of them. Once there he does not pass through the courtyard gate but dwells outside. Daily he circumambulates the city, oppressed by the fact his caste is an impediment to seeing God. To succour (*rakṣitum*) him, Śiva with smiling face comes to him in a dream and tells him that by entering fire he will conquer his caste and be able to worship him alongside the Brahmans. Then Śiva came to the Brahmans of Cidambaram and said to them in their dreams, 'If any person of the lowest caste should enter fire tomorrow, let him be honoured by you.' The perfect priests had a fire lit at the entrance and went into the temple.

'I am a slave and yet am I fortunate,' declared Nanda, and with joyful devotion he entered the fire. He lost his previous body and took on the glory of a Brahman. Chaste, pure, his upper body clad only with the sacred thread, reciting the Vedas he came forth from the fire, and as the gods showered down flowers entered the temple to be seen no more, having won identity with Śiva.

Especially for readers familiar with the Nāyaṉārs, there is a marked difference between the story of Nanda and that of Pulkasa, extending even to their names. The factitious quality of the latter means that his caste is all the name he needs. The *Cidambara Māhātmya* even leaves out the detail of the Brahman's occupation. Partly perhaps its redactors did not want to diminish the power of the central narrative by adding distracting details; and certainly not by introducing the well-known Nāyaṉārs. The story they had to tell was new, and its success was not assured.

We have still to deal with the son of Valkala. He is known from the *Cidambara Māhātmya* as a demon who defeated Indra, since Śiva had given him the boon of being unconquerable (7.17). More details are given in 41:

> Once in the past when Indra, lord of the gods,
> had his fine body struck by one called Vālkali
> he resorted to Viṣṇu and told him what had happened to him;
>
> with Viṣṇu, foe of Mura,
> he came to this holy place and worshipped the Lord;
>
> through His pure pity
> he obtained great strength and slew his foe.
>
> . . . (41)[17]

According to Kulke this episode, part of Vyāghrapāda's father's discourse to his son, is an interpolation, a Northern Vaiṣṇava text inserted into the original narrative, with only minimal changes. Kulke is clearly correct that the narrative was originally Vaiṣṇava, but there is no good reason to suppose that it was not part of the original mix of ingredients used to construct the *Cidambara Māhātmya.* It explains the presence of Viṣṇu in Cidambaram, and Viṣṇu is to play an important part in subsequent events – as Mohinī in the Dāruka Forest. It also refers to Viṣṇu bringing the Milk Ocean with him to Cidambaram. Kulke himself remarks that 'the account of the Vaiṣṇava origin of the Milk Ocean in Cidambaram was probably one of the motives for connecting the Vyāghrapāda legend in the *Cidambara Māhātmya* with the Upamanyu legend.'[18] Indeed, it is hard to think of a stronger motive. Within the *Cidambara Māhātmya* the subsequent event – Śiva bringing the Milk Ocean for the benefit of Upamanyu – is given more sectarian point by the earlier reference to the rival Vaiṣṇava event.

The appropriateness of the story of the Milk Ocean here prompts a reconsideration of the whole question of Upamanyu, who is again referred to near the end of the poem:

> Tigerfoot's baby boy obtained
> the very pleasant ocean of milk
> by constantly praising the desirable Lord
> Who dances in the heavens
> . . . (306)[19]

Kulke thus summarizes his own position:

> The starting point of the Vyāghrapāda-legend is seen in the Sanskritization of a Tamil name of Cidambaram, 'Puliyūr', as 'Vyāghrapura'. Thus, the legend of the Muni Vyāghrapāda was created, who up to this time had been known only as the father of Upamanyu, a saint of MBh XIII, 14. The Vyāghrapāda legend, created in Cidambaram, was brought into connection with this well-known Upamanyu legend.[20]

Yet it is not impossible that the legend is entirely Southern in origin. Its inclusion in the Critical Edition of the *Mahābhārata* may be questioned. The editor of the *Anuśāsana Parvan*, R. N. Dandekar, remarks, 'it is certainly strange that the well-known Upamanyu episode . . . should not have found place in the *Āndhra Bhāratamu*'.[21] The relevant part of this Telegu adaptation was written by Tikkana Somayājī (1200–80); I suggest the Upamanyu episode is a manifestly late insertion in the *Mahābhārata*, and that its origin is precisely a Śaiva take-over of the Milk Ocean, though Cidambaram may not be the earliest site for the attempt.[22]

A related incident is the story (found in the twelfth-century *Periya Purāṇam*) of the first *Tēvāram* poet, Campantar being fed with milk from Umā's breast in a golden cup. The 3-year-old's father was alarmed to see milk trickling from his mouth, and demanded to know who had fed him, fearful of pollution from a lower caste. The opening hymn of the *Tēvāram* is said to be the poet's reply to this question. A verse in another hymn is a more direct reference:

> When I was rebuked by my angry father,
> who rejected as a harmful thing
> the sweet dish of wisdom
> served in a flowerlike golden cup,
> the great Lord possessed me.[23]

9. Vyāghrapāda with son and wife, milk tank to the left, Mūlanātha Shrine to the right. Ceiling painting, Śivakāmasundarī *maṇḍapa*, Cidambaram. Seventeenth century.

Upamanyu was a noted Śaiva teacher, as in the *Vāyavīya Saṃhitā* of the *Śiva Purāṇa*, a text for which Umāpati is said to have written a commentary; and supposedly the author of a Sanskrit version of the lives of the Tamil saints, the *Upamanyubhaktavilāsa*; and in the *Mahābhārata* – a late insertion as noted above – the teacher of the worship of Śiva to Kṛṣṇa, mentioned by Umāpati in verse 54.

The central episode of the Cidambaram legend where Śiva appears as Bhikṣāṭana is considered in depth in chapter 7. We have not yet considered the date of the *Cidambara Māhātmya*. We shall now look at Kulke's dating on the basis of his highly systematic analysis; and at the account of its composition offered by one of Umāpati's biographers, Śivānandanātha Dīkṣita, who credits not only the Tamil version but the Sanskrit original to Umāpati.

Kulke claimed to discover a historical core to the sequence of events. He suggests that Siṃhavarman, the king from Gauḍa who gains a golden skin in the Śivagaṅgā tank and rebuilds Cidambaram, was based on the Cōḻa king Kulōttuṅga I (1070–1118). This hypothesis hinges on a few small points. Siṃhavarman's father is named Lokendravikrama, and is further described as *bhāgīrathīpūraparipanthin*. Kulke suggests that this was in fact Rājendra I, who captured the river Gaṅgā, and thereafter established a new palace and temple called the City of the Conqueror of the Gaṅgā (Gaṅgaikoṇḍacōḻapuram, 54 km by road west of Cidambaram).[24] This conquest of the Gaṅgā was no more than a raiding party led by one of his generals; but it is this Cōḻa king and no other who is to be distinguished by the epithet. He was the great-grandfather of Kulōttuṅga I. A minor but puzzling detail of the narrative of the *Cidambara Māhātmya* is that Vyāghrapāda adopts Hiraṇyavarman. Kulke sees this as the legitimation of an outsider, and connects it with the claim of Kulōttuṅga's court poet, Jayakoṇṭar, that the East Cāḻukyan Kulōttuṅga was named as crown prince by the Cōḻa Vīrarājendra.

Kulke relies on two other details for his *post quem* dating – a close correspondence between what he sees as an interpolated reference to a Varuṇa festival in the month of Māgha and an inscription of Naralōkavīraṉ (pre-1128/1129) concerning the building of a *maṇḍapa* by the sea, and road to it, for that same festival. Further, Kulke takes VII, 30 (misprinted in his book as VI, 30) to refer to the Viṣṇu shrine in Cidambaram.

The foregoing arguments are persuasive, but what is absolutely crucial for Kulke's bold claim that the *Cidambara Māhātmya* is an example of 'an historical king's biography being transformed into a legend during his lifetime'[25] is his assumption that after Kulōttuṅga II (1135–50) removed the image of Viṣṇu from Cidambaram there was no such sculpture there until it was replaced by Acyutadeva Rāya (1529–42). The only *ante quem* evidence is that the *Cidambara Māhātmya* must have been written before Kulōttuṅga II removed the image.[26] However, the image is in place in Umāpati's time:

> Even today to His right
> Viṣṇu in his jewelled shrine
> is lying on the couch of the coils
> of the five-headed Lord of Snakes
> with his feet to the south and his face to the north.
>
> Although he is always asleep,
> he constantly meditates
> on His praiseworthy foot.
> . . . (42)[27]

At present Govindarāja is lying in the opposite direction, that is, Viṣṇu's face is directed towards the south and his feet are in the north. There is no set rule as to which way that Śeṣaśayana Viṣṇu should be orientated, but the dual shrines in Cidambaram are a special case, and the head to the north, pointing to the Cit Sabhā, is a sign of submission to Śiva; to the south as at present, the reverse, a mark of Vaiṣṇava independence, as would be expected from the mighty Vaiṣṇava Acyutadeva Rāya.[28]

It follows from Umāpati's reference to the Viṣṇu shrine that the *Cidambara Māhātmya* could have been written at any time after the *post quem* dates suggested by Kulke. It should also be remembered that the building in Cidambaram in Kulōttuṅga I's reign was due principally to the general or warlord Naralōkavīraṉ. Kulke closely follows Nilakanta Sastri, the historian of the Cōḻas, but passes over the fact that Kulōttuṅga II had an extensive building programme in Cidambaram. Sastri declares, 'The renovation of the temple and city of Cidambaram is, in fact, the best known event of the reign.'[29]

The *Rājendrapura Māhātmya* by Śivānandanātha Dīkṣita, a life of Umāpati of uncertain date, its title taken from the place of Umāpati's *āśrama*, gives a different view of the composition of the *sthalapurāṇa*.

> One day the priest on duty was opening the door for the night *pūjā* when it was discovered that the Lord of the Sabhā and Ambā had disappeared! Hearing this incredible news the excellent sages, every one of them, assembled in the Deva Sabhā and reflected on the matter. They came to the conclusion that the Lord of Dancers now remained in the Sabhā only as space, bereft of qualities. Someone meditating on His lotus foot must have drawn the form of Lord to his own place and installed Him there!

Then the Lord, although bereft of qualities, spoke to them.
'I am to be found in the *sthalapurāṇa* that the priest (*makhin*) Umāpati is composing. I am dwelling within a golden casket in his *pūjā* room along with Umā.
O best of sages! You must invite him and enthrone him in the Jewelled Pavilion before the Cit Sabhā. Seated in front of him at the time of the morning milking every day for three fortnights, you, O Brahmans! along with Umā, must listen to the great Purāṇa of my city, and its abbreviated Tamil version, each of them a stream of nectar.
As soon as the first word is said I shall enter the great Sabhā and, O Brahmans! I shall be visible to all. Go quickly to his monastery.'
Thereupon the Lord rejoined his tangible form, accompanied by Ambā.
Going to the monastery the twice-born saw the best of sages and bowing to him loudly cried, 'We long to hear your Purāṇa poem. Come quickly, O knower of the Supreme Self.'
And Umāpati, hearing their words, came with them and entering the Sabhā, on a throne of brass and jewels in the middle of the *maṇḍapa*, facing east, his arms upraised in homage,
he meditated on the Lord of the Sabhā in the lotus seed-cup of his heart. Then he stood on the throne and looking at the Brahmans, he began to recite the beginning of the Purāṇa.
Then the Dancer was before all men. (*Rājendrapura Māhātmya* 81–95)

On the basis of the foregoing discussion and revision of Kulke's dating, Umāpati could, conceivably, have written at least the final redaction of the Sanskrit *Cidambara Māhātmya* at the same time as making the Tamil version (generally attributed to him). The very poetical account of Bhikṣāṭana's encounters with the wives of the Ṛṣis, for example, is almost identical in both versions, and since it is more appropriate in style and feeling to the *Kōyil Purāṇam* than to the rest of the *Cidambara Māhātmya*, could well be equally his composition. So too other sections of the *Cidambara Māhātmya*.

Noteworthy in the above passage from the *Rājendrapura Māhātmya* is the attitude to the image attributed to the priests. Not only is the image the object of intensely focussed attention, it can as it were be sucked away to the one who meditates upon it the most intensely. Again, note that Umāpati restores the image in a double sense, both physically and in his literary work. The interconnection of the physical image and its textual version is intensely close. So too throughout the *Kuñcitāṅghristava*.

CHAPTER 3

Temple, priests, and ritual

'O you excellent gods, why do you dwell on this peak?
'There's a sacred place called Puṇḍarīka, "White Lotus",
'in the heart-lotus of the earth
'that sustains all the sacred places of the Lord.

'There alone does God shine
'with all His thousand elements.
'Go there today!' –

with this kind suggestion
Nandin hurries them from the Mountain to see Him;
Him Whose foot is curved
I worship. (227)[1]

Nandikeśvara, leader of the Gaṇas, Śiva's doorkeeper, urges the gods to leave Mount Kailāsa and to go south to see Śiva in his full glory. A portion (*kalā*) of Śiva is in every sacred place, but only in Cidambaram is he totally present. Puṇḍarīka means 'white lotus'; Puṇḍarīkapura, 'White Lotus City', is another name for Cidambaram, and *Puṇḍarīkapura Māhātmya* the name of a later Cidambaram *māhātmya.*

Every day the sun sees the golden pinnacle of His stage,
mistakes it for Meru, stops his chariot
and stays there for a moment

until he hears again the auspicious sound
of Him being worshipped – the ringing of the bells,
and the Vedic mantras of the three thousand Brahmans –
and realises it is the city called Tillai Wood.
. . . (289)[2]

That the sun mistakes a high building for the cosmic mountain is a convention of Sanskrit poetry, but has added point here since in the virtual reality of the *sthalapurāṇa* Cidambaram itself is a cosmic mountain,

10. Roofs of the Kanaka Sabhā (on the left) and Cit Sabhā (on the right) viewed from the top of the East *gopura*, Cidambaram.

and Patañjali had to ascend through a vertical tunnel to reach it. The highest points of the temple are the gateway towers, the *gopura*s, and other structures within the temple are higher than the Cit Sabhā, but to think of the temple is to think only of the Cit Sabhā.

Several kings claim to have covered the Cit Sabhā in gold. The present situation is that the roof of the Cit Sabhā is said to have golden tiles, and the similar-shaped Sabhā right in front of it, which is called the Kanaka ('Golden') Sabhā, is roofed in gilded copper. However, the roofs look identical, save that the Kanaka roof is about a metre lower. As for the bells, today they comprise two large bells about 3 metres above ground in the north-east corner of the innermost courtyard and a row of little bells fastened to a pivoting board pulled by a string at the front of the Kanaka Sabhā. Prior to 1934 the large bells were situated directly in front of the Kanaka Sabhā, on the eastern side.

Another name for Cidambaram is Tilva, or Tillai in Tamil, this being the name of the type of tree with which the whole area was forested.[3] *Tilvavana Māhātmya* is the name of a later Sanskrit *sthalapurāṇa* for Cidambaram.

Although a few other temples in Tamilnadu are particularly closely associated with Naṭarāja and have their own myths of the Dance along with halls specific to their version of his Dance, Naṭarāja is above all the God of Cidambaram. A general introduction to the temple, with its buildings, priests, and rituals, is provided by Umāpati, and this is enlarged upon here; the symbolism and esoteric significance of the Cit Sabhā, the heart of the temple, will be discussed in detail in chapter 4.

Cidambaram has a good claim to be the greatest of all Śiva temples. From the days of the Śaiva saints of the seventh and eighth centuries it has been for southern Śaivas the *kōyil*, the temple *par excellence* which needs no other name to be known. Today it remains a popular temple, though not on the scale of the Mīnākṣī temple in Madurai, which has the economic advantage of being in the centre of a rapidly growing industrial city. The most popular and the richest temple in all India is the Vaiṣṇava shrine in Tirupati, Andhra Pradesh, notwithstanding its remoteness. Nevertheless, the increased popularity of Naṭarāja in the second half of the twentieth century along with the great revival of dance have assisted the temple's reputation in India at large. Within Tamilnadu the temple enjoys a very special position, being the only major temple to have remained outside the control of the state government. It did not entirely escape the DMK attack on Sanskrit and Sanskrit learning in recent decades,[4] but several learned priests have kept alive the scholarship and poetry that have been part of the Cidambaram tradition from earliest times.

The plan shown in plate 11 provides a clear conceptual model in the eye of an artist. The Śivagaṅgā tank is misplaced, but otherwise the essential features are in place. The prominence of the two sages, Vyāghrapāda and Patañjali, is characteristic of all post-eighteenth-century representations of Śiva dancing in Cidambaram. The South *gopura* is in reality no larger than the others, but its greater significance, since Śiva faces south, is signalled today by two orange flags that fly from its roof. The drawing clearly shows the enclosures, and above all the supreme importance of the Cit Sabhā.

The actual form of the temple is asymmetrical and atypical; its development hard to unravel. Its *gopuras* are the oldest group of four *gopuras*, and their irregular positioning suggests that the four-gateway ground plan had not been made canonical by the time of their construction.[5] These *gopuras* are a valuable expression of Cōḻa art, and a virtually complete statement of Cōḻa Śaiva iconography. The huge scale of the temple, the area defined by the positions of the *gopuras* being no less than 16,500 sqm, demonstrates the importance of the temple in the thirteenth century.[6]

சிதம்பரம்

11. Plan of Sabhānāyaka temple. Madras 1867 edition of *Kōyil Purāṇam*.

MŪLANĀTHA, THE ORIGINAL *LIṄGA* SHRINE

Of all the *liṅga*s and mobile images
to be found in the holy places He has favoured,
whether in the underworld, the world of mortals, or heaven,

the source is the blessed Mūlanātha, 'the Original Lord',
the best of Śiva *liṅga*s which ever shines
to the north of His Hall in the inner enclosure.
. . . (296)[7]

This is where Vyāghrapāda worshipped, though he also established his own *liṅga* shrine half a mile away.[8] The Mūlasthāna, 'The Place of the Original Liṅga', is now in the second enclosure, and presumably was so in Umāpati's day, since the wall enclosing the Cit Sabhā (and the Kanaka Sabhā; and the Viṣṇu complex) is said to have been built by Kulōttuṅga I (1070–1122).

Kulke, in his analysis of the *Cidambara Māhātmya*, declares with confidence, 'The older and conservative element in Cidambaram is represented by the *liṅga* cult and the younger and more dynamic one by the cult of the dancing Śiva.'[9] The author of the Vyāghrapāda legend 'was the apologist of a threatened *liṅga*-cult'.[10] This is too stark a contrast. On the evidence of the *Cidambara Māhātmya* itself, and as we shall see on the evidence also of the *Kuñcitāṅghristava*, the basic and constant worship of Śiva is always conducted by worshipping the *liṅga*. While Vyāghrapāda waits for Śiva to perform in this world age the *ānandatāṇḍava*, not only does he worship at the Mūlasthāna, he also sets up his own *liṅga* shrine; so too Patañjali. It is the natural thing to do, and does not in any sense contradict the dance. The principal activity in the Kanaka Sabhā in front of Naṭarāja is the worship of the small Crystal Liṅga which was given to the priests by Śiva himself. We have already seen the striking verse of *Kuñcitāṅghristava* where the drops of water from Naṭarāja's locks become *liṅga*s. Historically, Naṭarāja worship is later than *liṅga* worship, but there is not the least conflict between the two forms of worship. The earliest sculptures of Dancing Śiva represent him as ithyphallic. On the evidence of the *Cidambara Māhātmya* it is worship of the *liṅga* that brings the vision of the Dance. In the *Kuñcitāṅghristava* we find that for the planets and even the gods *liṅga*-worship is an integral part of worshipping Naṭarāja:

Desirous of seeing His dance
the planet lords, the sun, the moon and the others,
settled in Cidambaram.

They established *liṅgas* in their own names
beside the excellent edge of the Śivagaṅgā tank
and worshipped there;

and also constantly meditated
on His gentle radiant dance
that continued in their hearts just as it did outside.
. . . (119)[11]

Viṣṇu, Brahmā, delightful Lakṣmī;

Indra, Fire and Yama,
Nirṛti the lord of Rākṣasas,
Varuṇa with his noose,
Vāyu, Kubera, three-eyed Īśāna;

Aruṇa and other gods, the Moon and Sun,
have constantly beheld the dance of Paśupati
in His most holy place.

They have established *liṅgas* in their own names,
bowed before them,
and enjoyed perfect happiness.
. . . (38)[12]

The worship of Naṭarāja did not supplant but complemented the established worship of the *liṅga*. The worship of Śiva as dancer was well established from the time of Tiruñāṉacampantar, the first of the *Tēvāram* poets. There is neither evidence nor reason for the hostility Kulke supposes.

His house is resplendent with five walls,
with gleaming *gopuras* in each direction
to the number of the Vedas,

with five Halls
which are the sheaths of Brahman –
food and the others, –

with the holy waters,

and with the shrines of the Blessed Mūlasthāna,
Devī, Viṣṇu, Elephant-faced Vināyaka, and Skanda.

Him Who constantly performs His dance
there in the Sheath of Bliss,
Whose foot is curved,
I worship. (76)[13]

The most obvious feature of a South Indian temple is its *gopuras*. Those of Cidambaram are around 40 m in height, and are landmarks for sailors, Cidambaram being some 5 km from the sea, as well as for travellers by land. The Vedas here signify the number 4, there being four Vedas, but at the same time the special Vedic authenticity of the temple is asserted.

The *gopuras* are shining *(vilasad)*. *Vi-las* is an important word in Sanskrit poetry. It signifies the vibrant quality of light, and of life itself. Today there is a double contrast in the *gopuras* at Cidambaram, as elsewhere. The stuccowork of the tiered upper section, modern since it has to be periodically renewed, contrasts with the fine Cōḻa sculptures of the stone lower section. Again, the garish colours of the upper section contrast with the bare stone beneath. Originally, the stonework was probably finely plastered and painted, and the stucco work would have matched the stone sculpture in quality.

The *gopuras* were completed not long before the writing of our poem, and quite possibly within Umāpati's memory. For him they were relatively modern buildings. The West and East *gopuras* were probably completed around 1250. In Harle's opinion, the South *gopura* was entirely built at some time between 1248 and 1272, though some decorative detail and bas-relief figures were left unfinished. Because of slight differences between the West *gopura* and the three other *gopuras*, and because of the style of the West *gopura*, Harle argues that the West is the earliest. The South *gopura* bears the mark of Sundara Pāṇḍya, and it is called the Pāṇḍya *gopura*, but his claim to have built it is generally disputed by scholars. Although the South *gopura*, closest in time to Umāpati, displays an evident stylistic decline from the art of the first two *gopuras*, nevertheless, Umāpati may fairly be said to have lived amid the glories of Cōḻa art. It must indeed be stressed how dominant the *gopuras* are. Not only in entering and leaving the temple, but wherever one moves in the outer courtyard, one cannot but be aware of them.[14]

Harle begins his discussion of the iconography of the Cidambaram *gopuras* with these words:

> At the end of the Cōḻa period, the great *gopuras* succeeded the *vimānas* as the most important buildings of the temple in a physical sense and the stage was set for a new phase in South Indian temple iconography. The iconography of these *gopuras*, some with upwards of seventy niches containing images, was potentially far richer and more complex than that of any previous buildings, not excluding the great *vimānas* of Tanjore, Gaṅgaikoṇḍacōḻapuram, Dārāsuram or Tribhuvanam.[15]

Harle goes on to say that the Cidambaram *gopuras* 'are among the very first seven-storey *gopuras* to have been built and the earliest to have survived intact.' A point which I do not think has hitherto been made by any scholar is that it was precisely and uniquely at Cidambaram that such structures were needed because the centre of the temple contained no *vimāna* to carry the iconic statement of the forms of Śiva.[16] In every other temple of the period, the exterior of the *vimāna*, the towering superstructure of the *garbhagṛha*, bore the sculptures that were the temple's chief public statement after the essential form, the *mūlamūrti*, hidden within. The kings who built the four royal temples named by Harle were all devotees of Naṭarāja, and the creation of Cidambaram is intimately related to those other temples. Its grandeur could be no less than those statements of royal power, and the only way to achieve that was by building the great *gopuras*. It was not feasible to build a *vimāna* over the Cit Sabhā; and the form of the *gopuras* is manifestly based on that of the *vimāna*.[17] The lack of a *vimāna* over a central shrine necessitated the development of the *gopuras* in Cidambaram as major iconographic statements. I would add the thought that once the decision was made to shift the iconographic statement formerly found on the *vimāna*, the logic of the situation demanded four such *gopuras*, otherwise the centre of iconographic gravity would entirely shift away from the centre. With such *gopuras* in each direction, however, due weight was restored to the centre.

The first tier of all the *gopuras* is crowded with divinities other than Śiva; the second tier rises up grandly and spaciously and is devoted to forms of Śiva. The first tiers each have forty-six images, the upper tiers twenty-three. The sculptural programme of each *gopura* is the same.[18] We shall have occasion in further chapters to refer to particular images on the *gopuras*; note here that *vilasad* surely refers not only to the shining masses of the towers, but also to the throbbing presence of multiple sculptures.

Finally on the subject of the *gopuras* in this chapter, the fact that the *gopuras* are in each direction –

> His house is resplendent . . .
> with gleaming *gopuras* in each direction
> to the number of the Vedas –

merits discussion. The standard form of a great South Indian temple is that of a rectangle with an entrance in the centre of each side. In Cidambaram, however, although the 1867 drawing given above (page 49) showed the *gopuras* as situated centrally, they are in fact not so situated.[19] The true positions are shown in the scale plan in fig. 1 above (p. 6). These asymmetrical positions are difficult to account for. The South *gopura* is the only one in line with the axis of a shrine, the Cit

Sabhā. It may well be that the South and West *gopuras* are on the site of entrances of a very early period of the temple, whereas the other two had their positions determined only at the building of the *gopuras* now in existence, by which time the whole site had grown.

Let us turn now to one more other striking characteristic of the Southern temple in general, namely the series of enclosure walls. Jouveau-Dubreuil likened the procedure by which the temple precincts were expanded to the phenomenon of the growth of a tree trunk, the cross-section of which shows a number of concentric rings each an annual contribution to its thickness. On the same principle the earlier enclosures are those towards the centre, while each concentric wall with its gateways records successively a later addition. However, a full quota of enclosures seems to have been present at an early stage in Cidambaram. Not only does Umāpati speak of five walls, or enclosures (the word *prākāra* means both wall and enclosure), five enclosures are mentioned already in the *Cidambara Māhātmya.* In chapter 18, the *gaṇas* ask Nandikeśvara who is going to protect the boundaries of the temple Hiraṇyavarman has renewed.

Nandikeśvara appointed his own entourage to be the guards of the Sabhā, surrounding it (1). For the protection of the next courtyard he appointed *bhūtas* (2); for the next courtyard, *piśācas* (3); as protectress of the courtyard after that Kālī and her own attendants (4); beyond there, he ordained Bhairava and others as protectors (5).[20]

In the *Kōyil Purāṇam*, Nandikeśvara says,

> These ones will valiantly protect all this house:
> *pāriṭams* who crowd everywhere
> will protect the inner parts.
> Next, the middle portions will be guarded
> by many angry *kūḷis* and by Kāḷi.
> The outer parts will be guarded
> by appropriate classes
> of the Lord's hosts. (*Kōyil Purāṇam, Naṭarācaccarukam* 50)[21]

In both accounts, the preceding discussion shows the Gaṇas, Śiva troops under Nandikeśvara's command, to be indignant that mortals should freely behold Śiva's Dance. This angry jealous nature seems to be proper to door-keepers, and here perhaps increases along with distance from the centre. Kālī is mentioned only here in both texts.[22] The *Cidambara Māhātmya*, by referring to Kālī as she who stands beside the Lord, is perhaps referring to Śivakāmasundarī in her separate shrine in what is now the third enclosure. Alternatively, the Kālī temple is referred to. It may well be that the fifth enclosure is the remainder of the city. A variety of fierce boundary goddesses is to be found around the outskirts of the town, especially to the north, and such has doubtless been the case for centuries. But today there are not held to be any such dangerous presences within the temple itself.

Given that Umāpati does refer to five enclosures, it is also surprising that when he introduces the Upaniṣadic idea of the five sheaths of a human being, he links this idea not to the enclosures, but to the five halls. That the enclosures represent these sheaths is a notion which is popular in modern times at least. For example, G. Vanmikanathan:

> To Maanikkavaachakar and, indeed, to all the saints of Tamilnaadu, and, for that matter, even to the common man, the abode of God is his own body, his mind, his heart . . . This faith has been extended to the ground plan of the temples by the great sages who wrote the Aagamas . . . [The] five courtyards represent the five sheaths of a human body, viz. *annamaya kośa, prāṇamaya kośa, manomaya kośa, vijñānamaya kośa, ānandamaya kośa.* – . . . the sheath of food, i.e., food transformed into flesh, the sheath of breath, the sheath of mind, the sheath of intellect, and, ultimately, the sheath of bliss.[23]

And more pertinently the same claim with regard to Cidambaram itself was made in 1983 by Somasetu Dīkṣita in his introduction to the second volume of the Cidambaram ritual text, the *Citsabheśotsavasūtra.* Umāpati, however, unquestionably links the sheaths with the five halls –

> . . . five halls
> which are the sheaths of Brahman –
> food and the others –[24]

The five halls as understood today, and presumably then, are, in inverse order of proximity to the centre, the Rāja Sabhā (the Thousand-pillared Hall), the Deva Sabhā, the Nṛtta Sabhā, the Kanaka Sabhā and the Cit Sabhā.[25]

The five Sabhās do not correlate with the five enclosures. The Cit Sabhā and the Kanaka Sabhā, respectively the sheaths of bliss and knowledge, are in the innermost enclosure. The Nṛtta Sabhā, the sheath of intellect (*manas*) and the Deva Sabhā, the sheath of breath, are in the second enclosure. The Rāja Sabhā, the Thousand-pillared Hall, is in the third enclosure.

Other than the key identification of the Cit Sabhā with the Consciousness that is Bliss, there would seem to be no special force in the connections made here. Certainly none is spelled out. But the five halls do have both a certain unity and a clear progression of significance. All have the same type of roof, and are as it were variations on the basic theme of the Cit

Sabhā as an assembly hall. The Kanaka Sabhā is in many respects a duplicate of the Cit Sabhā. The Nṛtta Sabhā is an elegant and ornate pavilion containing principally the shrine of Śiva as Ūrdhvatāṇḍava, but also space for a dancer to dance. The Deva Sabhā houses the many bronze images of the temple and other precious objects; the Dīkṣitas hold their assemblies on the steps in front of it. The Rāja Sabhā, vast in extent, is only entered twice a year by devotees; kings were crowned there in Cōḻa times.

The Nṛtta Sabhā is the most ornate of these halls. It is also the only one easily examined. It is an extremely interesting structure in design, being a stone chariot, provided with two stone wheels, and two stone horses.[26] However only the top of one wheel and the head of one horse are now visible, having been concreted over to strengthen the basic structure as part of the Kumbhābhiṣeka of 1955. At an early period the structure was curtailed by part of the Viṣṇu complex to the south, and cut sheer away to the north to make a passageway. And as early as the construction of the wall of the first enclosure, its position in relation to the Cit Sabhā was clearly demoted.

Apparent in the representation of the temple in plate 11 above is the potentially significant position of the Nṛtta Sabhā. At present the lack of a southern entrance to this enclosure considerably reduces the architectural value of the Nṛtta Sabhā. But it is also noteworthy that Umāpati makes no reference to the Nṛtta Sabhā other than its presumed inclusion in the list of five Sabhās. It now houses the shrine for Ūrdhvatāṇḍava Śiva along with a small Kālī beside his feet, but this shrine is clearly a later addition, the original ornate pillars being crudely walled off here to enclose the shrine on three sides. This shrine faces east, which is at odds with the orientation of the Sabhā, which faces the Cit Sabhā, and towards which its now hidden horses were intended to be seen drawing it.

Also present in the innermost courtyard is the Viṣṇu shrine, set at right angles to the Cit Sabha. The present building of the Vishnu shrine which is known as Govindarāja is not old. The rectangular *garbhagṛha* has a barrel roof, and has an *ardhamaṇḍapa* and a *pradakṣiṇa patha* (circumambulation passage). Vaikhānasa priests (*arcakas*) officiate at this shrine. In the past there have been disputes with the Dīkṣitas, and the ownership of the Hundred-pillared Hall remains in dispute. It is significant that the ritual texts of the temple do not mention the Hundred-pillared Hall; nor does Umāpati. Either it was simply superseded by the Thousand-pillared Hall, or it belonged to the Vaiṣṇavas. The Vaiṣṇavas could have been allowed to use it after the construction of the Thousand-pillared Hall; or it could have been allocated to them by Acyutadeva Rāya when he rebuilt the Viṣṇu shrine in the sixteenth century. Although the shrine has established its autonomy in law, one public assertion of status is not permitted – a flag may not be raised on the shrine's flagpole.

Verse 76 quoted above includes the Viṣṇu shrine when it speaks of the five shrines:

> and with the shrines
> of the Blessed Mūlasthāna,
> Devī, Viṣṇu, Elephant-faced Vināyaka, and Skanda . . .

In modern times 'the five shrines are frequently spoken of by the priests, but the Viṣṇu shrine is no concern of the Śaivas, and the Cit Sabhā is included to make up the five.[27] The Viṣṇu shrine was clearly subordinate in Umāpati's day, as demonstrated by its orientation with the head submissively towards the Cit Sabhā, and it was perhaps under the overall control of the Dīkṣitas. The *Cidambara Māhātmya*, as we saw in the last chapter, establishes Viṣṇu as Śiva's helper.

THE PRIESTS

We come now to consider the personnel of the temple, the 'three thousand priests' whose mythico-historical origin was mentioned in the previous chapter. Their importance for this study is very great, for Umāpati was one of their number, they were his audience, and it is only among them that the poem has survived to the present. In the poem, they are frequently mentioned. Here is a typical example:

> Those who possess faith,
> who know the Vedas,
> learning the *śāstra*s and other sciences
>
> through the grace of supreme Śiva,
> abandoning meaningless speech,
> doing *pūjā* to Him, the Lord, several times a day,
> performing the ritual actions laid down by the Veda,
>
> they obtain the Awareness of the Self
> that is very hard to obtain for any one else,
>
> they, the Brahman lords, portions of Him
> Who bears the axe and the deer,
> . . . (92)[28]

However, to properly appreciate the position of the priests of Cidambaram, various factors must be understood. In the first place, the status of a temple priest is relatively low. Although he calls himself a Brahman, other Brahmans consider him degraded by his contact with worshippers at large, and consider his Brahmanhood to be only nominal. In Tamilnadu, Śaiva priests generally belong to the Ādiśaiva caste, said to have emanated directly from Śiva, rather than from Puruṣa as did the four *varṇa*s, the four main castes. The origins of the Ādiśaivas are described in the Āgamas, and it is the Āgamas rather than the Vedas that they are supposed to study. The Cidambaram priests are a special case, for they came originally from outside Tamilnadu; and they put special emphasis on their performance of ritual according to the Vedas. Although in the opinion of other Brahmans they are, so to speak, tarred with the same brush, as other temple priests, the Dīkṣitas marry only amongst themselves, and the women are supposed never to leave Cidambaram.[29] A remarkable feature is their democratic organization, where all priests have an equal say, and all are trustees of the temple. Young and old, they have far more self-confidence and pride in their temple than is usual among other temple priests, however dedicated they may be.

As in other large temples, menial tasks, especially cooking, are performed by low Brahman families. For chanting during the fire sacrifice and for *śrāddha* rituals ordinary, that is high-status, Brahmans, are employed by the priests, three families being authorized at present to provide this well-paid service. At the same time, several Dīkṣitas are studying the Vedas, that is to say, recitation of the Vedas; and a traditional school of Vedic recitation has been started by one of the Dīkṣitas. This is both a raising of status and the beginning of a return to the earlier glories of the temple.

We have also to consider the account of the priests in the *Cidambara Māhātmya* and the *Kōyil Purāṇam*. In both texts, there is the account of the priests' arrival from the north, and in the *Cidambara Māhātmya* an introductory account of the priests at the beginning of the text. The key episode in their arrival, and one that is often referred to today, is not referred to in the *Kuñcitāṅghristava*.

In the *Cidambara Māhātmya*, the king arrives with all his people and with the priests. The king witnesses the *ānandatāṇḍava* and faints, overwhelmed by emotion. He then displays to the sage Vyāghrapāda the sage-lords (*munīśvara*) he has brought back with him.

But among those *munis* who were devoted to Him, their selves perfected, 3000 in number, there was one the King did not see. Then the King's face went white, his heart was dismayed. When he had counted again and again, but could not see the sage who would complete their number, who indeed was not to be found amongst all the people, then even as the King was lamenting, a voice was heard, sweet and calm, audible among other voices but which came from no embodied person (*śrāvyā vāṇīnām aśarīriṇī*). 'O Hiraṇyavarman, one among these sages (*muni*) is missing. Do not grieve in your heart as to how this came about. For these of pure lineage, whose lustre is that of blazing fire, I shall be the one who makes their number total three thousand.' Hearing this speech which was like a proclamation of coronation the King lost his grief and considered those Brahman lords (*viprendra*) to be the Lord incarnate (*īśavigraha*).

(*Cidambara Māhātmya* 24.78–84)

In the *Cidambara Māhātmya*, the chapter concludes with the sages (*muni*), 'their faces and hearts bright, great in power', telling Vyāghrapāda that even if Brahmā again asks for them to attend his sacrifice, they must never again be sent from Cidambaram:

And the son of Madhyandina, hearing the words of those sages (*muni*) of unlimited power smiled gently and said, 'So be it.' Then settling the sage-lords (*munīśvara*) and the army to the west of the Golden Sabhā, the King, his joy unequalled, dwelt there with his armies, the sage-lords (*munīndra*) and all his people beholding the Tāṇḍava of Śambhu.

The version in the *Kōyil Purāṇam* is similar, but the account of the journey is expanded and poeticized. Mention is made several times of the chariots ('like red suns' *Kōyil Purāṇam, Iraṇiyavaṉma carrukam* 119) the priests are given to ride in; and when they reach Cidambaram, 'the great jewelled chariots' are drawn up in a straight line so that they can be presented to Vyāghrapāda (*Kōyil Purāṇam, Iraṇiyavaṉma carrukam* 127).

The priests' status is thus affirmed in the words of the *Kōyil Purāṇam*:

The Unblemished One who is
Mother and Father to all beings
Saw the sincere anguish of the prince
Who could not find one of those
Great ones of perfect truth and
Proclaimed for all the gods to hear,
'They are all equal to Us and we are equal to them.
We are one among them.'

Everybody heard these words of grace.
The prince realized that the Vedic Sages have the greatness
Of the Lord of the Vedas who
Dances in the hall of Tillai

Being one among them.
He came and bowed at their feet
With a trembling heart as the gods
Poured down a rain of flowers.

(*Kōyil Purāṇam, Iraṇiyavaṉma carrukam* 128–9)[30]

This is not unlike the *Cidambara Māhātmya*, though it does not repeat the Sanskrit text's mention of the great power and indeed the unlimited power of the priests; but the next verse of the *Kōyil Purāṇam* is very different:

The sages shining by their number
Were afraid of themselves because of the grace
Given by the Lord of the Gods.
They fell on the earth and arose revived.
They bowed and worshipped Him forgetting (themselves)
They said, 'Give us the grace of taking us
As slaves in seven births,' and danced
Holding their staves wrapped in cloth.

(*Kōyil Purāṇam, Iraṇiyavaṉma carrukam* 130)[31]

We are now in an altogether different environment. The falling to the earth, and the dancing, behaviour nowadays rigorously excluded from the temple even on the part of devotees, let alone the priests, belong to popular religion and are not countenanced by the Sanskrit tradition.[32] However, in the light of this version, we should perhaps look closely at the *Cidambara Māhātmya*'s account of the King fainting when on his return he sees the *ānandatāṇḍava*:

He beheld the Tāṇḍava of Śambhu. Then he experienced
the bliss of consciousness in Cidambaram, that steals the sight,
the *ānandatāṇḍava* of Śambhu that removes all taints.
He lost his power of speech and his power of movement.
He lost his power of sight. His heart lost its power.
He fainted, overwhelmed by his emotion (*rasa*).
And then when the confusion (*moha*)
generated by seeing the Tāṇḍava had departed,
the King bowed to Naṭarāja and went out.

(*Cidambara Māhātmya* 24.74–7)

The use of the rare word *analambhūṣṇu*, 'bereft of power', in verses 75 and 76 adds to the force of the account. Here, then, the phenomenon of trance, confirmed by the state of confusion (*moha*), is focussed by the author of the *Cidambara Māhātmya* entirely on the King, and not a breath of it touches the priests.

Also to be considered here is the account of the priests given as a kind of crescendo at the end of the introductory part of the *Cidambara*

Māhātmya that precedes the story of Vyāghrapāda. This account is given by Śiva to Nandikeśvara (so Sūta informs his disciples). Three main threads run through this lyrical effusion. One is that the priests are very good Brahmans.

Twice-born, of excellent birth, their minds purified by their *tapas*,
among the Vedas, O Gaṇa-lord, they are all a synonym for Brahmā.
Ever satisfying the gods with the great sacrifices where the fees are liberal
with honest hearts they perform *pūjā* to me.
. . .
There is ever very pure speech in their mouths,
the Goddess of prosperity in their glance, quietude (*śānti*) in their hearts,
beauty in their bodies.
. . .
Devoted to truth and religious observances, their radiance blazing like fire,
the topmost peaks of the mountain of Dharma, suns to the darkness of sin,
they bestow knowledge free from taint through the attainment of seedless yoga,
seeing Śiva in their hearts, these ascetics rejoice.
. . .
Husbands of the Muses (*kalāvilāsinī*), lovers of the Sciences,
moons rising from the oceans of the Śāstras, O Nandin!
cuckoos in the park of the Āgamas,
Ever attentive to their guests,
devoted to the performance of the six duties of Brahmans,
these supreme twice-born are the embodiment of true and pure behaviour.
(*Cidambara Māhātmya* 5. 2, 3, 5, 7, 8, 10, 11)

Beyond this standard Brahmanism, the Three Thousand have a special purifying quality.

Free of lust, anger and the other faults,
destined to good fortune (*bhāgyaśālin*),
. . .
the sight of them destroys other men's misdeeds.
Further, the pure-syllabled utterances of these twice-born
root out men's sins without extraneous aid.
. . .
Seeing them once has the fruit of long performance of asceticism.
Grave sins are quickly dissolved by thinking on these.
. . .
Seeing those twice-born just once, their bodies adorned with ash,
is very great *tapas* for the body and removes the taints.
(*Cidambara Māhātmya* 5. 6, 9, 14, 21)

Here the ambiguous status of the temple priest has been made into a positive virtue. The third element is the special relationship that the priests enjoy with Śiva.

> Though they do not have matted locks, nor the crescent moon,
> nor an eye on their foreheads, nor the woman
> in the left-hand side of their bodies, yet are they forms of me.
>
> ...
>
> I too am one of these twice-born, O Nandin!
> and dwelling only there with them I am pleased.
> They alone know my glorious nature which is beyond the supreme,
> but I do not altogether know their supreme and wonderful glory!
>
> ...
>
> Thus, O Nandin, they who meditate on those twice-born
> are meditating on me, the Great Lord,
> and are doing what is pleasing to me.
>
> ...
>
> They are playful manifestations of the Āgamas (*āgamalīlānāṃ*),
> their hearts are intent on me, and I am one like them.
> No one else in the three worlds is like them.
>
> ...
>
> This truth has been told to you, my principal Gaṇa.
> I am not able to speak of all their glory.
>
> (*Cidambara Māhātmya* 5. 4, 12, 13, 23, 25, 29)

Remarkable is the statement, 'They alone know my glorious nature which is beyond the supreme, but I do not altogether know their supreme and wonderful glory!' (*Cidambara Māhātmya* 5.13). The writer or writers of the *Cidambara Māhātmya* clearly felt it necessary to establish the credentials of the Cidambaram priesthood, but for the modern reader such praise might seem inappropriate to Śaiva theology, even to verge on the hysterical. Any judgement, however, needs to be tempered by consideration of the rituals of the priests.

Umāpati himself in the *Kuñcitāṅghristava* has moments of excess in praise of his colleagues, in which a degree of self-praise might be present:

> He is worshipped
> by the three thousand sages in the Sabhā –
> Patañjalis in the science of grammar,
>
> so many venerable Kaṇādas and Akṣapādas
> in the discourses of logic,
> embodiments of Vyāsa in the Vedānta,
> the equals of Kumārilabhaṭṭa in Jaimini's Mīmāṃsā,
> Bodhāyanas in the techniques of Vedic sacrifice,
> veritable Brahmās in the Vedas –

Him the best of teachers,
Whose foot is curved,
I worship. (89)[33]

The phrase 'veritable Brahmās in the Vedas' is reminiscent of the *Cidambara Māhātmya*'s 'among the Vedas they are all synonyms for Brahmā' (*Cidambara Māhātmya* 5.2). But there more stress is placed on their relation to the Āgamas. They are 'cuckoos in the park of the Āgamas' (5.10), and 'playful manifestations of the Āgamas' (*āgamalīlā*) (5.25). In the *Kuñcitāṅghristava*, Umāpati makes a careful statement of the relative weight of the two types of scripture.

For the enlightenment
of pupils excluded from the Vedas

the Brahmans, gods on earth,
read out the *Kāmika* and other Āgamas
which make known His glory
in their Conduct and Yoga sections.

But they themselves,
under white umbrellas held high
by the kings who come
when they perform the Vājapeya sacrifice,

worship Him
according to the way of the revealed Vedas.
. . . (107)[34]

Note the word 'pupils'. Priests today do not normally have pupils; nor are temples the cultural centres they used to be. But, as we shall shortly see, Umāpati had pupils while still a priest in the temple, according to his biography. Nor was this unusual. The *Citsabheśotsavasūtra*, the Festival Ritual text, includes a long series of prose prayers to be said on the raising of the flag at the beginning of the Brahmotsava festival, some of which praise the priests; and their pupils are mentioned: 'pressing at their heels are the tens of millions of their pupils who have come from various countries (*deśa*) to study Śruti, Smṛti, Purāṇas, the Epics, etc. and many sciences'.[35] It is not surprising that the priests were popular teachers if indeed, as the same prayer declares, 'they have studied all the Vedas and quite surpass Lotus-born Brahmā in their understanding of their meaning'.[36]

The performance of Vedic sacrifices by the priests is stressed here and elsewhere in the poem. The same emphasis is found in parallel Cidambaram texts. Thus the *Citsabheśotsavasūtra* says of the priests that they 'enshadow the entire circles of the fourteen worlds with the high lifted white umbrellas they earn through Vājapeya sacrifices'.[37] The *Citsabheśotsavasūtra* differs from the above verse of Umāpati and the *Cidambara Māhātmya* and *Kōyil Purāṇam* by not mentioning knowledge of the Āgamas as part of the priests' learning, although it does refer to twenty-eight pillars of the Cit Sabhā representing the Āgamas.[38]

Umāpati's verse seems to set the Dīkṣitas on a superior plane to the Āgamas; indeed we elsewhere learn that the Dīkṣitas are themselves the Vedas:

> In every *kalpa* the Vedas,
> to lose their fear of birth in the first half
> and of destruction in the second half,
> satisfy the Death of Death with manifold asceticism
>
> and at His command
> become three thousand Brahmans –
> a state unobtainable by the gods themselves,
> and in due order constantly worship Him
> according to the procedures of His path.
> . . . (176)[39]

The Āgamas are clearly second best, for Śiva's purpose in publishing them is

> So that those who have no right
> to perform the rituals laid down in the Vedas
> could attain Dharma and the other ends of man,
> . . . (146)[40]

In one verse the Brahmanhood of the priests contaminates, so to speak, the final goal, which is said to be Brahmā's palace, despite the continuous vision of Naṭarāja.

> The best of the wise,
> making their home in His holy place,
> meditating on Him in the lotuses of their hearts,
> chanting the Mantra,
>
> beholding Him with His consent
> all the time performing His dance
> in the Golden Hall where
> His praises are sung by Brahmā and Viṣṇu,
>
> live happily, all their desires fulfilled
> and after this life that is their last
> rejoice in Brahmā's palace.
> . . . (147)[41]

The priests are here called 'the best of the wise' (*vibudhaparibṛḍha*). The choice of names for the Three Thousand is significant. Although in this study it is convenient, and indeed entirely fitting, to speak of them of as priests, Umāpati never once does so. They are always Brahmans, ascetics, sages, or simply the pure, the wise. The term *munivara*, 'excellent sage', used five times, plus three times of particular *munis*, is possibly adopted under the influence of the Tamil for *muni*, namely *muṉivar*.[42] By contrast, *muni* alone is used only twice (106, 142), *munīndra* once; *yativara* twice (95, 210). Most frequently they are called Brahmans: *vipra* (17, 47, 69, 276), *viprendra* (92). One goal of the poem, as in the case of the *Cidambara Māhātmya*, is to persuade the reader of the true Brahman status of the priests, and the palace of Brahmā here is in some sense a vision of that goal.

The earliest mention of the priests of Cidambaram is in the eighth century with Cuntarar's listing of the Śaiva saints, the *Tiruttoṇṭattokai* hymn, where they hold pride of place. The hymn begins,

> I serve the servants of the Brahmans living in Tillai.

However, it has nothing else to say of them. A detailed, if idealized, picture is given in the twelfth century by Cēkkiḻār in his *Periya Purāṇam*, the key text of Tamil Śaiva devotion, written, it is said, in Cidambaram.

> With beauteous ornaments rich beyond reckoning
> They deck the Lord and perform the auspicious rites;
> They hail the Lord with the words of the Vedas;
> They render gloriously all other service, befitting them;
> Service within the Lord's temple and shrine is theirs.
>
> Poised in dharma, they cultivate and master the four Vedas
> And their sextuple components of radiant truths;
> They tend the Triple Fire that lives may thrive in grace;
> They are rich in their servitude divine
> Of the great Lord of the Grand Dance.
>
> They descend of a flawless race and are impeccable;
> By their sovereign acts sixfold, they have chased Kali away;
> They deem as wealth true, only the Holy Ash;
> Love of Śiva is all that they seek after; thus they thrive.
>
> Flawless is their mastery of Carya, Kriyā, Yoga and Jñāna;
> They are great in munificence and ascesis;
> They are everpoised in righteousness;
> They lack nothing; poised in patience and honour

They are the divine Brahmans whose intellect
Hath been by Śiva clarified; they are
Three thousand strong who have in this very life
Gained the Lord-God for their adoration.
What other beatitude are they in need of?
They alone are their equals; unique is their glory.
(*Periya Purāṇam* 353–7)[43]

This discussion of the priests of Cidambaram may be fittingly closed with the *Rājendrapura Māhātmya*'s description of Umāpati in his fifty-sixth year as he went out from the temple after worshipping Naṭarāja:

He got in the palanquin with its high poles topped by golden bulls on each side and set off while his sons and crowds of disciples, who knew the Vedas, recited the Three Vedas in due order.[44]

RITUALS

Umāpati's encounter with the Śaiva Siddhānta teacher Maṟaiñāṉa Campantar will be examined in some depth in chapter 5, along with a general description of the complex of ideas current at the time. We have now, however, to consider the work of the priests as described in the *Kuñcitāṅghristava*. Despite the careful absence of any word for functioning priest in the poem,[45] and the constant stress on the spiritual wisdom and purity of the Three Thousand, their daily work, then as now, was service of Śiva in the temple.

In his references to ritual Umāpati closely follows the ritual manual attributed to Patañjali. This differs from the ritual followed by all other Śaiva temples in that it is not centred on a fixed *liṅga* in a *garbhagṛha*, a central *sanctum sanctorum*; and in that the ritual procedures, though otherwise sharing common features, are punctuated throughout by Vedic mantras.

At Cidambaram, there are three key objects of daily ritual, for while Naṭarāja is supreme, ritual actions are focussed on the Crystal Liṅga and the ruby Naṭarāja. Cidambaram is not alone in having such special objects, but normally such supernumerary pieces supplement the *liṅga*, which is not the case in the Cit Sabhā.

Another factor is that while all temple ritual has a theatrical quality the daily ritual at Cidambaram, performed on the raised platform of the Kanaka Sabhā, is all the more like a stage performance. That this is so follows from the fact that both the Cit Sabhā and Kanaka Sabhā are modelled on a dancer's stage.

A connected account of the rituals and festivals of the temple is given in the opening section of the poem, following on its selective summary of the *sthalapurāṇa*. This section on ritual and festival is followed by a verse describing Brahmā and Viṣṇu searching for the top and bottom of Śiva's *liṅga*, the scene usually sculpted on the west face of the exterior of the *garbhagṛha* in other Cōḻa Śiva temples, and here indicating that the most intimate details of the temple have for the most part now been given.

> The boar whose name was Viṣṇu, Lord of Śrī,
> could not see the lotus of His foot.
>
> The goose whose name was Brahmā
> could not see the crest of His crown,
> so we are told.
>
> . . . (27)

Verse 27, then, marks the end of the poet's formal introduction to Cidambaram, with the allusion to the western outer wall of the *garbhagṛha* of other Śiva temples suggesting the leaving of the sanctum. Verses 14 to 22 refer to the daily ritual of the temple, verses 23 to 26 to the festivals. Verse 14 describes Patañjali's composition of the temple's ritual manual;[46] verse 15 –

> To the Brahmans, gods on earth,
> who delight the Lord of Dance with the worship
> they forever perform six times a day,
>
> and to all living beings, of whatever caste,
> who are His devotees,
>
> He the Performer gives happiness.
>
> To the worshippers in His temple
> He gave the Crystal Liṅga for lustrations.
>
> I worship
> Him Who gives very great happiness,
> Whose foot is curved. (15)[47]

> To their delight,
> for them to perform His worship
> at the appointed times,
>
> He gave the Brahmans a *liṅga*
> made from the solidified foam of nectar
> from the moon on His own head,
> like a diamond,
> surpassing in its lustre

the moon, fire, the sun,
lightning, and the stars,
always sparkling.

Him, Who takes away the fear of existence,
Whose foot is curved,
I worship. (276)[48]

The profound importance of the Crystal Liṅga, the Candramaulīśvara, in the life of the temple led Rājagaṇeśa Dīkṣita to devote fourteen pages of notes to it, whereas no other topic received more than three and a half pages. His enthusiasm led him to claim, for instance, that verse 1726 of the *Tirumantiram* referred to the Crystal Liṅga:

The human form is like the Śiva *liṅga*,
The human form is like Cidambaram
The human form is like Sadāśiva
The human form is like the Holy Dance.[49]

Some say that Umāpati gave the Crystal Liṅga to the temple, which would by no means rule out his praise of it. According to the biography of Umāpati entitled the *Rājendrapura Māhātmya*, the Crystal Liṅga was once in his possession, though unbeknownst to him, when he had been excluded from the temple as a consequence of becoming a disciple of Maṟaiñāṉa Campantar:

One day Umāpati Dīkṣita was about to enter the Temple of the Dancer. The sage-lords angrily said, 'O Umāpati! you must not enter the Temple of the Dancer.' The following day, when the priests attending Naṭarāja went to the Sabhā at the first period of the day, they at once noticed the absence of the golden casket of Candramauli. They went out and summoned all the sage-lords. Then they all came with the temple servants and entered into the assembly hall (the Deva Sabhā), and as they went in they called to the priest on duty. He was standing trembling in the presence of the Dancer but came as soon as called to the Deva Sabhā and throwing open the door told how on entering the Cit Sabhā he noticed that the box of the Moon-crested image was not there. Then the priest in charge of the worship of the Dancer went back to the Cit Sabhā to perform worship to Him.
A certain old man getting up there in the assembly declared, 'I am the blessed Lord of the Sabhā' and related the whole story of Umāpati the priest. 'You must listen.' The sage bulls were listening to his speech with deep devotion when a certain clever boy came in and wrote it all down on a leaf.
[Umāpati is praised by Śiva speaking through the old man, and it is implied, since he is said to have been the protector of Śiva's commands on Mount Kailāsa, that he is an incarnation of Nandikeśvara. The possessed man concludes,]
'Today by my command the box of my *liṅga*, which has my form, rests in Umāpati's faultless ashram. You must all go to this wise man, ask him for it and bring it back.'

So saying, this Lord of the Sabhā disappeared. [Then the priests decided to do as they had been told.] Thus deciding those lordly sages went to Umāpati who was dwelling with his disciples in his monastery which is splendid on the banks of the Śveta in the varied wood called Rājendrapurī and paying respect to him, declared, 'We have greatly offended. O knower of the Great Self! Just today we have learned your greatness from the mouth of the Lord of the Sabhā.' So said the sage-lords.
'Why have you come here?' he asked.
[They tell him what has happened.]
'Where am I, where is the *liṅga*, where is the Sabhā, where is the casket, where are you who are the equals of the Lord of Dancers who dances the Dance of Bliss? I do not know.[50] Nevertheless I will look for the casket.' Thus he spoke before them.
Going right then to the *pūjā* room he looked and saw it. Then the great man said, 'The casket is here today!' Opening the casket he saw the *liṅga*, closed it and gave it to them. Taking the *liṅga* the three thousand Brahmans went to the Cit Sabhā chamber and deposited the casket.
Bathing in the morning, beholding Brahman without qualities, in the middle of the day he worshipped, acted as priest for the *liṅga* and the image. After his meal he set his mind to writing books, at night he always taught two subjects.
[This must mean he started going again to the Temple, and served as priest in the Cit and Kanaka Sabhās, in the mornings.]
With the sounds of the lotus-shaped copper bell accompanying *śruti* and the music of the flute and the *vīṇā* accompanying the Dravidian Veda he constantly performed worship of the Lord of the dance, and of the *liṅga* and the yantra.
(*Rājendrapura Māhātmya*, 21–44)

This long extract throws light not only on the legendary history of our poet, but on the religious and psychological climate of much of Hinduism of whatever date – what for modernity is gross superstition is, in other terms, the frequent willingness of the divine to manifest both in human beings and in material objects.

The sequence of the ritual section of the opening of the *Kuñcitāṅghristava* continues as follows:

Brahmā of a Hundred Sacrifices
performed a sacrifice in great Antarvedi,
a sacrifice that took a thousand years to complete.

In that assembly at Vyāghrapāda's behest
the chief ascetics were present.

So that they could continue to worship Him
He gladly sent a Dancer made of precious stone
arisen from the best of fires.
He is the source of that image,
. . . (16)[51]

As in the case of the Candramaulīśvara, the antecedents of the Ruby Naṭarāja, the Ratnasabhāpati, are remarkable. Since the image came out of Brahmā's own super-sacrifice, the Vedic affiliations of the Cidambaram priests are the stronger. The Dīkṣitas possess, indeed, a kind of quintessential transformation of the whole sacrificial paraphernalia into Naṭarāja in little. Just as in the *Jaiminīya Brāhmaṇa* the daily *agnihotra* sacrifice is said to be an abridgement of Prajāpati's thousand-year sacrifice, and further the ultimate abridgement of all sacrifices, so too the ruby Naṭarāja is, implicitly and visually, an abridgment of the ultimate.

> The Brahmans perform the perpetual rites –
> first the auspicious day;
> reverencing the excellent gurus;
>
> the purification of the body down to the elements
> with the drying up and the other two procedures;
>
> all the affixings
> pertaining to hand, body, OṂ, the gods;
> muttering all the mantras.
>
> First worshipping Him within,
> their bodies made of Śiva,
>
> they conduct worship to Him externally.
> . . . (17)[52]

This verse is concerned with the priest's self-preparation before he begins the exterior ritual. 'The auspicious day', that is the declaration that the day is auspicious, is an old Vedic practice for special ritual occasions that becomes a constant feature of temple ritual. The temple ritual is a codified agglomeration of what were originally scattered special practices. The list of practices here follows the order of Patañjali's *Pūjāsūtra*. By and large, the ritual of the Cidambaram temple differs only from that of temples following Āgamic ritual by its use of Vedic mantras – the procedures are otherwise identical.[53]

The second topic mentioned by Umāpati is that of praising one's gurus. The *Pūjāsūtra* says simply that the priest should bow to Śveta and other gurus, one's own guru, and to Śiva.[54] The additional notes (*Vivaraṇa*) to the *Pūjāsūtra* explain that the other gurus are Gaṇeśa, Umā, Skanda, Viṣṇu, and Brahmā. Śveta heads a remarkable list, but who is Śveta? A Brahman called Śveta figures in the *Liṅga Purāṇa* as a staunch devotee of the *liṅga*; there is the notable Upaniṣadic teacher Śvetaketu. A more likely alternative is Meykaṇṭar who was born in Tiruvengadu, of which Śvetavana is the Sanskrit name, and was named Śvētavaṉapperumāḷ.

Not only was Meykaṇṭar the teacher of Umāpati's teacher, but, according to one life of Umāpati,[55] Umāpati was taught the essential Śaiva path by Śveta, as well as by Maṟaijñāṉa Campantar and Vyāsa and Śiva; not only that, Umāpati was given by Śveta a Gaṇeśa that was a wish-fulfilling creeper, an [*ardha-*]*meru* Cidambara yantra, and an incomparable crystal *liṅga*! Note how doctrine, thought, 'the essential Śaiva path', is inextricably combined with material objects. This kind of combination is a key feature of Hinduism.

Perhaps the most remarkable part of Śaiva ritual is the purification of the body by mentally reducing it to its constituent elements. The priest purifies the elements of his body by mentally drawing them upwards into the last of the yogic centres which is above the body, twelve thumb-widths above, which gives it its name in Sanskrit, 'the *dvādaśānta*'. The element of earth goes up as far as the knees, water from the knees to the navel, fire from the navel to the throat; wind from the throat to the mouth; ether from the mouth up. Each of the elements corresponds to a face of five-headed Sadāśiva. Safely outside the body and joined in the *dvādaśānta* with the radiance of the Lord of the Sabhā, the priest can now proceed with the 'drying up and the other procedures'. He dries up the body with the wind that he has bottled up within it, he burns it with a fire that begins from his big toe to consume all as it rises, and thirdly, as he returns to his body he drenches it in nectar from the body of Śiva.[56]

His body is now purified but it needs to be sanctified. This is achieved by affixing mantras to it. In fact, according to the *Patañjalipūjāsūtra*, this is done to the hands before the purification of the elements (*bhūtaśuddhi*), and the rest of the affixing after the *bhūtaśuddhi*, though normally in Śaiva ritual the hands-and-body affixings are considered as a unit.

He should affix the Praṇava, OṂ, in due order on his arms, elbows, wrists, ribs, stomach, thighs and ankles, mouth, and feet. The most elaborate of the procedures that Umāpati names – the *Patañjalipūjāsūtra* gives details of additional affixings – is that of the gods (*devatānyāsa*). In this, a deity is made to stand in each part of the body, and other deities all around the body, along with mantras from the *Taittirīya Brāhmaṇa*.

The priest now has a divine body, saturated with the power of mantras. With this divine body he can act as a Śiva in the ritual. That the priests every day follow procedures which make, as the verse says, 'their bodies made of Śiva', renders more comprehensible the bold claims of the fifth *adhyāya* of the *Cidambara Māhātmya* reviewed above. Śiva's remark, 'Though they do not have matted locks, nor the crescent moon, nor an eye on their foreheads, nor the woman in the left-hand side of their bodies, yet are they forms of me' (*Cidambara Māhātmya* 5.4), is the more plausible when we remember the ritual.

The next verse continues to follow the course of the daily ritual.

> Consecrating the place and the vessels,
> offering water for washing the feet
> and water for sipping,
>
> then worshipping the conch with flowers,
> performing the worship with the five products of the cow,
> the worship of the pots,
> the water-worship,
>
> the worship of the bull,
> the worship of the door,
> the worship of Gaṇeśa, Lord of Obstacles, and the other gods,
> and the bathing of the Crystal Liṅga and the Ruby Lord.
> They, the pure, worship every day His form;
> . . . (18)[57]

The place and the objects of the ritual, no less than the priest, have to be made pure. Then Śiva is invited as honoured guest, and is accordingly offered water to wash his feet and water to refresh his mouth. The worshipping of the conch involves the priest praising it, offering it flowers and incense, worshipping the sun within the conch, and further purifying it before sprinkling water from it on himself and all the equipment. Nine pots are set out and filled with water and other liquids to be used in the worship of the Crystal Liṅga and also the Ruby Naṭarāja. The pots and their contents are then worshipped.

> Six times a day every day
> the lordly sages free from sin
> worship His *liṅga*
>
> with the five products of the cow;
> with oil;
> with milk, with curds, and with ghee,
> with honey and pure sugar – the fivefold ambrosia;
>
> with sweet lime juice;
> with the water of tender coconut;
> with boiled rice;
> with fragrances,
> with the waters of the other Gaṅgā, the Śivagaṅgā tank.
> . . . (19)[58]

The *liṅga* is anointed with these liquid substances, and the boiled rice is placed before it. Anointing, however, is not quite the right word for the

Sanskrit *abhiṣeka*, since anointing, smearing or rubbing with oil, is the small-scale application of a substance, whereas *abhiṣeka* is large-scale application, the more the better. The root of *abhiṣeka* is *siñc*, 'to sprinkle', but the process of *abhiṣeka* is rather inundation. In the *abhiṣeka*s of the Naṭarāja bronze, the Sabhāpati, described below, thousands of litres of various liquids are used.

Umāpati continues:

> Honouring Her Who is in the Śrīcakra on the wall,
> and after Her
> the Lord of Dancers within the Śaivacakra,
>
> [then the Lord of Dancers]
> and on His left His Jñāna Śakti,
> She Who has two hands and holds a parrot;
>
> then worshipping
> the Bull, Brahmā, and the others;
>
> making all the kinds of reverential food offerings,
> making the external food offerings,
> and performing the *homa*,
>
> they honour Him every day.
>
> . . . (20)[59]

The Goddess in the Śrīcakra on the wall is worshipped, and then Naṭarāja within the Cidambaram cakra. Then, though this is not stated clearly in the verse, the bronze Naṭarāja and the bronze Śivakāmasundarī, as Pārvatī is called in Cidambaram, are worshipped. As part of this worship, the following verses are meditated upon:

> For the image of Śiva without form
> is to be meditated on by worshippers.
> This image has a blue throat,
> is supreme bliss,
> joyously delights in the Tāṇḍava.
> This image is to be worshipped
> by Brahmā, Viṣṇu and Mahādeva
> whose forms have qualities.
> Thus is this supreme image
> of the one who is bereft of all images
> and is the overlord of all beings –
> so says the eternal Śruti.[60]

In the case of the Goddess:

> On the two-eyed, two-armed, Gaurī,
> one-faced, dark in form,
> holding a beautiful lotus in one hand . . .[61]

The Bull and Brahmā are here two instances of the eighteen servants of the Dance (*nṛttasevaka*), whose number begins with Gaṇeśa and ends with Apasmāra.[62] Food offerings (*bali*) are made to Indra and the other gods on the *balipīṭha* in the second enclosure, and fire sacrifice is offered in the sacrifice hall (*yāgaśālā*).

They, the pure, worship Him with incense,
then with the lamps –

the snake-lamp, the man[-animal] lamp,
the bull-lamp, the pot-lamp,
the lamp with five wicks,
the fire-sacrifice-lamp,
the star-lamp, the camphor lamp;

and with ash, with fan,
with excellent white umbrella
and chowry;
with mirror, with mantras, with flowers;
with fine camphor flames held high.
Quickly they abandon ignorance
and see Him clearly every day.
. . . (21)[63]

The importance of lamps is indicated by the fact that of the 135 pages of the *Patañjalipūjāsūtra*, no less than 9 consecutive pages in section 24 are concerned with the lamps. Umāpati continues to follow closely the order of contents of *Patañjalipūjāsūtra*. The multiplicity of lamps shows the importance of fire in worship; and the agglomeration of precise physical objects here is closely related to the condensation of the divine into material form that is evidenced in the Crystal Liṅga and the Ruby Lord of the Hall. And yet it is through this visual bombardment of lamps that the priests are enabled to abandon ignorance. They see Naṭarāja clearly with the various illuminations – and enable the worshippers to see him – but also they see him with spiritual enlightenment. The physical light and the spiritual light are inseparable.

On the perimeter of His dwelling
are the ten lotus-pedestals with their ten bulls
in addition to the large-size pedestal
for the constant presentation of food-offerings
at the three times for Indra and the others.

To all the quarters,
outside on high
the flagpoles shine like nine mountains.
. . . (22)[64]

Umāpati now elaborates on the *bali* offerings referred to briefly in verse 20. It is the duty of every Brahman to make offerings of food (*bali*), usually grains of rice, to all creatures; and temple ritual follows suit, there being special altars (*pīṭha*) provided for the offering of *bali*. A temple always has one main *balipīṭha* in front of the flagpole and the Nandin bull, and then usually other, smaller *balipīṭhas* are placed around the outside of the *garbhagṛha*. In the case of Cidambaram, the minor *balipīṭhas* are, as one would expect, placed around the Cit Sabhā and Kanaka Sabhā, the two forming a single unit, on all four sides, each accompanied by a Nandin bull; the flagpole and the main *balipīṭha* are to the south, in the second enclosure. In the third enclosure, separated by a wall from the Nṛtta Sabhā, are two further massive *balipīṭhas*, and one large Nandin.

FESTIVALS

To provide a coherent account of the ritual life of the temple, I now interrupt Umāpati's opening sequence by including two verses from later in the poem which refer to the *abhiṣeka* of Naṭarāja himself.

> In order to constantly anoint along with mantras
> at the six times of daily worship
> the Crystal Liṅga
> and the image of the Lord of Dance made of precious stone
> with pure and sacred waters (*tīrtha*),
>
> and also at certain times
> the bronze image of the Lord of Dance himself,
>
> Gaṅgā, who forms the ornament of His head,
> by His command flows into the Well of Supreme Bliss,
>
> . . . (74)[65]
>
> It's well known that what is a year for men
> is a day for the gods.
>
> In six of the months
> of what is declared to be that day –
> in Sagittarius, Aquarius,
> Aries, Gemini, Leo, and Virgo –
>
> were the excellent forms of worship
> beginning with sunrise
> for His Dancing Form.
>
> . . . (202)[66]

On these six occasions the bronze Naṭarāja of the Cit Sabhā receives *abhiṣeka*. The time of day for this progresses through the year. Thus the *abhiṣeka* of *mārkaḻi*, December–January, concludes at sunrise, and that of *puraṭṭāci*, September–October, concludes at night. Two of these *abhiṣeka*s are part of the twice-yearly festival, in *āṉi* (June–July) and *mārkaḻi* (December–January), and take place in the Thousand-pillared Hall. The other four take place in the Kanaka Sabhā. Such *abhiṣeka*s today last about 4 hours. *Dīpārādhana*, worship with the waving of lamps, takes place after the image has had the following subtances applied to it: sacred ash, milk, honey, sugar, *pañcāmṛta* (a mixture of milk, sour milk, ghee, honey, and sugar), lemon juice, coconut water, Gaṅgā water, sandal paste. Some fifteen Dīkṣitas are involved in the ceremony. There is also simultaneously a fire offering. The *Śatarudrīya* is recited eleven times and also *Camaka*, sections of the *Yajurveda*, the *Puruṣasūkta*, the *Devīsūkta*, the *Durgāsūkta*, the *Sarasvatīsūkta*, the *Navagrahasūkti*, and the *Taittirīya Upaniṣad*. Finally, returned to the Cit Sabhā, Naṭarāja is decorated with flower garlands and cloths, as is Śivakāmasundarī. A thousand *laṭṭu*s, sweet-balls, are distributed to the Dīkṣitas and others.

The most important day of all is the Ārudra Darśana in *mārkaḻi*, which is a special day throughout Tamilnadu when many Śaivas offer sweet pudding (*kaḷi*) to Naṭarāja and Śivakāmasundarī. This is the day when Patañjali and Vyāghrapāda are said to have made the same offering before seeing the *ānandatāṇḍava* for the first time.

> For His Brahmotsavas every year,
> in the month of Taurus
> the nine flags with their bulls shine;
> in the month of Aquarius there will be five flags;
> and in Sagittarius just one flag;
> and there are respectively
> nine, five and just one fire.
> . . . (23)[67]

A Brahmotsava is the principal festival of a temple; the name sometimes explained by saying that Brahmā conducts the ceremony. On each flag Śiva's Bull is painted. Now only two Brahmotsavas are celebrated annually.

> In the first festival for Him,
> on the bright day of June–July
> for twenty-seven days
> there should be nine foremost priests;
> in February–March five foremost priests,
> and just one in the December–January festival.

For the daily *pūjās* there should be just one priest
in each of these festivals.

The performers of these acts of worship
are pure[st] among the best of sacrificers.
. . . (24)[68]

In His festivals –
first performing the Agnihotra,
the shaving, the purification,
the sipping with mantras,
the sprinkling with mantras,

the purification of the body
with the Pot-gourd verses,
the pacification of the Man of the Site, the Vāstupuruṣa,
that begins with the offering to his feet,

the offering to the Joyful-faced ancestors,
the clod of earth and the sprouts,
the protective amulets,
the sprinkling water on the bull on the flag,
– the pure ones then raise the flag.
. . . (25)[69]

The day before the ritual of setting up the bull flag (*dhvajapaṭavṛṣa*) is performed, the priest in charge of the festival ritual, the Ācārya, having performed the morning fire-offering (*agnihotra*), has his hair and beard cut, removes extraneous body hair, has his nails cut, bathes, puts on new clothes and, sitting facing east, performs purifying mantras, sips water, and scatters water to the accompaniment of mantras (*mantraprokṣaṇa*).[70]

The *kūṣmāṇḍa* or Pot-gourd verses[71] are often-used accompaniments to personal purification. The *Baudhāyana Dharma Sūtra* repeats the declaration of the *Taittarīya Āraṇyaka* II.8 that the man who offers burnt oblations reciting the Kūṣmāṇḍa mantras becomes free from any sin that is less than the murder of a learned Brahman (III.7.1). The Ācārya 'performs the *kūṣmāṇḍa homa.* By this his body is purified, all his sins are removed and he is fit to do good deeds.'[72]

The creative aspect of the raising of the flag which marks the beginning of the festival is brought out by the incorporation of two rituals which are essential features of the ritual for constructing a temple, namely the pacification of the Vāstupuruṣa, the embodied ground-plan of the temple, and collecting earth for the planting of seeds. The offering to the Nāndīmukha ancestors is used by Vaikhānasa Vaiṣṇavas as a ritual for conception, and here is used to promote the successful raising of the flag with which the festival, we might say, is given birth.

The protective amulets, which also feature in weddings, are of gold, silver, or cotton. The Ācārya has one, as do the festival deities and the flagpole. The bull on the flag is treated with great respect. Āgamic texts, though not the Cidambaram text, describe its representation in great detail.[73]

> In the three Brahmotsava festivals
> in His form as Somāskanda
> He rides in a canopy on vehicles
> in the form of
> the moon, the sun, a demon,
> a bull, a royal elephant,
> the Silver Mountain,
> and on a horse;
>
> on the ox-chariot,
> with the ox's eyes opened wide,
> He is the Beggar.
>
> Every day He progresses through the streets,
> bathes,
> and with Śivā enters His own abode.
> . . . (26)[74]

The chief participant deities in the festival are called the Pañcamūrti, the five images. The most important is Somāskanda, that is, Śiva accompanied by Umā and their son Skanda. The other four are Śivakāmasundarī under the name of Śivānandanāyakī, Skanda with his two wives, Gaṇeśa, and Caṇḍeśvara.[75]

On the evening of the second day of the festival, the deities process through the Car Streets for the first time. Somāskanda is seated on a crescent moon of silver-plated wood. On the third evening Somāskanda rides on a sun-shaped vehicle of gold-plated wood. On the fourth evening, Somāskanda is supported by a *bhūta*, a monster in human form, with fangs and four arms. On the fifth evening, Somāskanda is mounted on a bull, but the bull rides in a giant temporary *ratha* modelled on the form of a *gopura*. This special vehicle, which has sixteen wheels, has three compartments. Somāskanda of course takes pride of place, On his left, Śivānandanāyakī, on his right Skanda. On the sixth evening, Somāskanda rides on a silver elephant. On the seventh evening, Somāskanda rides on Mount Kailāsa, with Rāvaṇa shaking the mountain with his twenty hands. This is held to be the most special day of the festival. On the eighth evening, the usual deities, the Pañcamūrti, are not taken out. One *mūrti* alone, Bhikṣāṭana, Śiva the wandering beggar, is taken through the Car Streets, riding in a golden chariot. When Bhikṣāṭana has returned, Somāskanda is taken out on a plain wooden horse. It is said that Somāskanda is on horseback to check the Car Streets in preparation for the following day, when Naṭarāja himself, the *mūla mūrti*, will be taken round in a chariot.

We have now completed our peregrination through the temple, and we have looked at the priests and what they do in the temple. All this has been accomplished on the basis of what Umāpati tells us in his poem, with some help from relevant texts. In the next chapter we go into the Cit Sabhā.

CHAPTER 4

The Hall of Consciousness, the Heart of the Universe

All the Vedas know that I perform the Dance of Bliss,
but they do not know
the cause, the region,
the time, the place.
. . .
There is on earth a certain great and heavenly Hall
that is able to support my dance.

Cidambara Māhātmya 15.21–26

Vyāsa:
Now I will describe the wonderful character of the Sabhā.

Tilvavana Māhātmya 4.1

Two aspects of the complex of religions called Hinduism are crucial for much of its history. On the one hand the enthusiasm for idealism; on the other the perception of physical reality of the supernatural, that it is embedded in concrete things. The Cit Sabhā is a superlative example of the combination of both these aspects. The bronze image of Naṭarāja is pre-eminently present in the Cit Sabhā, which is both the heart of the universe and the consciousness that is found in the heart of every human being. The Cit Sabhā not only enshrines Naṭarāja, but embodies him: the Festival Ritual text says that the temple of the Cit Sabhā is made out of the body of the Lord of the Cit Sabhā.[1]

The supreme importance of the Cit Sabhā is evident in the opening of the *Kōyil Purāṇam*, where the first four verses each end by hailing it, under its Tamil name, *tirucirṟambalam*, 'the holy little hall'. Shulman brings out the contrast between the littleness of the hall and the greatness of Śiva in his translation of the refrain of Cuntarar's single hymn devoted to Cidambaram:

our great lord in the little hall at great Tigertown.[2]

Because of the holiness of the Cit Sabhā, the Tamil *tiruccirṟambalam* also signifies something like 'supreme holiness' and at some point became an invocatory expression used to preface the recitation of *Tēvāram* hymns or to head a document; indeed, it has something of the significance of OṂ in Sanskrit. As we shall see, for Umāpati in his Sanskrit poem, not only Naṭarāja, but the Cit Sabhā as well, are equivalent to OṂ. Two or three centuries before Umāpati, around the time of the composition of the *Sūta Saṃhitā*, the Tamil term *ciṟṟambalam* gave rise to the Sanskritization *cidambara*, the 'sky of consciousness', which was explained as referring to the 'heart teaching' of the *Chāndogya Upaniṣad*.[3] The heart was held to be the centre of consciousness, so that all the world was experienced within the heart and was therefore, in a sense, within the heart:

OṂ! [The teacher should say:] 'Now, what is here in this city of Brahman, is an abode, a small (*daharaṃ*) lotus-flower (*puṇḍarīkaṃ*). Within that is a small space (*daharo. . . ākāśaḥ*). What is within that, should be searched out; that, assuredly, is what one should desire to understand.'

. . . 'As far verily, as this world-space (*ākāśa*) extends, so far extends the space within the heart. Within it, indeed, are contained both heaven and earth, both fire and wind, both sun and moon, lightning and the stars, both what one possesses here and what one does not possess; eveything here is contained within it.'

(*Chāndogya Upaniṣad* 8.1.1 and 5)[4]

This teaching, which by the time of the *Sūta Saṃhitā* was known as the Dahara Vidyā, is promulgated in the Cidambaram *Māhātmya*s.[5] Another, related idea is also developed, namely that the geography of India corresponds to the physiology of the human body, in as much as key Śaiva sites occur as the *cakra*s, spiritual nodes, of the cosmic giant who is the world. In this, the Vedic idea of Puruṣa is linked with the much later ideas of Haṭha yoga.

In chapter 15 of the *Cidambara Māhātmya*, Śeṣa has been practising extreme *tapas* in his longing to see the dance that Viṣṇu has told him of, when Śiva appears and tells him about the Cit Sabhā and its site.

The earth and the body may be said to be the same, O wise one!
The earth has a great vein, the Iḍā nāḍī, that reaches Laṅkā.
There is another called Piṅgalā that reaches the Himalaya,
and between them is the famous Suṣumnā
which reaches the middle of Tillavana.
Very extensive, it (like the other two) belongs to the beautiful earth
which is thus shaped like Puruṣa.
Śrīparvata is said to be at his crown,
Kedāra mountain is at the forehead,
the great place called Kailāsa peak at the head,
O Śeṣa! Vārāṇasī, with the holy river, is between the brows,

Kurukṣetra is on the chest, and Prayāga is called the navel,
while Cidambaram is in the middle of the heart,
and Kamalālaya (Tiruvārūr) is the [Mūl]ādhāra *cakra.*
He who leaves this place and goes to other places
abandons a great jewel he has in his hand for a piece of glass.
The centre of that place is vast, divine, pure, like Brahman,
There is O Śeṣa a great *liṅga* named the Holy Mūlasthāna.
To the south of it, not far away there is a mighty hall, named Sky (*ambara*).
It is wonderful, the source of all good things.
In it I perform my invariable Dance of Bliss.

(*Cidambara Māhātmya* 15.31–9)

This clumsy passage is a conflation of a section of the *Sūta Saṃhitā* that moves from the account of *tīrtha*s to praise of the inner *tīrtha* in the self, for which the jewel in the hand is more appropriate praise.[6] But then Cidambaram itself is the heart!

The word 'invariable' (*abhaṅgura*) in the sentence 'I perform my invariable Dance of Bliss' is necessary not only because of the claimed eternality of the dance, but also to mask the fact that it is a new, Cōḻan, development of the iconography of Śiva. We see clearly here the invention of tradition, a novelty sought to be made the more secure by a double embedding in human physiology. Not only is Cidambaram the heart of the world, but it is the only port of call, as it were, of the world body's central canal (*nāḍī*).

A clearer version is given in the *Kōyil Purāṇam*:

Because the active body corresponds to the physical world
The Iḍā Nāḍī goes through Laṅkā.
The other bright and beautiful Piṅgala Nāḍī
Goes through the great Himalaya.
The Suṣumnā Nāḍī lies between.
That central Nāḍī, the Suṣumnā, which is hard to find
Goes through Tillai.
Shining with goodness,
The Mūla Liṅga is in that place.
To the south of it lies
A permanent hall, unseen
By the Vedas which surround it.
There we dance forever. So said
The Lord who takes us as His slaves.
Because the Hall of the space of wisdom is eternal,
It will not pass away with the things of Māyā.
It will continue forever.
If the souls do countless great *tapas*

And receive the hard won eye of permanent wisdom
They will see the dance.
Those who do not get to see it
Will be reborn. (*Kōyil Purāṇam, Patañcali carrukam* 70–2)[7]

The northern sites of the Sanskrit text are reduced to the 'Himalaya' in this briefer and smoother account. A more fully worked-out sequence is to be found in the *Vyāghrapura Māhātmya* (15.18–33), with Vārāṇasī as the highest, *ājñā*, cakra, preceded by southern sites: Tiruvārūr (Mūlādhāra), Jambukeśvara (Svādhiṣṭhāna), Aruṇācala (Maṇipura), Cidambaram (Anāhata, heart), Kālahasti (Viśuddhi). A yet further development is found in the Festival Ritual text, the *Citsabheśotsavasūtra*, where the great *abhiṣeka*s that take place six times a year in Cidambaram are identified with the six *cakra*s.[8]

Umāpati says that Naṭarāja dances in each of the *cakra*s:

He is the non-stop dancer
in the Mūlādhāra and the rest of the six centres,
even as He is in the heart-lotus of Virāj.
. . . (65)[9]

There is a third aspect of the symbolism of the Cit Sabhā to be mentioned. Not only is the Cit Sabhā the heart of the world and the heart of the individual self, but it also houses the Rahasya, the Secret. This has a specific location, on the wall to the right of Naṭarāja, and is hidden from profane view by a curtain. For Umāpati and the ritual texts of Cidambaram, the Rahasya is a *yantra*, a diagram, or rather a diagram with a picture of Naṭarāja and Śivakāmasundarī in the centre. This Rahasya Yantra is essentially a modification of the well-known Śrīcakra.[10] Umāpati several times speaks of Śiva dancing on the wall of the Cit Sabhā, which must refer to the Yantra, though one is reminded of the Citra Sabhā, the seventeenth-century Sabhā in Kutrālam, Tirunelveli District, where the shrine consists essentially of a wall whereon are painted Naṭarāja, Śivakāmasundarī, and the Śrīcakra.

It is striking that today the Secret is thought to be nothing but empty space. Thus S. Meyyapan, a well-informed resident of Cidambaram, says of the Rahasya:

No images are sheltered within, only a garland of golden *bilva* leaves is seen as a pendant. The mystic secret purport is that God exists in the form of Formless space. How to worship God who is present in every space of the expansive universe? Here it has been provided to worship the empty space itself as God.[11]

Sivaramamurti, in his brief discussion of Cidambaram in *Naṭarāja*, having mentioned the Golden Hall, comments::

It is very interesting that there is a hall beyond, all empty, to suggest space, *ākāśa*. A screen here, when pulled aside, reveals just space, with no real image in it except what fancy may imagine as present in the sky. The removal of the veil is just the removal of ignorance, and behind the veil is the real truth – *sat*, *cit*, and *ānanda*, representing the Naṭarāja form itself. This representation of ether, space or void, represents the *rahasya* of *chidambara*, or the mystery.[12]

Another popular idea is that a Liṅga of Space is within the Cit Sabhā. Harle, for instance, notes that 'the *ākāśa* ... *liṅga* is believed to be installed in the Cit Sabhā'.[13] The *Sūta Saṃhitā* declares that there is a *liṅga* made of each of the five elements, and each is identified with a particular site. Thus Tiruvanamalai, where Śiva is said to have appeared in the Liṅga of Fire before Viṣṇu and Brahmā is naturally the site of that *liṅga*. Umāpati refers to this list in verse 100, but it is significant that he does not site the *liṅga* in the Cit Sabhā:

> in the Tillai wood, on the crown of the Triple Peak,
> stands the Liṅga of Space.
> Each one of these *liṅga*s is the Lord of the Dancers.[14]

Here Umāpati is concerned to affirm the priority of Naṭarāja over the *liṅgas*; it is surely for the same reason that he has nothing else to say about the notion of *ākāśa liṅga*, if indeed, the *ākāśa liṅga* had become of any consequence by his day.[15] The *Cidambaramāhātmya* and the *Kōyil Purāṇam* state that Cidambaram is situated on the top of a subterranean mountain, the base of which rests in the world of Nāgas, but this mountain is not named, nor does it have more than one peak. Verse 103 describes Śiva as 'shining on the top of the Triple-peaked Mountain' (*triśikharaśikhare*). In verse 101 Śiva is said to be 'residing on the Triple Peaks' (*trikūṭasthitijuṣam*), which K. M. Rājagaṇeśa Dīkṣita takes to mean 'in the Triple Peak mantra'; and given the explicit mention of Śrīvidyā, known as the Triple Peak because of its threefold division, in verses 120 and 207, this is plausible. That the Śrīcakra is soon to be mentioned several times in the poem makes the identification still more likely.

The sanctity of the site to some extent foments the popular imagination. I was told by one intelligent resident of the city that the long-lived sage Tirumūlar entered into final *samādhi* in the Cit Sabhā and taught many mysterious things to Śiva before expiring. The scholar B. G. L. Swamy was led to suggest that the back of the Cit Sabhā was a secret chamber 'where *yogi*s entered into eternal *samādhi*'.[16]

Ramalinga Dikshitar says that the Rahasya is the formless (*arūpa*) aspect of Śiva, Naṭarāja is the form aspect of Śiva (*sarūpa*), and the Crystal Liṅga, Candramaulīśvara, is the form-and-formless (*rūpārūpa*),[17] but gives no source for this tripartite formulation which puts the Crystal Liṅga on a higher level than Naṭarāja. Śiva tells Śeṣa at the beginning of chapter 15 of the *Cidambara Māhātmya*, before mentioning the existence of the Cit Sabhā, that he has two forms, one with form, the other without form.[18]

THE ARCHITECTURE OF THE CIT SABHĀ AND THE KANAKA SABHĀ

Despite its extreme importance, little has been been written on the Cit Sabhā as a building. The building today consists of a massive stone plinth topped by walls, supporting pillars, and roof beams all of sandalwood. The tiles are of copper, plated in gold. A slightly smaller version of itself, the Kanaka Sabhā, stands directly in front of it, to the south, separated by a hallway 1.5 m in width. Such a wooden superstructure is found in no other Cōḻa temple, though subsequently other Śiva temples in Tamilnadu copied the basic form of the Cit Sabhā to house their own Naṭarāja festival bronzes. Provision for human dancers in Cōḻa temples is typified by the Nṛtta Sabhā, with an open area amid a mass of pillars, and everything of stone.

The shape of the roofs of the twin Sabhās is distinctive – rectangular with a curvilinear *śikhara*, resembling the roof of the Draupadī Ratha at Mamallapuram – and is repeated on the other halls in Cidambaram, and also over the other shrines there.

Given the wooden structure of most of the Cit Sabhā, it is not surprising that no early examples of similar buildings survive, but a seventeeth-century painting seems to show the kind of raised dance pavilion that the builders of the temple reproduced in a sacred version; see plate 12.

The best idea of the Cit Sabhā in Umāpati's day can be gained from the mural painting in the circumambulatory of Rājarāja I's Rājarājeśvara temple at Tañjavūr, consecrated in 1009/10, a painting which, contemporary with the founder, portrays him worshipping at the Cit Sabhā.[19] Sivaramamurti describes it as

> representing Naṭarāja in all his glory at Chidambaram, with the entire concourse of Dīkshita priests around him, the emperor shown at one end, accompanied by his queens and a large retinue, including his chosen soldiers and bodyguards. The ground plan of the temple is also wonderfully given here. It is a very interesting representation of the very high regard that the Choḷa emperors had for Naṭarāja at Chidambaram.[20]

12. Dance stage. Wall painting, Narumpunathar temple, Tirupudaimarudur, Tirunelveli Dist, *c.* 1700.

The painting clearly shows both the Cit Sabhā and the Kanaka Sabhā in front of it. The King and his three wives, hands in *añjali*, stand in the Kanaka Sabhā. They are in three-quarters profile, but the Sabhās are two-dimensional. The Kanaka has its roof supported by three pillars, of which only the right-hand, southern one is visible. (The orientation of the painting, on the inner eastern wall, matches that of the Sabhās.[21]) Soldiers, clad only in a cloth that is wrapped round their loins and then rises in a narrow strip up the centre of their chests and round their necks, stand to the right, outside the Kanaka Sabhā. Above the roof of the Kanaka Sabhā and part of the roof of the Cit Sabhā are seated eight women, either heavenly nymphs or dancing girls, clad only in dhotis tightly wrapped around their lower halves, each dhoti in a different and rich pattern; jewelled collars enclose their necks and delicate scarves float over their shoulders. These women are in a well-defined rectangle. To the left stand two bearded priests. The space immediately above the rest of the roof of the Cit Sabhā is blurred. Behind the figures above the

Kanaka Sabhā is a double tier of colonnades with a tiled roof, as exists today, though with a renovated frontage. The priests and women are therefore shown in the courtyard on the eastern side of the Sabhās. The right-angle of the buttress to the right of this picture portrays another wall of the surrounding colonnade. The right buttress itself has a massive structure painted on it, which must be a kind of gatehouse to the colonnade, having a similar set of tiled roofs, though also a triple set of smaller roofs above them. This structure is entirely missing today; but the two roofs, at least, of the twin Sabhās seem unchanged.

It is clear from this illustration that the architectural intention of the Sabhā was originally very different from that of the standard *garbhagṛha*, being intended to facilitate display. The gilding of the roof, carried out by several Cōḻa kings, fostered this display, making the Sabhā a beacon, as it were, rather than a dark receptacle; and in paintings the shrine is an open stage. By contrast, in Kramrisch's words, 'The cubical chamber of the Garbhagṛha is replete with static order.'[22] Yet Kramrisch twice refers to Cidambaram in her brief account of the *garbhagṛha* in her authoritative study of the Hindu temple, and compares the *garbhagṛha* to the heart.The open display of the Sabhā quickly regressed to the heart, if not the womb. The Sabhā, however different its original intention, has converged with the *garbhagṛha*. 'The world in which we live is indefinite in extent and open on all sides to question and uncertainty; within limits, number and measure is the Garbhagṛha.'

The Tāñjāvūr painting is around 200 years earlier than Umāpati. Some 300 years later than Umāpati were produced the paintings on the ceiling of the Śivakāmasundarī shrine. Here there are several paintings of the Cit Sabhā, the largest much damaged. Three smaller ones give considerable detail, but differ widely. One shows Vyāghrapāda worshipping at the Mūlaliṅga, with the twin Sabhās beside it. In fact the Cit Sabhā is empty, awaiting Śiva's performance of the dance.

The second painting shows the Cit Sabhā amid a stylized plan of the whole site, after the reconstruction work carried out by Hiraṇyavarman. Here the Cit Sabhā is given a double-tiered roof, much higher than that of the Kanaka Sabhā. In the sequence of registers the painting immediately following this overview of the temple as a whole represents the twin Sabhās as normal. Whether or not the artists are different, the second painting expresses the inherent demand in the logic of a temple for a *vimāna* over the central sanctum.

At the centre of the temple are the twin Sabhās, the Cit and the Kanaka. These adjoining edifices, of almost identical rectangular plan,

13. The Cit and Kanaka Sabhās as visualized by Vyāghrapāda, adjoining the Mūlanātha shrine. Ceiling painting in Śivakāmasundarī *maṇḍapa*, Cidambaram. Seventeenth century.

together measure 11.9 m (east–west) by 13.4 m (north–south). The Cit Sabhā is 1 m higher than the Kanaka Sabhā. A hall 1.5 m in width links the Sabhas, flanked by steps set against the plinth to east and west. The Cit Sabhā has wooden walls, made up of sections of four 35cm wide planks set between wooden pillars of the same width; the southern wall has window grills and wooden doors, and is covered in silver plates. The roof is said to be supported by twenty-eight free standing wooden pillars; and the roof of the Kanaka Sabhā by eighteen wooden pillars. Copper-plated folding doors take up much of the eastern and southern sides of Kanaka Sabhā.

THE INTERIOR OF THE CIT SABHĀ

Within the hall five silver-plated steps lead from the Kanaka Sabhā to the higher level of the Cit Sabhā, though the first silver step is on the same level as the Kanaka Sabhā. Within the Cit Sabhā is a further stone plinth set back about 1 m with a wall behind it, while beneath Naṭarāja and Śivakamasundari to his left, this is fronted with gilt panelling, with the plinths of the two *mūrtis* rising above this. To Naṭarāja's right is the Cidambaram Rahasya, where several strings of golden *bilva* leaves hang in front of a curtain. The curtain is 1.5 m high and 3.5 m long, extending behind Naṭarāja as well as covering the Cidambaram Rahasya. It is made of two layers, the inner one red, the outer one black: illusion outside, enlightenment inside. It is renewed twice a year, on the tenth day of the main festivals, old curtains being preserved in the Deva Sabhā.

In addition to Naṭarāja, Śivakāmasundarī and the curtain of the Cidambaram Rahasya, the Cit Sabhā contains a *mukhaliṅga*, representing the head of Brahmā that Śiva cut off; Śiva's *pādukas*, golden sandals mounted on a plinth; Balināyaka, a Candraśekhara *mūrti* taken round the second *prākāra* during food offerings to the various deities; Svarṇākarṣaṇa ('Gold-attracting') Bhairava, occasionally worshipped in the Kanaka Sabhā, and said formerly to have turned copper into gold for the Dīkṣitas; and, worshipped daily in the Kanaka Sabhā, the Ruby Naṭarāja and the Crystal Liṅga.

The exterior of the Cit Sabhā has a double colonnade of round columns of highly polished black stone; this colonnade is narrower on the eastern side, to allow passage round the Caṇḍeśvara shrine, though the present structure is not very old. The ceiling of the colonnade has paintings retelling the *sthalapurāṇa*, dating back perhaps to the beginning of the century. The plinths of both Sabhās have been recently faced with glazed white tiles interspersed with narrower columns of green tiles.

Adjoining the eastern side of the Kanaka Sabhā is a nineteenth-century *maṇḍapa* which consists of a copper-tiled roof of similar design supported by round wooden pillars similar to those around the outside of the Cit Sabhā. Under this roof worshippers gather to watch the lamp worship of the Ratnasabhāpati, the Ruby Naṭarāja.

A stone roof section on massive pillars adjoins the front of the Kanaka Sabhā, with a modern bronze Naṭarāja and Śivakāmasundarī enclosed in glass just beneath the ceiling and always on view. This was constructed in the 1930s, replacing an old and much lower structure. On the ceiling are modern paintings of Naṭarāja and the Śrīcakra, and various lotus-based designs.

On either side of the front of the Kanaka Sabhā hang wooden boards each with a verse from the *Kuñcitāṅghristava* in Tamil script. On the left, the opening verse, on the right verse 278.[23] The boards look contemporaneous with the publication of the printed book.

14. Naṭarāja in the Cit Sabhā. Painting by G. Parameśvara Dīkṣita. Courtesy: G. Parameśvara Dīkṣita.

THE CIT SABHĀ AND KANAKA SABHĀ IN THE *KUÑCITĀṄGHRISTAVA*

Umāpati refers to the Cit Sabhā throughout the *Kuñcitāṅghristava*.[24] A detailed account of the Sabhā is given pride of place at the opening of the poem. Umāpati takes his readers at once to the heart of the matter in the opening of his poem. We shall first consider verses 3 to 7, leaving till later the most esoteric verses 1 and 2.

> This Hall is formed out of the letters of the alphabet
> from the base plinth to the golden stones,
> and in it there are
> Brahmā, Viṣṇu, Rudra, Maheśvara,
> and five-headed Sadāśiva above with Ambā;
>
> and on the wall
> the Lord of the Cit Sabhā is dancing.
> His many deeds are praised
> by the five elements, the six sciences,
> and the four Vedas,
> each manifest in the form of pillars.
>
> I worship
> Him who gives limitless happiness,
> Whose foot is curved. (3)[25]

The first line of the Sanskrit, translated as –

> formed out of the letters of the alphabet
> from the base plinth to the golden stones,

– clearly parallels a passage in the description of the Cit Sabhā given in the Festival Ritual text, 'adorned with a base (*adhiṣṭhāna*) that is the form of all the mantras beginning with each of the letters from *a* onwards'.[26] The numbers of the elements, sciences and Vedas are not spelled out in the Sanskrit, but they at least are entirely conventional, and do not need to be stated to be understood.

The base plinth (*mūlapīṭha*) is a massive and architecturally complex structure, as are all Cōḻa plinths, and is similar in style to the basements of the *gopuras*.[27] The Festival Ritual text identifies the various groups of letters of the alphabet with specific mouldings of the plinth, in a very rare linkage of the highly formal structures of architecture with the more usual topics of intellectual discourse. In subsequent verses Umāpati compares the tiles and beams and so on of the building with religious topics, following the *Tilvavana Māhātmya*, but the architectural side of the equation remains rudimentary, and, as will be seen in the case of the number of pillars, somewhat removed from reality.

With the five gods named here we are brought into the world of Śaiva Siddhānta. The architectural structure contains an iconological structure: five-headed Sadāśiva is situated on top of the four lesser gods, themselves supported by the alphabet.

The roles of these forms of Śiva are clearly stated by Umāpati in verse 102:

> In the beginning He Whose form is the self
> created Brahmā for the creation of the worlds,
> Hari for their protection,
> and the form of Rudra for their destruction,
>
> and then Maheśa for concealing everything,
>
> the form of Sadāśiva with Pārvatī beside Him
> to show favour to those worlds.
>
> He performs the Dance of Bliss in the Hall.
> . . . (102)[28]

It is important to understand that Naṭarāja is the highest form of Śiva, surpassing as well as subsuming the other five forms.

We have seen Umāpati refer to the Upaniṣadic idea of the five sheaths; and he later refers to them again in the context of the five deities in question here:

> At His command
> Brahmā shines in the sheath of food,
> Viṣṇu whose excellent vehicle is Garuḍa
> shines in the sheath of breath,
>
> and Rudra in the sheath made of mind,
> and then Maheśa in the excellent sheath of consciousness,
> and Sadāśiva in the sheath called bliss.
> . . . (105)[29]

Each of these five forms of Śiva has his own throne (*pīṭha*) within the Cit Sabhā. Umāpati refers in verse 3 to three of these seats which are constituted by pillars:

> His many deeds are praised
> by the five elements, the six sciences,
> and the four Vedas,
> each manifest in the form of pillars.

The five pillars that are the elements constitute the throne of Rudra. The six pillars that are the *śāstra*s constitute the throne of Maheśvara. The four Veda pillars constitute the throne of Sadāśiva.[30]

In the lower part of His hall
The *Āgamas*, *Kāmika* and the others,
originating from Śiva's mouths,
have assumed the form of golden pillars
to the number of twenty-eight.

On every side their lower parts shine brightly;
their higher parts are hidden within.

They praise Him Who is worthy of praise
in His dancing form praised by hundreds of scriptures.
. . . (4)[31]

The twenty-eight pillars that are the Āgamas are said to constitute the throne of Brahmā. Conceivably the esoteric parts of the Āgamas are referred to here as well as the high parts of the pillars which are concealed within the overhanging roof. The Naṭarāja cult is considerably later than most of the Āgamas, and is therefore concealed within them, so to speak. The Vedas, the 'hundreds of scriptures' (*śrutiśata*), are also mentioned: there is no sense of antipathy between the two classes of revealed literature.[32]

In His assembly hall the stairway,
made up of the five letters of His mantra,
looks like the Silver Mountain.
Jaya and Vijaya are the principal guardians
who protect its doorway.

Within shine the five gods,
Brahmā and the others,
along with the ninety-six Tattvas.

I worship
Him Whose constant dance is there,
Whose foot curves. (5)[33]

Within the hall five steps lead from the Kanaka Sabhā to the higher level of the Cit Sabhā, though the first step is on the same level as the Kanaka Sabhā. The five steps are held to represent the five syllables of the Śiva mantra, *namaḥ Śivāya*. The steps were plated in silver by Manali Mudaliar in the eighteenth century, but given the image of the Silver mountain, it is likely they were also of silver in Umāpati's day. The comparison of these steps which rise about a metre from the level of the Kanaka Sabhā to that of the Cit Sabhā, with a mountain, may seem less of a gross exaggeration when it is remembered that Cidambaram is thought to be on top of a mountain in the *Cidambara Māhātmya*, and that the Cit

Sabhā as the supreme abode of Naṭarāja is superior to any Himalayan mountain.

Although the ninety-six *tattva*s are mentioned by Appar in the seventh century, systematic enumerations are late. Umāpati refers to them in his Tamil poetry but not in his treatises.[34] Since, as Umāpati says, these *tattva*s which sum up the phenomenal world are to be uprooted –

> He transform'd my very thought –
> Uprooting the *tattva*s six and ninety,
> Hard to narrate –[35]

their presence in the Cit Sabhā is perhaps less to be expected than any other of the constituent symbolisms. But as can be seen from the next verse, the Cit Sabhā is not only the heart of the world, but the world itself in essential form.

> Its finials represent the Śaktis.
> Shining below them, the tile-pins
> represent hairs.
> The golden tiles are the breaths
> and the rafters they're affixed to
> are the veins and arteries.
>
> Under these all the worlds
> take the form of the cross-beams
> and the arts the main beams.
>
> In this the Lord dances.
> Him Whose body is unparalleled,
> Whose foot is curved,
> I worship. (6)[36]

There are nine finials on the roof of the Cit Sabhā, and they are faithfully shown in all modern pictures. The nine Śaktis play an important part in the priests' mental representation of Śiva in the ritual of worship.[37] In the standard Āgamic form of worship on which the Cidambaram ritual is based, worship of Śiva is preceded by worship of his differentiated powers, the worshipper ascending towards Śiva as the levels worshipped rise. In the course of a series of visualizations, the worshipper mentally constructs a lotus throne, on which a stainless throne will be placed. Eight of the Śaktis are associated with the eight petals of this lotus; the ninth Śakti, Manonmanī, the undifferentiated Śakti of Sadāśiva, sits in the cente of the lotus. Each of the eight Śaktis presides over a male governor of the impure domain that is the phenomenal world. Aghora Śivācārya describes them thus:

Shining like the rising sun, three-eyed, four-armed, crowned with their matted locks which are ornamented by the crescent moon, they each hold a chowry, make the gesture of giving a boon and the gesture of 'Do not fear', and with their fourth lotus hand cling to their [representative of] Śiva.

(*Kriyākramadyotikā* p. 89)

Unlike this smooth and coherent meditational process taken by the Cidambaram ritual from the Āgamas and the standard ritual manuals of Śaiva Siddhānta, the symbolism of the Cit Sabhā is by contrast *ad hoc*, and somewhat incoherent, which is not altogether surprising since we have to do with an actual building rather than an idealized psychology.

In the Hall He has around Him,
in front, to right and to left,
Gaṇeśa, Skanda, Lakṣmī, Brahmā's fifth head,
the Astradeva, His sandals, the Crystal Liṅga,

the dancing image of ruby,
with to the west the Gold-attracting form.

And in the middle Blessed Śivā's Lord
performs His dance.

. . . (7)[38]

Although from a distance only Naṭarāja is visible in the Cit Sabhā, it is in fact additionally populated. Brahmā's fifth head was cut off by Śiva; in the Sabhā it takes the form of a *liṅga*, the Face Liṅga. In verse 30 it is said that Brahmā is to Śiva's right as mentioned, and to his left, that is beside Caṇḍeśvara in the Brahmā-Caṇḍeśvara shrine adjoining the Cit Sabhā. The Astradeva, the 'Missile Deity', is the Trident, an object of great ritual significance, providing protection for rituals and festivals, and worshipped in its own right. Śiva's golden sandals are prominent in morning and night-time rituals, for they are ceremonially carried in a palanquin to and from the bedchamber he shares with Śivakāmasundarī, she having an image permanently within that chamber.

These five verses, from verse 3 to verse 7, show the importance of the Cit Sabhā. Adjoining the Cit Sabhā is the Kanaka Sabhā, which is referred to only once by Umāpati.

He it is in front of Whom
the Kanaka Sabhā, the Golden Hall, shines,
supported by the *Purāṇas* in the form of pillars,
in which the lotus face of the Lord of Bulls,
the very form of Dharma, looks north,

in which the lordly sages perform grand *abhiṣekas*
on the Lord, Devī, the Crystal Liṅga,
the Boy Bhairava, and the Ruby Naṭarāja
. . . (75)[39]

Abhiṣekas are performed in the Kanaka, not in the Cit Sabhā. Unlike the Cit Sabhā which has a raised platform and a wall in its centre, the Kanaka Sabhā has a smooth floor, reputedly made with just five huge flag stones, and a channel so that the daily *abhiṣekas* flow smoothly away.

In the middle of the south edge of the floor of the Kanaka Sabhā is Nandin, Śiva's bull, facing north in constant adoration. In verse 178, Umāpati says that with the Goddess on his lap, Śiva speeds across the oceans on his lordly bull, incarnation of Dharma.

Scarcely less than a *liṅga*, the seated bull is the sign of a Śiva temple. In Cōḻa times bronze figures of the bull with a human body became popular, portraying Nandin as Nandikeśvara, Śiva's wise and learned chamberlain.[40] Umāpati mentions Nandikeśvara as the source of the lineage of his school.

As I have said, the above verse is Umāpati's one mention of the Kanaka Sabhā. No explanation, so far as I am aware, has been offered as to why the Kanaka Sabhā is so named. Umāpati several times refers to the Cit Sabhā as the Golden Hall – as indeed the hall is named in early inscriptions – but invariably uses some other term than Sabhā.

In verse 246 Nandikeśvara sees Śiva in all his forms in the Cit Sabhā, here called the Golden Hall (*kanakasadas*). One of these forms is OṂ.

The Lord of Dance Whom Nandikeśa
saw in the Golden Hall
as His form as Half-woman,
afterwards as Half-Nārāyaṇa,
then again as Pārvatī,
as the Formless Liṅga,
as OṂ, the Saving Syllable,

as the fire within that circle,
the unparalleled form of Saccidānanda –

for the moment
the supreme was easily accessible –
. . . (246)[41]

In another verse the Cit Sabhā itself, again called Golden Hall (*svarṇasaṃsad*), is OṂ.

By looking at His Dance of Bliss
from which streams forth
the radiance of supreme Śiva
in the Golden Hall which is OṂ itself

the lordly sages crossed over
fierce Being, that vast ocean,
the host of worlds are in His body
that is beyond comprehension and reasoning;

He is the teacher of enlightenment
through knowledge of the Supreme Spirit,
He is ancient, He makes darkness disappear,
. . . (222)[42]

The brightness of the Cit Sabhā is the brightness of Śiva:

By His light the whole world constantly shines;
His supreme radiance
being in the form of the Lord of Dance
accompanied by Ambā in the Golden Hall
in the heart lotus of Virāj,
. . . (85)[43]

We have now reached the point at which it will be fruitful to consider the two opening verses of the poem. The poem at once addresses the heart of the matter, in a way that is reminiscent of a teacher beginning with the *mūla sūtra*, the summation of what he will gradually expound to his pupils, rather than the normal beginning of a *kāvya*.

The universe is the body
of radiant Virāj, the Cosmic Man.
His feet are in the south, sun-born Yama's quarter,
his multiple heads in the north;

and in that Man, in the lotus of his heart,
in the centre, facing south
in the royal *yantra* called the Sammelana,
meditated on by the best of sages in their hearts,
the Lord dances, with His Śakti at His side.

I worship Him, the Lord of Dancers,
Whose foot is curved. (1)[44]

I worship the Lord of the Cit Sabhā
Who is dancing in the golden pericarp –
the great King of Yantras that stands on the wall –
of the single lotus, that is the heart

of the five hundred million miles of the earth,
the heart of the creator whose name is holy Virāj,

His feet constantly worshipped by the three Śaktis,
shining in the Nādānta, His dances ninefold,
His foot curved. (2)[45]

The Cit Sabhā may have architectural origins, as has been suggested, in a stage for a dancer, but it also goes back to the Vedas. The mysterious Virāj, the radiant sovereign, is Puruṣa, the Cosmic Man from whom the world was produced by the sacrificial process (*Puruṣasūkta*, *Ṛgveda* 10,90,5). As the temple of the most significant manifestation of Śiva, Cidambaram is the heart of the world; Cidambaram is the heart of the Cosmic Man.

The Cit Sabhā is named only incidentally, but the verses seek out its core. Here, in the opening of the poem, the focus is on the two-dimensional drawing or painting of Naṭarāja within the diagram of the *yantra*, rather than the metal image in three dimensions; and the *yantra* belongs to the Cit Sabhā, it is affixed to the wall.

The royal *yantra*, the Sammelana yantra, is a variant of the famous Śrīcakra, with the centre taken by a drawing of Naṭarāja with Pārvatī (Śivakāmasundarī) at his side.[46]

The *Devatāstotra*, a hymn in praise of the divinities of the Cidambaram temple, published with the *Patañjalipūjāsūtra*, contains two verses in praise of the Rahasya:

We praise the Cidambaram Rahasyam,
this place that is the wall,
where the specific *yantra*s of the Śrīcakra and others are fashioned,
wet with musk,
made of the knowledge of eternal bliss,
manifesting the mingling of Naṭeśa and Śivā,
marked with strings of garlands of golden *bilva* leaves.

I worship the great Cidambaram Rahasya whose glory is world-surpassing,
whose life-giving drug, the Pañcākṣara, gives good things to all the world,
in which at the end of the day,
shell-haired Śiva swallows all the Śaktis and is embraced by Gaurī,
from which at dawn the universe arises, Śakti shines
– let that shine forth in my heart.[47]

The Sammelanacakra, the King of Yantras, is the centre of focus. There is no mention of any curtain, and it may well be that the Cakra was not covered over in his day. Or it may be a question of the mind's eye. Umāpati is going to call before the reader all aspects of Dancing

Śiva in Cidambaram, and the core, so to speak, of this act of imagination is the mental construct that is the *yantra*. Just as the technical texts on *yantras* spell out dimensions and proportions, so too the dimensions of the universe are stated, for that also is a subordinate part of the grand construct centred in Cidambaram.

The heart is the seat of the imagination in Hinduism. The *yantra*, which is contained within a lotus, is at the same time contained within the heart of the world. Naṭarāja is the ultimate core of things; with the development of his cult he became ever more central. And yet within the diagrams and mental constructs the God retains his form, even if here his feet alone are mentioned. His feet are worshipped by the feminine principles who are comprised within his Consort. The three Śaktis are Icchā Śakti, Jñāna Śakti, and Kriyā Śakti. Their local manifestations in the Cidambaram temple are as follows: Icchā Śakti is beside Naṭarāja in the Cit Sabhā, Jñāna Śakti is Śivakāmasundarī in her separate shrine, and Durgā, whose small shrine is backed by the outer wall of Śivakāmasundarī's, is Kriyā Śakti.[48] In the theology of the Śaiva Siddhānta, Icchā Śakti is Śiva's desire when he is moved by the pitiable condition of selves, to save them, and for that end he creates the world; Jñāna Śakti permits Śiva to know what he creates; and Kriyā Śakti is his activity manifesting itself by multiple actions.

Like the nine Śaktis referred to above which are represented by the finials of the Cit Sabhā, these three Śaktis are also involved in the meditational process of invoking Śiva. After the nine Śaktis on the petals of the lotus throne, the worshipper visualizes three concentric circles on top of the lotus throne, outermost being the sun circle with which Jñāna Śakti is identified, then the moon circle, with Kriyā Śakti, and innermost the fire circle with Icchā Śakti.

Just as a standing bronze of Pārvatī accompanies every Naṭarāja bronze under worship, so too within the Yantra the standing form of Śivakāmasundarī is drawn.

There are two modern paintings hanging in the Naṭarāja temple, near the Deva Sabhā, on the main route to the Cit Sabhā, which show Pārvatī seated in a comfortable chair as she watches the Dance. I know of no Cidambaram text which so describes the Goddess, and the painters were doubtless influenced by the description of the 'evening dance' in the *Śiva Pradoṣa Stotra* quoted by Coomaraswamy in his famous essay on the Dance of Śiva: 'Placing the Mother of the Three Worlds upon a golden throne, studded with precious gems, Śūlapāṇi dances on the heights of Kailās, and all the gods gather round Him.'[49]

Śiva, our poet tells us, is 'shining in the Nādānta', and here we have to do with another matter given wide currency by Coomaraswamy. Coomaraswamy in his essay twice refers to Śiva's dance in Cidambaram as the Nādānta dance, but does not explain the term.[50] Dorai Rangaswamy in his detailed study of the *Tēvāram* poet Appar objects to Coomaraswamy calling the Cidambaram or Tillai dance the Nādānta Dance, roundly declaring that 'The *pañcakṛtya naṭana* cannot be the Nādānta dance.' The Nādānta, in Dorai Rangaswamy's view, is the Dance in the crematorium:

It is the void which is spoken of as the crematorium . . . 'When am I to reach Him who dances the great dance inside the wild [i.e. the crematorium], when the air, the fire and the world are dead?' (*Tēvāram* 7.84.3). The poet longs for this experience. This is really the Nādānta Dance. The universe [494] evolves; there starts the movement (*nāda*); a point of stress is formed (*bindu*), and the vibrations result in various forms becoming grosser and grosser till one reaches the world of the present. The involution is the reverse process and the final stage is the Nāda, and Nādānta is what is even beyond this incipient sign of creation. It is this void of Nādānta where nothing but Śiva exists; this grace is there inseparable from Him as the Mother.[51]

This is a correct and helpful exposition of the meaning of Nādānta, though no one else, I believe, has thus applied it to the pre-*ānandatāṇḍava* dance. Shulman's translation of this verse of Cuntarar differs considerably:

flawless radiance
becoming wind
and fire,
and earth –
when shall I reach him
whom I know
as the great Dancer in the forest.[52]

Cuntarar does not in fact refer to Nādānta, and it would not be unreasonable to suggest that Dorai Rangaswamy sees Nādānta as the supreme form of the dance and wishes to find his poet, Cuntarar, associated with it. In this wish, Dorai Ranagswamy passes over a significant reference to *nāda*. In 7.84.9, Cuntarar says –

The lord
who becomes primordial sound [*nāda*],
life within flesh
and the living lamp of wisdom – [53]

Within the standard tradition of the Tamil Śaiva Siddhānta, the one author to connect the Nādānta with the dance is a disciple of the founding father, Meykaṇṭar, who wrote a small primer spelling out the symbolism of Naṭarāja and the Pañcākṣara mantra.

O my gracious Guru! Thou hast explained to me beautifully the nature of the Nādānta dance. Let me now know the nature of the Five Letters (*pañcākṣara*). Can they be one with the letters which are imperishable?

(*Uṇmaiviḷakkam* 40)

Yet again, explanation for the use of the term is lacking. The earliest application of the term to the dance must be that of Tirumūlar, in his lyrical and obscure way.

The Primal Supreme danced;
The Fire in His hand danced;
The Holy matted lock danced;
In intoxication of joy He danced;
The crescent moon danced;
Merging in Nāda He danced
The Dance of Nādānta, heavenly.

(*Tirumantiram* 2751)[54]

A good instance of Tirumūlar's ecstatic manner is the following:

Nādānta that is end of Nāda (Principle of Sound)
Bodhānta that is end of Bodha (Jñāna)
Vedānta that is end of Vedas
Śivānanda that Bliss of Śiva,
Sadāśivānanda that is without end,
In all these, He dances the Śiva Naṭana,
He that is Nāda Brahma (Lord within the Sound Principle).

(*Tirumantiram* 2792)

The last detail in the two opening verses of the *Kuñcitāṅghristava* is that Śiva's dance is ninefold. The significance of this precision, however, is not clear. Tirumūlar says that Śiva danced nine dances to delight the nine Śaktis (*Tirumantiram* 2736); but also that he has eight dances and five dances. For Tirumūlar, 'Everywhere is Cidambaram, Everywhere is Divine Dance.' For Umāpati in the opening of his poem, the dance is in the Cit Sabhā, and every detail is precisely specified, even though in this instance the nine dances are not identifiable.[55]

He danced, Jīvas to delight;
He danced nine dances,
The nine Śaktis to delight;

He danced in forests;
He danced in the thoughts of His devotees;
He danced in the junction of Suṣumṇā within;
He danced in Jñāna Endless;
Thus He danced away,
He, my Lord.

(*Tirumantiram* 2736)

The ecstatic singing of Tirumūlar is far removed from the complex and sometimes tortuous syntax of Umāpati, and its complex of ideas, though parallel, is less constrained. After the tight and concentrated opening of his poem focussed on the Sabhā, Umāpati too, in Tirumūlar's words, dances away, flitting from one idea to another, but his Naṭarāja remains securely housed in the Cit Sabhā, the Cit Sabhā that is also the heart.

His dance that is pure consciousness
He, inconceivable, performs
in the heart more subtle than the subtle,

in the palace called the lotus of consciousness,
in the little cave.
Him Whose foot is curved,
I worship. (273)[56]

CHAPTER 5

Śaiva Siddhānta and Vedānta

Examination of the temple ritual and the symbolism of the Cit Sabhā has involved mention of elements of Śaiva Siddhānta, or the Siddhānta as it was called in the Sanskrit texts.[1] It is now time to set these elements in a wider context. It will also be necessary to consider the references to Vedānta and Advaita in the poem; the latter is not necessarily a subset of the former. By Umāpati's day there had been several centuries of development of Śaiva thought, development fostered by royal patronage over much of India. The Siddhānta had become an all-embracing system, encompassing temple worship and architecture. There was an increasing readiness on the part of that system to compromise with what was originally the alien thought of the Vedas. Why forego royal favour and patronage by antagonizing such conservative and purely orthodox forces as yet remained in society by asserting difference from the Vedas? Vedic recitation and Vedic sacrifice remained prestitigious, and continued to assist the sanctification of royal power. Although the Siddhānta system seems to have originated in individual practice, in the course of time its core texts, the Āgamas, become more and more concerned with temples. At the same time, the various Vedānta schools were developed in conjunction with sectarian affiliation; their monastic centres sought power and influence. To mention only Śaṅkara's Advaita, one important innovation was the worship of the Śrīcakra; and several Śākta texts, most notably the *Saundaryalaharī*, 'The Ocean of [the Goddess's] Beauty', were attributed to Śaṅkara. And it may be questioned whether the Śivādvaita of Śrīkaṇṭha's commentary on the *Brahma Sūtras* was a Siddhānta colonization of Vedānta, or *vice versa*.

The Siddhānta has three fundamental categories: *pati*, Śiva; *paśu*, the individual self; *pāśa*, the bonds. Māyā, one of the three bonds, is the material cause of the universe, Śiva is the efficient cause, and his female part, Śakti, is the instrumental cause.[2] Māyā evolves in a long series of *tattvas*, from *bindu*, the subtlest, to earth, the grossest. This evolution is in two stages, divided between Pure Māyā and Impure Māyā, the former being necessary for beings on a higher level than common humanity.

Umāpati chooses the following summation of the Siddhānta to open his annotated collection of key passages, the *Hundred Jewels Collection*, the *Śataratnasaṃgraha*:

Now, to liberate the self from the bonds of *mala*, *māyā*, and *karman*, and to manifest its Śivahood, knowledge proceeds from Śiva.[3]

Umāpati comments, 'Śiva is of like nature as the self, the difference being the self is bound and Śiva-ness is unbound . . . And here by the word *jñāna* is meant Śiva's Śakti which takes the form of both enlightenment (*avabodha*) and *dīkṣā*.'[4] The bonds are material, and because of this knowledge alone cannot liberate: the material process of *dīkṣā* is essential to remove bonds. The special feature of the Siddhānta system is the notion of *mala*, called *āṇavamala* when the term *mala* is applied to all three bonds.

Umāpati twice refers to the three bonds collectively as he nears the close of his poem and a personal note appears. In verse 300, the individual's awareness of the difficulties of existence is made a universal statement, but this rhetorical procedure may signify rather 'I am like all other people in feeling in this way.'

> 'O Lord, my heart is plunged in the ocean of *saṃsāra*,
> 'so terrifying, hard to cross, swarming with
> 'the crocodiles that are the bonds (*pāśa*).
>
> 'I have followed evil ways, an outright rogue. Depressed,
> 'I have turned away from the worship of Your feet,
> 'sinful that I am. Protect me, protect me.'
> so saying all people resort to Him.
> . . . (300)[5]

In the next verse, the Dīkṣitas are referred to:

> The lordly wise, they enjoy, oh yes they enjoy
> the unparalleled pleasure won by worshipping Him.
>
> By spiritual yoga they cross, oh yes they cross
> the ocean of existence, abundant in horrors.
>
> By meditating on Him in their hearts
> they burn up, oh yes they burn up
> the very hard set of bonds.
>
> They say His mantra again and again,
> and delight in the supreme glory of His foot.
> Him Whose foot is curved I worship. (308)[6]

In his *Neñcuviṭutūtu*, 'The Heart as Messenger', Umāpati considers the royal insignia of Śiva, following a convention of Tamil poetry; one of these insignia is the elephant, which

> quells th'vast cruel sorrowing
> *pāśas* and smites the sea of birth to turn
> Dustily dry.[7]

Common in Siddhānta texts is the notion of burning up the *mala*, either the *pāśa* of that name, the *āṇavamala*, or all three *pāśas* under the heading of *mala*. In the *Śataratnasaṃgraha* the individual self is said to have his *malas* burnt up by the fire of *dīkṣā*.[8] Later in that work Umāpati, on the subject of *āṇavamala*, quotes from the *Raurava Āgama*. A heap of cotton thrown in a blazing fire burns up and is completely destroyed. It can never become cotton again. Similarly, the soul that reaches the highest state after the purification by *dīkṣā* is never reborn.[9]

Umāpati refers to the bond of *karman* in one verse in the *Kuñcitāṅghristava*:

> Although the actions that have already begun to bear fruit
> will be worked out through experience in this life,
> the more frightening latent and future residues
> can be destroyed through knowledge:
> thus declare the statements of the Āgamas –
> that is well known –
>
> but fortunately for living beings
> He destroys all forms of karma
> just by His body in His dance being seen,
> and gives happiness:
> He is victorious in the Hall.
> . . . (268)[10]

This threefold classification of *karman* is extensively employed in Śaiva discussion of the efficacy of rituals that contribute to liberation. Active *karman*, *prārabdhakarman*, literally, '*karman* whose effects have already begun', has brought about the present embodiment of a self, and can be removed only by being consumed (*bhogāt*). In his *Śataratnasaṃgraha*, Umāpati gives as *sūtra* 87 the standard passage on this point:

> *Karman* from many existences is burnt like a seed by the mantras [of *dīkṣā*]; future *karman* is prevented. As for that *karman* by which this present body exists, that [can be ended only] by being consumed.[11]

In the *Civapirakācam* Umāpati says:

> The proper fruit of *karman* must unavoidably be eaten; much of *karman* may be removed by means of the *Āgama* and *Veda* (*Civapirakācam* 32).

However, Umāpati's verse 268 over-rides the Āgamas: the mere sight (*ālokamātra*) of Naṭarāja destroys all *karman*. Umāpati makes his point delicately, in that he says simply that 'they' are destroyed. I have translated *tāni* ('they', 'those') as 'all forms of *karman*' since Umāpati used the dual endings for the two sorts of *karman* that the Siddhānta says can be destroyed (by the knowledge that *dīkṣā* brings), and the word *tāni* has to apply to all three *karmans* for the plural to be justifed. Beneath the formal grammar of the verse there is also a certain frisson in the way that the *tāni*, those that are destroyed, follows closely after the neuter plural *nigamavacāṃsy*; and the Āgamas *are* over-ridden, though not destroyed.

Verse 308, ' . . . they burn up . . . the very hard set of bonds . . .', considered earlier, likewise departs from the doctrine of the Siddhānta, when it claims that meditating on Śiva in one's heart achieves what in the *Śataratnasaṃgraha* and all the literature of the Siddhānta is the sole province of *dīkṣā*. Meditation is a good thing, and should lead to *dīkṣā*, but the verse in question does not mention *dīkṣā*, nor does the poem at large. Again there is specific mention of something called spiritual yoga (*adhyātmayoga)*. As in verse 268, with its bold contrast between the statements of the Āgamas and the sight of Śiva's dance, so too in verse 273, Umāpati's most detailed reference to the teaching of the Siddhānta, the Siddhānta is distanced from intimate connection with Naṭarāja mysticism.

> Employing the Vidyā aspect in fire,
> the Pratiṣṭhā, establishing aspect, in water,
> and the Nivṛtti, solid aspect, in the earth,
> the calming aspect called Śānti in the air,
> His own aspect, Śānti Surpassed, in the ether,
>
> Inconceivable, He performs His dance
> that is pure consciousness
> in the heart more subtle than the subtle,
> in the palace called the lotus of consciousness, in the little cave.
> . . . (273)[12]

For the Siddhānta, existence below supreme Śiva takes the form of thirty-six *tattvas*. The highest Śiva is beyond them, and thus in verse 81 Śiva is called 'surpassing the *tattvas*' (*tattvātīta*). These *tattvas* descend from subtle to gross. At the top is *bindu*, at the bottom the five 'portions' or *kalās* which are referred to in this verse, and which are in one sense nothing more than the five gross elements which comprise the entire manifest world. An important role of these *kalās* within the ritual system has already been referred to, for the process of mental purification of the body that is part of the Cidambaram ritual was lifted from the standard Siddhānta texts. In discussing the verse that mentions *bhūtaśuddhi*[13] I pointed out that each of the elements corresponds to a face of five-headed Sadāśiva and that the element of the earth goes up as far as the knees, and by further stages, water to the navel, fire to the throat, wind to the mouth, and ether to the *dvādaśānta* above the head. Each of these elements is seen as a domain pertaining to a *kalā* ('portion'), with the names as given in the present verse. Each *kalā* is seen as a mode of the highest *tattva*, the *bindu*. *Nivṛtti kalā*, corresponding to the element earth, the solid aspect of *bindu*, is the energy that stops. *Pratiṣṭhā kalā*, corresponding to the element water, the liquid aspect of *bindu*, is the energy which establishes. (An instance of the establishing power of water would be vegetable growth. From within the poem, an instance of this establishing power can be found in the water drops from Śiva's hair that establish *liṅga*s all over the world.[14]) *Vidyā kalā*, corresponding to the element fire, the fiery aspect of *bindu*, is the energy which permits knowledge. *Śānti kalā*, corresponding to the element air, is the calm aspect of *bindu*. *Śāntyatīta kalā*, corresponding to the element ether, is that aspect of the *bindu* which is in no way shaken by the evolution of the realities of manifestation.

The *kalā*s play an important part in the key initiation, namely the *nirvāṇa dīkṣā*, in a more sustained and elaborate version of the daily *bhūta śuddhi*. In this *dīkṣā* a cord called the *pāśa sūtra*, 'bond cord', equal in length to the initiand's height, has transferred on to it all the constituents of that person, most notably the *kalā*s, along with the *ātman*. In this context the ontological framework of the manifest world is provided by the *kalā*s. Each *kalā* therefore contains a slice, as it were, of the complex series of realities that the Siddhānta perceives. Each slice is envisaged in detail by the guru, on whom all the activity of the ritual falls, though the true agent is thought to be Śiva. First the guru follows the order of emission of the world, beginning with the most subtle of the *kalā*s, the *śāntyatīta*, transposing them each into the cord. Coloured powders mark out the places of the respective *kalā*s on the cord. The next day the guru detaches each *kalā* section in turn from the cord, this time working upwards in the order of reabsorption, beginning with *nivṛtti*, and places it in the sacrificial fire. The bonds that each *kalā* contains perish with it in the flames.

Umāpati in his treatises stresses the importance of *dīkṣā*. In the *Śataratnasaṃgraha* he cites, for instance, the *Sarvajñānottama Āgama*:

The self is bound by these *tattvas* and associated with all their features. It can obtain release only through the Śaiva *dīkṣā*.[15]

Umāpati enlarges on this in his gloss, saying that the self is associated with the *tattvas* and their features (in other words, with *māyā*), and is tightly bound by the beginningless [*āṇava*] *mala* and by the river of *karman*. Near the end of his treatment of this *sūtra* he declares:

Because *mala* is material, knowledge alone cannot make it disappear, no more than it can a film over the eye. *Mala*'s disappearance is brought about only by the physical action of the Lord that is called *dīkṣā*, [and the cataract] only by the eye-doctor's surgery.[16]

Prior to this he cites three passages that dismiss the panorama of other religious actions – bathing in holy waters, sacrifice, vows, worship, meditation – nothing can bring about release save *dīkṣā*. This stern concentration of purpose is demanded by the constraints of the Siddhānta system, but it is as alien to the free-ranging of the poet of the *Kuñcitāṅghristava* as it is to religion at large.

UMĀPATI'S TEACHER, MAṈAIÑĀṈA CAMPANTAR

In the *Kuñcitāṅghristava*, Umāpati makes no mention of any teacher, but lineage is not relevant to a poet; he does assert his own status as teacher, and this assertion will be considered at the close of this section. Only in one of his works, the *Civapirakācam*, does Umāpati give the lineage of his teaching:

The following Gurus have a right to exercise authority over us, viz.: Nandikeśvara, the lord chamberlain of Mount Kailāsa, wherein shines the glory of the God of gods; Sanatkumāra, one of the disciples of the former; the immediate disciples of Sanatkumāra, who obtained a revelation of the true *jñāna*, and descended to the earth; the great *muni* Paraṃjyoti who was a disciple of the last-mentioned *jñānin*; Meykaṇṭar, a disciple of Paraṃjyoti, who obtained an insight into the true *jñāna*, who lived at Tiruveṇṇai Nallūr; Aruḷnanti, of immortal fame, and the disciple of Meykaṇṭar; the divine Campantar, possessed of glorious spiritual riches and never-fading benevolence.

I place on my head the glorious lotus-like feet of my spiritual father, Maṟaiñāṉa Campantar, who came into the world to enlighten it, to cause the many-headed Sāma-Vēdam to thrive, to cause to prosper the descendants of Parāsara-Māmuṉi [a class of Brahmans], and to secure the proper attainment of *ñāṉam* [in the world]. He is the crowning gem of the Śaiva school, who has graciously taken me as his servant. He is the lord of Marutūr, and is the glory of Tirupeṇṇākaṭam [the source of the river Peṇṇān], which is encircled by groves, and the mountain-tops of which, capped with cool, beautiful clouds, send out their arm-like flag-staffs, so as to intercept the moon in her course.[17]

In the *Caṅkarpa Nirākaraṇam*, 'Exposition and Refutation', perhaps the latest of his Tamil treatises, and dated by him (1313 AD),Umāpati refers only to Meykaṇṭar in the beginning, but mentions Campantar of Marutūr in the final verse.

Turning now to his Sanskrit treatises, the *Pauṣkara Bhāṣya* makes no mention of any teacher;[18] but Umāpati's *Śataratnasaṃgraha* is of great interest. After his prefatory verses Umāpati says that he bases his commentary (on the extracts that he has selected) on the commentaries of Sadyojyoti, Rāmakaṇṭha, Nārayaṇakaṇṭha, Aghora Śivācārya and others and also on the tradition handed down in the lineage of his own teacher.[19]

We must also note his earlier remarks in this work:

> In this world where through the malign influence of the Kali Yuga the meaning of the Āgamas has been lost, the heretical (*pāṣaṇḍa*) doctrines are increasing, and the succession of teacher and pupil is confused, the supremely compassionate Umāpati Śivācārya in order to benefit his own pupils . . . drew together one hundred Sūtra jewels.[20]

In his Tamil poems, Umāpati has much to say concerning his teacher. His messenger poem, *Neñcuviṭutūtu*, 'Message through the Heart', is directed to his teacher; Umāpati apostrophizes him as Campantar the great *muni*, who liberated him from his bonds, and as Campantar the Lord, *nātha*. Since Śiva appears in the form of the Guru, it is often difficult to discern when the Guru is specifically referred to, but the following passage seems to apply to Maṟaiñāṉa:

> He th'Lord ethereal came in procession;
> I adored him, seeing others Him adore;
> He threw his eyes on me; in that instant
> Abolished was the bunch of my *mala*
> Fivefold,[21] and He transformed my very thought
> Uprooting the *tattva*s six and ninety,[22]
> Hard to narrate; to me my inner spa
> of honied ambrosia, he did reveal
> And demonstrate that th'sacred ashes white,
> Th'form of Śiva's devotee and worship
> Of Śiva alone to be true; 'Riches
> and life domestic are false,' he declared;
> He did inculcate the inner content
> Of the Pentad of Syllables sacred
> And how to chant and count and meditate
> On it; He taught me to look within too

Fearless, and trim th'inner taper aflame
And merge with the inly light of that lamp
Bright with boundless effulgence beautiful;
. . . (*Neñcuviṭututūtu*)[23]

In his *Pōṟṟippahroṭai*, 'Multiple Hymn of Praise', an experiential account of the working of Śiva's Grace, Maṟaiñāṉa Campantar is again called Lord, *nātha*, and Umāpati declares that he gave him the full set of initiations (*samaya*, *viśeṣa*, *nirvāṇa*, and *ācāryābhiṣeka*):

Our befuddled *citta* He clarified
By his divine presence, but not content
With this, He did initiate us in th'path
Supreme of Śaiva wisdom infinite
Beginning with *samaya* and ending
In *abhiṣeka*; by his divine look
He caused the wound of cruel birth, and deeds
Twofold, to vanish; on our head He did place
His beauteous hand flowery and did melt
Our stony heart and did elucidate
Unto us Truth's nature; like recession
Of murk from sky into space at th'advent
Of ruddy sun, He the Just One did cause
Āṇava Mala, though it be deathless,
To cease its ceaseless hold on me henceforth.
May that Holder of Justice, us protect.
(*Pōṟṟippahroṭai* 235)[24]

Umāpati's *Viṉāveṇpā*, 'Questions in the *veṇpā* metre', a work of thirteen verses, is supposed to be addressed to Maṟaiñāṉa Campantar, the answers being found in Umāpati's other works; this differs from the works of his predecessors that also question the teacher, for they also provide the teacher's answers, the teacher in both cases being Meykaṇṭar.[25]

TEACHER AND INITIATION IN THE LIFE OF UMĀPATI

As mentioned in the Introduction, there are two Sanskrit lives of Umāpati which might be relatively early. The shorter, that of Śivānandanātha Dīkṣita, starts almost at once with what is clearly in all versions the central event of Umāpati's life, his meeting with Maṟaiñāṉa Campantar (in Sanskrit, Vedajñāna Sambandha). In Śivānandanātha Dīkṣita's account, Umāpati, in his 56th year, accompanied by his two sons and his pupils, having worshipped Naṭarāja went outside to his splendid ivory palanquin.

He got in the palanquin with its high poles topped by golden bulls on each side and set off while his sons and crowds of disciples, who knew the Vedas, recited the Three Vedas in due order.
A certain learned Brahman, Vedajñāna Sambandha by name, was sitting in the street with his disciples and when he saw that palanquin with the Brahman riding in it, with Vedic recitation, music, and the lamp on the pole he called his disciples to him and declared, 'This man is blind in the daytime. But you don't see the whole picture. Things will turn out well for him.'[26] Then the Brahman knew this speech to be true and got down from his palanquin.
After prostrating himself at his feet, he filled his stomach with the leavings of his meals, recognizing him to be the giver of knowledge; and thereafter he followed him for three years.
That teacher when he had provided instruction in true knowledge to that pupil born in the family of the lordly sacrificers (*yajvendra*) attained the form of the supreme self free from birth and death.
With his pupils Umāpati dwelt in the monastery built by the Cola called Vīra in the beautiful wood called Rājendrapura that is splendid on the outskirts of Cidambaram.
But the three thousand Brahmans, intent on worshipping the Dancer, when they heard all that had happened to Umāpati, all assembled in the second hall [the Deva Sabhā], and summoning both his sons, said to them, 'Today your father who has in his possession the Bull-flag of the Blessed Lord of the Original Liṅga Shrine has abandoned all the pure behaviour laid down by the Vedas. Intent on worshipping the feet of a mystic (*jñānin*) he has abandoned his kinsmen and has strenuously applied himself to the path preached by that man.'
When all the sage-lords had spoken thus, the two sons remained silent in the assembly. 'From now on, these sons, wife and daughter must refrain from sacrificing with, eating with and honouring this man.'
When they had heard the sentence of the sage-lords, the two sons, of excellent character, rose to their feet, prostrated themselves before the sage-lords, and went home mulling over what had happened. They bowed several times at their mother's lotus feet, and said, 'O Mother! hear the order given today in the assembly with respect to our father. "His daughter, his sons, and all his kin must entirely cease relations with him – they must not sacrifice, eat, speak with him; they must not honour him." Thus those sages pronounced in the assembly. What reply shall we two make to their sentence?'
'This very severe sentence must stand. We are forever bound by their sentence.'
Then one day Umāpati Dīkṣita was about to enter the Temple of the Dancer. The sage-lords angrily said, 'O Umāpati! you cannot enter the Hall of the Dancer.'

(*Rājendrapura Māhātmya* 9–21)

As presented in this version, Umāpati is wealthy and rides in great state. He is accompanied by pupils. The Śaiva Siddhānta teacher has pupils, but so has Umāpati; and it will be recalled from chapter 3 that the priests are described as having flocks of pupils.

Why the palanquin? This is always understood as an indication of the life of luxury of pampered priests.[27] The Dīkṣitas' socio-economic condition in the days of the glory of the temple would have been higher than today. In more recent times, such riding in state is normally the privilege of the head of a *maṭha*. Paintings from the seventeenth century onwards often show distinguished ascetics riding in palanquins. Just such a palanquin, though made only of wood, is to be found today in the *maṭha* in Cidambaram where Aghora Śivācārya is said to have lived in the twelfth century.

But it is by no means impossible for Umāpati to have been simply a successful priest at this time. I can point to a contemporary parallel. Several priests in Cidambaram today are wealthy, due in most cases to the system of tendering for annual contracts on each of the main shrines; and one priest, benefiting principally from foreign visitors to the temple, is the proud owner of a white Ambassador car, complete with driver, which stands resplendent outside his modest and shared house. In itself, then, the magnificence of conveyance is not impossible; though to have pupils would have meant some other claim to prestige than mere wealth. But what of the lamp? Not even the priest of today I have mentioned drives round with his headlights on in broad daylight.

Let us now consider the *Pārthavana Māhātmya*'s version of these events.

> [Umāpati] performed the midday *pūjā* and then mounted the beautiful palanquin brought by the temple servants who acted as bearers, and started to go to his home. But there on the road was the Śivācārya Vedajñāna, surrounded by his pupils.
> He was fervently teaching the Śaiva Siddhānta to his pupils. One among his pupils, hands in *añjali*, pointing out to his teacher the Dīkṣita lord, mounted in his palanquin, accompanied by lamps and music, in the very hot month of Madhu, politely asked him, 'What use is there now for lamp-bearers? The teacher said, 'How can you be in doubt? It is an owl-man going by!'
> Then, hearing the speech of the guru, Umāpati, the sacrificing Brahman, was startled and obtained a trace from a previous birth.
> Jumping down to the ground from his palanquin as if he had been burned by fire, he at once in haste began to praise the Teacher.
>
> (*Pārthavana Māhātmya* 72–7)[28]

This is similar, but the verses that precede provide a clue to another interpretation: Umāpati's father, after teaching him to perform the Vedic sacrifices (63), 'taught him the Five-Syllabled Mantra and other mantras, and the Patañjali ritual rules. Then he gave him, following the

Śāstras, the *bāṇaliṅga*'(64). This *bāṇaliṅga,* a pebble *liṅga* that is a personal and portable *liṅga*, is given at the end of the second of the three Siddhānta *dīkṣās*.[29]

His father teaches him how to worship his personal *liṅga*, then the performance of the worship of the Lord of the Cit Sabhā (65–68). After three years his father dies. The text then says, 'Autonomy of worship had come to Umāpati Dīkṣita. Rising on that day, then, in the aforesaid manner, he performed the midday *pūjā* and mounted his palanquin.'

This account has referred to Umāpati's *viśeṣa dīkṣā*. Could it be that what is now described is the celebration of the conclusion of his *ācāryābhiṣeka*, the fourth and greatest of the initiatory processes, wherein the use of a palanquin is actually prescribed? It would be because of this special celebration that there are lamp carriers! That the palanquin is carried by temple servants is perhaps mentioned because this is not their usual function. Aghora Śivācārya says that the *abhiṣeka* should be accompanied by recitation of the Vedas and auspicious noises; other texts call for a variety of musical instruments, singing, and even dancing.[30]

Yet there are grounds for rejecting this explanation of the circumstances surrounding Umāpati's meeting with Maṟaiñāṉa. Were the suggestion just made correct, there would be the paradox that no sooner was Umāpati formally made *ācārya*, than he happened to meet his true teacher. Furthermore, Umāpati himself tells us in the *Pōṟṟippahroṭai* that he received the full series of Śaiva initiations – 'beginning with *samaya* [*dīkṣā*] and ending with [*ācārya*] *abhiṣeka*'.[31] He seems to say that it was his teacher Maṟaiñāṉa who performed these ceremonies upon him, though because of the Guru being Śiva as far as the Siddhānta is concerned, ambiguity remains. Whichever Guru gave him *dīkṣā* would be Śiva. Could it have been a fellow priest? There is no evidence of the Dīkṣitas performing elaborate initiations.[32] Certainly they have not done so in living memory; and the glorious fact that they are the equals of Śiva by birth makes elaborate initiation unnecessary. It is then a possibility that Umāpati received in due course the regular and full initiation into the Śaiva Siddhānta from Maṟaiñāṉa.

Further, it may be that the way Umāpati is supposed to have met his teacher is entirely a fabrication. Umāpati often refers to light and darkness. In his *Tiruvaruṭpayaṉ*, 'Fruit of Divine Grace', Umāpati makes a striking comparison:

> Like the owl which cannot see even in bright sunlight, the soul (though present in God) cannot perceive God, owing to its connection with Āṇava Mala.[33]

It is likely that this striking phrase was enough to spark the imagination of a biographer. Also incorporated within the incident is a common Siddhānta simile, one cited by Umāpati in his *Śataratnasaṃgraha*:

Just as someone [looking for something in the dark] abandons the torch he holds in his hand when he has found the thing, so the soul being now able to perceive [Śiva] the One to be known, afterwards abandons the means of knowing [Him].[34]

Lastly, the whole tenor of Umāpati's writing on Śaiva Siddhānta is geared to the action of grace – that the key events in his life should pertain to conversion experiences is an expression in story form of the keystone of his thinking.

INITIATION BY UMĀPATI

Umāpati does not mention any teacher in respect of himself in the *Kuñcitāṅghristava*. In a poem, mention of a teacher would not be expected. Again, in so far as he was writing as a Dīkṣita, member of a democratic community all members of which were by definition the equal of Śiva, acknowledgement of a teacher would be less likely. And yet Umāpati claims himself to be a high-powered teacher, referring to an event that might otherwise have been thought biographical embroidery:

Śambhu, Lord of the Dance, has given me success
through great mantras of enormous power;
great magic power through yoga;

and the great enlightenment of the self
that removes birth and death;

and the rank of guru – confirmed in writing –
to give release to Sūta and others;
He has shown me His dance,
He has given me exceeding delight.
. . . (305)[35]

This is a reference to the other famous incident in Umāpati's life, his initiation of Sūta, an outcaste wood-cutter, when the latter hands him a letter from Śiva ordering the initiation.[36]

The *Rājendrapura Māhātyma* gives the following account.

'O Umāpati, I am "the Dancer who favours His devotees". Today, when you have read this, you must make that Sūta, a man of the lowest caste, receive release through the descent of Śakti from you.'

Placing this command of the Lord of the Sabhā on his head, and having brought before him the noble and very constant outcaste, he, the most excellent of enlightened men, looked upon him and by bringing down his own Śakti caused a surge of the radiance of the Supreme Self to enter him.

(*Rājendrapura Māhātyma* 70–1)

The wood-cutter's widow is most upset at the disappearance of her spouse in flames, and despite Umāpati's explanation complains to the King. Under investigation, Umāpati opts to demonstrate his powers by conferring enlightenment on a bush. The bush accordingly goes up in flames, to reveal a yogin who had been waiting for release within (or behind!) the bush. Lee Siegel's work on magic in India leads one to be on the lookout for conjuring tricks;[37] but more likely is that the account of the incident was inspired by an uninformed view of the fiery nature of extreme Śaktinipāta. As Umāpati says in the *Śataratnasaṃgraha*, 'Were the *dīkṣā* to bring about complete destruction of all the *pāśa*s and the true nature of one's being to be revealed, at that very moment the body would fall away'.[38] For the Siddhānta, that cannot happen because, as Umāpati goes on to say, the *karman* that has produced the body in the present life has to take effect. Assuming the event had a historical basis – he does after all refer to it – it might readily be supposed that the shock of the initiation was so great that the outcaste died of a heart attack, a *cause célèbre* that yet ended favourably for Umāpati.

The *Pārthavana Māhātmya* also describes Umāpati's giving of enlightenment to his wife, Pārvatī. When he became an ascetic, his wife went with him to the penance grove. He taught the *Pauṣkara Āgama* to devotees there for a month, then she asked for release from rebirth for herself, a wife not being dependent on a man who is a *yogin*. Umāpati, after other preliminaries, fed her *pañcagavya*, the five products of the cow, to remove her sins, blindfolded her, 'and entered her body through her vagina (*bhogamārga*), took out the particle (*kalā*) that is the support of life and coming out again through the vagina placed [her life force] in the supreme space of the *ātman*. He burned her lifeless body, bathed, and regained his purity.'[39]

The magical turn of these two episodes accords ill with the Śaiva Siddhānta treatises of Umāpati, but reflects a real and important current of Hindu thought, amply present in most Tantric schools. More to the point, it is not so far removed from the mindset of the *Kuñcitāṅghristava*, which is very much concerned with power over events sought by the adept (*sādhaka*) who seeks enjoyment (*bubhukṣu*).[40]

VEDAS AND ĀGAMAS

A key feature of the Tamil Śaiva Siddhānta, one might almost say its defining feature, is the claim that its source lies in the Vedas as well as the Āgamas, in what it calls the Vedāgamas.[41] There was already a movement in this direction when, around 1000, Bhaṭṭa Rāmakaṇṭha mentions that amongst other threats to the Siddhānta's purity some people sought to reconcile the established truth of the Siddhānta with the Veda.[42] As was suggested in the beginning of the chapter, this claim to Vedic orthodoxy was an attempt to broaden the base of the Siddhānta's appeal. With the further development of the Tamil Śaiva Siddhānta, the claim that 'the Siddhānta is the essence of the Veda' (made for instance in the late *Uttarakāmika Āgama*) comes to be an expression of indifference to both the Vedas and the Āgamas, implying that inspiration is found elsewhere – indirectly in the *Tēvāram* and other Tamil poetry, and directly in the writings of Meykaṇṭar.

A verse attributed to Umāpati makes an adroit summation of the school:

> The Veda is the cow, the true Āgama its milk;
> the liturgical Tamil of the Four
> is the ghee churned therefrom;
> the essence of the Tamil work fostering wisdom
> by Meykaṇṭar of eternal Tiruveṇṇainallūr,
> the 'Good Town of Sacred Butter',
> is the taste yielded by that ghee.[43]

The Four are the three poets of the *Tēvāram* plus Māṇikkavācakar. Aruḷnanti, Meykaṇṭar's disciple, says that the Vedas and the Śaivāgamas are both positioned beneath Śiva's sacred foot, and continues:

> The only real books are the Vedas and Śaivāgamas. All other books are derived from these. These two books were eternally revealed by the Perfect God. Of them, the Vedas are *general*, and given out for all; the Āgamas are *special* and revealed for the benefit of the blessed; and they contain the essential truths of the Vedas and Vedānta. Hence all other books are *pūrvapakṣa* books and the Śivāgamas alone are Siddhānta works.[44]

Umāpati is generally content to link the Āgamas with the Vedas in his Tamil works. Both he and Aruḷnanti do not seem to have differed from Tirumūlar's view:

> Veda and Āgama alike
> Are revelations of God,
> That is Truth.

The one is general
The other special.
Their goals two, they say.

Search them both –
For the truly learned,
There is no difference.

(*Tirumantiram* 2398)[45]

In the *Śataratnasaṃgraha*, based as it is entirely on the verses from the Āgamas, there is little scope for mention of the Vedas. Apropos of the five heads of Sadāśiva giving out pure knowledge in five streams at the time of creation, Umāpati says the knowledge that is enlightenment comes forth as *nāda* from formless Śiva; it then takes the form of the Tantras when it comes from Sadāśiva. One of the five streams is the Vedas. 'The four Vedas then just take the form of a stream.'[46] 'The entire intellectual universe (*sakalaṃ vāṅmayaṃ śāstrajālam*) is contained within these [streams and their subdivisions].'[47] 'The Siddhānta has superiority over the Vedas and all other [systems] . . . the knowledge that is the Vedas etc. is inferior, the knowledge that is the Siddhānta is supreme.'[48] Umāpati gives this *sūtra* one of the most extended discussions in the *Śataratnasaṃgraha*, but the Vedas are barely noticed. The situation is different in his *Bhāṣya* on the *Pauṣkara Āgama*, the *Bhāṣya* beginning with an explanation of why it is that the Āgamas are authoritative. Whereas the *Śataratnasaṃgraha* is a sealed world of a mass of Siddhānta texts, the *Bhāṣya* takes a more relaxed view, quoting freely, at least in this opening section, from Purāṇas and other sources outside the Siddhānta. The Śivādvaitin Nīlakaṇṭha is quoted as saying 'We see no difference between the Veda and the Śivāgama.'[49] Umāpati poses the question, why then were they both composed? And gives Nīlakaṇṭha's answer, 'The Veda is intended for the three [twice-born] castes, the other for all castes.' Umāpati then makes the point that the Veda's authority is for those who are 'unripe', the Āgama's for the 'ripe'. 'Both the Veda and the Śaivāgamas of the Siddhānta are supreme over all other [texts]; and of the two the Āgama [is supreme].'[50]

Umāpati takes a contrary view in the *Kuñcitāṅghristava*:

For the enlightenment of pupils excluded from the Vedas
the Brahmans, gods on earth, read out the *Kāmika* and other *Āgamas*
which make known His glory in their Conduct and Yoga sections.

But they themselves, under white umbrellas held high
by the kings who come when they perform the Vājapeya sacrifice,
worship Him according to the way of the revealed Vedas.

. . . (107)[51]

It may be significant that Umāpati mentions only the *caryā* and *yoga* sections of the Āgamas, especially that *kriyā*, the ritual section, is omitted, since the most significant difference lay in the distinction between the Cidambaram temple ritual ('Vedic' in that it used Vedic mantras) and that of the Āgamas.

> So that those who have no right
> to perform the rituals laid down in the Vedas
> could attain Dharma and the other goals of man,
>
> Pārvatī under His instruction
> published the multitude of Siddhānta Tantras
> that He, Supreme Śiva, had composed,
> in its divisions of the *Kāmika* and the others
> and their constituent parts; and the sixty-four arts.
> . . . (146)[52]

Both verses clearly assert the priority of the Vedas, and the former, verse 107, reminds us of the grand status assumed by the priests of Cidambaram. Embodiments of the Vedas and practising 'Vedic' ritual (in that it used Vedic mantras), the Dīkṣitas were committed to uphold the Vedas. But other verses refer to the Siddhānta alone. Here is another instance of the Goddess's association with revelation:

> Gaurī, hearing the seven crore mantras –
> that give the great magic powers,
> subjecting the three worlds and so on –
>
> originated from His five lotus faces,
> Sadyojāta and the others,
>
> by His command
> She Herself brought them down to those worlds,
> along with their usages and ceremonies.
> . . . (245)[53]

The seven crore of mantras are in principle a power of knowledge and action that is entirely unveiled. They are instruments of grace, for Śiva uses them to give either liberation (*mukti*) or superior enjoyments in the pure worlds (*bhukti*) to selves whose *mala* is ripe. The manifestation of these mantras is a standard part of the evolution of the universe as viewed by the Āgamas, but in the Āgamas the Goddess does not usually play a role in their promulgation, as here and in the preceding verse. However Umāpati's concluding *sūtra* in his *Śataratnasaṃgraha* is:

My fair-faced lady! reveal this knowledge to my devotees.[54]

In his commentary on this he cites from the *Vāyu Saṃhitā* Upamanyu's conclusion of the main account of Śiva that he gives Kṛṣṇa: 'Beautiful-necked Śiva told the Śivāgama, sole means to benefits, to Śivā [Pārvatī] out of compassion for his devotees'.[55]

Another verse gives the Āgamas priority over the Vedas:

At the beginning of the Kalpa there first appeared
from His excellent throat the two sounds
'OṂ, now (*atha*)!', excellent and auspicious,
making known the meaning of the Siddhānta.
Afterwards the Vedas and other sciences originated;
Brahmā, Viṣṇu and the other gods; all the worlds.

Him Who faces South,
the abode of the illuminating sun,
Whose foot is curved,
I worship. (251)[56]

Umāpati refers indirectly to one famous Āgama when he says in verse 299 that Śiva is 'praised by Viṣṇu the Man[-lion]' (*naraharivinutaṃ*). According to Bhaṭṭa Nārāyaṇakaṇṭha commenting on the *Mṛgendra Āgama*, Indra, stained by the sin of having killed Vṛtrāsura, who was a Brahman, praised Viṣṇu with a thousand names and with hymns from the three Vedas. Viṣṇu gave him a breastplate belonging to Narasiṃha (*nārasiṃhaṃ kavacam*) and ordered him to practise *tapas* while adoring Śiva. When a thousand years had gone by, Śiva taught him the *Kāmika*. Because the husband of Umā had thus taught it to Indra when he was in the form of Nṛsimha, 'Man-lion', this *Kāmika* was called *Mṛgendra*, from the fact that a lion (*mṛgendra*) had been the auditor.[57] The *Mṛgendra* is not one of the 28 Āgamas, appearing in the list of supplementary *Upāgamas* as the *Nārasiṃha*. Yet it is, in Brunner's words, 'one of the most famous anonymous texts of Śaivism'.[58] Very frequently cited by the Siddhānta masters, it was also often referred to by the non-dualist Śaivas. Mādhava (fourteenth century) based his account of the Siddhānta on it, and Umāpati uses it extensively in the *Śataratnasaṃgraha*.

Once or twice Umāpati refers to the Vedas without reference to the Āgamas, making the point that Śiva is the source of the Vedas:

He, Maheśa, the Great Lord, in the beginning
created Brahmā and gave him
the complete collection of scripture,
. . . (36)[59]

From Whom the Whole of Śruti,
which has the form of Brahmā's breathings,

and all the Smṛti which resembles it –
ritual texts, ancient songs, the Purāṇa,
the manifold excellent mantras
along with the epics and the sciences –

shine everywhere even today of their own accord;

He, through His pity, becoming the Naṭeśa in His Hall,
protects all the worlds. Him, matchless,
. . . (87)[60]

To round off this presentation of Umāpati's view of the Vedas and Āgamas, we shall look at a compromise position from the *Cidambara Māhātmya* and the *Kōyil Purāṇam*. At the beginning of the Hiraṇyavarman episode, creation is described according to the Siddhānta – though it seems to begin in the Cit Sabhā – but the Vedas are inserted into the schema and precede the emission of the Mantras. The Āgamas, which should follow the Mantras in the process of creation, are omitted. Once creation has been described, the Āgamas, despite not having been mentioned in creation, are now mentioned as of superior merit to the Vedas. Brahmans who sacrifice in the fire that is Śiva's own body to propitiate him win heaven. Those who are intent on the discipline, yoga, and ritual laid down in Śiva's Āgamas gain liberation up to the level of similarity of form with Śiva (*sārūpya*).[61] Brahmans who perform sacrifices without desire attain the threefold *mukti* – presumably the *sālokya*, *sāmīpya*, and *sārūpya* of the Siddhānta. Both those who are devoted to the Vedānta (the Upaniṣads), and those who are well established in the *jñānapāda* of the Āgamas attain *sāyujya* (*Cidambara Māhātmya* 20.7–22). The *Kōyil Purāṇam*, however, omits the Upaniṣads, and gives all the weight to the Āgamas:

We placed Our will on the powers,
The flawless formless great Māyā was animated and
Five elements starting from sound were produced from it.
The preserved letters and language beginning with
The Mantras of the Vedic texts
Were expanded in a pure way
And the impure elements were
Assembled from the beginning.[62]
The people who followed the way of the Vedas
Attained heaven. Those who followed
The paths of virtue, rituals, and yoga

According to the Agamic texts,
With Our help attained Our own world,
Our vicinity, and Our own form.
Those who attained great wisdom in Us
Got to be with Us without separation.[63]

There was inevitably considerable tension between the rival groups of scriptures, and Umāpati was, as it were, a fault line between the two. Many other writers must have been in a similarly complex ideological position, but he stands out with remarkable prominence. Of the four founding fathers of the Tamil Śaiva Siddhānta, Umāpati was the first to use the term Śaiva Siddhānta, though Tirumūlar used it among the many terms he freely coined. This was the term that caught on, but the colophon of the *Pauṣkara Bhāṣya* uses the more significant term Vaidikasiddhānta, the Vedic Siddhānta, to express Umāpati's position, and this would very well fit the *Kuñcitāṅghristava* too.

SIDDHĀNTA AND VEDĀNTA

At the beginning of the *Pārthavana Māhātmya* the teacher and his pupils have come out from the city to worship the *liṅga* which Arjuna worshipped. One of the pupils, being told they were passing by the site of Umāpati's *āśrama*, rejoins 'You previously said that the great mendicant Śaṅkara who wrote the Advaita commentary was born in the lineage of the Tillai Brahmans. How did it happen that they who expounded opposite views were born in one and the same place?' Brahmānanda then gives the story of Umāpati's life, but Śaṅkara is not referred to again. In the *Kuñcitāṅghristava*, Umāpati refers twice to Śaṅkara. Śaṅkara is said to have been born in Cidambaram, to have been a Dīkṣita:

He Who wears the Skin decided to spread
the knowledge of Advaita in all the worlds

and joyfully created from a portion of Himself
in the ocean of the family of the terrestrial gods
who allay darkness by worshipping His own foot,

a lord among ascetics, pure, called Śaṅkara,
who occupied the throne of omniscience.
He conferred His grace upon him;
. . . (295)[64]

The other verse explicitly mentions Śaṅkara's commentaries on ten Upaniṣads, and says they always praise the form of Brahman that they know to be the Dance (88).

These Upaniṣads that form the key statements
in the Vedānta, entail proximity to Brahman;

the principal ten of them are especially important
along with the great Commentary composed by the ascetic;
having the form of pillars they always praise
the form of Brahman they know to be the Dance;
. . . (88)[65]

Umāpati does not refer to the fact that Śaṅkara teaches Māyāvāda (against which he argues in his treatises), and assumes within the context of the poem that Śaṅkara's Advaita does not differ from his own. In verse 89 he celebrates the Dīkṣitas' knowledge of the *Brahma Sūtras*:

embodiments of Vyāsa in the Vedānta
. . .
veritable Brahmās in the Vedas – (89)[66]

Why in verse 88 does he refer to the Upaniṣads as pillars? Presumably this is a reminiscence of the earlier passage where core texts are part of the structure of the twin Sabhās, despite the fact that the Upaniṣads are not formally incorporated into the symbolic structure. Yet, even if the Upaniṣads are pillars, their value is limited, for they entail only 'proximity to Brahman'. In terms of Māyāvāda, of course, this makes no sense; in terms of Siddhānta, it grants a limited value to the Vedānta. Then again, Umāpati might have said *sāmīpya* rather than *sāyujya* to show that he did not accept the Vedānta version of Advaita.

Umāpati argues against Advaita Vedānta (Māyāvāda) at length in his *Caṅkaṟpa Nirākaraṇam*, 'Exposition and Refutation'.[67] This work of 975 lines devotes 58 of them to an exposition of Māyāvāda and 254 to its refutation. Whereas Aruḷnanti refuted Māyāvāda as eleventh in the fourteen systems considered in the *Civañāṉa Cittiyār*, Umāpati takes the Māyāvāda as the foundation of what is to be refuted. Māyāvāda is refuted by an advocate of Aikyavāda (the union of Śiva and the *ātman*, with the existence of *āṇava mala* denied), and so on in turn, each succeeding view a closer approximation to Siddhānta until the Siddhāntin himself, who refers the others to the *Civapirakācam*. In his refutation of Māyāvāda, Umāpati concedes that the Vedas declare that Brahman alone exists, but then why speak of even apparent duality? If the Veda is self-generated (*svayambhū*) then it is separate from Brahman, which cannot then be the one existent. If the Veda was uttered by Brahman, how can that be since Brahman has no parts, and no vocal organs? If Brahman uttered the Veda through gods or *ṛṣi*s, like a spirit speaking through the person it possesses, then the Veda would be the utterance of a *paśu*, and would not be free from *mala*, impurity. Moving from the *pramāṇa* to the *prameya*, Umāpati argues that the oneness of gold underlying all the forms, such as ornaments, that gold takes, nevertheless has had changes wrought upon it by a doer. 'The gold has not become ornaments without a doer.' Further, if Brahman is the creator, there must be a material cause upon which it acts, otherwise the creator and the created will be the same.

Umāpati then supposes that the Māyāvādin claims that the *acit*, the non-conscious, came from *cit*, the conscious. If the nonconscious phenomenal world (*prapañca*) emanates from Brahman, is this because such is the nature of Brahman? Then the world must be of the nature of Brahman and not *acit*. If Brahman giving out the world which is *acit* is said to be like a lamp giving out black smoke, Umāpati rejoins that the blackness pertains not to the lamp but to the wick and the oil, 'and in any case the black smoke does not go back into the brightness of the lamp.' If the world is said to be Brahman's play, *līlā*, the body assumed in play is separate from the player. 'Just as the silk worm binds itself with the silken thread of the cocoon and dies within it, so also Brahman which assumes an illusory body (*māyāśarīra*) in play (*līlā*) will find itself imprisoned and be devoid of its absoluteness and intelligence.' With regard to *mukti*, Umāpati argues that *tat tvam asi*, 'That art thou', is in fact the same kind of figure of speech as the statement 'You have become a tiger' addressed to a brave man. That person has not literally become a tiger. 'When the Vedas say I am Brahman this means that the I is different from Brahman. The Māyāvādin claiming a false Brahma-*jñāna* will neglect the virtuous conduct ordained by the Vedas. About to die, he receives no reassurance from God, and when dead the other gods will be angry with him because of his claim to be Brahman.'

Two verses might seem at first sight to express a position resembling that of Śaṅkara. It will be fruitful to consider them together.

> Inconceivable in terms of
> time or space or any other category,
>
> honoured by those who meditate on His own Mantra,
> He is the Essence of Advaita (*advaitasāra*),
> bereft of middle, beginning and end,
>
> He sees the hearts and thoughts of all men,
> He is the first One, the one beyond Māyā,
> quietened, the illuminator of all heavenly bodies,

truly named the Lord,
composed of lustre, the radiant One.
Him the supreme, the ultimate dancer,
Whose foot is curved, I worship. (267)[68]

Brahman alone is true,
not this world, nor anything else.

Reflecting on this statement of the *Upaniṣads*
the leaders of the wise constantly
look upon Him in their hearts,

the mass of consciousness, beyond perception,
His Dance of Bliss constantly repeated
like the flickering flame of a lamp,

free from illusion, shining white,
supporting the spheres of truth and being.
He is what is meant by Tat Sat
. . . (272)[69]

Verse 267 speaks of Śiva as the essence of Advaita, but calls him 'beyond Māyā', as in *tattvātīta*, that is, beyond the really existent phenomenal universe. The term Advaita is, of course, not necessarily synonymous with Māyāvāda. Most forms of Vedānta philosophy are versions of the notion of non-duality. The currently preeminent position of Śaṅkara's philosophy, which has left the West with a somewhat distorted view of Indian religious thought, is the culmination of a rising tide of popularity which was first beginning to be seen around the time of Umāpati. Thus, in addition to Umāpati's own references to Śaṅkara in the *Kuñcitāṅghristava*, Umāpati's younger contemporary Mādhava, made head of the Śaṅkara monastery at Śringeri in 1331, wrote the *Sarvadarśanasaṅgraha*, a review of sixteen systems of Indian philosophy shown as culminating in Śaṅkara's Vedānta.

In Umāpati's *Caṅkarpa Nirākaraṇam* the Nimittakāraṇapariṇāmavādin takes a position close to that of Nīlakaṇṭha, and which may be called Śivādvaita. Here all existence is a manifestation of Śiva. The world is a real manifestation of Śiva; Śiva and the self are *cit*; Śiva, the world, and the self are not separate entities.

The term *advaita* (Tamil: *attuvitam*) is used twice by the founder of the Tamil Śaiva Siddhānta. Explaining his second *sūtra*, Meykaṇṭar says, 'The Primal (God) is one with souls and other than souls: for the word *advaita* means "not two"; for if it be taken to mean "one", there is that which thinks it is one . . . like tune and sound, like fruit and its essential sweetness, the grace (*tāḷ*)[70] of the omnipresent Lord is in *advaita* relation (with souls), the precious Scriptures do not say "one" but "not two".'[71]

In verse 267 Śiva is called 'the one beyond Māyā (*māyātīta*), but this is not saying that the world is an illusion; rather, it is saying that Śiva is beyond the really existent phenomenal universe, and is equivalent to the expression *tattvātīta*, 'beyond the *tattvas*'. He is honoured by those meditating on his Mantra, and he sees men's thoughts: God is clearly separate from humanity.

In verse 272,

> Brahman alone is true,
> not this world, nor anything else.

might sound like Māyāvāda, but not when read with the rest of the verse. The words *Satyaṃ brahmaiva* are reminiscent of *Bṛhadāraṇyaka Upaniṣad* 5.4.1:

> This, verily, is That. This, indeed, was That, even the Real. He who knows that wonderful being as the first-born – namely, that Brahma is the Real (*satyaṃ brahmeti*) – conquers these worlds. Would he be conquered who knows thus that great spirit as the first-born – namely, that Brahma is the Real (*satyaṃ brahmeti*)? [No!] for indeed, Brahma is the Real (*satyaṃ hy eva brahma*).[72]

This passage of the *Bṛhadāraṇyaka Upaniṣad* immediately follows mention of Brahman as the heart:

> The heart (*hṛdaya*) is the same as Prajāpati (Lord of Creation). It is Brahman. It is all.

Another relevant passage is from the Śāṇḍilyavidyā section of the *Chāndogya Upaniṣad*:

> Verily, this whole world is Brahma. Tranquil, let one worship It as that from which he came forth, as that into which he will be dissolved, as that in which he breathes.[73]

The point is not that the world is illusion, but that Brahman is everywhere.

I turn now to three verses which can be fruitfully considered as a group.

> On the best of mountains, the lotus-eyed Viṣṇus,
> who had each in turn relinquished their authority,
> greeted Kṛṣṇa Govinda come for a boon for the gods.
>
> After embracing him in delight, and asking how he was,
> they enlightened him as to Him:
> 'Dear one, it's because you don't
> 'comprehend the Essence of Brahman in your heart,
> 'that you ask for action –
> 'action is the cause of suffering!'
> . . . (215)[74]

In 215 when Kṛṣṇa comes to seek Śiva's help against the demons, the Viṣṇus of former ages, the earlier *avatāras*, welcome him and explain that it is because he does not understand the truth of Brahman, *brahmatattva*,[75] that he seeks action – but action is the cause of suffering. They enlighten him as to the true nature of Śiva as Brahman. And the following verse has Brahmā as exasperated teacher of Vedānta:

> 'So to win wisdom you must go this very day
> 'and take refuge with the Lord of the Sabhā.'
>
> Thus the Creator informed the throng of sages
> and sent them to that Lord of the Sacred Place,
> . . . (216)[76]

Appropriately, these two verses concerning failure to understand the true nature of reality are followed by one that breaks the run of exasperated instruction and yet continues the theme on another plane:

> Once the Daughter of the Mountain
> seeing her son Gaṇeśa
> when playing on the Silver Mountain
>
> quickly pick up the Mountain of the Gods
> between his great tusks
> because he thought it was a golden banana,
>
> in her love for him she called Him at once
> and proudly showed Him the deed of their son,
> . . . (217)[77]

Here at the back of the poet's mind is a variation of the Vedāntic trope of mother of pearl mistaken for silver, and the rope for a snake; Gaṇeśa mistakes golden Mount Meru for a banana. This verse is an involuntary allusion to the Māyāvāda type of error. There is a switch from the strain of propaganda to maternal satisfaction – the mother's pride in her strong if silly son is all part of the process of relief. Māyāvāda would have been in Umāpati's mind because of his two references to Śaṅkarācārya.

Another verse describes the teaching of the Vedānta, in this case by Śiva to Pārvatī:

> He was delighted to tell in private
> the Daughter of the Mountain
> the truths of the Vedānta
>
> but, infuriated by Her inattention,
> cursed Her to be born in the family of a fisher king.
> Him She chose as Her husband in marriage

when He caught the mighty fish in the ocean.
She took up Her dwelling in His left side.
. . . (157)[78]

This story is part of the Madurai cycle, very popular from at least the sixteenth century; the cycle is represented in bas-reliefs on the colonnade plinth of the west side of the innermost courtyard, which seem to be part of the modern renovation of the temple. The fish in question is Nandin, Śiva's bull and doorkeeper. The divine couple's sons were enraged to find their mother banished and throw Śiva's books into the sea. For letting the boys into his room, Śiva curses Nandin to be born as a fish in the sea. He is thereby enabled to rescue the books that had been so summarily disposed of. In the sixteenth-century version of Parañcōtimuṉivar, the book Subrāhmaṇya snatched from Śiva's very hand was not an Upaniṣad but Meykaṇṭar's *Civañāṉapōtam*!

The lord of all, source of all living beings,
His nature unchangeable,
giver of all, ornament of all,

all surpassing, His name is Being,
eyes full of compassion,
the essence of all the Vedānta,

truth, existence, dwelling in the sky,
worshipped by Sanaka and the other sages

energy in the singing of the Sāma Veda,
the Lord of the Hall (*saṃsad*),
praised by all poets,
. . . (284)[79]

VEDĀNTA AND NAṬARĀJA

A verse that gives a straightforward account of the iconography of Naṭarāja, begins by affirming an origin in the Vedānta.

His form is sung in the Vedānta.
He bears the fire and the drum in two hands,
. . . (108)[80]

The same claim is made in more general accounts of Śiva. Thus,

His form is the Self as described in the Vedānta,
Brahmā and Viṣṇu are his sons,
He is the Lord of the Universe,
He is present in the Hall,
. . . (66)[81]

And again,

> My mind is aware of no Lord of the Gods but Him –
> the moon His crest, His mouth softly smiling,
> His throat blue, He has three eyes,
>
> the Vedānta sings of His deeds,
> He creates Brahmā and Viṣṇu,
> His play is universal Māyā,
> the woman occupies the left half of His body, . . .
>
> (302)[82]

In both these verses the mention of the Vedānta is followed by the statement that he created Brahmā and Viṣṇu. There is also mention of Māyā. In verse 284 Śiva is the essence of all the Vedānta (*sarvavedāntasāram*). At the end of the poem the Vedānta and contemplation of Brahman are linked with the general practice of Śaivism:

> Running, constantly running
> to the place that is dear to Him,
>
> adorning, constantly adorning
> their bodies with ash and *rudrākṣa* beads,
>
> listening, constantly listening
> to His deeds that are sung in the Vedānta,
>
> performing, constantly performing intently
> worship three times a day,
>
> the lordly ascetics, absorbed in contemplating Brahman,
> attain the place of Bhava that is beyond being.
> Him Whose foot is curved
> I worship. (311)[83]

The obvious meaning of Vedānta here is the Upaniṣads. Śiva is, of course, sung of in the *Mahānārayaṇa Upaniṣad* and the *Śvetāśvatara Upaniṣad*, but his deeds and iconography are only to be found in the late temple-oriented Āgamas; and it may be that the Āgamas, seen as the culmination of the Vedas, are referred to here by Vedānta, with a deliberate ambiguity. By this ambiguity, Umāpati would, within the poem, absorb Śaṅkara, and perhaps other Vedāntins, within the ambit of the Siddhānta.

TAMIL ŚAIVA SIDDHĀNTA AND NAṬARĀJA

Although the four great Tamil poets often sing of Śiva's dance, they were writing before the Cōḻa codification of Naṭarāja. The three masters of the Tamil Śaiva Siddhānta tradition have almost nothing to say about Śiva's dance. Only Maṉavācakam Kaṭantār deals with it, and it plays a prominent part in his *Uṇmaiviḷakkam*:

O my Teacher, explain to me the following! What are the 36 *tattvas*? What is *āṇava*? What is that Karma which arose even then? What am I who seem to differ from these? Who art Thou? What is the Lord's Sacred Dance (*nāṭaṉṉaṭam*) and what is the truth of the Pañcākṣara?

...

O Meykandanatha, graciously expound so that I may understand the nature of the Sacred Dance (*niṉṟāṭal*) seen by the sages that takes the form of the Five Letters beyond the Nāda *tattva (nādānta)*.

O my son, hear. The Supreme Intelligence dances in the soul formed of the letter YA, with a form composed of the five letters, SI VA YA NA MA for the purpose of removing our sins.

Hear now how the Dance is performed. In his feet is NA; in his Navel is MA; in his shoulders is SI; in his face is VA; in his head is YA.
[These letters are to be contemplated in those parts.]

The hand holding the drum is SI, the hand held out is VA, the hand holding out protection is YA; the hand holding the fire is NA; the foot holding down Muyalaka is MA.

The arch (*tiruvāci*) over Śrī Naṭarāja is OṂ; and the *akṣara* which is never separate from the OṂ is the filling Splendour. This is the dance of the Lord of Cidambaram. They understand this who have lost their self (*ahaṅkāra*). Understanding, they have left their births behind.

Creation starts from the Drum. Protection proceeds from the Hand of Hope. The fire produces Destruction. From the Foot holding down proceeds Tirobhava; the Foot held aloft gives Mukti.

By these means, Our Father scatters the darkness of Māyā, burns the strong Karma, stamps down Mala (Āṇava) and showers grace, and lovingly plunges the soul in the Ocean of Bliss. This is the nature of His Dance.

The silent Jñānins, destroying the three kinds of Mala, establish themselves where their selves are destroyed. There they witness the sacred Dance (*niṉṟāṭal*) filled with Bliss . This is the Dance (*kūttu*) of the Sabhānātha whose very form is Grace.

The One who is past thought and speech assumes graciously the Form composed of the Pañcākṣara in the Dancing Hall of Parā Śakti, so as to be seen by his Consort , Umā, Haimavatī. They never see births who see this mystic Dance.

O my gracious Guru! Thou hast explained to me beautifully the nature of the Nādānta dance. Let me now know the nature of the Pañcākṣara, Can they be one with the letters which are imperishable?

(*Uṇmaiviḷakkam* 3; 31–40)[84]

Umāpati briefly links the Pañcākṣara with the Dance in his *Tiruvarutpayaṉ*:

> On one side mystic darkness of 'Weakness', on the other
> dance of mystic 'Wisdom', – Soul between the two.

Commentary. The syllables MA and NA represent the energetic whirl of Impurity in itself, and as operating in the Soul; the syllables ŚI and VĀ represent the mystic action of Śiva and of Grace. Between these stands YA, which represents the Soul.[85]

Umāpati contrasts Śiva's manifestation in nature (*ūṉanaṭaṉam*), *ūṉa* being 'flesh', 'weakness', with his dance of knowledge (*ñāṉanaṭam*). This distinction is based on Meykaṇṭar's ninth *sūtra*:

> Let the soul by spiritual vision (*ñāṉakkaṇ*) discover the Lord in its own consciousness – the Lord who cannot be known by imperfect knowledge (*ūṉakkaṇ*) and sense-perception.[86]

PAÑCĀKṢARA

A major difference between the Siddhānta and the Tamil Śaiva Siddhānta is the prominent role of the Five-letter Mantra (*pañcākṣara*), *namaḥ śivāya*, in the latter system. (The order of the syllables is variable.) The Five Letters are mentioned briefly but emphatically by Meykaṇṭar. The ninth *sūtra* referred to above continues as follows:

> When the self abandons the world of sense (*pāśa*) as a quickly passing mirage, the Lord becomes cool shade [for it]. It will ponder the Five Letters in the manner prescribed.

Meykaṇṭar adds:

> If the self knows by the Five Letters that it belongs to Hara; if in the heart it worships Him by them; if in the navel it offers oblation by them; if between the eyebrows it meditates; then in that meditation God will appear and the soul will become His servant.[87]

Umāpati declares in the *Tiruvarutpayaṉ*,

> The Āgama and the Veda and other *śāstras*
> only explain the truth of Pañcākṣara.[88]

C. N. Singaravelu, the editor of the journal *Śaiva Siddhānta*, explains the logic of this view:

> The holy hymn Sri Rudram occupies the central position among the four Vedas. The Panchakshara has been mentioned in the middle of Sri Rudram. The Panchakshara may therefore be considered to be the core of the Vedas. It may also be considered to be the quintessence of the twenty eight Saiva Agamas which form the basis for Siddhanta Saivam.[89]

Like the Vedas and Āgamas, the Pañcākṣara is present in the Cit Sabhā as the five silver steps leading up from the Kanaka Sabhā (5).[90] There are three other direct references to the Pañcākṣara in the *Kuñcitāṅghristava* – it does not have here the preeminent position it enjoys in the Tamil Śaiva Siddhānta. The gods of the five divine functions won their respective powers by reciting it along with other mantras (112); Vasiṣṭha and the other sages muttered it every day for a year in Cidambaram (59); Daśaratha got his sons by reciting it in Cidambaram (116). The *Śrī Rudra*, or *Śatarudrīya*, in which the Pañcākṣara first occurs, and on which Umāpati is said to have written a commentary, is mentioned thrice. This section of the *Taittirīya Saṃhitā* plays a prominent part in temple ritual, both in Cidambaram and all other Śiva temples. Nandikeśvara, Śiva's chamberlain, won his position by reciting the *Śrī Rudra* three crore times (153). But as Umāpati says, he himself was given by Śiva 'success through great mantras of enormous power' (305): this statement refers not to the Pañcākṣara mantra alone, but to a wide variety, some of which are considered in the chapter following. In the case of mantra, as in other respects, Umāpati's Sanskrit poem takes a much wider view than that merely of the Tamil Śaiva Siddhānta, or of the Siddhānta.

YOGA

In verse 305 Umāpati also says that Śiva gave him 'great magic powers through yoga'. Yoga plays, in fact, a more important role in the poem than Siddhānta or Vedānta, being a more or less constant part of worship of Śiva. However, Yoga is not necessarily separate from Siddhānta. As Umāpati himself mentions, Yoga (along with Caryā, Proper Behaviour) is one of the four parts of an Āgama. Now, as Brunner has shown, this fourfold division of the Āgamas is in fact a relatively recent phenomenon in the history of those texts.[91] Yet, as Brunner also shows, the Yoga sections, although not contradicting the Ritual sections, nevertheless are either redundant or extraneous.[92]

The Siddhānta school was in a commanding position in many parts of India; this position would only have been bolstered by an extension of the appeal of the school, and the inclusion of Yoga, however modified from that of Patañjali, was clearly such an extension. The *Mṛgendra Āgama*, on present evidence the most popular of Āgamas by Umāpati's time, and a major source for his *Śataratnasaṃgraha*, has a Yoga section.

The position of Siddhānta in general provides a parallel for Umāpati's mention of Śaṅkara. Umāpati in writing his poem, sought to broaden the appeal of both his poem and the philosophy to which he owed allegiance, by including within the horizon of his ideas Śaṅkara's version of Vedānta, which by his day had at last attained prestige and growing favour. Śrīkaṇṭha had established Advaita as applicable to monistic Śaivism. Why therefore not go all the way – so what may be seen as the logic of the *Kuñcitāṅghristava* suggests – and subsume within the Śaiva Siddhānta, at least within the confines of the poem, what was otherwise a principal rival of the school?

Śiva is the great yogin, and even when Dakṣiṇāmūrti the teacher, he is at the same time yogin. Umāpati describing Dakṣiṇāmūrti says that he is handsome with his yoga posture band (*paṭṭa*), the band of cloth that makes comfortable prolonged yoga posture (142). In Cidambaram Dakṣiṇāmūrti is the most important initial *mūrti* for devotees after one or another of the Gaṇeśas; his shrine is on the outer wall of the Mūlanātha shrine, and the passageway is often impeded by worshippers prostrating themselves before him. This importance of Dakṣiṇāmūrti is further shown by the placing of another Dakṣiṇāmūrti shrine in front of the main *balipīṭha* – the first shrine seen on entering through the South *gopura*.

Śiva's most famous action as yogin is the destruction of Kāma, the god of love. Kāma was sent by the gods to shake Śiva's 'unwavering gaze out of the state of absorption (*samādhi*) He'd attained through yoga' (37). Śiva's action is that of yoga – 'His form is the Self as described in the Vedānta . . . through His meditation (*svadhyānāt*) destroying darkness and delusion in all the worlds' (66).

Great yogins are a fact of life. The Siddha Tirumūlar lived underground for a world age,

> being in *samādhi*,
> in the state of supreme bliss
> that arises from seedless yoga;
>
> . . .
>
> his knowledge free from constraint
> he meditates constantly
> within himself upon Him. (185)[93]

Tirumūlar is only the first of the Siddhas. There are many others.

> The great yogin-lords, by yogic practices
> such as drawing the senses into their heart-lotuses
> take their breath to their own entrance to Brahman
> and live for a divine host of years –

their bodies adamantine
through taking herbs, jewels, and pills
according to the science of the Siddhas,
they worship Him as their own self
. . . (226)[94]

Śiva of course is synonymous with yoga. It is He

on Whose form the best of yogis
constantly meditate in their heart-lotuses
. . . (73)[95]

These specialists aside, yoga is of universal importance:

He is the Lord and has given all creatures
two hands to worship the lotus of His feet,
two eyes to see Him,
eloquence to praise all His deeds,
two feet to circumambulate Him,
and mind to meditate on Him: –
He ever protects us.
Him Who bears the Gaṅgā as His watery crown,
Whose foot is curved,
I worship. (94)[96]

In the case of Bhuṣuṇḍa, the wonderful crow who lives forever on Mount Meru, the practice of yoga seems to parallel if not coincide with grace:

By His grace,
he attained freedom from fear of death,
hard for anyone else to attain.
Thanks to meditating on Him (*yaddhyānayogāt*)
he sits on the excellent Golden Mountain,
. . . (168)[97]

Dhyānayoga is a term used several times. When Śeṣa swallowed Vāyu, Vāyu gained a mighty body by meditating on Śiva (*yaddhyānayogāt*) and burst free (254). The Vaiśya Iyaṟpakai 'had as his manifest wealth the splendour of meditation on His foot' (*yasyāṅghridhyānabhānuprakaṭitavibhavo*) (214). A certain king defeated all his foes by the yoga of meditation on His feet (*yatpadadhyānayogāt*) (204). It is Śiva 'from Whom the best of yogins attained skill in directly experiencing union with the universal self,' (*yasmāt sārvātmyayogānubhavanipuṇatāṃ lebhire yogivaryāḥ*) (269); Śiva 'ever protects all disposed to meditate on His lotus feet' (*sarvān svapadasarasijadhyānaśīlān ajasraṃ rakṣaty*) (190). Vyāsa's son, Śuka, and others, burning up through the yoga of knowledge (*jñānayogāt*) the impenetrable forest of Tamas ... win the true happiness that is enlightenment (*prabodham*) (307).

When Arjuna tells Kṛṣṇa he has seen a strange figure on the field of battle, holding a trident, sparks coming from his mouth, Kṛṣṇa momentarily goes into a yogic trance (*muhūrtaṃ* ... *yogād dhyātvā*) before telling Arjuna that this is Śiva (271). We are to understand that this trance was hardly necessary for Kṛṣṇa to make the identification, but so used is Kṛṣṇa to meditate on Śiva that Śiva is inseparable from meditation for him. Draupadī in her previous birth commutes her husband's curse upon her by meditating on His mantra (*yanmantradhyānayogād*) (224).

It must not be forgotten that Patañjali, the incarnation of Śeṣa, was a key figure in the history of the temple. An universal intellect in contrast to his yet more mythical comrade in devotion, Vyāghrapāda, Patañjali included the standard treatise on yoga among his other works:

> As Patañjali he wrote those books named after him
> on yoga, grammar, medicine and ritual
> ... (278)

Our review of the Śaiva Siddhānta and Vedānta in the poem has ended in yoga, and meditation on Śiva in one's heart, which brings us back to a point close to the dance in the heart with which the last chapter ended. More complex meditational forms are considered in the chapter on the Goddess.

CHAPTER 6

The Goddess

In several ways the Goddess as presented in the *Kuñcitāṅghristava* can be seen in Cidambaram today virtually as she was in Umāpati's time. In the first place she is present as Śiva's consort Śivakāmasundarī in the Cit Sabhā, as a standing figure in bronze who watches his dance. She shares his worship in this most sacred place. Secondly as Śivakāmasundarī she has her own extensive shrine on the west bank of the Śivagaṅgā tank. This dates back to the reign of Kulōttuṅga I, and was perhaps the first of the series of monumental Goddess or Amman̲ temples erected in the thirteenth century. Thirdly there is the Tillai Kālī temple on the northern edge of the town, built under Kōpperunjinga in the mid-thirteenth century. A pilgrimage to Cidambaram is usually concluded by a visit to this temple. And fourthly, there is a small image of Kālī in the shrine to Ūrdhvatāṇḍava Śiva within the Nṛtta Sabhā.

This list by no means exhausts the presence of the Goddess. Just outside the Śivakāmasundarī shrine is a tiny shrine to Akhilāṇḍeśvarī (spouse of Śiva at the Jambukeśvara temple, Trichy), and adjoining that a shrine to Durgā. In the town are several Goddess temples, to Durgā, to Draupadī, and others; annual firewalking is a popular event in one or two. In these respects also, the picture may not have been so very different for Umāpati. Finally, worship of Śrīcakra and Śrīvidyā continues.[1]

ŚIVAKĀMASUNDARĪ

The Goddess in Cidambaram is Śivakāmasundarī, the beautiful lady who is Śiva's love, and is specific to Cidambaram in the same way that as Kāmākṣī she is specific to Kāñcīpuram and as Mīnākṣī to Madurai.

The representation of Naṭarāja in metal seems always to have been accompanied by the Goddess. She stands, leaning slightly to one side, as the principal witness of the dance. The most significant aspect of this form of the Goddess is simply that she is not dancing, and not attempting to rival Śiva. An early myth of Cidambaram, though perhaps first found in Tiruvalangadu, is that of the dance competition, where the wild goddess who is the original inhabitant of the Tillai forest attempts to surpass the male intruder.

From the eighth to the eleventh centuries stone sculptures representing Naṭarāja tend to portray Pārvatī on one side witnessing the dance and Kālī dancing beside Śiva. The earliest example of this comes from a cave excavated by one of the commanders of the Pāṇḍya ruler Parāntaka Neṭuñcaṭaiyaṉ in the eighth century.

The Goddess in the Cit Sabhā is emphatically different from Kālī. Śivakāmasundarī is the housewife of the God. In the two great festivals of the temple when the two bronze images have gone round the city in their festival cars, in the final stage of their return to their home when the images are carried on the shoulders of devotees, the Goddess moves ahead of Naṭarāja so that she enters the home first to prepare it for her Lord. The temple has a fine collection of bronzes, and of these bronzes, those of the Goddess are particularly notable. Indeed, Nagaswamy remarks of the Cidambaram bronzes belonging to the twelfth century, 'The quality of these female images . . . seems to suggest a specialisation in portraying feminine form more elegantly than the male one.'[2] The images of Śivakāmasundarī are the most numerous. As we noted above, such images are usually made to complement a Naṭarāja, and their predominance in the Cidambaram hoard is hard to explain.

In the opening of the poem, the presence of the Goddess is played down. Umāpati mentions the Sammelanacakra, as we saw in chapter 4, and by implication the Goddess is present beside Śiva in this *cakra*, and the poet then says Śiva 'dances with His Śakti [at His side]'. The second verse of the poem remarks that the Lord of the Cit Sabhā has his feet 'constantly worshipped by the three Śaktis' – *citsabheśaṃ trisṛbhir api sadā śaktibhiḥ sevitāṅghriṃ.* These are Icchā Śakti, Jñāna Śakti, and Kriyā Śakti. Theologically, Icchā Śakti, the Power of Desire, is the power by which Śiva, moved by the pitiable condition of individual selves, desires to save them, and for that end creates the world; Jñāna Śakti, the Power of Knowledge, permits Śiva to know what he creates; and Kriyā Śakti, the Power of Activity, is the activity manifesting itself by multiple actions. Their local manifestations in the Cidambaram temple are nowadays said by the Dīkṣitas to be as follows. Icchā Śakti is beside Naṭarāja in the Cit Sabhā as Śivakāmasundarī, Jñāna Śakti is Śivakāmasundarī in her separate shrine, and Durgā, whose small shrine is backed by the outer wall of Śivakāmasundarī's, is Kriyā Śakti.[3]

15. Śivakāmasundarī. Parāntaka I period, *c.* 950. Courtesy: Dr R. Nagaswamy.

There is no further reference to the Goddess until verse 20. This is a distinctly low-key approach to the Goddess, and contrasts with, for instance, the invocation of Umāpati's *Civapirakācam*, with the first verse on Naṭarāja and the second a full account of the Goddess:

> The great Parā Śakti pervasive Who is
> In sooth Tirodhāna Śakti, doth stand
> As the Lord's Icchā, Jñāna and Kriyā
> Śaktis and is of the form of Grace that grants
> Unto the souls their ordained bodies,
> And experience; to cause unto souls
> Out of Māyā – pure or impure,
> Their bodies, instruments, locales
> And experience, the Goddess is
> In union with the First Causes, and yet
> She is One only Who is *mala*-free;
> She is the seed of the Lord's five-fold acts;
> She, the Mother, to deliver to souls
> From their misery of transmigration
> Witnesseth in Tillai's golden forum
> The dance of the Lord; we wear on our crown
> Her lotus feet of grace, and Her adore. [4]

In the *Kuñcitāṅghristava*, it is not until verse 77 that there is a significant reference to the Goddess:

> The Goddess Who is the visible form of Saccidānanda
> is resplendent in Her palace
> shining on Gaṅgā's western side.
>
> Her lotus mouth
> the abode of all intellectual systems,
> she has as many hands as there are Vedas.
> She is His Jñāna Śakti,
> the companion of final liberation.
>
> Kāmasundarī is her name.
> She it is Who beholds His dance.
>
> . . . (77)[5]

The shrine of the Goddess in Cidambaram has changed little since the fourteenth century.[6] It is substantial in size. The gateway and the surrounding colonnades are clearly early. The original Cōḻa shrine was subsequently enclosed, perhaps when the elegant *maṇḍapa* was built in the sixteenth or seventeenth century. But also early are the very fine sculptures of dancing girls and musicians that line the base of the portico. The shrine for the wall-mounted Śrīcakra on the north wall of the portico is modern. Modern paintings on the *maṇḍapa* portray Śuka teaching the Śrīcakra to Ādiśaṅkara; and scenes from the *Lalitopākhyāna*. It is not known what the modern paintings replaced in the centre: the centre is flanked by Nāyaka paintings (seventeenth-century) – to the north the *sthalapurāṇa*, with the famous Bhikṣāṭana and Mohinī scene; to the south another unidentified variant of the *sthalapurāṇa* and the life of Māṇikkavācakar.

This form of the Goddess is associated with learning. K. M. Rājagaṇeśa Dīkṣita notes that 'Sage Patañjali wrote *Vyākaraṇamahābhāṣya* with her blessings. She was worshipped by Hayagrīva, Agastya, Lopamudrā, Durvāsas and Paraśurāma. Ādiśaṅkara wrote his commentaries on the *Upaniṣads* in her temple.'[7] Nowadays a few students from Annamalai University are often to be seen sitting studying in the colonnades.

THE DIVINE COUPLE

'Your face is beautiful, O lady!
'This is all the money I've made
'since I was a boy.
'Please, it's for you. Take it,
'and hold me tight in your arms.
'I'm desperately hit
'by Love's arrows.
'Console me here and now.'

Thus spoke the Blessed One
as He followed Umā on the mountain,
she hurrying away
though held back by her companions.
. . . (256)[8]

Can it really be that Śiva is approaching Pārvatī as a courtesan? Reminiscent of Kālidāsa's description of the divine couple's honeymoon is this:

Under the pretext of showing the flocks of geese
energetically besporting themselves
in the land-lotus bed on the peak of the Golden Mountain
He was tightly embraced by Śivā,
His constant companion.

The white ash on His forehead
was rubbed off by the noble lady's nipples
as she moaned in unparalleled sexual delights
experienced in manifold ways.
. . . (200)[9]

Waterfowl are noted for their energetic and highly mobile copulation. Poetry has a greater freedom than sculptural art.

> Conquering the circle of rays
> from the young disc of the sun
> with the colour of His lower lip –
>
> for it was reddened
> by the betel served with longing
> by the Daughter of the Snow Mountain
> in her eagerness for play –
>
> in His keenness to display
> His skill in music
> He's playing the veena
> His moving hand never quits,
>
> Him who is made of the first *rasa*,
> Whose foot is curved, I worship. (212)[10]

The importance of betel in royal life comes out well in the story told by Kalhaṇa (twelfth century) in his history of Kashmir, wherein the exiled king Jayāpīḍa while watching a dance performance reveals his original status by continual reaching behind his back in expectation of being handed betel by the maid appointed for that purpose.[11] So too Pārvatī serves her Lord, though her service is prompted by her desire to make love.

Yet, in contrast to the instant gratification abruptly sought in verse 256 above, here physical love is subjected to the claims of art. There is perhaps a tension here between the desire on the part of the Goddess and the claims of Śiva's musical art, a tension that enhances both, and all constitute the 'first *rasa*', that is, *śṛṅgāra*, erotic aesthetic emotion.

All of the verses considered in this section have been instances of *śṛṅgāra rasa*, *rasa* that is made graphically explicit here:

> His wide eyes are bees
> agitated by the river of sweet *rasa* –
> the wine of love –
>
> coming from the mountains
> that are the jutting breasts –
> golden pots –
> of Gaurī ever ready to play. (149)[12]

Breasts are of great and manifest importance in Hindu culture. Women in the South had bare breasts until modern times, and milk is of supreme importance in a vegetarian culture. The pot in daily life and even more in ritual is an open symbol of the female, of the womb as well as the breast. Special place is made in the *sthalapurāṇa* for the providing of divine milk for the young Upamanyu, in reminiscence of the poet saint Ñāṉcampantar, similarly fed. In this verse the nutritive mother becomes the nutritive lover, feeding Śiva's passion, and promoting a liquid flow in which the poet and reader also participate.

If three verses describe the happy love of the two, another three speak of jealousy.

> Seeing the smearing of musk paste
> and the forehead mark of musk
> and the fresh garland of flowers,
> as He came to her
>
> the lotus-eyed Daughter of the Mountain,
> inferring He had been up to something,
> asked, 'O Lord,
> for the joy of which woman
> was this marking made
> while I am your good wife? Speak!'
> . . . (261)[13]

This reference to adultery is part of the language of *kāvya*, a reflection of the life of the court, and is to be found even in such texts as the *Saundaryalaharī*. It is equally consonant with the mainly Southern figure of Bhikṣāṭana, the utterly handsome naked ascetic, his loins clad only in a rearing cobra, who entrances wives wherever he wanders. Still more redolent of the court and the harem is this:

> 'You frolic in secret
> 'with my companions Jñāna and Icchā!
> 'You don't stop playing with them all night!
> 'How dare you come to the Sabhā in the morning!
> 'You enjoy being inconsiderate!
> 'Go off to the Divine river: she's just there!
> 'No one wants me.'
>
> When the Daughter of the Mountain
> was annoyed and spoke thus,
> He placated her.
> . . . (235)[14]

The multiple forms of the Goddess might easily be seen to lead to emotional complexities. The demands of the verse force the poet to reschedule Devī, since properly speaking it is the Icchā Śakti who is

16. Gaṅgādharamūrti. South *gopura*, Cidambaram.

present in the Cit Sabhā (normally, in other temples, under the parallel name of Bhoga Śakti). Kriyā Śakti, the third of the trio, is usually considered to be Durgā in Cidambaram.

In one verse Śiva lists his liaisons; in another verse when he and Pārvatī are reconciled he lists the most famous places of his worship:

'You are her friend.
'You must soothe My noble lady.
'Her heart has been filled with anger
'towards Me
'through
'My fun and games
'with the women dwelling in the Dāruka forest;
'My rape of Hari
'when he was a woman on Mount Meru;
'My connection with the Divine River;
'and My burning up of Love.'

So saying in all frankness
He sent Jayā to the women's quarters.

I worship Him –
He's hard to get –
Whose foot is curved. (257)[15]

There are many famous Śiva temples, and in accord with a long standing poetical fancy in India, Śiva takes to the air with Pārvatī and gives her an aerial view.

Often He and His Beloved mount the Bull
and He shows her –

'Look, Gaurī,
'Here's My excellent abode,
'the golden peak called Kedāra;
'here's Kāśī,
'and here's Kāñcīpuram,
'here's excellent Aruṇagiri,
'Śvetāraṇya, Vedāraṇya,
'and the Causeway,'

but every day He comes back
to His own place,
Cidambaram,
His home.
. . . (231)[16]

In addition to moving through space, the divine couple often move through time to suit the exigencies of various *sthalapurāṇas*, Pārvatī taking human birth, and then being married to Śiva. Umāpati gives just one instance of this.

Gaining the lotus-hand of Kātyāyanī
in her father's ashram –

that ascetic
who put down darkness,
whose heart experienced bliss
through understanding the meaning of the Vedas
learned from the face of the sun –

He, constantly protecting the mass of beings
drowning in the exceedingly frightening ocean of *saṃsāra*,
is eternally victorious in Śivapuram.
. . . (180)[17]

KĀLĪ

The Nṛtta Sabhā contains a shrine to Ūrdhvatāṇḍava Śiva.[18] Here Śiva is today said to have defeated Kālī in the dance competition by raising his leg to his head. A small image of dancing Kālī is on the ground beside the Ūrdhvatāṇḍava *mūrti*. However, the walls of this shrine are clearly an addition to the original structure, the fine pillars being partly concealed within plain stonework. The shrine has its own wood-framed copper-plated roof, as does an open area before it of some 36 sq m which thereby constitutes a *maṇḍapa* to the shrine within the main Nṛtta Sabhā, the rest of the structure having a flat roof. The open area would have been sufficient for the performance of a single dancer.

The small statue of dancing Kālī here is her only representation in a shrine of the temple; in the alcove of Ūrdhvatāṇḍava on the East *gopura* a small Kālī stands to Śiva's left, and to his right in the South *gopura*.[19] Kālī's dance is not mentioned in the chief *sthalapurāṇa*, the *Cidambaramāhātmya*, nor in the Tamil version, the *Kōyil Purāṇam*, but one of the minor Sanskrit *sthalapurāṇa*s does deal with it. This is how Umāpati refers to the dance competition:

> Paśupati in ancient days
> once danced with Kālī.
>
> In the assembly of gods and sages,
> raising up His foot
> and performing the elevated dance
> He defeated Kālī then
> as prelude to her expulsion.
>
> And all the gods and chief sages call Him Lord,
> and the sinless ones worship Him every day,
> Lord of the High Dance.
> Him Whose foot is curved
> I worship. (46)[20]

THE TILLAI KĀLĪ TEMPLE

The classic simplicity of Cōḻa art was created at the height of the dynasty's power. Of Rājarāja III who reigned until 1256, the historian of the Cōḻas says, 'an incompetent ruler under whom confusion increased and the dissolution of the Cōḻa kingdom was hastened'.[21] Refusing tribute to Sundara Pāṇḍya, he was subsequently captured by that king's ally, the Kādava Kōpperunjinga, and held in the fortress at Cēndamangalam. In 1231 Rājarāja was released by his Hoysaḷa allies. It was this warlord, Kōpperunjinga, who built the shrine of the present-day Kālī temple, about half a kilometre to the north east of the Naṭarāja temple, on the northern boundary of the city.

Tillai Kālī has the unusual feature of four heads, which are said to represent the four Vedas, though I know of no textual explanation. Brahmacaṇḍeśvara in the main temple might be relevant, for this too is a unique combination with Brahmā, and perhaps relates to the claimed Vedic affiliations of Cidambaram; the Tillai Kālī temple also claims to follow 'Vedic' ritual.

> When Kālī who is Brahmacāmuṇḍikā,
> born from the fire of Gaurī's anger,
> terrifier of demons,
> a portion of Brahmā the Creator,
>
> at His fierce high dancing
> hung down her four faces
> in shame
> and so exceedingly praised Him
> to assuage her sin,
>
> He, His eyes filled with compassion,
> took care of her
> and made her the protector of His holy place.
> . . . (283)[22]

Alone of the Sanskrit *sthalapurāṇas*, the *Vyāghrapura Māhātmya* deals with the dance competition. It does not mention the four heads of Kālī, and might therefore predate the installation of that *mūrti*. The three thousand Dīkṣitas, the *munīndras*, witness her defeat, her dance not being described, only Śiva's plethora of technical movements, culminating in a non-technical conclusion – 'placing one foot on the ground he put the other in the sky'.[23] Kālī hangs her head, and draws in the dust with her toes, a reminiscence of Pārvatī doing so in happier circumstances in Kālidāsa's account of Śiva's wooing. Not only do the Dīkṣitas in the *Vyāghrapura Māhātmya* witness Kālī's defeat, they proceed to lecture her on proper behaviour: one should not boast in the presence of the great, and so on. Kālī's role as protector was already brought out in a verse earlier in the poem:

> When Kālī had eaten a portion of the *hālāhala* poison
> and slain in battle the demon called Dāruka,
> as Bhadrakālī She shook the world
> with Her horrific power.
>
> He went forth to meet Her,
> countered Her,
> and showed Her the Dance of Bliss in the cremation ground.

It is through Her
that the Lord protects all the worlds.
Him who is worshipped by the sun and the moon
. . . (192)[24]

This is closely based on an episode in the *Liṅga Purāṇa*, with one important omission. The *Liṅga Purāṇa* gives the following account.

O Brahmans, they approached Brahmā and told him everything. Accompanied by Brahmā they went to Śiva . . . 'Dāruka is really fierce. He defeated us at the outset. You must protect us and kill the demon Dāruka who can only be killed by a woman!'

Hearing Brahmā's submission, the blessed Lord Śiva, Destroyer of Bhaga's eyes, faintly laughed and said to the Goddess, Daughter of the Mountain, 'I ask you now, O beauteous woman, for the welfare of the worlds, to slay this Dāruka who can be slain only by a woman, O woman with a lovely face!'

Hearing his words, she, Mother of the World, intent on taking birth, entered the body of God (Deva), she who is the Queen of the Gods (Deveśī). A portion of her entered the Lord of the Gods (Deveśa), the best of the gods; but Brahmā and the other gods with Indra at their head did not know this. Even all-knowing Brahmā was deluded by her Māyā and saw the beautiful Daughter of the Mountain at Śiva's side just as before. Pārvatī, having entered into the body of the God of the Gods, made a body for herself out of the poison in his neck. And being aware that she had so transformed herself, Śiva, the Foe of Kāma, emitted Kālī with his third eye – her neck was blue and her hair was matted.

When she was born, her throat black with the black poison, then the other gods became confident that there would be complete victory – though it had not yet occurred – for the Supreme Lord (Parameśvara) and his consort (Bhavānī). But when the hosts of gods and Siddhas got a good look at her they fled in terror, for she was like fire, black, her black throat embellished with poison – Viṣṇu, Lotus-born Brahmā and Indra led the way. An eye was manifest on her forehead, the white digit of the moon was prominent on her head, the terrible [poison] on her neck, the sharp trident terrible in her hand, and she had her ornaments. Along with her, Siddha-lords and Siddhas, and Piśāca-demons were born . . .

At Pārvatī's command the Supreme Mistress (Parameśvarī) slew the demon Dāruka who had been slaying the lords of the gods. By the excessive pervasion of her violent emotion, by the fire of her anger, all this world was afflicted.

But Śiva who is Being (Bhava), to drink up the fire of her anger, cried in the form of a baby boy in the burning ground full of ghosts, through illusion (Māyā). She saw the baby boy who was the Lord (Īśāna) and was deceived by his Māyā. She picked him up, sniff-kissed him and gave him her breast. Then along with her milk he drank up her anger. With this wrath the boy became the Protector of Holy Places (Kṣetrapāla). And of that wise Kṣetrapāla there became eight forms. And thus by that boy her anger evaporated.

Then to show favour to her, the God of Gods performed the Tāṇḍava dance at dusk, he the delighted Trident-bearer along with all the goblin-lords and ghosts. The Supreme Queen (Parameśvarī) after drinking her fill of the nectar of Mild (Śambhu) Śiva's dance herself danced for her own delight, like a *yoginī* amidst the ghosts. All around the gods, Brahmā, Indra and Viṣṇu in their midst, bowed down and praised Kālī and then Queen Pārvatī too. Thus the Fierce Dance of the Lord Who bears the Trident has been briefly described to you; but others say that the Fierce Dance of the Lord is brought about by the bliss of yoga (*yogānanda*).[25]

What is omitted in Umāpati's verse is the giving of milk by Kālī to the baby Śiva. To have included this would have demeaned Śiva. The striking exchange with which the episode ends, Kālī's milk for the nectar of the dance, places Kālī in too favourable a light to be appropriate for the *Kuñcitāṅghristava*. With regard to the *Liṅga Purāṇa*, we may note that this episode there follows the story of the origin of Gaṇeśa, and is itself followed by an account of Upamanyu receiving the Milk Ocean; this is to say, the unnatural son who does not receive milk is followed by two instances of extraordinary giving of milk.

The mention of Upamanyu reminds us of his appearance in the Cidambaram *sthalapurāṇa*; and the name of the demon, Dāruka, reminds us of the Dāruka forest which is prominent in the *sthalapurāṇa*. Even for a demon remarkably little is said about him – the only information is his name. The only other occurrence of this word is as the tree and forest. It is in this Dāruka forest, according to the *Cidambara Māhātmya*, that the first performance of the *ānandatāṇḍava* takes place. The *Liṅga Purāṇa* episode closes with two dance performances – Śiva's evening *tāṇḍava* dance (*tāṇḍavam/ saṃdhyāyām*),[26] and Kālī's dance after drinking the nectar of Śiva's dance. The occurrence of the *tāṇḍava* dance arouses the suspicion that the demon Dāruka is somehow a transposition of the Dāruka forest episode. This suspicion is confirmed by the closing words of the episode: 'Thus the Fierce Dance of the Lord Who bears the Trident has been briefly described to you; but others say that the Fierce Dance of the Lord is brought about by the bliss of yoga (*yogānanda*).' This is an alternative explanation of the dance of Śiva, designed to pull the rug, so to speak, from beneath the Cidambaram story. The chapter begins with the sages asking Sūta how Śiva's dance began (*nṛttārambha*). The term *yogānanda* is cunning: nowhere is Śiva's dance said to be brought about by yoga, though as we have seen in chapter 5, it is identified with the *ānanda* of the Upaniṣads. Reference to *yogānanda*, then, is an oblique reference to the *ānandatāṇḍava* without a formal recognition of its existence. The alternative version of Upamanyu that follows might also be an attempt to detract from the Cidambaram version.

There is yet one more element in the *Liṅga Purāṇa*'s story that points to Cidambaram, or rather another element deliberately designed to refute the Cidambaram version of events, though in this case not the version of the *Cidambara Māhātmya*. I refer to the dance of Kālī. It seems to me to be a deliberate inversion of the dance competition between Śiva and Kālī. That Kālī drinks her fill of the nectar of Śiva's dance , and literally 'up to her throat' neatly complements her earlier drinking of Śiva's poison, and Śiva's drinking of her anger along with her milk; nevertheless, I suggest the primary intent of the narrative is to refute the story of the competition. (The *Liṅga Purāṇa* is said by Hazra to be no later than 1000, but he admits the possiblity of later interpolations.)[27]

There is also the question as to why Umāpati should refer to this account. In answer it must be said that the above interpretation would probably not have occurred to him; and what interests him is that Śiva counters Kālī's horrific power, and transmutes it to protective power. Further, Umāpati's verse suggests that it is on her account that Śiva danced in the cremation ground. The cremation ground was the only place of Śiva's dance for Kāraikāl Ammaiyār, and the usual place as far as the *Tēvāram* trio were concerned. But Māṇikkavācakar seldom refers to it. Umāpati continues this trend. It is precisely the *ānandatāṇḍava*, the creation of the Cōḻa court, that makes the burning ground an inconvenient site. Śiva's dance is now beneath the golden roof of the Cit Sabhā.

The *Liṅga Purāṇa* does not use the name Bhadrakālī, but the Goddess under this name would have been constantly before Umāpati's eyes, since she figures on the Cidambaram *gopura*, the identification spelt out by the incised caption on the statue on the West *gopura*. Similar images are on the South and North *gopura*s. However, what the image in question actually represents is not clear. Its form holds the attention. Harle describes it thus:

> The goddess has eight arms and apparently stood with her right leg raised and placed on the recumbent 'asura'. Both her legs are now broken. The goddess wears a crown (ratna mukuṭa?), with a large flame aureole behind it. Both contain snakes and other figures. From the goddess' right ear-lobe dangles a small human figure; from her left ear hangs a large circular ear-ring in the interior of which is a bird. She has a third eye and tusks, but her excessively ghoulish expression is probably due in part to a broken nose. There is a rope of snakes above the goddess' breasts, which are particularly fat, and a sacred

(a)

(b)

17 (a). Bhadrakālī. West *gopura*, Cidambaram. Courtesy: Dr James C. Harle.

(b). Bhadrakālī. South *gopura*, Cidambaram.

thread of small spheres (skulls?) passes between them. Many of the goddess' hands have been broken off and it is not easy to distinguish any of her hand emblems or gestures.
The 'asura', holding a sword in his right hand, has fallen to a crouching position on his knees. He has a human head, with slightly grotesque features, and wears a crown. Behind him, a bhūta-like creature with tusks and a small sword holds one hand around the top of the asura's crown.[28]

Harle attempts no identification other than noting the similarity of the goddess's pose with that of Mahiṣamardinī, and declaring 'This is evidently a representation of the *Śakti* in combat with an *asura.*' R. Nagaswamy makes a clear identification, saying of the West image, 'Kālī here appears as *Sumbha* Nisumbhasūdani in which form she was popular in the Cōḻa period.'[29] His italicization of Sumbha is significant, for the one other instance of this form is called only Nisumbhasūdani. The name itself comes on high authority, for the Tiruvalangadu copper plates of Rājendra Cōḻa I state that when Vijayālaya conquered the city of Tanjavur he installed the image of Nisumbhasūdani and ruled his country by her grace. This image has been identified as that worshipped as 'Vadabhadrakali near the eastern gate'.[30] Nagaswamy observes that it is a 'unique sculpture . . . exhibiting the tremendous power with which the Devi shook off the mighty asuras and emerged victorious. It is also illustrative of the grim determination with which Vijayālaya Cōḻa was able to throw off the yoke of the Pallava power of the north and the menacing power of the Pāṇḍyas of the south . . . We may say the great period of Kāli worship begins with the installation of Nisumbhasūdani at Tanjore.'[31]

Nagaswamy does not give a description of the image he publishes, but there seem to be two figures beneath the goddess rather than one, which would strengthen Nagaswamy's argument.[32] However, although our understanding of the nature of Kālī is augmented by consideration of the Tanjavur image, Nagaswamy's suggestion does not bear close examination. In the case of the West *gopura* image, the crucial one because the earliest, the middle figure, between the goddess and the '*asura*' is clearly attacking the *asura.* If we turn to the South *gopura* image, although the matter is made more complicated by the middle figure appearing feminine, certainly there too the middle figure is, so to say, on the side of the Goddess rather than the victim's; and its erect hair is in the Kālī–Bhairava style.

How, then, is the image to be explained? Umāpati provides the clue in verse 52:

When Dakṣa proceeded to sacrifice
without inviting Paramaśiva,

Gaurī his daughter
going there to her father
and seeing her husband put to shame
entered the fire.

He, the Lord, creating
the thousand-headed hero Vīrabhadra
and Kālī used them to bring about
the destruction of Dakṣa, and of others.
. . . (52)[33]

I suggest that the 'demon' is Dakṣa and the middle figure Vīrabhadra.

This myth has a long and complex history, going back to Rudra's exclusion from the sacrifice in Vedic times, and from the *Mahābhārata* onwards affirming Śiva's superiority to the Vedic sacrifice. Umāpati's is a late version, the historical development being first Śiva himself doing the destruction, then Vīrabhadra, then Vīrabhadra and Kālī. This development perhaps mirrors the growing importance of Kālī. The Goddess is called Bhadrakālī in the versions of, for instance, the *Kūrma Purāṇa*, the *Śiva Purāṇa*, and the Tamil *Kanta Purāṇam*. In the Cidambaram *gopura* versions she becomes the dominant partner in the assault, though Vīrabhadra retains the executive role. That Vīrabhadra is decidedly unlike the powerful figure of the texts is to be explained not only by the artist's desire to promote Bhadrakālī, but also the sculptural impossibility of fitting two overwhelming images in the same niche.[34] In the version of the *Śiva Purāṇa* both Vīrabhadra and Kālī are thousand-headed, but the iconographic texts prescribe only the one head for their images. In the West *gopura* image Vīrabhadra is clearly in the act of beheading Dakṣa. It might be questioned why Dakṣa, if it is he, is holding a sword. The version of the *Kanta Purāṇam* states that Dakṣa thought it shameful to run away and resolved to fight Vīrabhadra[35] – hence the sword. The head of the victim is also significant, for it looks much more like the head of a Brahman than of a demon, and a Brahman with a goat-like beard.

KĀLĪ AS ŚIVA'S DESTRUCTIVE FORCE

When Viṣṇu took on the body of the Man-lion
and had his great body broken in battle,
yet he came roaring before Him.

A mighty parrot did He become,
the chief of *śarabha* birds,
and from the fire-pit of the eye on His forehead

at once created a Kālī
with ten thousand faces –
the Fierce Antagonist was her name –

and sent him, like a good oblation,
to the fire of the tip of her tongue.
. . . (126)[36]

Kālī is thus made a product of Śiva's special form assumed to put down Viṣṇu's fiercest form. The Śarabha was a popular *mūrti* in the twelfth century, as will be discussed in chapter 8 on the other forms of Śiva in the poem. It is especially noteworthy that the Nṛtta Sabhā that commemorates Ūrdhvatāṇḍava's defeat of Kālī also contains a Śarabha shrine.

Kālī emanates from Śiva in a way parallel to her earliest historical appearance in the *Devīmāhātmya* (*c.* sixth century), when she comes forth from Ambikā, as alluded to above in verse 283, 'born from the fire of Gaurī's anger'. An obvious element in the origin of such stories is the way a person's face becomes black with rage. This hypostatization of emotion is perhaps most powerfully developed in the sequences of goddesses that populate the sections of the Śrīcakra. In this verse the distortion of Śiva's face into that of a bird's then reverts to human form, but form that is feminine and multiply feminine.

A point of contrast is a passing implication, in a verse where all compounds begin with *k*, of Śiva smiling at Kālī: 'His heart is delighted by Kālī's dance.'[37] Umāpati may have in mind Māṇikkavācakar's *Kīrti Tiruvahaval*:

He dances 'mid the company of beauteous Tiger-town,
That golden beauty like Himālaya wears,
There to Umai, whose roseate mouth is filled with sweetness,
And to Kāḷi grants the beauteous smile of His blest countenance.[38]

DRAUPADĪ

In Cidambaram, in addition to the great temple and the minor stone temples already mentioned, there is a variety of hut temples to various Goddesses, with low-caste *pūjāris*. There is no reason to think the situation very different in Umāpati's day. The inclusion of Goddess shrines within great temples that can be traced from the thirteenth century onwards, demonstrates the intrusive pressure of such deities on formal and official Sanskrit gods. Although only Durgā is admitted to the *devakoṣṭha* of the standard Cōḻa temple, she is the representative of a whole throng of Goddesses.

There is at least one Draupadī temple in Cidambaram today, to the north-west, and one passes by it when going to Singarattottam, the site of Maṟaiñāṉa's *āśrama*, where Umāpati would have stayed with his new teacher on being banished from the temple, if his biography is accepted. The importance of the Draupadī cult in historical times should be remembered when we read Umāpati's verse on her former incarnation:

> A certain woman named Nālāyanī
> was the good wife of Māṇḍavya, a famous ascetic;
> she desired to do
> what was pleasing for her husband.
>
> To allay the fire of the curse he uttered
> she clouded over the radiance of her beauty.
> By meditating on His mantra
> she acquired five kings as her beloved husbands,
> such as could hardly have been won by any other woman;
> and also the state of Śiva free from rebirth.
> . . . (224)[39]

This story is a striking expression of the power of female sexuality. Nālāyanī is a good wife (*satī*) not least because she remains devoted to her foul-smelling and eventually leprous husband. She is unperturbed when one of his fingers drops off into the rice bowl, and eats the rice. Pleased by this action, the husband grants her a boon. She asks for him to take on a fivefold body and grant her sexual fulfilment. He accedes to this request, but after thousands of years tires of it. She begs him to continue, but, angered by her importunity he curses her to have five husbands in her next life to assuage her lust. She is greatly upset at this fate, and practises severe austerities, amid the five fires, to seek Śiva's help – dulling the radiance of her beauty in the process. Śiva promises five husbands each the equal of Indra – these, of course, will be the five Pāṇḍavas she will marry as Draupadī. The *Mahābhārata* makes no mention of the *pañcākṣara*. The story is a doubled mirror-image of what happens in the epic: she wants the fivefold sexuality, but then she doesn't. Here as throughout events are painted over with a high gloss, so that brightness is the prime characteristic. The epic story is reduced to a good wife praying to Śiva and gaining success. The brightness of Śiva's grace overshadows everything else. Nevertheless it is permissible for us to look into the shadows, which are made more emphatic by the dynamic of the poem.

ŚRĪVIDYĀ AND ŚRĪCAKRA

From this subsidiary form of the Goddess, we turn now to her highest manifestation. As we saw in chapter 3, the poem begins boldly with the most esoteric form of divinity in Cidambaram, which is a modification of the pan-Indian esotericism of the Goddess in the form of Śrīcakra.

The role of *yantras* in worship in Cidambaram is a complex issue, concerning which I have only limited information. Somasetu Dīkṣita in his Sanskrit introduction to the Festival section of the Cidambaram ritual text, declares that there are five principal *cakras* in the Rahasya part of the Cit Sabhā, namely the Śrīcakra, the Śivacakra, the Dhvanicakra, the Cintāmaṇicakra, and the Sammelanacakra.[40] However, this comes at the end of thirteen sets of five elements constituting the temple, and is perhaps constrained by numerical determinism. When Patañjali in the text speaks of the Śrīcakra and other *yantras* on the wall of the Cit Sabhā, the editor gives as footnote a verse listing nine *cakras*, adding the Tāṇḍava, the Lalitā, the Gaṇeśa, and Skanda *cakras* to the above five. All seem clearly to be based on the Śrīcakra, and there can be no doubt that by Umāpati's day Śāktism had penetrated to the core of Cidambaram worship.

The first two verses to be considered in this section come at the beginning of a group of verses that is of exceptional interest. This group as a unit will be considered at the close of the chapter. The first verse concerns the Śivacakra, 'His Cakra', the Śrīcakra so to speak commandeered by Śiva; but the second verse concerning their joint presence in the centre of the *cakra* – which I take to be the Sammelanacakra – is so closely connected with the central Śākta tradition and the most famous and accessible of Śākta texts, the *Saundaryalaharī*, that it seems best to discuss it here in the chapter devoted to the Goddess; and as we shall see the group as a whole concerns the Goddess.

> The faultless worship His Cakra every day,
> His body, within the radiance of true form,
> shines brightly on all sides
> as far as the fourteen-cornered enclosure,
> joined with His Śakti on His left
> He comprises the beauty of the golden filaments
> of the eight-petalled lotus.
>
> His Cakra is pervaded with the Śiva mantras,
> Mohana etc. in the Chamber of the Thousand [Petals].
> . . . (109)[41]

The 'faultless' (*anaghāḥ)*, as throughout the poem, are the Dīkṣitas,[42] but the term in the case of Cakra worship has a special significance, in as much as worship of the Śrīcakra lays greater stress on personal purity than does any other Hindu ritual system.

Śiva with the Goddess beside him fills the fourth enclosure marked out by the fourteen corners that stands within the eight-petalled lotus. Mohana might refer to the outermost of the nine enclosures of the Śrīcakra (and those *cakras* based on the Śrīcakra), which has the name Trailokyamohana. Śiva stands within the *prabhāvali* that is OṂ.

Rājagaṇeśa Dīkṣita says that this verse is a further description of the Cidambaram mantra with which the poem begins (verses 1 and 2); he then quotes two verses from Tirumūlar's section on the Tiru-v-ambala Cakram:

> Letter Five is the seat of Nandi
> Letter Five is Holy Mantra
> Letter Five is Divine Chakra
> Letter Five is Lord's abode.
>
> How do you see the Dancer?
> Many are the ways;
> Chant first Letter of Dance (Ci),
> Thou with Dancer will one in thought be;
> That is the way to see the Dancer truly. (*Tirumantiram* 934, 935)

B. Natarajan, the translator of these verses, notes, 'Even the chanting of the first letter of Sivayanama is enough to enable the devotee to envision the Dancer.' The *Tirumantiram* is one of the most important texts in the history of Southern Śaivism, and without doubt, because of the lack of early commentarial tradition, the most obscure. This quotation does not at first throw much light on Umāpati's verse, but we should surely bear in mind the two verses that follow in the *Tirumantiram*.

> Kindle the Fire (Kuṇḍalinī) where it dormant lies
> Chant letter *na* that is in the chakra
> Then the symbolized *na*
> Brings the Lord there.
> She Herself Grace grants
> If upward you lift Kundalini;
> She Herself granting Grace
> High above in Sahasrāra places thee;
> There do you chant Her syllable *ma*
> You shall indeed be placed
> Like a gem of ray serene. (*Tirumantiram* 937, 938)

Should this mention of the thousand-angled *cakra* be connected with the verse in hand? Tirumūlar's ecstatic sequences remain tantalizingly obscure.

At all events, from the point of view of the structure of the poem, it is notable how closely verse 109 relates to verse 110, which follows, an intimacy of connection that is found perhaps only in the first verses of the poem and in another couple shortly to be discussed. It is as if, in these cases, the symbolic density of the topic has some magnetic force that influences its successor; or, to put it another way, as if the density of the subject-matter demanded a second verse for proper expression.

> In the middle of the earth circle,
> within the eight and sixteen-petalled lotuses,
> within the forty-three angles,
> in the Bindu,
> in a delightful jewelled palace surrounded by
> continuous multitudes of Kalpa trees,
>
> He, with Devī,
> seated on a golden couch
> whereof the legs are formed by Brahmā and the others,
> and [Sadā]Śiva forms the plank,
>
> is worshipped by the gods with Viṣṇu at their head;
> . . . (110)[43]

The most famous source for this is the notable and most widely read Śākta text, the *Saundaryalaharī*, 'The Ocean of Beauty', attributed to Śaṅkara.[44]

> Fortunate but few
> are those who worship you
> the swelling wave of consciousness
> and bliss
> amid the ocean of nectar
> on the island of jewels
> encircled with groves
> of heavenly wishing trees
> within the mansion of wishing gems
> with its groves of *kadamba* trees
> on your couch formed by Śiva
> where you recline
> on the lap of Paramaśiva. (*Saundaryalaharī* 8)[45]

The same idea is expressed in *Saundaryalaharī* 94, with the further point that Śiva as the Goddess's seat seems to be her bedspread, since, himself white in colour, he now reflects her red colour and further seems to be erotic *rasa* incarnate. We saw the reverse above in verse 149 where *rasa* seems to flow from the Goddess's golden breasts. And yet for Umāpati, Śiva is firmly and dominantly *śṛṅgāra rasa* in himself; he is only apparently so in the *Saundaryalaharī*, where the source of power is the Goddess. And for Umāpati, Śiva is seated beside the Goddess, insinuated into the heart of Śāktism.

The sequence of verses following 8 in the *Saundaryalaharī* is interesting here and perhaps parallel. Verse 9 states that the Goddess rising up from the *mūlādhāra cakra* through the other *cakras* sports in secret with her lord in the thousand-petalled lotus. In verse 10 she goes back down again; in verse 11 there is a description of the Śrīcakra. There may here be a convergence between all three texts, our poem, the *Saundaryalaharī* and the *Tirumantiram*.

Also to be noted here is a passing reference to Śiva as *trikoṇasthitijuṣam*, 'present in the Triangle', (280, where most words begin with *tr* or *tṛ*) which plainly refers to Śiva's position in a *yantra* and which Rājagaṇeśa Dīkṣita takes to be the Śrīcakra. Indubitably, the basic *yantra*, the core reality here, is the Śrīcakra, which is subjected to various and perhaps ill-defined modulations. But ill-defined is an inappropriate qualification here – it is rather a question of the shimmering, the rippling of imagination's power.

I turn now to the Śrīvidyā, the intimate correlate of Śrīcakra worship. There are some grounds for claiming that the second century of verses has near its beginning, from verse 109, an injection of Śākta, or modified Śākta esotericism that parallels the Naṭarāja esotericism of the poem's two opening verses, discussed in chapter 4; and this new element could be said to be signalled in verse 101 which includes a brief reference to the Śrīvidyā, and Śiva's colonization of it: he is '*trikūṭasthitijuṣam*', 'Who is present in the Triple Peak mantra, the Trikūṭa'. Rājagaṇeśa so takes it. These peaks are the three divisions of the mantra: Vāgbhava, Kāma, and Śakti.

> His Jñāna Śakti,
> enrapturing in the world of the Secret Place,
>
> She who is the blessed great Sixteen Syllables,
> the knowledge praised
> by the gurus, Śrīnātha and Tantric heroes,[46]
> she who is worshipped by Yoginī *dūtīs*,
>
> She who is Śivā undivided from [His] Self,
> She it is that the yogi searches for in his heart
> and becoming free of mental constructions
> is praised by mighty yogis.

Him, free of qualities,
Whose foot is curved,
I worship. (207)[47]

A pair of verses, an exceptionally close pair, remains to be mentioned. They refer to the story of Lalitā, a Kāñcīpuram-based form of the Goddess whose principal narration is the *Lalitopākhyāna*, appended to the *Brahmāṇḍa Purāṇa*. The scene the first verse describes can be seen today on the central ceiling of the *maṇḍapa* of the Śivakāmasundarī shrine. The paintings here, in oils, damaged by fire in 1989 look impressively Victorian but were executed in 1972.[48]

He was satisfied when He saw Bhavānī
standing in Her chariot which was the Śrīcakra,
preceded by Her Śaktis mounted on elephants and horses,
accompanied by Her companions
the Nityās, Vārāhī, and Mantriṇī,
displaying the Weapon Science of the Young Girl,

Her hands grasping all weapons,
on the battlefield,
in Her shining battledress.

I worship Him
that friend of Kubera, the Lord of Wealth,
Whose foot is curved. (128)[49]

Here the static ultimacy of the Śrīcakra, diagrammatic form transcending all phenomenal movement, is pressed into service as war transport. According to the *Lalitopākhyāna* Lalitā riding in the Cakrarāja chariot is accompanied by Mantriṇī in the Geyacakra chariot and Daṇḍanāthā in the Kiricakra chariot. Bhāskararāya (seventeenth-century) explains in his commentary on the *Lalitāsahasranāman* of the *Lalitopākhyāna* that *kiri* means 'boar' and that Daṇḍanāthā is Vārāhī.[50] The Nityās are the goddesses presiding over the fifteen days of the lunar fortnight; in the *sahasranāman* Lalitā is She who rejoices at beholding the rising valour of the Nityās.[51]

Creating the *avatāra* portions of Viṣṇu
on the battlefield with her ten nails,

the Goddess destroyed the Lord of Obstacle's *yantra*
with the trunk of her elephant face that came upon her
from looking at the Lord of Love.

With His missile she destroyed the Daitya Bhaṇḍa
along with his city and the host of his sons.

She it is who resides in the Śrīcakra.
Him who performs auspicious deeds,
Whose foot is curved,
I worship. (129)[52]

These two verses are based on the *Lalitāsahasranāman* rather than the *Lalitopākhyāna.*

I now return to the sequence of verses 108-14 (see p. 154). Peculiar force is provided by what can be seen as the concluding verse of the series. Umāpati goes quite outside the usual Southern geography of the poem by referring to the great poet, *mahākavi*, of the twelfth century, Śrīharṣa, author of the *Naiṣadhacarita* – and the identification is exceptionally precise since Śrīharṣa names both his parents in colophons:

A Brahman called Harṣa,

[here just a Brahman rather than a poet]

making use of the Cintāmaṇi mantra,
the Wish-fulfilling jewel,

obtained from his father, Śrīhīra,
sat in the cremation ground
fearless in the night
on the lifeless body of his mother, Māmalladevī.

Through His excessive compassion
he won back his mother
and attained all knowledge and other magic powers.

I worship Him Who bears a drum in His hand
and Whose foot is curved. (114)[53]

Here there is indeed a complete absence of a nutritive maternal breast; or rather the son nourishes the maternal breast. The connection with Naṭarāja seems particularly slight, though a Cintāmaṇi mantra does feature in the ritual of the temple. This Cintāmaṇi mantra, however, has nothing in common, other than its name, with the Cintāmaṇi Śrīharṣa claimed to be the driving force behind his work. Note also the possibility of a degree of fellow-feeling on the part of Umāpati, himself a master of mantras. If we accept the biographies, there might also be a degree of wishful thinking, in as much as our poet, our Śivācārya, had some embarrassment concerning a missing person. When Umāpati gave Śaktinipāta (immediate release through the power of the Goddess, Śiva's grace) to Sūta the wood-cutter, that man disappeared in a flash of flame. At all events, the verse remains somewhat bizarre and out of place on a first reading.

If, however, we consider Harṣa sitting on his dead mother in relation to the verses immediately preceding it, an explanation suggests itself. In the six verses (from 108 to 113), we have found a sustained presence of the Goddess, even if slightly muted by Śiva. Thus, in 109, we are told that Śiva is present in the Śrīcakra; in 110, Śiva forms the plank of the bed in the centre, but we are to understand Śiva here as Sadāśiva and Śiva sits beside the Goddess on the golden couch. Verse 111 is a change of topic – Śiva's matted locks stream out; yet is there not an essential femininity in long hair notwithstanding its being a badge of asceticism, and further a certain consonance with Gaṅgā in Śiva's own nature as presented here? Verse 112 returns to the Goddess with mention of the Śrīvidyā, along with other mantras. And then,

> Those who know the heart
> of revealed scripture know
>
> He Whose form is the dance
> has but one Śakti to be praised.
>
> She is Kālī in Her anger, Durgā in battle,
> She takes the form of Viṣṇu to protect the world,
> in enjoyment She is Bhavānī.
> Jñāna, Kriyā, and Icchā
> comprise Her varied bodies.
>
> At the time of universal destruction
> She calms down and is absorbed into Him.
>
> Him Whose son has an elephant's face,
> Whose foot is curved,
> I worship. (113)[54]

Although the manifestations of the Goddess are duly subordinated to Śiva, nevertheless there has been an irruption of feminine power that provokes a probably unconscious reaction in the poet's mind, and the next thing he does is think of Śrīharṣa on his dead mother, inverting the dominance of Kālī over Śiva, of Kālī sitting on Śiva as a corpse, not referred to, but brought to mind. There is a fine Cōḻa bronze in the Tillai Kālī temple of Kālī with Śiva beneath her feet.

This strange verse aside, Umāpati's presentation of the Goddess, of which a full account has just been given, is remarkably judicious and well balanced, her various aspects given even-handed attention. However, as we have seen, Umāpati was slow to give full attention to the Goddess, and she is allowed only a restricted role in the poem as a whole.

CHAPTER 7

Bhikṣāṭana

Naṭarāja and his temple, Śaiva Siddhānta and yoga, the Goddess and the Śrīcakra – these form the core of Umāpati's worldview. They do not, however, provide a complete picture of Umāpati's understanding of the Dance of Śiva. Other aspects are of some importance.

As was noted in chapter 1, Śiva's first performance of the Tāṇḍava Dance followed his appearance as Wandering Beggar in the Dāruka Forest. Śiva as beggar, Bhikṣāṭana, features in a dominant position on the *gopuras* of the temple, three of which must have been completed around the time of Umāpati's birth. The architecture of the *gopuras* is such that there are two especially large niche sections on each of the main façades, one either side of the doorway. Each *gopura* having an inner façade and an outer façade, there are on the *gopuras* a total of sixteen statues whose position is particularly imposing.[1]

On all four *gopuras* each of these dominant niches contains one of four images, Somāskanda, Kalyāṇasundara, Bhikṣāṭana or Kaṅkāla. The four images form two pairs. Bhikṣāṭana differs very little from Kaṅkāla; the former is naked, the latter is clothed. Kalyāṇasundara represents the marriage of Śiva and Pārvatī; Somāskanda shows the married couple seated side by side, with their son Skanda between them. The opposition between the pairs is stark: the wandering ascetic as opposed to the married man and his family. In the case of the East and West *gopuras*, both inner and outer façades have one married and one ascetic image. On the South and North *gopuras*, this opposition does not obtain: each façade has either two ascetic or two married forms. On both South and North *gopuras* the ascetic forms face south, and the married forms face north.

The notion of God as Beggar is tautologous. Bhikṣāṭana is a sublimation of the wandering ascetic who defends himself with his trident and his magical powers, and whose model is Śiva. Moreover, in the South the dominant literature, the *Tēvāram*, codified a hundred years or more before Umāpati, was the work of itinerant singers who, if not

18. Bhikṣāṭana. East *gopura*, Cidambaram.

beggars, had a parallel lifestyle. Then again, although the Sanskrit tradition, and the Tamil tradition also by Umāpati's time, saw Bhikṣāṭana as principally active in the Deodar forest of the sages, this is arguably not the case with the writers of the *Tēvāram*, who speak of the women of one village after another calling out to the beggar. There is a marked change with Māṇikkavācakar, for he makes only three or four references to Śiva seeking alms; this is no doubt a reflection of his very different lifestyle. All four saints poured much of themselves into their poetry, and in Māṇikkavācakar's case it may be supposed that for the former royal minister Bhikṣāṭana was an uncongenial version of his deity.

We are dealing with a figure manifestly based on the human wandering Śaiva ascetic. The technical term must be a Kapālin, Skull-bearer, since in all cases he holds a skull cup, but more generally surely any numinous wanderer is the model for this divine form. He is an outsider, who scares by his look; and sometimes charms. Dorai Rangaswamy notes

the great transformation effected, by the Tamilians in the horrid and terrific forms . . . these terrific forms with which Śaivism started from its early beginnnings, are not so very prevalent in the Tamil Country ... It is the lovable forms and the dance of Śiva that have captivated the Tamilians. More than this the Tamilians have made the terrific forms themselves beautiful and lovable ... By transplanting the terrible and horrible form of Kāpāli to this atmosphere of love and beauty, the Tamilian has worked a miracle; one gets the sublimation and universalization of this story.'[2]

Although Bhikṣāṭana is mentioned in Umāpati's poem only briefly, in the *Tēvāram* he is scarcely less important than Naṭarāja. Here is a typical example of Cuntarar's presentation of Bhikṣāṭana. Note the intimate connection of begging and dance in Śiva.

Draped in bark clothes,
a tiger's skin upon his waist,
he begged a serpent for its skin.
He loves to go begging
for food.
When he stops, it is to dance
with fire, in the night:
his place
is Valampuram.

. . .

With the burning ground,
beloved of jackals,
for a stage,
our lord dances,
spinning steadily
as the music swells.
His Woman,
        her curls twisted into braids,
is happy
        as half of
that Fire Dancer whose place
is Valampuram.

Hawks haunt the reeking
        begging bowl he carries;
his ornament
        is ash;
matted hair is piled
        high upon his head.

Palymra fruits fall
with a thud
to the ground

as he wanders from door to door
seeking alms
with his skull,

carrying off the women's dresses
with the alms he receives.[3]

There is an element of grim reality here, with the reeking begging bowl; occasionally concern for modern taste leads Shulman to overstress the grimness, as in Cuntarar's

He has trudged through the village streets
as he begged for paltry alms.[4]

The poet-saints themselves may have trudged, but surely never Bhikṣāṭana. The essential grace of the God's movement is well brought out by Appar in this hymn, also to the Śiva of Valampuram:

The Lord has a blackened throat.
He is the Kapālin,
who destroyed Kāla
by kicking him.
He wears the skin of the elephant
and carries the skeleton,
accompanied by *munis* and *gaṇas*;
he wanders playing on a *vīṇā*.
With his charming smile he lures me.
With a certain swagger,
he entered Valampuram
and resides there.
He wears the silken garment on his waist
and sandal paste on his body.
He came here gently dancing.
I asked him which was his native place.
He laughed, and as if taking my soul away
with his captivating smile
moved towards another house and entered Valampuram.[5]

Nagaswamy has pointed out that several features of this description are notably present in the fine bronze (plate 19) the Valampuram temple possesses – the movement of the God's legs, playing the *vīṇā* – very rare in the case of a Bhikṣāṭana image, and the charming smile; and that an inscription in the temple, made in the reign of Rājādhirāja II, referring to this image, uses Appar's very words in respect of it: *vaṭṭanaikaḷ paṭa naṭantu*, 'with a certain swagger' (literally 'slightly turning his leg').[6]

19. Bhikṣāṭana. Melamparamballam, Valampuranathar temple.
Courtesy: French Institute of Pondicherry/École Française d'Extrême-Orient.

Bhikṣāṭana is often superbly rendered in bronze. Whereas the form Naṭarāja undergoes a long development, Bhikṣāṭana is simply a handsome naked man. Here lies the earliest essence of Tamil sculpture, the human figure and nothing but the human figure. Again, whereas the Naṭarāja is an attempt to capture the movement of a dancing god at the centre of the cosmos, and carries an increasing theological load, the wandering beggar has no such accretions and moves slowly and languidly to show off his beauty. His essence is thus the more easily captured in the immobility of plastic art.

The fullest expression of Bhikṣāṭana in stone was achieved in the royal temple at Darasuram. The impressive tableau originally in the *maṇḍapa* in the north-east corner of the first enclosure is at present in the Museum at Tanjavur. Śiva as Kaṅkālamūrti is flanked on one side by the wives of the seven sages and on the other by five *gaṇa*s playing musical instruments.

BHIKṢĀṬANA IN THE CIDAMBARAM TEMPLE

A Kaṅkāla in a significant position is the one in the Nṛtta Sabhā, facing north, but though the pillars of its niche are original the sculpture is a poor modern copy. A naked woman of the type common in modern *gopura*-stucco is to the God's left. However, its position shows the implicit connection of Bhikṣāṭana with dance. Of no less interest is the modern painting on the wall above the Dakṣiṇāmūrti shrine, where a properly youthful Bhikṣāṭana shows, however facilely, a grace of movement which is hard to capture in stone.

Where Bhikṣāṭana does his begging is an interesting question. The general impression seems to be that Śiva begs only from the wives of the *ṛṣi*s in the Dāruka forest en route to Varanasi to gain release from the sin of cutting off one of Brahmā's heads. But this is to reduce the significance of his begging, and to subordinate it to other stories. This aspect of Śiva is clearly modelled on the universal Śaiva wandering ascetic, and is limited neither in time nor space. The limitation of which I speak is applied even by David Shulman in his translation of Cuntarar, Shulman declaring in his Introduction that Cuntarar's 'favourite myth' is 'the myth of Śiva's entry into the Pine Forest'.[7] However, this bears no relation to the text, which shows women in a variety of villages addressing Śiva the beggar. He is from the wilderness – 'O handsome lord from the wilderness'[8] rather than visiting the Pine Forest sages in their forest seclusion.

Even the Sanskrit Purāṇas which mainly situate the begging in the Pine Forest, do not do so exclusively. In the *Kūrma Purāṇa* Śiva wanders as

20. Kaṅkālamūrti from Darasuram. *c*. 1170.

a beggar for alms, in the usual sequence, after cutting off Brahmā's fifth head, as Kālabhairava:

> He put on a strange appearance
> that shone with his radiance,
> a holy sacrificial cord,
> his gleaming three eyes.
>
> . . .
>
> After drinking the divine nectar,
> the bliss of the Supreme Sacrificer,
> the Lord comes to all the worlds,
> rich in graceful playful delights (*līlāvilāsabahulo*).
> When they saw Śaṅkara
> the black-faced Kālabhairava,
> endowed with the beauty of a handsome body,
> women followed him.
> They sang all sorts of songs,
> they danced in front of the Lord,
> and when they saw the smile on his face
> they arched their brows. (*Kūrma Purāṇa* II 31,71–6)

He then goes to Viṣṇu's world and kills his gatekeeper. Only then, in this account, does he go to the Pine Forest.

In Umāpati's verse, although the demands of the Cidambaram story mean that the scene has to be the Pine Forest, there is no sense of place: it is generic and universal begging and response.

> 'Sir monk, where do you live,
> in town or mountain, or in the forest?
>
> Why do you wander here?
> Speak, lord,
> where will you go?
>
> Stop and do your begging right here.
> You must play with us.'
> Thus the women, beside themselves,
> rushed up to Him in the forest
>
> . . . (232)[9]

Note the use of *straiṇam*, meaning both an assemblage of women and also women in general. The same word is used in the *Kūrma Purāṇa* passage quoted above: the Lord comes to all the worlds, . . . women (*straiṇam*) followed him. Both verses take for granted the glorious beauty of the wanderer. This beauty is clearly stated in another verse:

It was He who made known the 32 *rāgas*,
His face all the more like a night lotus come alive
from the stream of clear nectar from the moon on His crown,
delightful with His unrestrained song.

In the forest He held immobile
the throng of the sages' wives,
He, the complete embodiment of the erotic,

Seeing Him, Viṣṇu's illusory form
determined to marry Him.
. . . (130)[10]

This powerful verse begins with technical enumeration – Śiva makes known the fundamentals of music by example. But this singing, produced so effortlessly and gracefully that there is no call to mention the God's mouth, flows out alongside the radiance of moonlight that bathes his face. Although it is day, emotionally it is the night. By implication, the lotus faces of the women are no less brought to life by the unearthly radiance of the intruder. Brought to life, yet held motionless. So far, the revealer of the complete complex of music reaches out to the complete group of women, from the elements of music to the audience – then, like a hammer blow in the course of the verse, or a drumbeat, the conclusion to this the principal part of the verse, the phrase of consummation – *sarvaśṛṅgārarūpaṃ*, 'He, the complete embodiment of the erotic.' The verse carries on, with a kind of coda. Viṣṇu forgets the part he is playing, and so far forgets himself that he wants to marry Śiva. Śiva's performance is universal, and Viṣṇu is only apparently a fellow performer. In fact he too cannot resist the show.

Here only the deer and Kuṇḍodara show that this is Bhikṣāṭana. This majestic figure is truly regal, and a fold of fat separates the deep and expansive navel from the Kīrtimukha of the sumptuous waistband. The skull and three peacock feathers form the front of the magnificent headdress, which is topped by the elegantly folded locks suggestive of the foliage of the fig-tree Dakṣiṇāmūrti sits beneath. Absorbed in his art, Śiva holds an absent *vīṇā* with supreme self-confidence.

It is as *sarvaśṛṅgārarūpaṃ* that Śiva sends Pārvatī's handmaid, Jayā, to soothe her when she sulks about his misdeeds:

My fun and games
with the women who live in the Dāruka forest;
My rape of Hari
when he was a woman on Mount Meru;
. . . (257)[11]

In the *sthalapurāṇa* it is this form of Śiva that leads into Naṭarāja. The erotic ascetic, winning the hearts of wives, defeats the husbands' attack and dances a dance of triumph in Sarga 11 of the *Cidambara Māhātmya*, as we saw in chapter 1. Umāpati's Tamil version follows the Sanskrit especially closely, and both texts must have profoundly informed his picture of Śiva. As I suggested in chapter 3, it may be that Umāpati produced the final version of the *Cidambara Māhātmya* and himself wrote some of the verses that the Tamil follows so closely.[12]

The following extracts from the *Māhātmya* are from Viṣṇu's account of events to Śeṣa. When Viṣṇu comes to seek his daily audience, Śiva informs him that they are to visit the sages in the Pine Forest:

For that reason I will take on
a wonderful handsome form,
infatuating,
radiant to the eyes
like the rise of the moon.

. . .

Then God Mahādeva, adorned with all ornaments,
the Lord, shone with the radiance
of the headjewels of gods and demons.

Divine jewelled sandals were touched by His feet-lotuses,
His body shone with the dazzling white *dhoti* He wore.

He was adorned with a sacrificial thread shining on His chest.
He gleamed with a showering of the ash
carried [in a bowl] on the head of a large *bhūta* [beside Him].

He flourished a skull in His left hand and a drum in His right
He was splendid with the bud of beauty
on the vine of His neck.
The Lord adorned His holy body
To make its beauty shine.

There was the sprout of a smile
on His lotus face that shone
with the petal of the lower lip.
He was charming with His ear-ring
that was a wave of the ocean of beauty.

The coquetry of His eyes shone out
and achieved the delusion of the world.
The disc of the moon on the expanse of His forehead
shone in the drops of sweat there.

He really shone with a shining bright round *tilaka* mark.
His smooth curls were delightful with crooked rows of bees.

O Śeṣa, with His supreme body that surpassed coral,
the Lord began slowly to move, like a mountain of coral.

(*Cidambaram Māhātmya* 11.37–46)

Accompanied by Viṣṇu as a voluptuous woman, Śiva goes to the Dāruka forest.

Going then to the beautiful *āśramas*
where the great ascetics dwelt
He stood in the outer courtyard of each.

Sounding His drum there again
with a joyful face,
the jingle of His priceless anklets
brightened the three worlds.

Then when women were coming
from inside the *āśrama* to give alms
He gave them the eye
and made a million suggestive gestures.

Then from here to there
the Blessed one, Śiva the Mild, Śambhu,
in His disguise as mendicant
was besieged by women
whose minds were thrown into confusion
by passion.

Some, their hands busy arranging their unsteady tresses,
let their girdles and clothes
drop right there.
Some praised the very bright radiance of His smile.
Some asked straight out
for the pleasure
of embracing Him.

Some, not having any cooked rice to give Him
took grains
and approached –
the grains were cooked in their hands
by the fire of Love.

Tormented by Love
who had released his irresistible arrow,
they placed His alms on the ground,
thinking it a vessel.

21. Wives of the Ṛṣis. Ceiling painting, Śivakāmasundarī *maṇḍapa*, Cidambaram. Seventeenth century.

Some, eager to show respect,
put a flower in a vessel
and threw it at His feet,
while looking at
His lotus face.

Some left hastily to get Him rice for alms,
But the rice became cooked
By resting in their hands. They spilled it
On the ground rather than in His bowl.

Some were confident He was a lover they had known before,
some believed He was Kāma, the God of Love, bereft of his wife Rati.

'Crocodile-bannered Love
has taken this form
and fired all his five arrows
simultaneously',
declared some.

'Where are you off to,
leaving me delusion
as I come to give you alms,
as the sun leaves darkness
for night?'

'Though I drink the nectar of your beauty,
it's fire to my deluded heart!
Make my wish come true!'
said one to Him.

'Seeing you – that made my bangles drop off.
Give them back right now
and be off with you!
If you can't give them back,
you mustn't go on from place to place!'
So one woman,
delighting in Him,
held Him back.

Saying 'Come hither',
some showed their firm breasts
to the holder of the begging bowl skull
as they showed the way to their ashrams.

Some said,
'Do whatever you please
where you please!
Anywhere on the ground
can be home!'

Some declared,
'O lord! whatever piece of ground
takes your fancy –
even in another wood –
take us to that ground.'

One said to Him,
'O lord! a lot of alms
will be given you in my house.
Don't go to any other house.'

'Our lives seem to be in danger.
Embrace us and give them back to us!'
So said some.

Lest Love torment us
in the guise of Yama who is Death,
protect us!'
some in their fear besought the Beggar.

Gazing at handsome Śiva as He was there,
some women danced for joy
in their delight at seeing Him,
and kept on dancing.

Even while the dance, a lovely sight, continued
some women, smitten with love,
gestured theatrically.

As though driven by Love's arrow shots,
so hard to bear,
some young women ran swiftly after Maheśa.

'Why do you hold out this skull of yours as an alms bowl?'
some, oppressed by love unconquerable,
asked the Lord.

As if asking the Lord
'If you don't respond,
think what will happen to us, Lord!'
some kept beside Him.

Seeing Him come for alms
the women pressed against Him,
disturbing their braided hair,
their garlands, necklaces,
and all their ornaments.

Some other lotus-eyed ladies,
as their girdles and saris slipped down,
suddenly fell on Him,
pierced by Flower-bowed Love's arrows.

In such ways did the lovely wives
of the ascetics all behave,
young ones drunk with their youth,
those in their prime, and the old.

Greatly deceived, the women there
were splendid in their wiles, for the moment.
Long and loud laughed the Trident-bearer.

(*Cidambara Māhātmya* 11. 37–46)

The *gopuras* are evidence of the importance of Bhikṣāṭana in Cidambaram; and the paintings on the ceiling of the Śivakāmasundarī *maṇḍapa* may well have been substituted for faded Cōḻa originals elsewhere in the temple.

THE FIRST PERFORMANCE OF THE ĀNANDATĀṆḌAVA DANCE

In the beginning Śambhu the Mild along with Mohinī
was strolling in the dense wood called Dāruka.

Deluding with His beauty the wives of the Brahmans,
and that throng of silent sages by Viṣṇu's illusion,
nullifying the magic attack the Brahmans staged,

He took pity on the Brahmans, and displayed His Dance.
. . . (40)[13]

Thus Umāpati describes in the *Kuñcitāṅghristava* how the first performance of the Dance of Bliss came to happen. The account in the *Cidambara Māhātmya*, Viṣṇu's narration of events to Śeṣa, continues as follows:

And I shall tell how I behaved towards all their husbands,
great-souled ascetics that they were,
even in front of their wives.

I instantly became a woman
such that the great sages would think me
neither chaste nor a courtesan,
and stood beside the Great Lord
who was gently laughing.

Looking intently on my face,
supremely intent, as if upon Brahman,
they committed a succession of offences,
bringing about rebirth for themselves.[14]

Then some of the old men among them,
rich in asceticism, were extremely angry.
'Who is this man in the guise of a Kāpālika,

22. Viṣṇu as Mohinī. Ceiling painting, Śivakāmasundarī *maṇḍapa*, Cidambaram. Seventeenth century.

a Skull-bearer, who has boldly come into our hermitages
and at once puts an end
to the conjugal fidelity of excellent wives
– fidelity that is the foundation of the universe.'
They released the arrows of fierce curses.

They released them
but saw them come straight back
without hitting Him.
The fury of all those eminent sages was not allayed.

Some maintaining restraint
tended the pits of their sacrificial fires
– as though they wanted Him to stop
and perform the Tāṇḍava dance.

In the pits they put fires – and made them blaze,
so too blazed the mantras they muttered.

With the whole range of materials fit for such ritual,
there in the divine Devadāru wood,
the resort of sages, directing them at the Lord of Viṣṇu,

stainless Śiva, who destroys all faults,
those ascetics unreflectingly performed black magic (*ābhicāra*).

As they performed that terrible ritual in the wood,
their hearts and eyes blazing with the fire of anger,

an extraordinary tiger shot from the fire,
seemingly created by the flaming circles of their furious eyes.

It seemd to split open all the quarters with its roaring
and the sage-lords hurriedly directed it
against the auspicious Lord who is the destroyer of all.

Then the great Lord softly smiled
and with His fingernail joyfully
killed that tiger which terrified everyone.

With His nail He cut off its skin and put it on.
Accustomed as He was to divine clothes,
yet He shone, the skin gleaming like a silken cloth.

And then a snake arose from the fire,
attended by *bhūta*s, the burning fire of its poison
unstoppable, its eyes blazing, a gem on its hood.

Terrible, like a heap of darkness,
hissing unbearably, directed by the sages
it rushed towards Śiva the Mild.

23. Apasmāra produced from the Ṛṣis' sacrificial fire. Ceiling painting, portico of Cit Sabhā, Cidambaram. Nineteenth to twentieth century.

24. Combined assault of the products of the Ṛṣis' sacrificial fire. Ceiling painting, Śivakāmasundarī *maṇḍapa*, Cidambaram. Seventeenth century.

The snake rushing at Him,
a gem blazing on its hood,
the God made a bracelet
on His auspiciously marked hand.

Before the ascetics
who while behaving hostilely because of delusion
were yet His devotees,
He took His own form out of compassion for them.

Those lovely locks of His
became tawny matted hair.
He started to perform
the preliminary step (*prastāvanāpada*) of the Tāṇḍava dance.

And two more excellent hands
were seen on Him by the sage-lords,
and the Great Lord bore an eye on His forehead
and black on His throat.

There arose a Creature – as if the darkness
that previously had been swallowed by those blazing fires
was vomited forth again by them in a compact lump.

Its hair was tawny with the flames
from the hot coals that were its eyes.
It had the body of a dwarf,
a great mouth with long tusks,
and its arms moved frenetically (*lasadbhujam*).

Massed ranks of snakes attended it.
Casting fear aside it hurtled at Śaṅkara.

The Great Lord was about to begin His dance
but, when He saw it, joyfully crushed it with His lotus foot
and made it there a foot rest.

They, finding Him unconquerable
by the highly dangerous means at their disposal,
hurled the fire itself upon Him, infuriated.

But He playfully caught it
as it hurtled towards Him with its ring of flames
and kept it on His auspicious palm.

And then the sages of great strength
wondered what was happening.
Overwhelmed by their anger,
they threw mantras at Him.

Śiva caught the mantras used by the sages,
made them into a heavy foot ornament of heavenly beauty,
and put it on to His foot.

Then Mahādeva,
His charming burden of matted locks swaying,
concentrated on the Tāṇḍava dance,
beginning gently,
for He is an ocean of compassion.

Then those sages who in their delusion
had sent fires and mantras, exhausted,
were briefly filled with alarm,
feeling themselves weaponless.

Then in a flash with the great speed
of His Tāṇḍava they lost consciousness
and fell down on the ground.

I too was not at ease.
At His side when He began the Tāṇḍava,
I felt great fear like never before.

He speedily put my fear at rest
with His hand resplendent with the snake bracelet.
He thought of Pārvatī and she came.

When the daughter of the Himalaya
came beside Him, then the gods in heaven
in delight rained down flowers;

and at the same time, by His command
I left off the extraordinary form of a woman
and again assumed my divine form,
auspicious and innate.

Then Pārvatī, the supremely illustrious
wife of Śarva, 'Śiva the Bowman', Śaṅkara's darling,
adorned as before the side
of Him Who is the Teacher of the World.

She, the Goddess, Mother of the Universe,
her face like a blooming lotus,
when she saw me said, 'Well done, well done!'
and was much amused for a good while.

Then Lord Śiva Himself, resplendent,
the embodiment of compassion,
His tawny matted locks undulating
as they stretched to the horizon on either side,

a lotus hand gleaming with the flickering
light of the fire, His blazing eyes
now flooded with overflowing compassion,

filling all the quarters with the terrible beat
from His *ḍamaru* drum which rivalled
the extraordinary hurricane that explodes at the end of time,

the jewelled anklets tinkling on His lotus feet
that are praised by all reverent people
in the eight points of the compass,

and greatly frightening Pārvatī at His side
with His hand that shone
with the gleaming snake bracelet,

then Śambhu, Whose form is the world itself,
began to perform the Tāṇḍava quickly,
His tiger-skin garment fluttering
in the speed of His circular movements.

Faster than even I could see,
He made 'Unending' Śeṣa into a bracelet
for Himself with His slightly curved foot
that was charming with its mobile anklet.

Umā, the Goddess, at His side,
was distraught with fear
– upon her He looked with intense compassion.
And all the while
He performed the Dance of Bliss (*ānandatāṇḍava*).

Then to Pārvatī the Lord said,
'Drink the *rasa* of this Tāṇḍava'
and He commanded Nandikeśvara,
'O bull, enjoy!'

And then all those sage-bulls
who had been stupefied were humble
and said 'O Śiva! O Śaṅkara! O God!'

They said, 'Glory to Umā's Husband,
to the Moon-crested God, to Śambhu!'
He gave them the eye of wisdom
so that they could see the Tāṇḍava.

Then Śambhu was splendid in the dance,
His eyes dancing with compassion,
purifying the forest with the lustre of His gentle smile.

As if He wanted to trample to death
that Creature which looked like
the agglomeration of their sins,
He stood with one foot on it.

To destroy the sins
that they had accumulated in life after life,
He showed that auspicious foot that was slightly curved.

Through the compassion of the God of Gods,
those ascetics saw the festival for the eyes
that is the divine Tāṇḍava Dance of Supreme Bliss.

When they had seen the supreme dance of Śambhu
they were filled with joy and wonder.
Taking their water-pots and staves
and holding them aloft,

thrilled to the depths of their being,
possessed by the *rasa* of Śiva's bliss,
they danced, reddening the forest
with the shaking of their matted locks.

Praising Him, the gods surrounded the Great Lord,
heaping handfuls of beautiful flowers before Him,
crushing some with the tips of their crowns
as they bowed at His feet.

Nārada and other skilled musicians,
their hands adorned with *vīṇā*s,
stood stock-still, not singing,
not knowing what to do.

Then all His *bhūta*s there in front of Him
performed a weird and wonderful dance at speed.

All the *gaṇa*s, overexcited,
performed all sorts of dance routines,
falling down and getting up over and over.

Then the God who is the Great God,
pleased at heart, said to those sages
whose goal was Brahman
and whose hearts were deeply satisfied,

'O Brahmā, Viṣṇu, Indra and you other gods!
O great sages! Listen. What I have to say
has never ever been heard before.
Praised by all the gods,

my Ānanda Tāṇḍava, Dance of Bliss,
is the rise of the full moon
from the great ocean of supreme bliss.
Think of it as the symbolic form (*liṅga*) of Śiva,
and with that in mind

25. Naṭarāja. Vedaranyam, *c.* 1200.

set up a Śiva *liṅga* in this very wood
that is my auspicious dance hall,
and worship it unweariedly.
Worship of this *liṅga* will be
the sole cause of enjoyment and release,
and by it you will attain the supreme unending state,
unobtainable by other means.'
Having spoken thus, the Blessed One,
the Mountain-lord, with a glance at Gaurī,
quickly disappeared into the sky,
O Śeṣa! with His great spouse, Mahābhavānī.
Then the gods bowed joyously
in the direction in which He had gone,
and returned whence they had come,
deeply satisfied with having seen Śiva.

O Śeṣa, with my mind fixed on it,
I have continuous and measureless bliss.
Now I think on that alone,
and am indifferent to my Yoga-sleep.

(*Cidambara Māhātmya* 13.1–74)

CHAPTER 8

Bhairava the Terrible and other forms of Śiva

Although Bhikṣāṭana is far more popular in the South, and indeed is characteristically Southern, the form of Bhairava, 'the Terrible', is closer to the general view of the essential nature of Śiva. In the North Bhairava is often a dancer; or rather Dancing Śiva, when mentioned, is likely to be called Bhairava, the dance being a destructive dance. While Bhikṣāṭana, in the South, expresses the eroticism that underlies Naṭarāja, Bhairava is the pure destructive power that Naṭarāja transmutes into rhythmic motion. Bhairava also carries a philosophical load. In terms of mythology, Bhairava is often considered to be a manifestation of Śiva, but in terms of much Tantric philosophy he is indeed the full form (*pūrṇarūpa*) of Śiva.[1] At the beginning of the *Śataratnasaṃgraha*, Umāpati discusses the variety of scriptures that issued from the five faces of Sadāśiva. On one view each face promulgates five types of scriptures. Both the Siddhānta and the Bhairava Tantras are of the type called *māntrika* – the former gives *mukti*, the latter destroys one's enemies.[2]

In Tamilnadu the destructive power of Śiva is conveniently summed up in the Eight Heroic Deeds, each of which is assigned a particular place. *Tirumantiram* 339–46 seems to be the earliest listing of the *aṭṭavīraṭṭānam*. In Tirumūlar's order, these actions are 1. The killing of Andhaka. 2. The beheading of Dakṣa and the substitution of a goat's head. 3. The cutting off of one of Brahmā's heads and the draining of Viṣṇu's blood into his skull. 4. The beheading of Jalandhara with a discus marked out on the ground. 5. The destruction by an arrow of fire of the Triple Cities of the demons. 6. The skinning alive of the elephant demon. 7. Rescuing the boy Mārkaṇḍeya by banishing Death with yogic fire, though this means seems specific to Tirumūlar, and the norm is kicking. 8. Burning up Kāma, the God of Love. Three of these deeds involve decapitation. This decapitation may relate to the self-castration of Śiva.

The following verse dramatically switches to the Northern version of the Pine Forest myth, as given by the *Kūrma Purāṇa*:

Śiva the Mild in his gracious play
plucked out His *liṅga* – the cause of pleasure –

because of what the ascetics said,
and threw it away in the forest,
watched in fear by the gods
wondering what was happening.

But through the praises of Brahmā and Viṣṇu
He made those sages realize the truth,
and disappeared.

I bow to that Lord Whose foot is curved,
Who fulfils those who bow down to Him. (258)[3]

This divine gesture of self-mutilation is variously described in the *Purāṇas*.

When the *liṅga* was cut off the Blessed Bhava, 'Being', vanished, no beings were visible in the universe. And then all was confused. Nothing gave off light. The sun gave no heat at all, and fire had no light. And even the planets and constellations were topsy-turvy. (*Brahmāṇḍā Purāṇa* 1.2.27. 35–6)

When they saw Śiva, the Mountain-dweller, in disguise, walking along naked, they cried, O you scoundrel, rip off that *liṅga*! Śaṅkara, the Great Yogin, said to them, 'I will do so, if you really hate my *liṅga*.' So saying the Blessed One, the Gauger out of Bhaga's eyes, ripped it off. And from that instant they could see neither the Lord nor Viṣṇu nor the *liṅga*. Then indeed there were bad omens, spelling danger for the world. The thousand-rayed sun did not shine. The earth shook again and again. All the planets lost their lustre and the great ocean heaved. (*Kūrma Purāṇa* 2.37.40–3)

In the *Śiva Purāṇa* the sages said:

'Your behaviour is immoral and violates the Vedic path. Therefore let your penis fall to the gound.' And when they said that the *liṅga* instantly fell on to the ground. . . . And that *liṅga* like fire burnt everything before it. And wherever it went it burned things. And it went into the subterranean world and it went to heaven. It went everywhere on earth. In no place did it become stationary. All the worlds were thrown into confusion. Those sages were deeply troubled. (*Śiva Purāṇa, Koṭirudrasaṃhitā* 4.12.17–18a, 19–21)

Śiva's *liṅga* while on his body had provided order and stability for the universe, performing there the role it performs within shrines. In the first two versions, everything collapses without this vital element. In the third, where there is release of energy rather than just its absence, the sages rather than Śiva are the active cause of the *liṅga* falling, and its response is reactive. In the Cidambaram myth, all opposing forces are absorbed within the dance. The complexity of the iconography of the dance absorbs its rivals. The *liṅga* is simple – it is either present or absent; it lacks the accommodating spirit of the dance.

Here is a summary of the version given in the Tamil *sthalapurāṇa* of Kāñcīpuram, a version based largely on the *Kūrma Purāṇa*.

On the Muñjaman peak of Meru, five-headed Brahmā appeared before some sages, and told them, 'From me the universe originated, and in me it will dissolve. All beings are under my protection.' The Vedas heard this claim and rushed up to declare that the Śaṅkara is the Supreme Being. Brahmā denied this, and said that Rudra could never be the essence of OṂ. OṂ thereupon took form to declare that Maheśa was its sole master. Brahmā paid no heed, and continued to vaunt his own glory. Viṣṇu then claimed to be the Supreme. The two gods began to fight. Seeing this from on high, Śiva presented himself before the combatants. Brahmā, still living in a world of his own, dared to say, 'Welcome, my son!' These words angered the Lord. His anger manifested itself. The god Bhairava came from his body and throwing himself on Brahmā cut off one of his heads. Brahmā then recognised his error, and begged the Lord to spare his life. Śiva forgave him, but informed him he would have to make do with four heads. To abate the arrogance of Viṣṇu and the other gods, he commanded Bhairava to seek the 'alms of blood' from them. Bhairava went first to Viṣṇu's world. He drove off the guardians of the palace and confronted the commander of Viṣṇu's army, Viṣvaksena. With a thrust of his pike, he speared him on the end of his weapon. Viṣṇu quickly appeared. Bhairava ask him for a gift of blood. The god did not hesitate. He cut an artery on his forehead and let the blood flow into the skull that Bhairava held out. The blood flowed for years and years, but the skull did not fill up. Viṣṇu fainted and fell to the ground. Bhairava helped him up, gave him back his strength and fulfilled his desires. He then went to the other gods and in the same way made them give up their arrogance, by asking them for the 'alms of blood'. Then he went to Kāñci. He put the skull on the ground and removed Viṣvaksena from his pike. He handed him over to Viṣṇu. Bhairava then set up a *liṅga*, Bhairaveśvara, to worship. Compassionate Śiva appeared and told him to be the guardian of Kāñci and to distribute the blood in the skull among all the *gaṇas*. Those who worship Bhairaveśvara (Vayiravēccuraṉ) are absolved from all their sins. (*Kāñcipura Māhātmyam* 34)[4]

For Umāpati, and for Naṭarāja this dramatic event is domesticated within the temple. Not only is Brahmā accommodated within the temple, albeit in a subordinate role, and shared subordinacy at that, but the head which in the Northern myths leads to such difficulties, is installed beside Śiva for all to see, now become a *liṅga*. Thus are the pretensions of Kāpālikas and *liṅga*-worshippers in general effectively dealt with!

Once in the past removing one of Brahmā's heads
and placing it on His right side for all people to see,

He placed him, the Creator whose faces
are the four Vedas, on His left.
His command was, He Whose form is space,
'O Self-born Brahmā, from today onwards
do you enjoy the remains of the offerings made to me.'
. . . (30)[5]

But Bhairava is also said to perform a very active role:

Bhairava dwells in His holy place
and all creatures who die there have their sins,

including those from previous lives, turned to dust
in a fraction of a second at His command
with a blow of Bhairava's trident,

though many years would otherwise have been
required to work off their consequences.

Bhairava, dwelling in His Hall,
quickly teaches the essential saving truth
that destroys birth and death.
. . . (159)[6]

Umāpati must here be referring to the bronze image of Bhairava present in the Cit Sabhā today,[7] in the form of Svarṇakālabhairava, though the guardian aspect of this Bhairava is not emphasized today.

This Bhairava holds a *ḍamaru* drum and a trident in his right hands,
and a noose and a skull in his left hands.
Very handsome, he is accompanied by a dog.
Formerly he turned copper placed at his feet
into gold and gave it to his devotees.
I seek refuge with Svarṇakālabhairava.
Maheśvara as Svarṇakālabhairava
holds a trident in his hand and is accompanied by a dog
which is the embodiment of the Vedas.
He ever gives all things to those who seek refuge with him.
He is the embodiment of the former merit
of the lineage of the lords of sacrifice [the Dīkṣitas].
I seek refuge with him. (*Devatāstotra*)[8]

In *The History of Chidambaram*, Somasekharendra Dikshitendra remarks,

Two hundred years ago Dīkṣitas placed copper plates at the feet of this Bhairava Mūrti at night and found them changed into gold plates the next morning. Then it became their livelihood . . . Even today people who seek wealth offer special *pūjās* to this God.[9]

Ramalinga Dikshitar says that the dog is an incarnation of 'Kuṇḍodara who carries Śiva's umbrella'.[10] Kuṇḍodara, however, can also be the *gaṇa* who carries Bhikṣāṭana's laden begging bowl, and this identification of the dog brings out the Bhikṣāṭana aspect of Bhairava, the two forms of Śiva being closely related. It is also true that the standard iconographical identification of the dog with the Veda is not such as to appeal to the priests when the image has been admitted into the holy of holies, the Cit Sabhā.

Apart from the attribute of 'Gold', similar Bhairavas are met with elsewhere in the temple, and in the poem, as boundary guardians, and will be discussed at the close of the Bhairava section of this chapter. The Bhairava who produces or attracts gold is a standard iconographic form and is not unique to Cidambaram. Nevertheless, the presence of Bhairava in the Cit Sabhā is thought-provoking. Bhairava is the chief deity and apex of an important set of Northern Śaiva systems which had a notable exponent in Cidambaram around the time of Umāpati. In his wide-ranging *Mahārthamañjarī*, Maheśvarānanda makes the intriguing statement,

Once long ago Lord Bhairava, who brings the universe into being (*viśvabhāvana*) stayed in the great jewelled pavilion that is the space of consciousness.[11]

Sanderson suggests that Maheśvarānanda may be referring to the Cit Sabhā.[12] Although the description of the Cit Sabhā as a jewelled pavilion (*maṇḍapa*) is unexpected, it is made plausible by the fact that Maheśvarānanda subsequently refers directly to the Cit Sabhā, and indeed seems to associate his own complex Tantric monism with Naṭarāja. Out of affection for his pupils he composed his book 'So that, O wonder! like the Lord dancing in the middle of the Golden Hall (*kanakasadas*), Śiva who is self-reflected consciousness (*vimarśa*) is easily here before our eyes.'[13]

And again,

This book is as sweet as the Kāverī,
as fragrant as the water lily,
its importance is like that of Naṭeśa's dance.[14]

There is also the tantalizing quotation of just one couplet from his teacher's *Ānandatāṇḍavavilāsastotra*, a text otherwise unknown:

We for our part praise your shining down
through the universe when you look outwards,
and when you look inwards
we praise your inner composure
composed of the bliss of autonomy
arising from bringing about the dissolution of the universe.[15]

Maheśvarānanda teaches the philosophy of absolute (*anuttara*) non-dual consciousness 'which leads to liberation in this life in which freedom and enjoyment (*mokṣa* and *bhoga*) are united'. In his commentary to verse 66 of his *Mahārthamañjarī*, 'By this Reality whose essence is nectar, even if its touch is only for a moment, every being that surpasses everything, obtains perpetual and universal glory', he quotes this line from the *Śivadṛṣṭi* – 'When one has once known the gold of true reality, what good are contemplation and the bodily organs?'[16] This kind of affirmation makes one wonder how the Bhairava who attracts gold arose. This standard iconographic form is a severe reduction in power and status of the supreme Bhairava on whose authority *mokṣa* and *bhoga* are enjoyed in this life. Could it not be a deliberate reduction in status of a hitherto supreme Bhairava? Such a reduction need not have originated in Cidambaram, though it may well have done so in the South.

In addition to the core story of his chastisement of Brahmā, Śiva decisively demonstrates his authority over Viṣṇu. Bhairava terrifies the baby Kṛṣṇa:

> At the Kalpa's end the oceans swell
> and cover the earth seven times:
>
> in the middle of the oceans lies Hari on a peepul leaf.
>
> No sooner did he say, filled with pride:
> 'Here is no man other than me'
>
> than he saw Bhairava carrying His trident,
> and fearfully venerated Him with fresh praises:
> . . . (236)[17]

Nor is it Bhairava's appearance alone that alarms Viṣṇu.

> Portions of this Lord –
> Śarabha, Baṭukarāja, Vīrabhadra and the others –
>
> destroy the fierce actions of cruel beings
> assumed by lotus-eyed Viṣṇu and Brahmā and others
> in every *kalpa*;
>
> also protect the whole world the whole time.
> Meditating on Him in their hearts, they are victorious.
> Him, Whose glory streams forth,
> Whose foot is curved,
> I worship. (203)[18]

One of the most striking sections of the *Kuñcitāṅghristava* is from verses 122 to 133, a section which begins with an irruption of terrible power as

Śiva destroys one *avatāra* of Viṣṇu after another: each *avatāra* goes off the rails once it has achieved its intended purpose and has to be terminated (122–5). There is a flutter in the rhythm as Kālī in verse 126 repeats the destruction of Narasiṃha wrought by Śiva in verse 125. Back to Śiva in verse 127 for the concluding destruction by Śiva of a form of Viṣṇu, as the Dwarf's expanded form is ripped up. Two verses on the Goddess, one on Viṣṇu as Mohinī in the Pine Forest, then back to the sequence of *avatāras*, though no longer to be destroyed. Paraśurāma gets his axe by praying to Śiva (131); by worshipping Śiva Paraśurāma killed the demon and got other benefits also (132). The limited *avatāra* sequence ends with Kalkin coming at the end of each Kali *yuga* with a sword given by Śiva (133). The clear sequence of *avatāras* makes a radical shift after the interval of the Goddess, now propitiating rather than opposing Śiva. A nice touch is the reference to the Goddess's creation of all ten *avatāras* from her shining fingernails (129). Then as a coda to the sequence there is reference to a purely local myth of a multi-headed Viṣṇu swallowing up a Śaiva pilgrim only to be killed by Śiva (134).[19] The theme of Śiva defeating Viṣṇu is then abandoned.

After the opening section, which we have looked at in detail, this is by far the longest coherent section. It is not without interruptions (shown in italics in the list below), but this is because the alternating rhythm here makes a larger and louder beat.

122 Viṣṇu as Fish recovers Vedas from the ocean.
123 Viṣṇu as Turtle intimidates – Śiva cuts him up.
124 Viṣṇu as Boar defeats the demon Hiraṇya.
125 Śiva as Śarabha defeats Man-lion.
126 Thousand-face Kālī defeats Man-lion.
127 Śiva defeats Vāmana become Giant.
128 The Goddess defeats the demon Bhaṇḍāsura; creates the 10 avatāras.
129 The Goddess is in the Śrīcakra.
130 The sages' wives and Viṣṇu as Mohinī want Śiva.
131 Paraśurāma meditates on Śiva's dance.
132 Paraśurāma meditates on Śiva, goes to Śiva's holy places.
133 Śiva gives Kalkin the sword he uses.
134 Multi-headed Viṣṇu kills a Śaiva and is killed by Śiva.

Two instances of Śiva destroying Viṣṇu are of considerable religious significance and merit discussion here.

ŚARABHA

All the gods trembled in fear of Viṣṇu
when he took on the body of the Man-lion,

so Brahmā sang His praises and He took on
the excellent body of Śarabha, the king of birds.

Speedily He cut him up with the tips of His claws
and adorned Himself with the skin,
illuminating the world with his fangs.

Him Who grants the wishes of all,
Whose foot is curved,
I worship. (125)[20]

In the first place, the presence of a Śarabha shrine in the Nṛtta Sabhā must be noted. At the back, against the enclosure wall, facing north, its proximity to Ūrdhvatāṇḍava and the small Kālī is significant in that there seems to be here a conglomeration of fierce power amid the elegant panelled pillars. The Nṛtta Sabhā was probably built by Kulottuṅga III (1178–1216), and there may be a special connection of the Śarabha with royalty. There are only four known Cōḻa images in stone, and the other three are found in royal temples. The earliest is in the Vikramasolisvaram at Tukkachchi not far from Kumbakonam, the only big temple definitely constructed by Vikrama Cōḻa (1118–35). There is a Śarabha image at Darasuram, and also in the Kampaharesvarar at Tribhuvanam, the last of the four great temples built by the Cōḻas, by the last great Cōḻa king, none other than Kulottuṅga III. At Tribhuvanam, the image is housed in a separate independent shrine north-east of the central shrine, with a metal image in addition to the stone one. L'Hernault remarks,

The sectarian aspect of this representation is undeniable for its appearance was more or less contemporaneous with the moment when there existed strong tensions between the Śaivas and Vaiṣṇavas at Cidambaram when the king Vikrama Cōḻa (1118–1135) had thrown into the sea the statue of Tillai Gōvindarājapperumāḷ. With the pacification of the quarrels from the time of the following reigns it is not surprising that a form of such manifest agression on the part of Śaivism was abandoned and is not found after the 12th century.[21]

The royal aspect of the cult should also be stressed, and the bizarre form could be seen to reflect the growing political stresses as Cōḻa power waned – desperate measures calling for desperate means. One might contrast Rājarāja's preference for the calm and stately Tripurāri *mūrti*, which exclusively occupies the niches on the second storey of the *vimāna*

26. Śarabhamūrti. Airavatesvara temple, Darasuram, *c.* 1170.
Courtesy: French Institute of Pondicherry/École Française d'Extrême-Orient

of the Great Temple of Tanjavur. In the *Kuñcitāṅghristava*, the destruction of Tripura is remarkable for its absence.[22]

ŚAṬṬANĀTHA

An image of this form of Bhairava is to be found on the south wall of the Deva Sabhā at the eastern corner. This is an important deity of the nearest major Śiva temple to Cidambaram, namely Sirkali.[23] This temple has two storeys above the *garbhagṛha*; the higher, with only a small square window-like entrance, contains a shrine to Śaṭṭanātha. This deity takes his name from his coat-like garment (Tamil: *caṭṭa*) which is made out of Viṣṇu's skin.

The temple *Devatāstotra* has this to say of Śaṭṭa or Kañcuka Nātha:

> The god who bears the name of Bhairava
> and stands before a dog,
> by Mahādeva's command went
> to Viṣṇu the Dwarf when he became large
> and struck him on the chest with one hand.

Umāpati puts it thus:

> Viṣṇu as the Dwarf,
> having shrunk his body
> to make his petition in Bali's hall of sacrifice,
>
> and made his body grow from earth to sky
> and placed his foot – itself the triple world –
> on the demon's crown.
>
> But then he terrified
> the whole world with his roaring.
>
> The hosts of gods praised Him
> as He slew the dwarf
> and ripped out his skeleton and tore off his skin.
> Him Whose foot is curved
> I worship. (127)[24]

VĪRABHADRA

We have met Vīrabhadra as Bhadrakālī's assistant in the beheading of Dakṣa; Umāpati gives another description of this event, omitting Kālī.

> Viṣṇu's *cakra* lost its fire,
> Brahmā's heart was in a whirl,
> the sun had lost his teeth,
> Indra's cheeks were split, Agni lost his flame,
> and everyone else lost his life –

He was satisfied
when He saw Vīrabhadra cut off Dakṣa's head
and roam the sacrifice ground with the *gaṇas*.

Him Whose heart was delighted,
Whose foot is curved,
I worship. (240)[25]

KṢETRAPĀLA

All of the violent forms of Śiva so far considered have been agents of punishment and retribution. Three verses refer however to the 'protector of the holy place', *kṣetrapāla*. One verse refers to Kālī, and has been considered in chapter 6; of the others, one refers to Bhairava, one to a local form.

Holding in His hand Brahmā's skull
that cannot be filled even by
pouring into it the stream of blood
flowing from Viṣṇu's forehead;

with hounds at His side,
His spreading matted locks
reddened by the lustre of the tips of His fangs,

Bhairava as Protector of the Field, Kṣetrapāla,
protecting the universe from torment, worships Him.
Him Whose foot is curved, I worship. (183)[26]

This Bhairava does not differ from the Bhairava previously considered, except that his protective role is specified. Given the importance of protecting a holy site, not the least because its holiness is demonstrated by the fact of its being protected, it is likely that the fierce forms of Śiva already considered are extensions of a primary protective function. The guardian has to be terrible to scare off the terrifying foe; indeed, he has to be more terrifying than what is feared, if he is to be effective. Shortly afterwards, a less imposing guardian is mentioned.

A wicked astrologer who lived on Godāvarī's bank,
was an inveterate liar.

Reborn as a lizard, that rebirth took place
in His holy place thanks to the fraction of merit he'd earned.

In order to burn up his inauspicious actions
of falling on people and making ominous sounds
he long worshipped Him with hymns of praise.

By His command he was reborn with a handsome body
and was victorious as the Protector of His Holy Place.
Him who has no equal, Whose foot is curved,
I worship. (191)[27]

This refers to the Lord of Lizards, Pallīśa, whose image is near Dakṣiṇāmūrti on the west side of the Mūla Liṅga shrine, though the temple *Devatāstotra* merely has the prayer, 'Ward off the fault of a lizard falling on us, make us happy.' Pallīśa is a far cry from being a full-fledged protecting deity, but then again it might be asked why Śiva, Lord of the Universe, needs a protector.

The answer to this is given by Biardeau:

The god of the great pilgrimage temple is – regardless of his name and his myth – the pure divinity, withdrawn into himself, the god of ultimate salvation. Furthermore, his most 'terrible' forms border on being considered improper for worship, so dangerous are they even for the devotees themselves. These are relegated to the most inaccessible of locations, where they are surrounded by all kinds of taboos, and only appeased by the appropriate offerings . . . In short, even though the god is the master of the universe of which his temple is the centre, he does not have direct function as its protector *hic et nunc*. This role is delegated to an inferior god, with Bhairava being the classic territorial guardian or *kṣetrapāla*.[28]

Should a king be his own doorkeeper? But in the case of Śiva the distinction in forms is slight. We now turn to two fierce forms of Śiva mentioned by Umāpati but not represented in the Cidambaram temple.

ŚIVA AS KILLER OF DEMONS (ANDHAKA AND JALANDHARA)

Although the trident is an emblem of Śiva, and he always carries it as Bhikṣāṭana and Kaṅkālamūrti, in these instances it is as ornament rather than weapon to be used. When the sages send magical adversaries against him, he does not use the trident. There are, indeed, grounds for suggesting that it is emanations of Śiva, rather than Śiva, who typically and essentially employ this instrument of assault. In what might be seen as the standard iconography of Śiva, the one important instance of Śiva using his trident is in the myth of Andhaka, where he impales this demon on his trident, and holds him aloft, in a powerful upward thrust of 45 degrees. It could be that the Southern tradition preferred to make the separation, to see Bhairava or Vīrabhadra use the trident rather than the stately Śiva, and by this hiving off of Śiva's terrifying aspects helped to make, in Dorai Rangaswamy's words, 'the terrific forms [of Śiva] beautiful and lovable'. The *Kāñcīmāhātmya* has Śiva depute to Bhairava the task of dealing with Andhaka: Bhairava impales the demon, and a pool formed when he fixed his spear in the earth to remove Andhaka from it.[29] Today the trident is closely associated with goddesses – a shrine marked only with a trident will always pertain to a female deity. The trident is not a common weapon. It is best suited for catching fish, as befits the weapon of Neptune, and it is essentially a ritual implement, used to induce possession.[30]

The Andhakāri is rare in the South, so much so that Dorai Rangaswamy is not certain whether or not Cuntarar refers to Andhaka, the Tamil version of the word being Antaka, and thus referring either to Andhaka or Antaka, the Sanskrit for Death, the 'Ender'. In considering Umāpati's reference to Andhaka, it will be fruitful to consider also another demon, Jalandhara. Not only does Umāpati mention them in consecutive verses, in itself of course at first sight a sign of logical incoherence, so too did Cuntarar, in both of his two mentions of Andhaka.

> You cut off one of the Lotus-Dweller's heads.
> You destroyed Andhaka with your fiery trident.
> Once when Neṭumāl,[31] lord of Tirumakaḷ,
> was offering splendid worship
> for many days,
> a single flower was missing
> from the (garland of a) thousand;
> to fill the gap, he adorned you with the lotus
> of his eye,
> and you graciously gave him
> the discus, victorious in battle,
>
> O pure lord of Tirupputtūr rich in groves.[32]
>
> He took the bright discus that cleft Jalandhara,
> who wanted war,
> and gave it to that excellent one
> who used his bright eye as a lotus.
> The lord who crushed Indra's shoulders
> impaled Andhaka, who lived in darkness,
> upon his trident.
> and gave it to that excellent one.[33]

The myth of Jalandhara is much richer in the South: not only is Śiva the source of Viṣṇu's unique weapon, but Viṣṇu becomes an exemplar of the utmost devotion, since he gives an eye to make up for the missing thousandth lotus in his offering to Śiva. Umāpati stresses Śiva's destructive power:

He, Śambhu, the Mild One,
He, Death's Destroyer,

slew the demon Jaladhara
with the discus created by His foot
and protected all beings,
their bodies struck by the missiles and blades
of that one's wicked deeds.

All beings declare
He who slew the manifestation of His anger,
the demon Jaladhara, is to be venerated.

. . . (48)[34]

The version of the Tamil *Kanta Purāṇam* is that Indra went to visit Śiva. To test him, Śiva takes the form of a naked yogi with matted hair and blocks the way, not replying when Indra asks who he is. Indra threatens the unknown person with his thunderbolt. Śiva gets angry at this but, not wishing to harm Indra, directs the fire of his fury into the ocean. There Śiva's anger takes the form of a boy, the boy becomes a righteous demon, but his doom to is be beheaded by Śiva with a discus that is then given to Viṣṇu.[35] Note that the story begins with Śiva acting as door-keeper, and that this role is the origin of the appearance of the demon who embodies Śiva's anger. In the version of the *Śiva Purāṇa* there is a subsidiary parallel. When the demon, led astray by Nārada, demands Pārvatī be sent to him, Śiva's anger manifests from his forehead and starts to devour the messenger. Śiva restrains it, as he does his anger at the beginning of the story, and makes it devour its own body. When only its head is left, he makes it his door-keeper, Kīrtimukha.[36]

So potent is Śiva, anger is not necessarily required to produce emanations from him.

Once on Mount Kailāsa,
when the Mountain's Daughter was having fun
she covered over Paśupati's eyes.

From the darkness a demon arose.
They called him Andhaka, 'the Blind',
and he was very wicked.

Being praised by all the worlds –
they were unable to bear the wickedness
streaming forth from the demon into the world –

by killing him He protected them.

. . . (49)[37]

Śiva's destruction of this demon is the first of the heroic deeds of Śiva in Tirumūlar's enumeration, but the story was never popular in the South, and the priority Tirumūlar gives it might be a sign of Northern influence. According to Dorai Rangaswamy, 'No sculpture of Andhakāsura Saṃhāra comes from the Tamil Country. Nor is there any description of it in the Āgamas.'[38] It is, however, worthy of note that both the demons Andhaka and Jalandhara are 'sons' of Śiva. Vīrabhadra is likewise an emanation from Śiva. In the case of Kṣetrapāla, cited from the *Liṅga Purāṇa* in chapter 6 above, Śiva takes the form of a baby boy in 'the burning ground full of ghosts'. David Knipe has described a contemporary Vīrabhadra cult in Andhra where dead boys are said to become Vīrabhadra, and to possess men.[39] Despite the long time interval, this little-known cult suggests a parallel with perhaps all of these myths that see Śiva become or generate an angry boy.

KIRĀTA, ŚIVA THE MOUNTAINEER

A story from the *Mahābhārata*, particularly popular in Karnataka, is Arjuna's wrestling match with Śiva. Practising penance in the Himalayas to win the dread Pāśupata missile from Śiva, the great bowman is attacked by an *asura* in the form of a boar. Arjuna kills it with an arrow, but a mountaineer comes up to claim the prey. The two men fight, and eventually Arjuna recognizes the mountaineer to be Śiva. He submits and wins the deadly missile.

> Arjuna who wears a diadem was astonished
> to be confronted by Him
> in the playful guise of a mountaineer
>
> with Gaṅgā on His crest,
> poison in His throat,
> a bracelet of a row of snakes on His arm,
>
> the moon on His brow, a third eye,
> a trident with prongs like flames,
>
> the skull of Unborn Brahmā,
> an army of sprites and ghosts,
> a dog that is the Vedas.
>
> . . . (260)[40]

The same event is referred to early in the poem, though probably with a different iconography in mind. As Pāśupatamūrti Śiva stands erect, not unlike Bhairava, with hair upright, and figures on a side façade of each *gopura*.

Once He, Paśupati, Protector of the Bound,
on the Silver Mountain
made a gift of His own missile
to Arjuna, descendant of Pṛthu

– He'd taken on the body of a forester,
fought with Arjuna
and received a broken head.

. . . (31)[41]

There is a local connection for this story, for Tiruvetkalam, where the university town of Annamalai now stands, some 3 km from the temple, is believed to be the place where Śiva gave the missile to Arjuna. Ñāṉacampantar and Appar sang of this place; the temple, recently renovated, is dedicated to Paśupateśvara and Nallanāyakī. The shrine has two fine images dug up nearby, a Pallava Kirātārjuna and a late Cōḻa Pārvatī.

As with Bhikṣāṭana, there is a masking of Śiva's true nature that at the same time is not a masking, since he has always been a wild god of the mountains. To be noted is the contrast between the physicality of the wrestling match, so well expressed in Hoysaḷa sculpture, and the hieratic purely formal representation of the Pāśupata weapon. The absolute power of Śiva playfully finds muted expression in hand to hand conflict, but the reality under the illusion is the Doomsday weapon.

THE SLAYER OF DEATH

Mainly restricted to the South and very popular there is the representation of Śiva as the slayer of Death (Death of Death, *kālakāla*, 176, 241). The *ṛṣi* Mṛkaṇḍu, offered by Śiva the choice between one good son to die at 16 and many bad sons, chooses the one, whose devotion to Śiva is such that when Death comes at the appointed time Śiva bursts forth from the *liṅga* and tramples on Death.

When once Mārkaṇḍeya was worshipping
the *liṅga* of the Lord of the Silver mountain,

then Death, son of the Sun,
of dread visage, drew him with his nooses.

The Great Lord came from the middle of the *liṅga*
to protect that sage.
Then God killed Death the Suppressor.

That eternal Lord of Dance,
praised by all kings,
Whose foot is curved,
I worship. (35)[42]

27. Kālāntakamūrti. East *gopura*, Cidambaram.

To the north of the Nṛtta Sabhā a relief of Kālasaṃhāramūrti on the south side of a massive nineteenth-century pillar has been turned into a shrine. Special *pūjā*s are offered on the full-moon day in the month of *kārtikai* when every house is beautifully lit with lamps.

Of all the forms of Śiva considered in this chapter, only Śiva as the Ender of the Ender has direct connections with the dance. Early versions of this image show Śiva dancing on Death in a manner that resembles dancing. Indeed, some images of this have been mistaken for early instance of the *ānandatāṇḍava*, with Death seen as Apasmāra.[43]

SOMĀSKANDA

Somāskanda is the group of seated Śiva and Pārvatī with Skanda standing or sitting between them. In Cidambaram, the one shrine to Somaskanda is on the north face of the same pillar as that of Kālāri, the two sides of the pillar having iron railings added to protect both shrines. Beneath Somāskanda are the five Pāṇḍava brothers. To worship this image, says Somasetu Dīkṣita, is 'to be blessed with beautiful children'. He reports the tradition that the five Pāṇḍavas performed their Rājasūya sacrifice here, winning the throne by Naṭarāja's grace. Along with the image of Kalyāṇasundara, Śiva marrying Pārvatī, Somāskanda is prominent on the *gopuras*. Umāpati's reference in the poem is indirect, in that he is principally concerned to mention Tiruvārūr, where Somāskanda, under the name of Tyāgarāja, is the principal deity. The importance of Tiruvārūr is apparent in the *Cidambara Māhātmya*, wherein under the name of Kamalālaya it ranks with Kāśī (Varanasi) as worthy of mention beside Cidambaram. These three places are great. One attains liberation by being born in Kamalālaya, by dying in Kāśī, and by seeing Cidambaram.[44]

> Once Moon-crested Śiva had betaken Himself
> with the Daughter of the Mountain
> to the park land of Kailāsa.
> As He sat there underneath an *indira* tree,
> He was all at once worshipped by a lordly monkey.
>
> To him He gave universal lordship
> and a complete armoury of missiles.
>
> I bow to the Lord
> Who wears *pārijāta* and all other flowers,
> and Whose foot is curved. (57)[45]
>
> Once it came to pass that Indra, the Lord of Heaven,
> had his enemies destroyed by the king with a monkey's face.
> Indra gave him the Tyāgarāja deity
> and also sent six other Tyāgarājas to the king.
>
> He worshipped these through the first-born
> in excellent temples at the principal site and at all the seven.
> I worship Him Who is the basis of those divine forms,
> praised by the throng of sages,
> His foot curved. (58)[46]

These two verses are Umāpati's most extensive reference to another holy place, and reflect the importance of Tiruvārūr, a Śaiva temple scarcely

28. Somāskanda. East *gopura*, Cidambaram.

less important than Cidambaram, though lacking Cidambaram's identification with a unique form of Śiva.[47] Six other temples share Tiruvārūr's connection with Somāskanda. Somāskanda, moroever, was of significance much earlier than Naṭarāja, being found in the central shrine of Pallava temples. Naṭarāja was a Cōḻa conception. Somāskanda's continuing importance is demonstrated by the fact that it is the chief processional deity in all Śiva temples.[48] Even in Cidambaram, Somāskanda is the chief image in the Brahmotsava processions, except when Naṭarāja is brought out. Somāskanda comes out every day.

> During the three Brahmotsava festivals
> in His form as Somāskanda He rides in a canopy
> on a vehicle in the form of:
>
> the moon, the sun, a demon, a bull,
> a royal elephant, the Silver Mountain, and a horse;
>
> as the Wandering Beggar on His own
> in a chariot drawn by a wide-eyed bull,
>
> daily He progresses through the streets,
> bathes, and with Śivā enters His own abode.
>
> . . . (26)[49]

Of all these forms, Somāskanda is furthest removed from the dance, though it was of almost equal importance. Tiruvārur has three times as many *Tēvāram* hymns dedicated to it as Cidambaram. The importance of the image is manifest on the Cidambaram *gopuras* and in the Cidambaram festival. Its power lies in its inclusivity, joining the old indigenous god Murukaṉ with the Goddess and Śiva, and it is the perfect iconographic expression of the family unit. The two images, Naṭarāja and Somāskanda, did not rival each other in their forms, the one full of energy, tension, power, the other utterly relaxed and complete, the only expressed energy in the bent legs of the baby boy.

We have in this chapter diverged widely from Naṭarāja, considering other forms of Śiva, and other temples. This has given some idea of the incredible richness of the religious contexts amid which Śiva performs his Dance of Bliss. I close this chapter with a verse that sets the Dance against the panorama of Śiva's other principal actions.

> Performing His dance
> in the company of His lotus-eyed Śakti,
> cutting off the head of Ka, Brahmā,
>
> slaying Time with His lotus foot,
> Love with the eye in His forehead,
> and the Cities with a smile,

protecting Mārkaṇḍeya, the son of the Brahma rishi,
and all the gods,

the Lord praised by the gods, the Lord of the Cit Sabhā,
Who has a thousand faces, Whose foot is curved,
Him I praise. (90)[50]

CHAPTER 9

Saints, dancing girls, 'gaṇas' – and Apasmāra

This chapter conjoins three very different sets of figures. The saints and dancing girls (*devadāsī*, or *rudrakanyā*) both played significant roles within the temple, and together constitute the major human presence within the imagery of the temple. These two are discussed in relation to Śiva's attendants, the hosts, or *gaṇas* – multiple goblin-like figures, who are in turn discussed in relation to Apasmāra.

About dancing girls Umāpati has little to say, partly it may be supposed because the centre of his attention was the dance of Śiva; but also it is likely that he felt no need for their presence within his poem. Their activity of dancing and singing before Śiva was in some sense a rival activity to the writing of poetry to Śiva. Like the saints, the Nāyaṉārs, they were specialists in devotion. As Reiniche says, 'dancing and singing are also acts of devotion, and the dancing girls of the Śaiva temple are, following the pattern (*mode*) of the Nāyaṉmār, equally *aṭiyār*, servants of the salvatory divinity'.[1]

SAINTS

Let us first consider the saints. The Nāyaṉārs, the sixty-three saints of Tamil Śaivism, constitute a significant element of the poem.[2] A row of images of these figures is found in every major Śiva temple in Tamilnadu, and their massed presence is an affirmation of the significance of the devotee, who therein worships the archetype of himself. The Sanskrit poem here treats in its characteristic manner material that is peculiarly Tamilian. Six Nāyaṉārs are each accorded a single verse, and they are also referred to collectively. The relevant verses will be discussed in turn, and then assessed in relation to the poem as a whole and to the life of the poet.

The Nāyaṉārs originate in a period prior to the Cōḻa cult of Naṭarāja and for the most part have no special connection with this form of Śiva. Their worship of Śiva is focussed on the *liṅga* and on the veneration of

29. Śiva placing a wreath on Caṇḍeśvara. Bṛhadīśvara temple, Gangaikondacolapuram, *c.* 1025.

other devotees of Śiva.[3] Their names are listed by Cuntarar in his 39th hymn, the Tiruttoṇṭattokai ('the holy assembly of the devotees [of Śiva]'), and therefore belong to the eighth century or earlier, Cuntarar himself being the latest and making the number up to sixty-three. Their stories find full expression in the *Periya Purāṇam* of Cēkkiḻār. In a short poem entitled *Cēkkiḻār Purāṇam* Umāpati gives an important account of how Cēkkiḻār came to write the *Periya Purāṇam*. It is also Umāpati who describes the discovery, and then the redaction, of the *Tēvāram*, the collected works of the three Nāyaṉār poets, in his poem entitled *Tirumuṛaikaṇḍapurāṇam*. A fourth poet, or poet-philosopher, Tirumūlar, is included in the list of Nāyaṉārs, though his writings seem considerably later than the others.[4] Māṇikkavācakar, who is often considered the greatest Tamil poet, is not included in the list of the sixty-three Nāyaṉārs, and is not mentioned by Cēkkiḻār, though he is generally dated around the ninth–tenth centuries, and is considered to be the sixty-fourth Nāyaṉār. There is in addition in the ranks of the Nāyaṉārs an important poetess, Kāraikāl Ammaiyār, who, however, though she figures also in the general iconography of Naṭarāja, is not mentioned by Umāpati in his poem. The poetry of these poet-saints will be considered in the final chapter.

Other than these great figures, the Nāyaṉārs are a varied collection of historical and legendary people, whose claim to fame as devotees usually consists in one startling and extravagant action of devotion. Of this remainder, Caṇḍeśvara is the most important, since he is the guardian of every major Śiva temple: in his charge are the keys, and his forgiveness is sought for any errors in worship. From Cōḻa times, property dedicated to a Śiva temple is made over to Caṇḍeśvara. His iconography is modelled on that of a god in body and ornaments, though he has only two arms, and is always in *añjali*, palms pressed together in devotion, his axe tucked under one arm. The major expression of this figure in art is found on the north-east wall of Rājendra's temple at Gangaikondacolapuram (*c.* 1020–30), and similar statues modelled on this are found on the *gopuras* at Cidambaram, the three earlier of which were completed around the time of Umāpati's birth.

This is how our poet gives the story.

A Brahman's lad, tending a herd of cows
pastured on the bank of a river, used their milk
to anoint a *liṅga* made of earth and so please Him.

He was meditating on it
when his worship was interrupted by his father.

In his anger he cut off his father's leg
and continued his worship of Him.

He became the chief of His attendants.
. . . (145)[5]

Annoyed at the use made of the milk, the father, according to Cēkkiḻār, kicks over the bowl. His son picks up his cowherd's stick to punish this interruption of worship, but by the power of Śiva the stick becomes an axe, and we have, in Shulman's words, 'the standard conjunction of blood and milk'.[6] The violent power of *bhakti* is shown to be all-conquering, subverting social norms without a qualm. It is immediately rewarded. In contrast to the fierce anger shown by the devotee, the iconography of Śiva blessing Caṇḍeśvara, winding a garland as a crown on the young man's head, is perhaps the most benign of all the God's images. Alone of the Nāyaṉārs Caṇḍeśvara receives a niche of his own on the outside of the *garbhagṛha*.

Amongst the remaining Nāyaṉārs, Kaṇṇappār is probably the most famous. Later representations show him with his foot raised against a *liṅga*, but he is not kicking it as did Caṇḍeśvara's father in the earlier version of Ñāṉacampantar.[7] He is marking the place of the *liṅga*'s damaged eye, so that when he removes his own remaining eye – having already given one of his eyes to the *liṅga* – he can insert it correctly.

Once a certain hunter
on a mighty mountain
where the woods were thick with animals
beheld His lordly *liṅga*

and performed *pūjā* to it
with mouthfuls of water,
the flowers he carried in his hair,
and the remains of meat he'd eaten.

In his intense devotion
he placed his own excellent eye
as a substitute for His eye.

He went to heaven.
. . . (144)[8]

The sacrifice of the second eye is not demanded. Before Kaṇṇappār completely blinds himself an arm comes out from the *liṅga* and grasps Kaṇṇappār's arm. Umāpati does not mention the attempted sacrifice of the second eye. For the Hindu the sacrifice of the eye is scarcely more horrible than the ostensible pollution of the *liṅga* by the saliva of the hunter. Neither seeming enormity is of any consequence in the face of love for Śiva.

Another notable Nāyaṉār, the second individual in the traditional list, is Iyaṟpakai, 'who never said no'. His name signifies 'Enemy of Nature', and indeed that could be an epithet for several of the Nāyaṉārs.

At the time of entering into battle
with his family who were furious
at him giving his wife away,
all his slender body trembling with apprehension,
he was bathed in tears of joy when
he saw Him looking pleased,

Him on Whose feet he meditated and
he, son of a Vaiśya, excellent devotee that he was,
his manifest wealth being the splendour of meditation on His foot,

he was mounted upon Nandin, the lord of bulls,
and went to the Silver Mountain –
. . . (214)[9]

Note that it is the body of the Nāyaṉār that trembles, not that of his compliant wife. The Śiva ascetic who asks for the wife is at once given what he asks, for all Śiva ascetics are Śiva himself; fortunately that is indeed the case here.

Midway between the verse on Caṇḍeśvara and that on Iyaṟpakai Umāpati refers to Cōmācimāṟar:

When Lord Śiva along with His *gaṇas*
disguised His true form and entered
the sacrificial enclosure of a Brahman called Māra,

alerted by Heramba, the man
with great devotion and delight
willingly gave into His lotus hand

the heap of oblation in the pressing
of Soma sacrifice called Jyotiṣṭhoma, 'Hymn of Light'.

Through this sacrifice he went to Śiva's city.
. . . (170)[10]

This Nāyaṉār receives only five verses from Cēkkiḻār, and in the *Periya Purāṇam* there is no reference to the appearance of Śiva as an outcaste; but the legend continued to develop, and is found, for example, in the *Agastyabhaktavilāsa*, with the difference that it is Cuntarar (Sundara), not Gaṇeśa, who alerts the sacrificer to the true nature of the intruder. Śiva enters the sacrificial ground as a drunken Caṇḍāla outcaste, a dead calf on his shoulder, accompanied by four dogs and Pārvatī and his two sons, likewise Caṇḍālas. Pārvatī too is drunk, and offers the Brahmans present a drink from the pot of alcohol she carries on her head. Only Māra, who had previously requested the presence of Śiva in any form whatsoever, does not flee in the face of this intrusion, and gives the oblation to the outcaste who is God.

Six verses later, the Vedic status of Cidambaram is most powerfully affirmed:

> In every *kalpa* the Vedas,
> to lose their fear of birth in the first half
> and of destruction in the second half
>
> satisfy the Death of Death with manifold asceticism
> and at His command
> become three thousand Brahmans –
> a state unobtainable by the gods themselves,
>
> and in due order constantly worship Him
> according to the procedures of His path.
> . . . (176)[11]

These three thousand are praised in the first chapter in *Periya Purāṇam* after the account of Cuntarar's life; Cuntarar's own hymn to the saints begins,

> I serve the servants of the Brahmans living in Tillai.[12]

and this is quoted by Cēkkiḻār.

The last Nāyaṉār to be mentioned in *Kuñcitāṅghristava* is the first individual saint to be named in the *Periya Purāṇam*, and the only one other than the Dīkṣitas who hails from Cidambaram, namely Nīlakaṇṭha. The 'sages' (*munis*) referred to in the following verse are the Dīkṣitas.

> This jewel in the ocean of the family of makers of pots,
> called Nīlakaṇṭha, seeing Him constantly,
>
> to maintain his good faith with the king among yogis –
> on the unanimous advice of the sages –
> he and his wife each holding the end of the stick
> entered into the water as an ordeal.
>
> He regained his youth thanks to His grace.
> Him Who is not great, Who is not small,
> . . . (298)[13]

Is there a touch of humour in the grandiose phrase 'jewel in the ocean of the family of makers of pots'? Or perhaps Umāpati was influenced in his choice of phrase by the size of the tank the couple entered? The tank as it exists today, before the Iḷamaiyākkiṉār temple, half a kilometre to the west of the Naṭarāja temple, is vast, almost as large as the Śivagaṅgā itself. An old stone panel set in the wall of the tank entrance portrays the scene. The story is as follows. Nīlakaṇṭha, though pious, and always giving free alms bowls to the devotees of the Dancer in the Hall,

> on account of the sap of youth coursing through his veins,
> he made a fool of himself
> in the region of sensual pleasures. (*Periya Purāṇam* 362–3)[14]

Because he has visited a prostitute, his wife refuses to touch him and he too swears not to touch her. They live without sexual contact for many years. At last, in their old age, Śiva appears in the form of a wandering yogin, king among yogins, to resolve the conflict. He leaves a bowl in the potter's safe-keeping, but when he returns it cannot be found. To prove that he has not stolen the bowl, the potter is asked by the yogin to immerse himself in the tank, holding his wife's hand, and again affirm his innocence. The potter's vow makes this impossible. The Śiva yogin takes him before the Dīkṣitas, who declare that he must do as asked to prove his innocence. Going back to his house, he does as asked, with the expedient of a stick between his hand and his wife's. When they come out of the water, their youth has returned, and they are bathed in a shower of flowers from heaven.

The initial fault of the husband becomes mere bad luck in the version of the *Hemasabhānātha Māhātmya* (which includes the stories of just two Nāyaṉārs, Nīlakaṇṭha, and Nandana): he is returning from the temple at night when there is heavy rain. He shelters outside a prostitute's house when the maid throws betel juice water (from a spittoon?) out of the window. Wet through, shaking his head, confused, he is seen by the prostitute. Full of apologies, she has him thoroughly soaped and scented. Thus sent home, his wife refuses to listen to his explanation.

Umāpati is restrained in his references to doctrine and philosophy, but one verse sets out the four categories of salvation according to Śaiva Siddhānta: *sālokyaṃ, sāmīpyam, sārūpyaṃ, sāyujyaṃ*:

> The sixty-three devotees of the Brahman and other castes
> by their particular forms of worship of Him
> attained assimilation to Him;
>
> and by frequently reciting His names
> the perfect power of attaining His presence;

by keeping in the company of devotees
and talking only with them
His world;

by meditation
peerless union with Him.
. . .
(292)[15]

As Schomerus notes, the legends of the Nāyaṉārs are a kind of folk theology[16] and at first sight Umāpati seems to be attempting an improbably formal classification of disparate and even wild phenomena; but in fact he is surely saying only that they exemplify all the categories of salvation. In keeping with *kāvya*'s delight in random order, these categories are not in order of merit; that order is clearly set out by Umāpati in his *Civapirakācam*: Those who understand the truth of the three eternal entities (*paśu, pāśa, pati*) when their guru explains it to them, their ears and other organs inclining to the instruction, just as water tends to the valley below, will enjoy *sālokya* when they die. Those who understand, and continually reflect upon, *paśu, pāśa, pati* graciously made known by the guru will enjoy *sāmīpya* when they die. Those have *pāśa* removed by the power of grace (*jñānaśakti*, or *aruḷ*), join with that grace and after death enjoy *sārūpya.*

In the final stage the self is filled with joy, has the power of intuitively apprehending all things, without the necessity of discriminating individuals, and is absorbed in union with God – this is *sāyujya, paramokṣa,* final liberation.[17]

In addition to the Nāyaṉārs, other famous humans are mentioned. There are the well-known figures whose stories are told in the *Mahābhārata*, Hariścandra and Sāvitrī; lesser-known figures from such texts as that fascinating story book, the *Brahmottara Kāṇḍa* of the *Skanda Purāṇa*; and other figures from unknown sources. One story is strikingly similar to those of the Nāyaṉārs:

A certain Brahman called Riṭa,
when he cremated his good wife –

so good she was ever trembling
in fear of disobeying
the restrictions her husband imposed –

he used the ashes from her pyre
to smear the image of Śiva and the Mother
Wishing to make the offering of food he called to his wife,

'Bring the pot here,' and by His grace
his wife was again at his disposal.

At his own death he enjoyed the place of Śiva.
. . . (155)[18]

A similar story is to be found in the *Brahmottara Kāṇḍa*, though in that text there is a touch of humour, mocking an ignorant tribal person – here a Brahman – and most significantly there the wife volunteers to burn herself to provide the ashes, while here the husband seems to take the initiative, in Nāyaṉār fashion.[19]

The natural order is again opposed by Tirumūlar, though his literary stature makes violence unnecessary:

The blessed primal Siddha, Holy Mūla by name,
maintaining his body underground for a Kalpa,
was hidden beneath an anthill,

being in *samādhi*,
in the state of supreme bliss
that arises from seedless yoga;

his deeds praised by the king,
his knowledge ever free from constraint,
he meditates constantly within himself upon Him.
. . . (185)[20]

The king who discovers the long-hidden sage praises his deeds. Tirumūlar, a Śivayogin from Mount Kailāsa came south to meet Agastya but *en route*, finding a dead cowherd beside his distressed charges, left aside his own body to resuscitate and carry out the duties of the cowherd. Subsequently he was unable to find his own body again, and realizing that Śiva wanted him to set out the truths of the Sanskrit Āgamas in Tamil, he meditated for 3,000 years, composing a verse every year.

Let us now consider the Nāyaṉārs in relation to the poem as a whole. Apart from a reference in verse 43 to the four great poets, the Nālvar (Appar, Tiruñāṉacampantar, Cuntarar, and Māṇikkavācakar), the references to the Nāyaṉārs cluster around the centre of the poem (144, 145, 155 the Nāyaṉār-like Riṭa, 170, 185) and at the end (281, 292, 298). These clusters must be seen in relation to the dynamic of the poem as a whole. The poem begins with the esoteric diagram of the Sammelanacakra and the Cit Sabhā, describes the Cidambaram temple in detail, with its *sthalapurāṇa* and rituals (1–26) and thereafter it opens out to wider and wider spheres of reference, though every verse concludes with worship of Śiva's upraised foot. In the final verses the poet himself speaks (300, 302,

303, 304, 305, 312, 313 and two further verses), so that there is a clear overall movement from the very highest significance of Naṭarāja in the Cit Sabhā described in detail at the beginning, to the poet himself at the end. The Nāyaṉārs come in the centre, and at the end, leading up to the poet himself. Most of the verses of the poem deal with worshippers of Śiva, Gods, heroes and sages for the most part from pan-Indian texts, in seemingly random order. The positioning of the Tamil saints is clearly coherent. They have a central place, for they have a central role in the literature of Tamil Śaivism, and a final place through linkage with the humanity of the poet himself. What seems to be the random logic of the poem has, it transpires, structural significance. It is vital for the proper appreciation of Sanskrit *kāvya* that detailed consideration be given to such questions.

Finally, the poet himself may be contrasted with the Nāyaṉārs. Cuntarar in his *Tiruttoṇṭattokai* declares himself the servant of each of the Nāyaṉārs, and says in verse 10 'I am the servant of all who serve as *bhaktas*'; Umāpati's perspective is quite different. The Nāyaṉārs are just one of the groups that as poet he marshals according to his whim, and all of which are effectively on a level before Śiva's upraised foot. In his commentary to his *Śataratnasaṃgraha*, Umāpati calls himself *paramakāruṇika*, 'supremely compassionate', in respect of his pupils.[21] Signally lacking in the stories of the Nāyaṉārs is the traditional relationship of guru and pupil, for that relationship is part of the natural order to which the saints are inimical.

Miraculous events occur in the life of Umāpati, most notably the fiery Śaktinipāta, (descent of divine Grace) he gave to the wood-cutter Sūta; and when the king came to investigate Sūta's demise, Umāpati sent up a bush in flames, to reveal a yogin within who had been waiting for release. In verse 305 Umāpati does not hesitate to mention his own magic powers though he properly acknowledges Śiva.

> Śambhu, Lord of the Dance, has given me success
> through great mantras of enormous power;
> great magic powers through yoga;
>
> and the great enlightenment of the self
> that removes birth and death;
> and the rank of guru – confirmed in writing[22] –
> to give release to Sūta and others;
>
> He has shown me His dance,
> He has given me exceeding delight.
> . . . (305)[23]

The Nāyaṉārs belonged to the past, and their ranks formed a sacred number. But Umāpati was himself one of the holy three thousand, the Dīkṣitas, who head the list of Nāyaṉārs. Certainly he was acutely aware of holiness of the saints, and he includes an excellently chosen selection of these saints effectively placed within his wide-ranging poem. Just as the varied histories of the saints are summed up in the line of their images in the temple, and each saint is an image of standard basic proportions, so too each *sragdharā* verse encapsulates a saint or other figure, with a widely heterogeneous series of events reduced to the standard number of syllables. The necklace of Sanskrit verses subordinates the Nāyaṉārs, like all else, to Śiva's raised foot; their iron will inimical to nature, yet they become so many pearls.

Few of the Nāyaṉārs are directly involved with dancing Śiva, a sign of their antiquity. But their stories remained a living presence within the temple. All but one, the early poetess Kāraikāl Ammaiyār, are men. Umāpati does not refer to her, and she does not appear anywhere in the art of the temple, although she is prominent beneath the Naṭarāja sculpture at Gangaikondacolapuram. The presence of Kālī in Cidambaram may have been perceived as leaving no scope or no need for the wildness of the female saint.[24] Umāpati refers, as we have seen, to two instances of the total submission of women. Women are given away or burnt, and this is typical of the general spirit of the stories of the saints. Nīlakaṇṭha's discomfiture by his wife is an exceptional story in the series.

Most worshippers of Naṭarāja cannot but be aware of Kāraikāl Ammaiyār. Umāpati quotes one verse from her *Arputa Tiruvantāti* in his *Caṅkarpa Nirākaraṇam*:

> He knows. He makes known. He is knowledge
> which knows. He is truth, object of knowledge.
> The blazing fire, earth, space,
> all that, is He.[25]

A typical verse by this poetess is the following:

> This is my greatest desire: without fail,
> one day you'll show yourself to us,
> My Father with locks twisted like the flames of a lighted fire,
> the place where you dance, in full night,
> over the high flames.[26]

Sometimes even mistaken for Kālī, her skeletal form is usually shown seated cross-legged and shaking castanets; she is also shown, as at Darasuram, walking on her hands up the Silver Mountain to see Śiva, following her biography in the *Periya Purāṇam.* Abandoned by her husband despite her beauty on account of fear of the power Śiva gave her to produce a melon out of thin air, she long searches for him only to find him remarried with a daughter named after her. Her husband wants to worship her feet – her response is to fix her mind on Śiva's ankleted feet, and to pray to be reduced to a skeleton, and companion of Śiva's demons. She then sings her poem *Arputa Tiruvantāti*, which includes the verse, 'I've become one of the faithful choirs, hosts who adore the superb lotus feet [of Śiva]'. Inspiring fear in all who saw her, she travelled north to the Silver Mountain. When she reaches Śiva's Mount Kailāsa, she dare not touch it with her feet, and ascends it 'by her head'. Reaching Śiva at the top she falls at his feet, only to be addressed by him as 'Mother'. She hails him as father, and prays to be ever beneath his feet, singing his praises where he dances. He tells her she may ever witness his great dance in Tiruvalangadu, and ever sing its praises there, companion to his *gaṇa*s. She goes all the way back to the South travelling on her head, and dwells in Tiruvalangadu, constantly beneath his pink feet.

DANCING GIRLS AND THE *GAṆAS*

Kāraikāl Ammaiyār does not dance. Kālī did, in her attempt to defeat Śiva. Apart from Śiva it is women who are dancers.[27] Male dancers are the teachers of dancing girls, whose presence must have been very noticeable in temples. It is difficult to say how many there were in Cidambaram. The 400 dancers who were called to Tanjavur at the founding of the great temple there by Rājarājeśvara were an exceptionally large number. Their presence in stone in Cidambaram, however, is overwhelming. In the first place a large portion of the inner walls of the entrance of each *gopura* displays from top to bottom the whole range of more than a hundred dance poses defined in the ancient canonical work on dance, the *Nāṭya Śāstra.* A dancing girl performs in each of the panels. As one enters into the temple, one enters into a world of dance, and a world of dancing girls. Extensive sets of dance sculptures are found also round the plinth of the Thousand-pillared Hall, and the base of the colonnade of the Śivakāmasundarī shrine. Here there is no didactic purpose, and there is no evident sequence in the dance poses presented; merely a joyous affirmation of dancing girls and musicians, each dancer being flanked by musicians. Small dancing figures are found on the pillars of the Nṛtta Sabhā, and in that Sabhā there was space for one dancer to perform.

On the Nṛtta Sabhā, and elsewhere in the temple, a dancer is shown raising her leg above her head.[28] There is a piquancy in her doing this on the Nṛtta Sabhā, where Śiva is said to have defeated Kālī by that very action. Marco Polo, a contemporary of Umāpati, describes that very pose being performed in Tamilnadu (Ma'abar):

they begin to sing, dance, leap, tumble, and make different entertainments to move the god and goddess to joy and to reconcile them, and thus they say as they make entertainment, O Master, why are you vexed with the goddess and do not care for her? Is she not beautiful, is she not pleasing? May you thus truly be pleased to be reconciled together and take pleasure with her, for truly she is very pleasant. And then she who has said so will lift her leg above her neck and will spin round for the pleasure of the god and goddess.[29]

All around the golden walls of His Hall
unparalleled heavenly nymphs
to please Him carry in their lotus hands

mirrors and all the eightfold auspicious objects
made of gold and precious stones,

and perform His worship.
. . . (291)[30]

Umāpati also refers to them as singing:

His stage filled with all the hosts of heavenly nymphs
moving hither and thither,
eager for singing the beginning
of the praising with the seven notes,
sa ri ga ma pa dha nī
. . . (252)

Umāpati is speaking of dancing girls here, though he does not mention dance as such. Gros remarks in his introduction to the *Tēvāram*, 'The musical and choreographic environment of the temple . . . has its archetype in the troupes of *gaṇa* musicians and in the celestial dancers.'[31] But the *gaṇas* are not only musicians but also dancers themselves. They as well as Śiva are exemplars of masculine dance. In sculpture they no less than the dancing girls form a *corps de ballet*.

Dhaky observes,

In gay gambolling parties these *gaṇa* goblins are found in various, though definite, situations in the fabric of sacred buildings. From weird and impish, bizarre and demonic to peaceful, serene, sublime, these dancing, music-making, frolicking and fighting genii of Śambhu . . . frequently are the liveliest creations in the minor figural art of India from the fifth to the tenth centuries.[32]
. . .

While in northern India the depiction of *gaṇas* or *pramathas* decreased after the eighth century – indeed they are rarely encountered after the tenth century – the temple sculptors in Tamil̲nāḍu continued to carve them until at least the end of the thirteenth century with undiminished vigor.[33]

Theologically, the *gaṇa*s, and more so their leaders, the *gaṇa*-lords, have a serious role to play, and Umāpati states it:

> He, independent,
> creating the hosts of Rudras and *gaṇa*-lords
> their excellent bodies deformed,
> sent them forth to protect the world,
>
> He Who is without end,
> has always protected the world and the universe beyond;
> Him, Who gives happiness to those who bow down to Him
> . . . (228)[34]

Dhaky describes them from the point of view of an art historian, an Indological art historian:

> In their kinds and functions these *bhūta* entities cover the entire range of Nature and her inherent, as well as cohering forces. From the dark powers of the underworlds, through the brown and green forces of the earth's skin (*tvac*), from the transparent phantoms and spirits of the intermediate and astral regions to the Shining Ones of the celestial quarters, every conceivable minor and major force of the Dynamic Reality, in its apparent and penultimate functional divisions, is represented by Śiva's troupe of elementals.[35]

As Umāpati says in the verse quoted above, they are deformed, though excellent in that deformity. They are human in appearance, though sometimes with animal heads. Short and round in shape, they are pot-bellied and lacking necks. They have two arms. Their poses are often contorted. Umāpati mentions them as the companions of Nandin, under whose direction they attend on Śiva.

Whereas in Pallava and Cāḷukya art they tend to be atlantides, at ground level supporting the weight of temples, for the Cōl̲as they float upwards, and are often found high on walls and under eaves. Kramrisch stresses their inherent lightness:

> The inward realisation of lightness, weightlessness, non-existence of the physical body in a state of concentration on the Supreme Spirit and on His manifestation, the Word, and the hearing of its music are shown in the images of the Gaṇas who, while resembling the shape of man, are unlike. Their bodies made of breath move in the air.[36]

In the story of the Nāyan̲ār Cōmācimār̲ar mentioned above, Śiva bursts onto the sacrificial ground with his *gaṇa*s. These companions of Śiva are prominent in sculpture and mythology. Umāpati mentions

30. Kālī, Apasmāra, Kāraikāl Ammaiyār and *gaṇas*. Bṛhadīśvara temple, Gangaikondacolapuram, *c.* 1025.

them several times as under Nandin's command, dwelling at the foot of Mount Kailāsa. The musicians who accompany his dance are *gaṇas*. At the same time they are natural forces, accommodated within the Siddhānta scheme of creation.

In their most important appearance for us, at the time of Śiva's first performance of the Ānanda Tāṇḍava, it is their childlike quality that is most apparent; along with their ability to join in with Śiva rather than merely watch:

> Praising Him, the gods surrounded the Great Lord,
> heaping handfuls of beautiful flowers before Him,
> crushing some with the tips of their crowns as they bowed at His feet.
>
> Nārada and other skilled musicians, their hands adorned with *vīṇās*,
> stood stock-still, not singing, not knowing what to do.
>
> Then all His *bhūtas* there in front of Him performed
> a weird and wonderful dance at speed.
>
> All the *gaṇas*, overexcited,
> performed all sorts of dance routines,
> falling down and getting up over and over.
>
> (*Cidambara Māhātmya* 13. 63–6)

APASMĀRA

Kāraikāl Ammaiyār, the Mother, becomes the companion of Śiva's hosts, the multiple *gaṇas*, and she is vividly shown in a marvellous panel beneath Naṭarāja at Gangaikondacolapuram (twelfth century). What is also interesting in this panel, in the present context, is not the presence of Kālī near Śiva's feet, but the conjunction of the *gaṇas* with Apasmāra. The similarity of the *gaṇas* and the 'demon' is, I think, apparent.

Let us look again at what the *Cidambara Māhātmya* has to say about Apasmāra:

> There arose a Creature (*bhūta*) –
> as if the darkness that previously had been swallowed
> by those blazing fires was vomited forth again
> by them in a compact lump.
>
> Its hair was tawny with the flames
> from the hot coals that were its eyes.
> It had the body of a dwarf,
> a great mouth with long tusks,
> and its arms moved frenetically (*lasadbhujam*).

Massed ranks of snakes attended it.
Casting fear aside it hurtled at Śaṅkara.

The Great Lord was about to begin His dance
but, when He saw it, joyfully
crushed it with His lotus foot
and made it there a foot rest. (*Cidambara Māhātmya* 13. 29–33)

Then Śiva dances.

As if He wanted to trample to death that Creature (*bhūta*)
which looked like the agglomeration of their sins,
He stood with one foot on it.

To destroy the sins they had accumulated
in life after life, He showed
that auspicious foot that was slightly curved.
(*Cidambara Māhātmya* 13. 58–9)

Throughout the description of Apasmāra, he is referred to as a *bhūta*, exactly the same word that is applied to the *gaṇa*s. It is true that his eyes are flaming, and he probably has multiple arms, but these characteristics are also found among *gaṇa*s. In verse 150 Umāpati described how Śiva danced to the sound of

the drums
rapidly struck
by the bristling throng of arms
of the excellent *gaṇa*s
such as Bāṇa the Daitya.

Umāpati himself mentions Apasmāra only once:

He bears the fire and the drum in two hands.
The other two hands
make the 'swinging' and the 'fear not' gestures.

Placing His right foot ever on Apasmāra,
with His left foot slightly bending
He ever gives everything to those who bow down –
. . . (108)

Noting that Apasmāra is made into Śiva's foot-rest, let us leave him for the moment and consider the forest sages.

Then those sages who in their delusion
had sent fires and mantras, exhausted,
were briefly filled with alarm,
feeling themselves weaponless.
. . .

Then in a flash with the great speed of His Tāṇḍava
they lost consciousness and fell down on the ground.

. . .

Then to Pārvatī the Lord said,
'Drink the *rasa* of this Tāṇḍava'
and Nandikeśvara He commanded,
'O bull, enjoy!'

And then all those sage-bulls who had been stupefied
were humble and said 'O Śiva! O Śaṅkara! O God!'

They said, 'Glory to Umā's Husband,
to the Moon-crested God, to Śambhu!'
He gave them the eye of wisdom
so that they could see the Tāṇḍava.

Then Śambhu was splendid in the dance,
His eyes dancing with compassion,
purifying the forest with the lustre of His gentle smile.

Through the compassion of the God of Gods,
those ascetics saw the festival for the eyes
that is the divine Tāṇḍava Dance of Supreme Bliss.

When they had seen the supreme dance of Śambhu
they were filled with joy and wonder.
Taking their water-pots and staffs
and holding them aloft,

thrilled to the depths of their being,
possessed by the *rasa* of Śiva's bliss,
they danced, reddening the forest
with the shaking of their matted locks.

(*Cidambara Māhātmya* 13. 38–9; 54–7; 60–2)

The sages are stupefied by Śiva's dance (*Cidambara Māhātmya* 13. 55), they are given 'the eye of wisdom' (*Cidambara Māhātmya* 13. 56), and 'possessed by the *rasa* of Śiva's bliss' they dance. The word for 'possessed' is the standard term used for being possessed by a spirit. Other references to possession in relation to Śiva's performance of the Ānanda Tāṇḍava were noticed in chapter 3. When King Hiraṇyavarman had moved his court to Cidambaram and watched Naṭarāja dance, he lost his power of speech, sight, movement. 'His heart lost its power. He fainted, overwhelmed by his emotion (*rasa*).' And in a rare variation from its source, the *Kōyil Purāṇam* describes the priests themselves first falling to the ground and then dancing. It is very surprising for the priests to dance. It is also interesting that they fall to the ground before dancing – is this not an inversion of the more likely sequence of events?[37]

In discussing Apasmāra as found in bronze sculpture, I suggested that he was originally merely a supporting figure, a mere pedestal, such as supported a variety of other figures. One of the earliest of such appearances was beneath standing women on the Mathurā *stūpa* railing, where crouching creatures indistinguishable from Apasmāras are clearly not being crushed by Śiva.

The word *apasmāra* means not 'evil', but 'forgetfulness', and also 'epilepsy':

> The *apasmāra-puruṣa* was . . . sent against Śiva. *Smṛ* is to remember; *apasmāra* is the forgetful epileptic fit. The man in an epileptic fit perhaps must have been expected to effect murder much more easily and with supernatural forces. The Tamil name for the epileptic fit is *muyal vali* because the patient breathes like the hare whilst following a scent; it is also called *muyalakaṉ* as is made clear by the *Periyapurāṇam*.[38] Therefore the *apasmāra-puruṣa* is known in Tamil as *Muyalakaṉ* of which the colloquial form is *musalakaṉ* as found in Tanjavur Temple inscription. The unconscious epileptic demon has to be under control with great force and the Lord presses him down under His feet. The Tamil term *muyalakaṉ* occurs for the first time in Ārūrar [another name for Cuntarar] and that only once [7.2.3] where he describes Śiva as the Lord of the burning ground. He calls the Muyalakaṉ *Mūṭāya muyalakaṉ*, the idiotic epileptic.[39]

Here is the verse, in Shulman's translation:

> Foolish Muyalakaṉ,
> raging serpents,
> demons swarming around
> a stinking skull,
> howling ghosts,
> a tiger's skin,
> goblins ignorant
> of what is right,
> richly flowering *konṟai*,
> thick *erukku* blossoms,
> the serpent with its great jewel
> bound to your waist:
> how wild
> are your deeds,
> great lord,
>
> Master! We are afraid
> to serve you.[40]

The reference to Muyalakaṉ is far from explicit. Note also the terms in which Śiva's *gaṇas* are referred to: 'howling ghosts', 'goblins ignorant of what is right'.

More significant, perhaps, is the other reference in the *Tēvāram* to Apasmāra:

> He wears a crown of matted hair,
> bears the waxing moon and the winding snake
> on his head.
> He wears the ringing anklet
> and the sounding hero's band on his legs,
> he cast defiant *muyalakan̲* under his foot.
> In his right hand he bears the sharp battle-axe
> and holds Māl in loving embrace
> in the left half of his frame.
> He carries a bundle of bones on his shoulder,
> and the *tuṭi* drum in his hand.
> He cured my painful disease and took possession of me.[41]

Dancing Śiva in the *Tēvāram* is wild and dangerous. Apasmāra is mentioned only a couple of times in the *Tēvāram*, but another demon, of the very greatest fame, Rāvaṇa, who steals Sītā and is killed by Rāma in the *Rāmāyaṇa*, is referred to very many times as being crushed beneath Śiva's foot. At the end of the *Rāmāyaṇa* it is mentioned as an earlier event that Rāvaṇa tried to uproot Mount Kailāsa when he found his passage in his aerial car impeded by it. His arrogant attempt at dislodging the divine court is stopped by Śiva pressing down his toe and crushing the demon. Rāvaṇa then sings Śiva's praise and becomes a devotee. Tiruñān̲a Campantar and Appar refer to the incident in each one of their hundreds of hymns. Cuntarar refers to it frequently.[42] The massive presence of the crushing of Rāvaṇa, I believe, may well have led to the view that Apasmāra, originally a supporting figure, was also crushed by Śiva, and that part of the Cidambaram myth invented to incorporate it.

In tandem with that possible explanation is the appropriateness of a figure sprawling on the ground in the context of dance. Dance in India, perhaps especially in South India, is both the sophisticated dance of the court and temple, with its extensive textuality, and the dance of possession, with its loss of control and of consciousness. The Ānanda Tāṇḍava, by incorporating Apasmāra, refers to both forms of dance. In the logic of the development of the image, the great virtue of Apasmāra is that he removes from Śiva all the lower aspects of dance, the random movement of limbs, the twitching, the loss of control, and expresses them in himself.[43] The refinement and purity of Naṭarāja is all the greater because of Apasmāra. Whereas with Kāraikāl Ammaiyār and the writers of the *Tēvāram*, Śiva when he dances in the burning ground is often little more than a very special goblin or ghost, a goblin among goblins, the artistry of the bronze elevates him to a position of superlative mastery and balance. There is beneath Naṭarāja and subsumed within the Naṭarāja bronze a whole subterranean world of human experience that is omitted from the discourse of *ānandatāṇḍava*.

CHAPTER 10

Last words

A. K. Coomaraswamy concludes his essay, 'The Dance of Śiva', with these words:

It is not strange that the figure of Naṭarāja has commanded the adoration of so many generations past: familiar with all scepticisms, expert in tracing all beliefs to primitive superstitions, explorers of the infinitely great and infinitely small, we are worshippers of Naṭarāja still.[1]

Coomaraswamy's essay was first addressed to the Hindu readership of the Madras journal *Siddhānta Dīpikā,* but when included in the volume of essays given the same title, its audience became the educated citizens of the world. Coomaraswamy and his readers are knowledgeable in the history of religion and in modern science, and Naṭarāja pertains both to the distant past and to the present. The range of abilities Coomaraswamy here credits to modernity might be seen as paralleled in scope by those Umāpati asserts for the Dīkṣitas and himself amongst them.

He is worshipped
by the three thousand sages in the Sabhā –
Patañjalis in the science of grammar,

so many venerable Kaṇādas and Akṣapādas
in the discourses of logic,
embodiments of Vyāsa in the Vedānta,

the equals of Kumārilabhaṭṭa in Jaimini's Mīmāṃsā,
Bodhāyanas in the techniques of Vedic sacrifice,
veritable Brahmās in the Vedas –
. . . (89)

Umāpati refers here to the mainstream intellectual preoccupations of classical India. For both writers, Naṭarāja is a synthesizing image, an image that encourages synthesis.

For the purposes of this book, Umāpati's poem has been seen to contain a kind of essay on the Dance of Śiva. How did Umāpati himself see his poem?

UMĀPATI'S ORIGINALITY

In the introduction to his most important work, the *Civapirakācam*, Umāpati does not hesitate in laying claim to a pioneering boldness. In verse 11 of that work while worshipping the feet of his predecessors Meykaṇṭar and Aruḷnanti, he collates them not only with the Śaivāgamas but also 'with what was revealed by holy grace in my mind'. He continues in verse 12:

Whatever is old cannot be deemed to be good [on account of its antiquity alone] and whatever book comes forth today cannot be judged ill because of its newness. Men pledged to seek good in everything will not mind the dust that covers a beautiful gem but only appreciate its true worth. People of middle calibre will investigate and welcome the beauty and antiquity of a work. Men who have no capacity to judge of the faults, excellences and substantial work of a production will praise it, if many admire it, and will in the same breath condemn it on hearing others speak ill of it, because they have no opinion for themselves.[2]

This is reminiscent of the well-known words of the Director in Kālidāsa's play *Mālavikāgnimitra*:

Not every old text is excellent
nor is every new poem to be censured.
The wise make their selection
only after careful examination.
The mind of a fool
follows the opinion of others. (*Mālavikāgnimitra* Prologue)[3]

Umāpati makes no claim for the originality of the *Kuñcitāṅghristava*.

UMĀPATI'S LITERARY PERSPECTIVE

Umāpati had a keenly developed literary sense. His *Tiruvaruṭpayaṉ* has been seen as an attempt to complete the highly venerated *Tirukkuṟaḷ*, written in the same metre and style, and treating of *mokṣa*, the fourth and final goal left unnoticed by Tiruvaḷḷuvar. Umāpati calls Tiruvaḷḷuvar 'the divine poet' in the *Neñcuviṭutūtu*.[4] In his *Caṅkaṟpa Nirākaraṇam* he refers to specific Tamil verses from the poets of the *Tēvāram*, and also Kāraikāl Ammaiyār. He had an intimate knowledge of the *Tēvāram*, manifested by his compilation of an anthology, and his listing of the places referred to by the *Tēvāram* poets. He wrote an account of the discovery of the *Tēvāram* hymns in Cidambaram. He summarized the lives of the sixty-three saints, and wrote a life of Cēkkiḻār, author of the *Periya Purāṇam*.

In the *Kuñcitāṅghristava*, there are several references to poets, Tamil and Sanskrit. Umāpati's work is a *stotra*, a hymn of praise. This is a genre of great importance in Sanskrit literature, and indeed in the history of Hinduism. Umāpati was well aware of this tradition. He refers to specific texts – including the *Mahimnastava* of Puṣpadanta, the *Vedapādastava* of Jaimini, and the poem in praise of Śiva attributed to the demon Rāvaṇa, worshipper of Śiva and enemy of the God Rāma. *Stotras* such as these are very much alive for Śaivas who know Sanskrit. A verse from Jaimini's hymn heads the programme for the Cidambaram festival in *mārkaḻi* (December) 1994.

Umāpati's references to the great Tamil poets, however, are more detailed, and more significant.

The opening verses of the *Kuñcitāṅghristava* are dedicated to the Cidambaram temple. A change is signalled in verse 27 which describes Śiva appearing in the *liṅga* of fire before Brahmā and Viṣṇu. This image commonly appears on the west outer wall of Cōḻa Śiva shrines, and thus suggests a departure from the innermost part of the poem. Verse 28 refers the poet Māṇikkavācakar, 'He whose words are rubies', whose story is included the Madurai cycle of Śiva *līlās*.[5] As soon as Umāpati has finished dealing with the temple of Cidambaram he turns to his most eminent predecessor: Māṇikkavācakar, who is still by many considered the greatest of Tamil poets. Later than the three poets of the *Tēvāram*, he belongs probably to the ninth or the tenth century; too late to be included in the list of the sixty-three saints, he is included with the *Tēvāram* poets in the group known as the Four, and is referred to as the sixty-fourth saint.[6] His image, holding the manuscript of his collected verses called the *Tiruvācakam*, is normally in front of the Naṭarāja bronze in Śiva temples. He is said to have ended his days in Cidambaram, and the *maṭha* near the Kālī temple he is supposed to have occupied has recently been renovated; what is said to have been the original manuscript is now in Pondicherry.

Verse 28 neatly resumes Māṇikkavācakar's history. This is worth giving, not just because Umāpati mentions it, but because of Māṇikkavācakar's admission into the standard Naṭarāja shrine. Śiva took the form of a guru and with his disciples sat beneath a Kunda tree (*trichilia spinosa*) at Tirupperuntuṟai. Vātavūrar, minister of Arimarttaṉa Pāṇṭiyaṉ, King of Madurai, sent with money to buy horses, meets the sage, who naturally looks like Dakṣiṇāmūrti, and who holds in his hand the *Civañāṉapōtam*. Vātavūrar is initiated, filled with wisdom, and begins to sing the glory of his guru. Śiva, delighted with his song, names him Māṇikkavācakar (Skt. Māṇikyavācaka), Māṇikkavācakar spends the money for the horses in honouring Śiva. Ordered to return, he is first spared royal displeasure by Śiva promising Himself to bring excellent horses to Madurai, and Śiva becomes a horseman and does so. The horses brought by Śiva turn into jackals. Māṇikkavācakar is severely punished, and prays to Śiva for help. Śiva causes the river Vaikai to flood. The king orders a barrage to be built to protect Madurai. Śiva enrols as a labourer, but fails to fill in his section of the barrage. The king, enraged, strikes him on the back with his cane. Śiva at last throws his load of earth in its proper place in the barrage and disappears. The king, his wives, his ministers, and the whole world besides all feel the blow on their backs. A voice from heaven explains all that has happened and Māṇikkavācakar departs for Cidambaram.[7]

> Once in the past He sat at the foot of a Kunda tree
> and taught true knowledge
> to Māṇikkavācakar whose words are rubies;
> and He became the horseman.
>
> Once He received a blow
> from the golden staff shining in the hand of the king.
>
> Then, satisfied by the songs he uttered,
> filled as they are with sweet emotion,
> He gave salvation to him.
> He is the Lord, a friend to all.
> . . . (28)[8]

'Sweet emotion' – Pope remarked in 1900, 'These poems [of Māṇikkavācakar] . . . are daily sung throughout the Tamil country with tears of rapture, and committed to memory in every Śaiva temple by the people, amongst whom it is a traditional saying, that "he whose heart is not melted by the *Tiruvācakam* must have a stone for a heart".'[9]

Umāpati shortly afterwards refers to all four of the great Śaiva poets, whose connection with the Cidambaram temple today is demonstrated by stucco statues in the entrance of each of the *gopuras*, each of the four being supposed to have entered by one of the *gopuras* – Campantar by the South, Appar (Tirunāvukkaracu, 'King of the Tongue') by the West, Cuntarar by the North, and Māṇikkavācakar by the East. There is also a shrine to the four poet-saints in the third enclosure.

> Campantar, Cuntarar, blessed Māṇikkavācakar
> whose words are rubies,
> and he who is called the King of the Tongue,
> with their own hymns of praise
> rich in varied emotion won salvation;
>
> all four praising Him, the Lord,
> as present in their own respective places
> though He is one, non-dual in form.

Him Who is the First,
Who has made the moon His crown,
Whose foot is bent,
I worship. (43)[10]

The sense of place features greatly in the religion of the South, and the Śaiva poets' experience was highly localized:

As the Śaivite saints travelled through the countryside, they sang the praises of the god and of the temples and shrines believed to be sacred to him. Each hymn is said to have been composed at a particular place, and either the name of that place or the name under which the god was worshipped there was usually mentioned in the text of the hymn.[11]

Māṇikkavācakar did not roam from place to place in the same way as the *Tēvāram* trio, nor did he exalt Bhikṣāṭana, the wandering form of Śiva. In both verses referring to the great Tamil poets, Umāpati mentions *rasa*. Māṇikkavācakar's poems are filled with 'sweet emotions' (*madhurasa*); the hymns of each of the four poets are 'rich in varied emotions'. *Rasa*, aesthetic emotion, the suggestion and creation of a sustained and pure emotion, or a series of such emotions, in the reader or audience, is a primary goal of Sanskrit poetry and drama.

In his *Tēvāra Aruḷmuṟaittiraṭṭu*, Umāpati compiled ninety-nine verses from the *Tēvāram* hymns under ten headings on the basis of the chapters given in his *Tiruvaruṭpayaṉ*.[12] Umāpati's deep knowledge of the *Tēvāram* is often to be sensed underlying the *Kuñcitāṅghristava*, as for instance in his verse 32:

Meru was Śambhu's bow.
And the Earth was His chariot.
His bow string was the Lord of Snakes.

Lotus-seated Brahmā was His charioteer,
present as His horses were the Vedas,
and as His quiver He had the ocean,

when He wished to destroy the Triple City.

Him, the cause of the creation,
destruction, and preservation of the world,
Whose foot is curved
I worship. (32)[13]

Tripurāntaka, a form of Śiva popular with the Cōḻas, is dominant in the imperial statement that is the Rājarājeśvara temple at Tanjavur. At Cidambaram it appears at the far right of the upper tier on the outer face of each of the *gopuras*. This verse is reminiscent of one from a poem of Cuntarar described as 'perhaps Cuntarar's most powerful expression of the emotional and metaphysical state of separation (*pirivu*, Skt. *viraha*)'.[14]

The mighty serpent was the bowstring,
the mountain the bow,
Agni the arrow's tip,
Hari the shaft,

when he drew back the bow
until it touched his breast
and set fire to the (Triple) City.

Fool that I am,
I failed to think of him
long ago;

why, then, do I bear this body,
why remain apart

from my lord of Ārūr?[15]

Another example shows Umāpati developing and going beyond a verse of the *Tēvāram* he quotes in his anthology – this time from Appar, built on the counting out of numbers:

The Lord is of dazzling form.
He is as one sound in *ākāśa*,
as two in air that blows abundantly,
as three in ruddy fire,
as four in water that flows,
as five in earth,
as the ever-abiding form that is our unfailing refuge,
as the tender shoot of the splendid coral creeper,
as the pearl, as the light that ever grows,
as the diamond, as the form of pure gold
He abides in Puḻḻirukku Vēḷūr.
I have wasted countless days without adoring Him.[16]

The numbers refer to the sensory qualities of the elements. *Ākāśa* has one, sound; air two, sound and touch; and so on to earth with all five.

As one He is Brahman
without a second,
but He is also threefold.
He comprises the four forms of speech.
The foe of five-arrowed Love,
He is praised by the foes of the six enemies.
The eye on His forehead has seven-tongued fire.
His crest is adorned with the one-eighth digit of the moon.
in His dance exemplifying the nine *rasa*s,
His clothes wave to the ten quarters.
And at His feet constantly bow the eleven Rudras
along with the twelve Ādityas.
. . . (182)[17]

The great difference between the Tamil verse and the Sanskrit is the constant personal note in the former. According to Tamil tradition, Śiva is supposed to say of the *Tēvāram* poets, 'My Appar sung of myself, Campantar sung of himself, Cuntarar sung of women.' This brings out the marked differences between the three, but from the Sanskrit perspective all three sing insistently of themselves, in addition to singing of Śiva. Yet, just as the two typical *Tēvāram* Tamil verses quoted here end on a personal note, so too does Umāpati's poem. Sanskrit poets often include a personal statement to round off their work, but in the final verses of the *Kuñcitāṅghristava*, Umāpati reproduces something of the fervour of the *Tēvāram*, a note made stronger by its oscillation between personal and impersonal.

THE CONCLUSION OF THE *KUÑCITĀṄGHRISTAVA*

The finale of the *Kuñcitāṅghristava* clearly begins at verse 300: People call out to Śiva, 'O Lord! I am drowning in *saṃsāra*.' Verse 301 is impersonal: the Vedas say Rudra is the supreme God. Verse 302 is personal only in the last line: my heart is aware of no God but Him. Verse 303 is personal, and reminiscent of the Tamil manner: shamelessly intent on filling my belly I flitted from place to place like a crow. Verse 304 defines the poem itself and says that Śiva accepts it. Verse 305 is personal and contains the important statement that Śiva confirmed in writing Umāpati's rank of *guru*, and empowered him to give release to Sūta, the wood-cutter.

From verse 306 to verse 313 there is a marked change in style, for in this last section three or all four lines of each verse begin with an emphatic repetition, usually of the verbal absolute in *am* (*ṇamul*). Thus verse 306 begins *krośaṃ krośaṃ* 'By wailing, by wailing' before Him, Rati got back her husband, Upamanyu got milk. This repetitive and vivid syntactic change tells us the end is coming. But at the same time, the subject-matter becomes impersonal, in the sense I have been using it – personal refers to Umāpati, impersonal to others; but where people in general are referred, as in the case of those who are drowning in *saṃsāra*, Umāpati is probably to be understood also. Note that this emphatic section begins on a highly emotional note, with the wailing of a widow and a baby boy crying for milk. Verse 307 is impersonal, with Śuka and other sages 'gently gently' worshipping the *liṅga* with Gaṅgā water. Verse 308 is very powerful. Speaking of the 'lordly wise', it very probably refers to the Dīkṣitas and Umāpati in their number. They 'enjoy, constantly enjoy' (*bhojaṃ bhojaṃ*) pleasure (*bhogam*) by worshipping Him; they 'cross, constantly cross' (*tāraṃ tāraṃ*) the ocean of *saṃsāra*; they 'burn up, constantly burn up' (*dāhaṃ dāhaṃ*) the three bonds; they 'utter, constantly utter' (*jāpaṃ jāpaṃ*) His mantra. Verse 309, impersonal in that it refers to the three great devotees of Cidambaram, Patañjali, Vyāghrapāda and Jaimini. They 'are aware, constantly aware' (*bodhaṃ bodhaṃ*) of His dance; they 'meditate, constantly meditate' (*dhyāyaṃ dhyāyaṃ*) on Him in the lotus of their hearts; they 'carry, constantly carry' His foot in their thoughts. These two verses begin each line with emphatic forms of virtually all the key religious verbs. The next two verses are in a similar vein, probably referring again to the Dīkṣitas and Umāpati as one of their number. Verse 312 is entirely personal: 'Bowing, constantly bowing to the compassionate Lord of Dancers I obtained a good wife and a handsome son.' So too is the final verse.

Śiva's foot plays a large part in the conclusion. In verse 300, human beings regret not worshipping Śiva's holy feet; not until verse 303 does he speak solely of himself in relation to the divine feet. Personal statements oscillate for a while with verses about the devotion of others. In verse 311 devout Śaivas end by mingling with Śiva's foot. In verse 313 Umāpati declares that he continually drank in the wine of the lotus of Śiva's foot in the assembly; and as an afterword he declares that those who read his verses will ultimately attain the holy foot, the foot that has been present throughout in the poem's refrain.

But let us return to *rasa*.

> His wide eyes are bees
> agitated by the river of sweet *rasa* –
> the wine of love – coming from the mountains
> that are the jutting breasts – golden pots –
> of Gaurī ever ready to play.
> . . . (149)[18]

The Tamil poets produce *rasa*; Śiva drinks *rasa* from Pārvatī, the 'Golden yellow lady' (Gaurī). He is himself the first *rasa*, that is to say, *śṛṅgāra*, the erotic *rasa* –

> Conquering the circle of rays
> from the young disc of the sun
> with the colour of His lower lip –
>
> for it was reddened
> by the betel served with longing
> by the Daughter of the Snow Mountain
> in her eagerness for play –
> in His keenness to display His skill in music
> He's playing the veena
> His moving hand never quits,

Him who is made of the first *rasa*,
Whose foot is curved, I worship. (212)[19]

In this world of aesthetics, of connoisseurship, Umāpati too has taken his place and played his part:

My hymn of praise in fine metre
for it is in the Sragdharā metre,
excellently adorned with many good qualities,

clearly excellent in style
for it brings great joy to the wise
with its sweet maturity and basic emotions, *śayyā*,
rasa and so on, excellent in its modes,

expounding the meaning of the Vedānta,
proceeding with meritorious words.
He accepts it and gives me great joy.
. . . (304)[20]

Umāpati uses a variety of terms from poetics, not all of which are easily determined in the present context. However, the mention of *pāka* ('maturity') and *śayyā* ('arrangement') suggests that he is following one or other of two thirteenth-century poeticians who were the first to use both terms. Both the terms *pāka* and *śayyā* can be seen as especially significant, given the deep complexity of the poem's composition. Rājaśekhara in discussing the varieties of *pāka* says that nine types are to be found among poets, each one linked to a particular fruit. Thus some, like the raisin, are at first not sweet but are sweet when they ripen, while those like the coconut are sweet from beginning to end.

UMĀPATI CONTRASTED WITH ŚAIVA MONISM

Abhinavagupta, the greatest of Indian poeticians as well as being the mastermind of Kashmir Śaivism, speaks of consciousness itself as a high-powered digestive process (*haṭhapāka)*:

All existing things are hurled into the fire in the stomach of our consciousness, where they lose all difference and become fuel for the fire. When the finite form of all things is dissolved by this fierce digestion, then the All, which feeds and sustains the divinities of consciousness [the senses and the intellect], becomes the ambrosia of immortality. These divinities, once satisfied, become absorbed in Bhairava, who is totally full, the sky of consciousness, the God who reposes in the Heart and not elsewhere.[21]

This is to switch from Umāpati's technical statement of his poetics to the core of the Northern theology of Bhairava, and yet this 'sky of consciousness' (*cidvyoman, cidambara*), the God reposing in the heart, is reminiscent of Cidambaram and the Cit Sabhā, the 'sky of consciousness' and the 'hall of consciousness'. Nor should it be forgotten that the Cit Sabhā contains a Bhairava once capable of turning copper into gold. Umāpati the poet has thrown into his and the reader's consciousness all things relating to the worship of Śiva in Cidambaram, and they have fed the fire that is the poem. One does indeed need a forceful intellectual digestion to deal with it. Umāpati did as it were hurl all existing things into the fire of his own consciousness as an offering for Śiva.

Abhinavagupta says:

> The wise one, in order to worship properly should offer back into the highest abode that essence (*rasa*) which flows and trickles from the multitude of existing things because they are heavy with their nondifference with Śiva . . . O God together with the Goddess, day and night, I adore you continuously washing with the *abhiṣeka*s of the essence of my astonishment . . . This triple world, full of various tastes and flavours, is cast into the *yantra* that is the *cakra* of the heart. I squeeze it . . . The supreme nectar of consciousness, which removes birth, old age and death, gushes from it. Opening my mouth wide, I devour it . . . and in this way O Supreme Goddess, I gladden and satisfy you day and night.[22]

For Abhinavagupta here the essential aspect of worship is a rendering back to Śiva of the essence (*rasa*) that flows from all things. Extracting this blissful concentrate from reality, one offers it back to the highest abode as the only truly worthwhile gift that can be offered to Śiva and the Goddess.

Despite his frequent praise of the Vedānta, Umāpati's Siddhānta position is far removed from the monism of Abhinavagupta, even if his several references to drinking wine – 'Drinking, constantly drinking the wine of His Lotus feet in the Sabhā', in the final verse of the poem – have an almost Kashmirian ring. But these words of the Northern master, of whom Umāpati comes not a million miles from being a Southern counterpart, serve to point up the differences between the two views. For Umāpati the poet, the temple is the essence of the triple universe, the temple is the universe. The paraphenalia of the temple are in themselves a multitude of existing things.

> They, the pure, worship Him with incense,
> then with the lamps –
>
> the snake-lamp, the man[-animal] lamp,
> the bull-lamp, the pot-lamp,
> the lamp with five wicks,
> the fire-sacrifice-lamp,
> the star-lamp, the camphor lamp;

and with ash, with fan,
with excellent white umbrella
and chowry; with mirror,
with flowers sanctified with mantras;
with the camphor-topped lamp.

Quickly they abandon ignorance
and see Him clearly every day.
Him Whose foot is curved
I worship. (21)[23]

And the dominant *rasa* in the temple is sheer material liquid:

Six times a day
every day
the lordly sages free from sin
worship His *liṅga*

with the five products of the cow;
with oil;
with milk, with curds, and with ghee,
with honey and pure sugar – the fivefold ambrosia;
with sweet lime juice;
with the water of tender coconut;
with boiled rice;
with fragrances,
with the waters of the other Gaṅgā, the Śivagaṅgā tank.

He is the Lord, the Unborn.
Him Whose foot is curved
I worship. (19)[24]

In a manner analogous to the ritual, Umāpati Śivācārya heaped together all the good things he could find, and showered them over Śiva's foot. It is only fitting to conclude with Umāpati's own words this presentation of the Dance of Śiva of which he is the source.

Listening, constantly listening
with full attention to His pure deeds,
drinking, constantly drinking with my tongue
the wine of His lotus feet in the Sabhā,

remembering, constantly remembering
Him the Lord in my heart,

seeing, constantly seeing
Him Who is the culmination of the Vedas,
Who, being pleased is the giver of enjoyment and salvation,

I am enlightened by His great eye of wisdom.
Him Whose foot is curved I worship. (313)[25]

Those mortals who read every day
this hymn, the product of my eloquence,
I who am Umāpati,
in praise of Śambhu
Who performs the Dance of supreme bliss in the Hall of Consciousness,
will first win all they desire in this world,
son, wife, and so on,
and at the end for sure
His foot, the state called pure consciousness.[26]

I, Umāpati by name,
in the forest-dwelling stage of life,
when I'd uttered
this royal hymn of praise of the blessed curved foot
in three hundred and thirteen verses,
saw with my very own eyes
the Dance of the Lord of the Hall.[27]

Notes

INTRODUCTION

1 More accurately, 'The fierce dance (*tāṇḍava*) [modified to become the dance] of bliss (*ānanda*)'.
2 A. K. Coomaraswamy, *The Dance of Śiva* (New York: The Noonday Press, 1957), pp. 77f. This citation omits the final sentence, which is given at the beginning of the final chapter of this book, p. 228.
3 Fritjof Capra, *The Tao of Physics: An Exploration of the Parallels between Modern Physics and Eastern Mysticism* (London: Fontana, 1976), pp. 258f.
4 D. H. H. Ingalls, *An Anthology of Sanskrit Court Poetry*, Harvard Oriental Series vol. 44 (Cambridge, Mass.: Harvard University Press, 1965), p. 69.
5 Beryl de Zoete, *The Other Mind* (London: Victor Gollancz, 1953), p. 44.
6 This is discussed at the close of chapter 9, p. 226f.
7 *Nāṭya Śāstra* 8.53. A photograph of a dancer's foot in this position is given in Shveni Pandya, *A Study of the Technique of Abhinaya in Relation to Sanskrit Drama* (Bombay: Somaiya Publications, 1988), p. 35. Every bronze of Naṭarāja shows the raised foot in this position.
8 'With his pupils he dwelt in the monastery built by the Cola called Vīra in the beautiful grove called Rājendrapurī that is splendid on the outskirts of Cidambaram' (*Rājendrapura Māhātmya* 14).
9 Hermann Kulke, *Cidambaramahātmya: Eine Untersuchung der religionsgeschichtlichen und historischen Hintergründe für die Entstehung der Tradition einer südindischen Tempelstadt*, Freiburger Beiträge zur Indologie, vol. 3 (Wiesbaden: Otto Harrassowitz, 1970).

1 THE NAṬARĀJA BRONZE

1 Douglas Barrett, 'The "Chidambaram" Naṭarāja', in *Chhavi 2*, ed. Anand Krishna (Varanasi: Bharat Kalā Bhavan, 1981), pp. 5–20, p. 17.
2 This painting is discussed in chapter 4, pp. 85–7.
3 Barrett, 'The "Chidambaram" Naṭarāja', p. 17.
4 See, for example, Sivaramamurti, *Naṭarāja in Art, Thought and Literature* (New Delhi: National Museum. 1974), p. 223, fig. 74.
5 For the musicians, see verses 9 and 151 and comment (pp. 19f.); for the flames, see verse 9 (p. 19). *Prabhāvali*,'continuous line of light or radiance'; the Tamil

term is *tiruvāci*, 'ornamental arch over the head of an image', 'ornamental arch under which anything sacred is carried'.

6 *yallīlārabdhanṛttaprasṛtavarajaṭājūṭasammardavega-*
prodyatsvargāpagāmbhojanitakaṇagaṇā yatra yatra prapetuḥ /
te 'py āsan tatra tatra svajanimamukharā mūrtayaḥ kṣetrarāje
taṃ devaṃ nandimukhyapramathagaṇavṛtaṃ kuñcitāṅghriṃ bhaje'ham //111//

7 In major temples a separate shrine within the central courtyard is dedicated to Naṭarāja. The earliest of such subsidiary shrines is probably the one in the Bṛhadīśvara in Tanjavur, though it was rebuilt by Sarfōji about 1802. In Cidambaram temple, the *liṅga* is in the second enclosure, and is called the Mūlasthāna, the original sacred place, for it predates the Cit Sabhā (in this world age, according to the *sthalapurāṇa*). There exist a number of minor temples dedicated to Naṭarāja in imitation of Cidambaram, e.g. in Madras, the Naṭarāja temple in Lingi Chetty Street, Muthialpet. A Northern version of the Cidambaram temple has been built within the last ten years at Satara in Maharashtra: see B. Natarajan, *Tillai and Nataraja* (Madras: Mudgala Trust, 1994), chapter 27.

8 The *liṅga* is in fact of stone, but the sunken *garbhagṛha* is regularly flooded by an internal spring. In Cidambaram, in the Cit Sabhā to the right of Naṭarāja there is said to be a *liṅga* made of space (*ākāśa*), and consequently invisible. Umāpati refers to this once, briefly, 246, but three or four times refers to the Mūla *liṅga* as the source of all *liṅga*s and the *ākāśa liṅga* seems not to be very important to Umāpati.

9 *āryāvāmāṃsabhūṣānavamaṇigaṇabhāsaṃgavaivarṇyanīla-*
grīvālokātiśaṅkiprasṛtaviṣabhayākrāntadikpālavargam /
cūḍācandrājihīrṣādaravivṛtaphaṇākuṇḍalīkarṇalolad-
gaṅgākūlāyamānasvasaṭavaravanaṃ kuñcitāṅghriṃ bhaje'ham //163//

10 *vedāntodgītarūpaṃ jvalanaḍamarukau dhārayantaṃ karābhyām*
anyābhyāṃ ḍolamudrām abhayam api sadāpasmṛtau dakṣapādam /
vinyasyākuñcitena praṇamadakhiladaṃ vāmapādena nityaṃ
devyā sākaṃ sabhāyāṃ racayati naṭanaṃ kuñcitāṅghriṃ bhaje'ham //108//

11 See my paper 'The Dance of Śiva', in *Perspectives on Indian Religion*, ed. P. Connolly (Delhi: Sri Satguru Publications, 1986), pp. 87–98. Apasmāra receives further discussion and interpretation in chapter 9.

12 *phāle bhasmatripuṇḍraṃ phaṇinam api gale pādapīṭhe ca bhūtaṃ*
bāhvor vahniñ ca ḍhakkāṃ vadanasarasije sūryacandrau śikhīndram /
oṃkārākhyaprabhāyāṃ surabhuvanagaṇaṃ pārśvayor vādyakārau
yaḥ kṛtvānandanṛttaṃ svasadasi kurute kuñcitāṅghriṃ bhaje'ham //93//

13 *dharmaṃ datvā janānāṃ ḍamarukaninadair artham apy agninā yaḥ*
kāmaṃ datvā 'bhayena svapadasarasijān mokṣarūpaṃ pumartham /
lokān samastān avati naṭapatir nāyakaś citsabhāyāḥ
taṃ devaṃ nṛttamūrtiṃ visadṛśacaritaṃ kuñcitāṅghriṃ bhaje'ham //104//

14 Coomaraswamy, *The Dance of Śiva*, p. 70.

15 According to M. Dhavamony, *Love of God According to Śaiva Siddhānta* (Oxford: Clarendon Press, 1971), p. 252.

16 Dated as early as the sixth century in the new and generally authoritative *Encyclopedia of Tamil Literature* under publication by the Institute of Asian Studies, Madras, but Graefe is more likely to be correct in postulating the eleventh century (W. Graefe, 'Legends as Mile-Stones in the History of Tamil Literature', *P. K. Gode Commemoration Volume* (Poona, 1960), vol. II, pp. 129–46, p. 145).

17 Trans. by B. Natarajan (slightly altered), *Tirumantiram* (Madras: Sri Ramakrishna Math, 1991), p. 430. All quotations from the *Tirumantiram* are from Natarajan's translation. The relevant passage from the *Uṇmaiviḷakkam* and further discussion are to be found in chapter 5, pp. 129f.

18 *sṛṣṭyai brahmāṇam ādau harim atha jagatāṃ rakṣaṇāyātmarūpaḥ*
saṃhṛtyai rudramūrtiṃ tv atha nikhilatirodhānahetor maheśam /
tallokānugrahārthaṃ himagiritanayāsaktasādākhyamūrtiṃ
yaḥ sṛṣṭvānandanṛttaṃ sadasi vitanute kuñcitāṅghriṃ bhaje'ham //102//

Umāpati always refers to Sadāśiva as Sādākhya. This verse is further discussed in chapter 4.

19 *bhūte saṃsthāpya caikaṃ caraṇasarasijaṃ dakṣiṇaṃ vāmapādaṃ*
śiñjanmañjīraśobhaṃ vidhimukhadiviṣatpūjitaṃ bhaktibhājām /
dharmādīṣṭān pradātuṃ dhanalipisahitaṃ kiñcid uddhṛtya tiryak
cākuñcyānandanṛttaṃ kalayati varadaṃ kuñcitāṅghriṃ bhaje'ham //70//

20 The Cidambaram ritual text gives a list of *nyāsa*s for each of the letters of the alphabet, the letters being distributed among the four arms of Naṭarāja, and *nyāsa* being performed on various parts of the worshipper's body in turn, with reverence to particular *śakti*s. Thus, to the hand holding fire (which receives half the alphabet) there is included *oṃ dhaṃ nāṃ śrutyai namo vāmapādāṅgulimūle, oṃ naṃ thaṃ sāvitryai namo vāmapādāṅgulyagre*, *Citsabheśotsavasūtra*, p. 243. However, when I asked G. Parameśvara Dīkṣita about *dhanalipi*, he paused and then informed me that his guru, the deceased K. M. Rājagaṇeśa Dīkṣita, the learned editor of the *Kuñcitāṅghristava*, was constantly present for him and that Rājagaṇeśa Dīkṣita had at that moment informed him that the true reading should be *kṣamalipi*. This would appear to correspond to the last syllable in the alphabetic sequence just referred to, which concludes, still directed towards Naṭarāja's *agnihasta*, *oṃ kṣaṃ maṃ mahālakṣmyai namo vāmapāde*.

21 Harle declares, 'The impact is made almost exclusively by the human–divine form', and adds in a note, 'To appreciate to what extent this is true one has only to compare Coḷa bronzes to those of Kashmir, with their fascinating iconographical diversity and inventiveness and frequently inferior craftsmanship. Similarly, the elaborate surrounds of most Pāla and Western Indian metal images tend to detract from the main figure.' J. C. Harle, *The Art and Architecture of the Indian Subcontinent* (Harmondsworth: Penguin, 1986), p. 302 and p. 519.

22 *yasmin nṛtyaty anādau nikaṭataṭagatau bhānukampākhyabāṇau*
śaṅkhadhvānair mṛdaṅgadhvanibhir api mahāmbhodhighoṣaṃ jayantau /
yasyoṅkāraprabhāyāṃ dhvanimanusahitā raśmayaś caikaviṃśā
vidyante taṃ sabheśaṃ naṭasuranikaraṃ kuñcitāṅghriṃ bhaje'ham //9//

Is a correspondance intended between the 23-syllabled *dhvani mantra* and the 21 flames of the *tiruvāci*? The *dhvani mantra* (*śivaśivaśaraṇaṃ śivānandaṃ śiva śiva śivāya śivāya namaḥ*) is defined and described in the *Cidambarakalpa*.

23 *nṛtteśaṃ bāṇadaityapramukhagaṇavaroddaṇḍadorbṛndavarya-*
krūrodvegāhatodyadghaṭadhimidhimitakśabdabhāvānukalpam /
tānātānātaneti kvaṇitadaśaśatītantrivīṇānugāno-
nmododgrīvāhibhūṣāvalayam abhayadaṃ kuñcitāṅghriṃ bhaje'ham //150//

24 *sāhasrakrūravaktraprabhavagurumarutpūrahuṃhuṃbhabhaṃbhaṃ-*
jhaṃjhīkṛcchaṃkhaśṛṅgapramukhavaramahāvādyabhṛdbhānukopam /
dṛṣṭvā hāhāhaheti bhramitasuragaṇābhītisaṃdāyipārṣad-
vyāpte raṅge ya īśo naṭati tam anaghaṃ kuñcitāṅghriṃ bhaje'ham //151//

Line b. Bhānukopa. Both the Sanskrit text and the Tamil translation (Pāṉukōpaṉ) have this, but surely Bhānukampa is in question here, and I give his name in my translation.

25 They are mentioned in the *Cidambaramāhātmya* (17.22–6), *Kōyil Purāṇam* (*Naṭarāja* section, 6–7) and in the *Cidambareśvaranityapūjāsūtra* they are included in the list of servants of the dance (*nṛttasevaka*), p. 98.

26 Citrasena, son of Viśvāvasu, taught Arjuna music (*Mahābhārata*, *Vana Parvan*).

27 T. Satyamurti, *The Nataraja Temple: History, Art and Architecture* (New Delhi: Classical Publications, 1978), p. 18. Śiva is rarely shown in this way. An early and perhaps unique instance of Dakṣiṇāmūrti as a drummer is found on the Pāṇḍyan rock-cut temple at Kalugumalai – illustrated in C. Sivaramamurti, *Kalugumalai and Early Pandyan Rock-Cut Shrines*, Heritage of Indian Art Series, no. 3 (Bombay: N. M. Tripathi Private Ltd, 1961), p. 5.

28 *padme māstv adya līlā phaṇipatiśayanaṃ vainateyo 'pi nālaṃ*
bhūmi tvaṃ śīghram āyāhy aham api naṭane tillavanyāṃ purāreḥ /
hastābhyāṃ vādayiṣyāmy ahaha caṭutaraṃ mardalaṃ cety udīrya
prāyād yadraṅgam ādau harir api tam ajaṃ kuñcitāṅghriṃ bhaje'ham //230//

29 R. Dessigane, P. Z. Pattabiramin and Jean Filliozat, *Les Légendes Çivaïtes de Kāñcipuram* (Pondicherry: Institut Français d'Indologie, 1964), pp. 86f.

30 *Ibid.*

31 *satyaṃ brahmaiva nānyaj jagad idam akhilaṃ ceti mīmāṃsayitvā*
traiyantoktyā budhendrā hṛdi ca yam aniśaṃ cidghanaṃ durnirīksyam /
dīpajvālāśikhāvat satataparicayānandanṛttaṃ vimāyaṃ
śubhraṃ paśyanti tatsatpadaviṣayam araṃ kuñcitāṅghriṃ bhaje'ham //272//

Line d. *araṃ*: cf. *nirbabandhādhikaśapatham araṃ kuñcitāṅghriṃ bhaje'ham* //261//

32 *phāle bhasmatripuṇḍraṃ phaṇinam api gale pādapīṭhe ca bhūtaṃ*
bāhvor vahniñ ca ḍhakkāṃ vadanasarasije sūryacandrau śikhīndram /
oṅkārākhyaprabhāyāṃ surabhuvanagaṇaṃ pārśvayor vādyakārau
yaḥ kṛtvānandanṛttaṃ svasadasi kurute kuñcitāṅghriṃ bhaje'ham //93//

33 *dhṛtvā yaḥ sarvadeśaḥ padajalajamukhe śreṣṭhamuktālim aṅge*
sauvarṇaṃ kañcukañ ca prathitamaṇicitaṃ bhūṣaṇaṃ divyavastram /
nṛttaṃ kṛtvāgatānāṃ sakalatanubhṛtāṃ dharmamukhyān pumarthān
dattvā rakṣaty anādir munikṛtayajanaḥ kuñcitāṅghriṃ bhaje'ham //106//

Line d. It is to Him that sages conduct their sacrifice, *munikṛtayajanaḥ*. Far from being excluded from the sacrifice, as he was as Rudra in Vedic times, Śiva is now seen as the object of the entire array of Vedic sacrifice.

34 *śrīmān bhṛṅgī munīndro mṛgaparaśukaraṃ devam evaikam īśaṃ*
natvā tatpārśvagāyā nijavimukharuṣaś caṇḍikāyāś ca vākyāt /
śāktaṃ māṃsādivargaṃ svatanuvaragataṃ protsṛjan yatprasādāl
lebhe daṇḍatripādaṃ svadhuri ca vasatiṃ kuñcitāṅghriṃ bhaje'ham //154//

Pārvatī is here called Caṇḍikā, 'the Fierce Lady', a name often given to Durgā, slayer of the buffalo demon. P. Z. Pattabiramin summarizes M. R. Dessigane's French translation of 'the Tamil treatiseç *ivaparakkraman*', p. 162 ('Notes d'iconographie dravidienne', *Arts Asiatiques* VI (1959), pp. 13–16): On Mount Kailāsa Śiva was seated with his wife Umā, amid his court, on a splendid throne. Gods and Ṛṣis came to pay their respects and to receive blessing. When Bhṛṅgi's turn came, he approached the throne of the Lord and revered only Śiva, without paying attention to Umā. Angered, she asked her husband who the *ṛṣi* was. Śiva said to her, 'My dear, it is a devotee who firmly believes that I am all and that everything depends on me. His name is Bhṛṅgi.' Then Umā decided to repress the arrogance of Bhṛṅgi. She withdrew from his body all the elements pertaining to vitality or energy (*śakti*): blood, flesh etc. The *ṛṣi* began to sway without being able to hold himself upright, having in his body only bones and nerves, the elements pertaining to Śiva. At this moment, Śiva, in his compassion, gave him another leg. Umā is led to demand that she and Śiva share one and the same body. [My translation from the French.]

35 R. Venkataraman, *Rājarājeśvaram: The Pinnacle of Chola Art* (Madras: Mudgala Trust, 1985), p. 157.

36 For some details, see Anne-Marie Gaston, *Śiva in Dance, Myth and Iconography* (Delhi: Oxford University Press, 1982), p. 131.

37 Always present in paintings of Śiva dancing in Cidambaram are the two sages, Vyāghrapāda and Patañjali, and sometimes a third, Jaimini. These three belong to the local tradition, and are discussed in chapter 2.

38 *kālyā sākaṃ purā yaḥ suramunisadasi svāṅghrim udyamya cordhvaṃ*
nṛttaṃ kṛtvātha kālīṃ paśupatir ajayat tadbahiṣkārapūrvam /
sarve devā munīndrāḥ prabhur iti ca vadanty ūrdhvanṛtteśamūrtiṃ
yaṃ devaṃ pūjayanti pratidinam anaghāḥ kuñcitāṅghriṃ bhaje'ham //46//

39 *bhāsante naiva yasmin raviśaśihutabhuk tārakāś cāpi vidyut*
yasmād bhītyendravāyūmihirakiraṇajo dūrato yānti nityam /
yadrūpaṃ yogivaryā hṛdayasarasije cintayanty anvahaṃ taṃ
śrīmantaṃ citrarūpaṃ vasukarakamalaṃ kuñcitāṅghriṃ bhaje'ham //73//

E.g. Tirumūlar, refers to eight arms, *Tirumantiram* 2728 trans. Natarajan, p. 119.

40 *cakṣūṃsy arkāgnicandrāś caraṇam ahibhuvi vyomni keśāś ca yasyāpy*
aṣṭāv āśāś ca vastraṃ nikhilabhuvanasaṃlagnahasto'dvitīyaḥ /
kukṣir vārāśijālaṃ naṭanaśubhatalaṃ rudrabhūmiś ca nityaṃ
taṃ devaṃ citsabheśaṃ śrutigaṇavinutaṃ kuñcitāṅghriṃ bhaje'ham //67//

41 *āviḥ smerānanasya dyutibhir abhinavaiḥ pāṇipadmāntarāla-*
prodyatkāntiprarohair nabhasi ca racayañ jālam ahnāṃ patīnām /
navyām ambhodamālām adhidharaṇi rucā pārśvagāyāḥ śivāyāś
citraṃ yo nānaṭīti bhramaranaṭanakṛt kuñcitāṅghriṃ bhaje'ham //220//

42 *āyur yat kaiṭabhāreḥ paramam abhimataṃ pūrṇatām eti tāvat*
kalpo yasya kṣaṇārdho bhavati ca sugamaḥ kiñcid aṃśena hīnaḥ /
ity āhur vedavācaḥ kim uta śatadhṛteḥ kiñcid dikpālakānāṃ
taṃ kālaṃ kālabhakṣaṃ phaṇiphaṇanaṭaṃ kuñcitāṅghriṃ bhaje'ham //282//

2 THE CIDAMBARAM MYTH

1 Dated by Kulke as early as the twelfth century; evidence from the *Kuñcitāṅghristava* throws doubt on that. See above, p. 44.
2 Cf. Shulman's review of this literature, 'The Mythology of the Tamil Talapuranam', unpublished PhD thesis, London University (1976), p. 30. Subsidiary Sanskrit texts on Cidambaram include *Tilvavana Māhātmya*, *Vyāghrapura Māhātmya*, *Puṇḍarīkapura Māhātmya*, and *Hemasabhānātha Māhātmya*.
3 The first published account in English is perhaps that of Pope: G. U. Pope, *The Tiruvaçagam* (Oxford: Clarendon Press, 1900), pp. lx–lxvii.
4 For details see Kulke, *Cidambaramāhātyma: Eine Untersuchung*, p. 32.

5 *pūrvaṃ mādhyandinir yacchivajanimavaraṃ pūjayan yatprasādāl*
labdhvā vyāghrāṅghribhāvaṃ tanayam api śivānugrahād dugdhasindhum /
ānīyāsmai pradatvā sadasi ca paramaṃ draṣṭavān yasya nṛttaṃ
taṃ devaṃ citsabheśaṃ nigamanutaguṇaṃ kuñcitāṅghriṃ bhaje'ham //10//

6 *yannṛttadhyānayogadviguṇitatanubhṛcchrīśasaṃvāhabhugna-*
svāṅgaḥ śeṣaḥ kadācid dharimukhakamalotpannayadvṛttamādhvīm /
pītvā taptvātighoraṃ rajatagiribiladvāramārgeṇa yasya
kṣetraṃ prapyānvapaśyan naṭanam adhisabhaṃ kuñcitāṅghriṃ bhaje'ham //11//

7 Both are now substantial temples, having been extensively renovated. The temple on the site of Patañjali's *āśrama* bears the oldest inscriptions in Cidambaram (Vijayālaya, 870; Parāntaka 907–57); see S. R. Balasubrahmanyam, 'The Oldest Chidambaram Inscriptions', *Journal of Annamalai University* XII/2&3 (1943).

8 The only instance I have seen outside Cidambaram is in the Bhikṣāṭana shrine (early twentieth century) in the Mārgasahāyeśvara Temple at Viriñcipuram, 11 km west of Vellore.

9 *ādau māse mṛgākhye suragurudivase puṣyabhe pūrṇimāyāṃ*
bhittau śrīcitsabhāyāṃ munivaratapasā dattavākpūtaye yaḥ /
nṛttaṃ kṛtvāvasāne phaṇadharavapuṣaṃ vyāghrapādaṃ maharṣiṃ
cāhūyābhyām adād yo niyatanivasatiṃ kuñcitāṅghriṃ bhaje'ham //8//

Line a. Read *puṣyabhe* for *tasya bhe*, which makes no sense. Umāpati refers to *Cidambaramāhātmya* 15.56–58a: *pūrṇimāyāṃ pauṣamāse 'mṛtayogena saṃyute //56// vāre ca gaurave tatra puṣyarkṣe ca śubhāvahe / dinasya madhyamaṃ bhāgaṃ samprāpte ca divākare //57// tāṇḍavaṃ darśayiṣyāmi tava tasyāpyanuttamam/.* Line b. *bhittau* 'against the wall'. For discussion, see chapter 4.

10 *antarvedyāṃ svayajñe diviṣadadhipatau sāmagānais tathoccair*
āhūte 'nāgate 'smin yadamalanaṭanaṃ dṛṣṭavantaṃ surendram /
sadyobudhvātmabhūs taṃ svayam atitarasānīya yasyātideśād
vipraiḥ sākaṃ svayajñaṃ suranutam akarot kuñcitāṅghriṃ bhaje'ham //47//

11 *antarvedyāṃ mahatyāṃ śatadhṛtir akarod abdasāhasrasādhyaṃ*
yajñaṃ tasmin munīndrāḥ sadasi samabhavan vyāghrapādoktibhir ye /
tatpūjārthaṃ śikhīndraprabhavamaṇinaṭaḥ preṣito yena modāt
tanmūrter mūlabhūtaṃ navamaṇimakuṭaṃ kuñcitāṅghriṃ bhaje'ham //16//

12 *gauḍeśaḥ siṃhavarmā svatanugatarujā vyākulaḥ svīyadeśād*
āgatya svarṇapadmākaravarasalilasnānanimuktarogaḥ /
bhūtvā śrīhemavarmā munivarasahitaḥ śambhunṛttaṃ ca dṛṣṭvā
yatprāsādaṃ vicitraṃ maṇimayam akarot kuñcitāṅghriṃ bhaje'ham //13//

13 The *Cidambara Māhātmya* says that he has the form of a lion, *siṃharūpadhara* (20.36). The *Hemasabhānātha Māhātmya* calls him *citrin* (7.35), perhaps in the sense of being mottled. The appendix to the *Tilvavana Māhātmya* summarizing the *sthalapurāṇa* says plainly that Siṃhavarman had leprosy (*kuṣṭha*).

14 *āmnāyeṣv apy ananteṣv anitarasulabhān bhinnasaṃsthān vidhīn*
apy āhṛtya śrīphaṇīndro naṭayajanamahaprokṣaṇārthañ ca sūtram /
ṛtvādau dattavān yat taduditavidhinā yaṃ sadārādhayanti
traisāhasraṃ dvijendrāḥ tam api naṭapatiṃ kuñcitāṅghriṃ bhaje'ham //14//

Line a. *anitarasulabhān*: literally, '[precepts] which no one else could easily find'. But Umāpati would hardly suggest any lack of authenticity in the temple ritual text, and the looseness of his style makes likely the adverbial turn of my translation, 'in a way that none could emulate'.

15 *ādau yaḥ karmakāṇḍapravacanamahimā jaiminir nāma yogī*
vyāsoktyā citsabheśaṃ prabhuvaram urasā namya gatvā sabhāntaḥ /
pādānte vedayuktaṃ stavavaram akarot svasaubhāgyadaṃ yaṃ
paśyann adyāpi devaṃ sadasi vasati taṃ kuñcitāṅghriṃ bhaje'ham //12//

Jaimini's 'excellent hymn of praise', the *Vedapādastava*, is a well-known *stotra*, and is included in collections of *stotras*. It continues to be read in Cidambaram: the brochure for the 1994 Kārttikai *mahotsava* at Cidambaram is headed by a verse from the *Vedapādastava*.

16 *devo yaḥ pulkasāya dvijakulajanuṣe valkalasyātmajāya*
nandābhikhyāya muktiṃ kaṇatṛṇasudhiye dattavān bhaktivaśyaḥ /
nityatvaṃ vyāghrapādaprathitaphaṇipatistotrakṛjjaiminibhyaḥ
tāṃs tān kāmāṃś ca sarvāṃs tam ajaraṃ amaraṃ kuñcitāṅghriṃ bhaje'ham //29//

Line c. *nityatvaṃ* 'eternal presence [in Cidambaram]'.

17 *pūrvaṃ vālkalyabhikhyān nihatatanuvaro devarāḍ viṣṇum āptvā*
coktvā svodantam asmai saha muraripuṇā prāpya yatkṣetram īśam /
ārādhyāptvā suvīryaṃ yadanaghakṛpayā mārayām āsa śatruṃ
taṃ devaṃ citsabheśaṃ vararucivinutaṃ kuñcitāṅghriṃ bhaje'ham //41//

18 Kulke, *Cidambaramāhātyma: Eine Untersuchung*, p. 182.

19 *śārdūlāṅghreś ca ḍimbhaḥ sukhataram abhajad dugdhakallolarāśim* /
stāvaṃ stāvaṃ vareṇyaṃ gagananaṭapatiṃ . . .

20 Kulke, *Cidambaramāhātyma: Eine Untersuchung*, p. 222.

21 *Anuśāsanaparvan*, Part 1, p. xxxi. David Shulman has pointed out to me (personal communication) that the Telugu *Mahābhārata* is extremely selective and often leaves enormous gaps.

22 As far as Cidambaram is concerned, precise details may be given. The Tiruppāṟkaṭal tank, the tank filled with Divine Milk for Upamanyu, is believed to have been situated to the north of the great temple, and west of the Tillai Kālī temple. The site has been filled in to make a school playground. Adjoining is a Mutt on the site where Māṇikkavācakar is said to have written his two poems.

23 *Tēvāram* III.282.2, trans. Peterson, *Poems to Śiva: the Hymns of the Tamil Saints* (Princeton University Press, 1989), p. 271.

24 We should remember that names are easily changed. In the later *Hemasabhānātha Māhātmya*, for example, Siṃhavarman's father is called Nairṛta, and rules in Ayodhyā (8.32).

25 Kulke, *Cidambaramāhātyma: Eine Untersuchung*, p. 224.

26 *Ibid.*, p. 208.

27 *yaddakṣe'dyāpi viṣṇur maṇimayasadane dakṣiṇe svāṅghriyugmaṃ*
kṛtvāsyaṃ cottarasyāṃ śaramukhaphaṇirāḍbhogatalpe śayānaḥ /
nityaṃ nidrāṃ prakurvann api hṛdi satataṃ yat padaṃ dhyāyatīdyaṃ
devyā taṃ citsabheśaṃ sutagajavadanaṃ kuñcitāṅghriṃ bhaje'ham //42//

28 Further evidence of the Vaiṣṇava zeal of Acyutadeva Rāya is provided by the family history of a group of *gurukkaḷs* now living in Kumbakonam, namely that they were brought from Andhra Pradesh by Acyutadeva Rāya to serve as priests in Cidambaram, only to be later expelled by the Dīkṣitas.

These people are Śaivas, and there is no reason to suppose that they were not so when brought in by the Vaiṣṇava king. The presumption is that the Dīkṣitas resisted his reforms, and were for a time ousted. Under such circumstances, it is only to be expected that the Śeṣaśayana image would have its feet towards Naṭarāja. There is evidence of Dīkṣita resistance to a Vaiṣṇava king at the end of the sixteenth century. The Jesuit Pimenta reports in 1597 a score of priests leaping to their deaths from the top of a *gopura* rather than see Krishnappa Nayaka improve the Viṣṇu shrine (Samuel Purchas, *Hakluytus Posthumus or Purchas His Pilgrimes*, vol. x (Glasgow: James MacLehose, 1905), pp. 208f).

29 K. A. Nilakanta Sastri, *The Cōḻas*, 2 vols., Madras University Historical Series (University of Madras, 2nd edn., 1955), vol. I, p. 348. In addition to inscriptions Sastri also notes the evidence of the Tamil court poetry of Oṭṭakkūṭṭaṉ, the *Kulōttuṅgacōḻaṉ Ulā*, and also the *Rājarājacōḻaṉ Ulā* and the *Takkayāgapparaṇi*.

3 TEMPLE, PRIESTS, AND RITUAL

1 *sānāv asmin kim arthaṃ vasata suravarā gacchatādyākhileśa*
kṣetrādhāraṃ dharāyā hṛdayakamalagaṃ puṇḍarīkābhidhānam /
kṣetraṃ tatraiva devo daśaśatakalayā rājatīti priyoktyā
nandī yaddarśanārthaṃ tvarayati ca gireḥ kuñcitāṅghriṃ bhaje'ham //227//

2 *yadraṅgasvarṇakumbhaṃ dinakṛd anudinaṃ vīkṣya merubhrameṇa*
rathyaṃ saṃrudhya madhye kṣaṇam api nivasan yatsaparyā sujātam /
ghaṇṭābhāṅkāraghoṣaṃ triśatadaśamakhīvedamantrāṃś ca bhūyaḥ
śrutvā tillīvanākhyaṃ puram iti manute kuñcitāṅghriṃ bhaje'ham //289//

3 *Tillai*, 'blinding tree', *Excoecaria agallocha.*

4 For the DMK (Dravida Munnetra Kazhagam, 'Dravidian Progress Party'), and the anti-Brahman movement, see Franklin A. Pressler, *Religion under Bureaucracy: Policy and Administration for Hindu Temples in South India* (Cambridge University Press, 1987), chapter 7.

5 Several major temples in Tamilnadu do not have four gateways. Śrīraṅgam, the largest of Vaiṣṇava temples, has entrance gateways on only one side. Moreover, perhaps the majority of significant temples are asymmetrical and atypical. Śrīraṅgam, for instance, is aligned to the South.

6 Cf. S. R. Balasubrahmanyam, *Later Chola Temples: Kulottunga I to Rajendra III*, (Madras: Mudgala Trust, 1979), p. 207: 'Kulottunga II continued to rule from the old capital of Gangaikondasolapuram or Gangapuri. It is likely that he had a secondary and well-frequented capital at Chidambaram'.

7 *pātāle martyaloke divi ca puraripor yāni priyāṇi*
kṣetrāṇy āsan tadantasthitim adhijuṣatāṃ liṅgaberādimānām /
hetuḥ śrīmūlanāthaḥ śivajanimavaro yatsabhodīcibhāge
kakṣyāyāṃ bhāti nityaṃ tam akhilajanakaṃ kuñcitāṅghriṃ bhaje'ham //296//

8 The now extensive Iḷamaiyākkiṉār temple. See J. M. Somasundaram Pillai, *The University's Environs: Cultural and Historical*, 4th imprint. (Annamalainagar: Annamalai University, 1963), pp. 137f.

9 Kulke, *Cidambaramāhātyma: Eine Untersuchung*, p. 222.

10 *Ibid.*

11 *yannṛttaṃ draṣṭukāmā raviśaśimukharāḥ svābhidhānair gṛheśā*
liṅgān saṃsthāpya gaṅgātaṭavaranikaṭe pūjayitvā sabhāyām /
tejorūpaṃ ca lāsyaṃ bahir iva hṛdaye saṃtataṃ cintayanto
vāsaṃ cakrus tam īśaṃ nikhilatanumayaṃ kuñcitāṅghriṃ bhaje'ham //119//

12 *viṣṇur brahmā ramendro dahanapitṛpatī rākṣasānām adhīśaḥ*
pāśī vāyuḥ kuberaḥ tridṛg aruṇamukhā devatāś candrasūryau /
nityaṃ yatkṣetrarāje paśupatinaṭanaṃ dṛṣṭavantaḥ svanāmnā
liṅgān saṃsthāpya natvā sukhavaram abhajan kuñcitāṅghriṃ bhaje'ham //38//

Of these, eight are the World-protectors, from Indra to Īśāna (*tridṛg*). But why the mention of Aruṇa?

13 *yadgehaṃ pañcasālair diśi diśi vilasadgopurair vedasaṅkhyair*
annādibrahmakośatvam upagatasabhāpañcakair bhāti tīrthaiḥ /
śrīmūlasthānadevī harigajavadanaskandagehaiś ca nityaṃ
tatratyānandakośe viracitanaṭanaṃ kuñcitāṅghriṃ bhaje'ham //76//

14 There is one place at ground level from which all four *gopuras* are visible from within the temple. This point is outside the entrance to the Śivakāmasundarī shrine.

15 Harle, *Temple Gates in South India*, p. 86.

16 An important *gopura* in considering the development of form is the one added to the Sembiyan Mahadevi Vriddhagirisvara temple at Vriddhachalam around 1186 (see K. V. Raman, 'Gopura Sculptures from Vriddhagirisvara Temple', in *Śrīnidhiḥ: Shri K. R. Srinivsan Festschrift* ed. K. V. Raman *et al.* (Madras: New Era Publications, 1983), pp. 203–12). But in fact its single and miscellaneous tier throws into greater relief the majestic Śaiva statement of the second tiers at Cidambaram.

17 As Harle, *Temple Gateways*, p. 21, and Susan L. Huntington, *The Art of Ancient India* (New York /Tokyo: Weatherhill, 1985), p. 531, both note. Harle, in his *The Art and Architecture of the Indian Subcontinent* (Harmondsworth: Penguin, 1986), refers also to textual prescriptions: 'Prescriptions in the *śāstras* for the construction of multi-storey *gopuras*, moreover, appear to be little more than mechanical transpositions of those for *vimānas*.' (p. 320).

18 Harle notes minor variations of position, *Temple Gateways*, p. 90.

19 'At first glance, the great *gopuras* would seem to have been purposely placed in such a way as to avoid any symmetry whatsoever.' Harle, *Temple Gateways*, p. 35.

20 *Cidambara Māhātmya*, 18.82–6.

21 *Kōyil Purāṇam, Naṭarācaccarukam* 50, trans. John Loud. Both *pāriṭam* and *kūḷi* resemble the *gaṇa*, being dwarfish, malformed, and multiple.
22 In the *Kōyil Purāṇam* Kālī is mentioned again three verses later.
23 G. Vanmikanathan, *Pathway to God through the Thiruvaachakam*, Sri Kasi Mutt Publication New Series, no. 4 (Thiruppanandal: Sri Kasi Mutt, 1980), p. 114.
24 The five sheaths are mentioned again in verse 105, but in another context. See p. 92.
25 F. L'Hernault points out that the Nṛtta Sabhā was not originally a Sabhā, since architectural features prove that it was not designed for a Sabhā-type roof, the roof being the defining feature (L'Hernault *et al.*, *Darasuram.*, vol. 1, p. 6. fn. 17).
26 For an instructive comparison of this Sabhā with the *ratha-maṇḍapa* at Darasuram, see *ibid.*, pp. 6f.
27 Somasetu Dīkṣita in the Sanskrit introduction to his edition of the *Citsabheśotsavasūtra* lists the five principal shrines as 1. Naṭarāja, 2. Śivakāmyumāmbikā, 3. Śrīmulanātha, 4. Mahāgaṇapati, 5. Subrahmaṇya, called the ŚrīPāṇḍyanāyaka (p. 3 of unpaginated sequence).

28 *śraddhāvantaḥ śrutijñāḥ paraśivakṛpayādhītaśāstrādividyā*
vyarthāṃ vācaṃ tyajantaḥ pratidinam asakṛt pūjayantaḥ prabhuṃ yam /
kurvantaḥ śrautakarmāṇy anitarasulabhāṇyātmabodhaṃ labhante
viprendrāḥ svāṃśabhūtāḥ paraśumṛgadharaṃ kuñcitāṅghriṃ bhaje'ham //92//

29 Such restrictions on the wives of a caste are not unique in Tamilnadu; another instance is the Kottai Pillai, a tiny Vellala subcaste that for generations lived in a mud-walled fort in Srivaikuntham, practising endogamy with the wives not allowed to leave the fort. See K. Ganesh, *Boundary Walls: Caste and Women in a Tamil Community* (Delhi: Hindusthan, 1993).
30 Translated by John Loud.
31 Translated by John Loud.
32 Ecstatic dancing is well documented in the Tamil tradition. For its place in Tamil culture of an earlier period see F. Hardy, *Viraha-Bhakti: The Early History of Kṛṣṇa Devotion in South India* (Delhi: Oxford University Press, 1983). Just how far ecstatic dancing was considered to be popular religion, to be low as distinct from high religion, is a difficult question. As Yocum mentions in his discussion of possession in Māṇikkavācakar, Umāpati's predecessor in the Tamil Śaiva Siddhānta lineage, Aruḷnanti, says that those who attain *jñānasamādhi* 'become like children and mad men and possessed persons, and they may delight in singing and dancing also (*Civañāṉacittiyār* 3.8.32 trans. Nallasvami Pillai)' (Glenn E. Yocum, *Hymns to the Dancing Śiva: A Study of Māṇikkavācakar's Tiruvācakam* (New Delhi: Heritage, 1982), p. 192); and Umāpati himself in his *Tiruvaruṭpayaṉ* compares *samādhi* to possession by a demon (8.7). Dancing on the part of worshippers may well have been the norm until modern times, perhaps until the ban on *devadāsīs*: Gopinath Rao wrote in 1916 that 'at the present time all Vaidika or Smārta Brāhmaṇas are

worshipping the *liṅga* and are even seen dancing and making *huḍukkāra* noise [the noise Pāśupātas were supposed to make] while worshipping in temples, a strange survival of the Pāśupata customs' (*Elements of Hindu Iconography* (Madras: Law Printing House, 1914–16), vol. II, Part I,. pp. 31f.).

33 *śābde śāstre phaṇīndraiḥ pramitibhaṇitiṣu śrīkaṇādākṣapādair*
vedānte vyāsarūpair jiminasutakṛtau bhaṭṭakaumāratulyaiḥ /
kalpe bodhāyanais taiś śrutiṣu vidhisamaiḥ pūjyate yo munīndraiḥ
traisāhasraiḥ sabhāyāṃ tam api guruvaraṃ kuñcitāṅghriṃ bhaje'ham //89//

34 *śiṣyāṇāṃ vedabāhyasthitim adhijuṣatāṃ bodhanārthaṃ paṭhantaś*
caryāyogāṅghribhedaprakaṭitavibhavān kāmikādyāgamāṃs tān /
bhūdevā vājapeyakratugatanṛpatiproddhṛtoddāmaśukla-
cchatrā yaṃ pūjayanti śrutipathavidhinā kuñcitāṅghriṃ bhaje'ham //107//

35 *nānādeśasamāgataśrutismṛtipurāṇetihāsādyanekavidyādhyetṛkasvaśiṣyakoṭisamākrāntapārṣṇibhāgānāṃ*, *Citsabheśotsavasūtra*, p. 88.

36 *samadhītasakalavedatātparyāvabodhasuvaśīkṛtābjasaṃbhavānāṃ. Ibid.*

37 *Ibid.*

38 Verse 4 of the *Kuñcitāṅghristava* mentions this symbolism; see below, chapter 4, p. 93.

39 *kalpe kalpe svakīyaprabhavalayabhayaṃ tyaktum ādye parārdhe*
vedā yaṃ kālakālaṃ bahuvidhatapasā toṣayitvā yaduktyā /
traisāhasraṃ dvijatvaṃ diviṣadasulabhaṃ labdhavantaḥ krameṇa
nityaṃ yaṃ pūjayanti svasaraṇividhinā kuñcitāṅghriṃ bhaje'ham //176//

40 *yeṣāṃ vedoktakarmasv anadhikṛtir abhūd adrijātā pṛthivyāṃ*
teṣāṃ dharmādim āptyai paraśivaracitaṃ kāmikādiprabhedam /
sāṅgaṃ siddhāntatantraprakaram api catuṣṣaṣṭisaṃkhyāḥ kalāś ca
yasyādeśāt prakāśaṃ tv anayad aganutaṃ kuñcitāṅghriṃ bhaje'ham //146//

For discussion of the rest of this verse, see chapter 5, p. 118.

41 *kurvantaḥ kṣetravāsaṃ hṛdayasarasije cintayanto japanto*
vidyāṃ sauvarṇaraṅge yam ajaharinutaṃ svecchayāvāptanṛttam /
paśyantaḥ sārvakālaṃ vibudhaparibṛḍhā labdhakāmāḥ sukhitvā
brāhme saudhe ramante caramavayasi taṃ kuñcitāṅghriṃ bhaje'ham //147//

42 The root of Umāpati's persistent use of the adjective *vara* is that the *sragdharā* metre demands six consecutive short syllables in each line, and *vara* takes up two of them. The choice of the word *vara* as filler is an instance of intensification in *kāvya*. See my *Ratnākara's Haravijaya: An Introduction to the Sanskrit Court Epic* (Delhi: Oxford University Press, 1985), p. 147.

43 Translated by T. N. Ramachandran, *Periya Puranam Part I* (Thanjavur: Tamil University, 1990), pp. 83–4. In his prose version of verses 355–6, Āṟumuka Nāvalar (1822–76) adds, 'They undergo the four Dīkṣās: the Samaya-dīkṣā, the Viśeṣa-dīkṣā, the Nirvāṇa-dīkṣā and the Abhiṣeka-dīkṣā' (trans. H. W. Schomerus, *Śivaistische Heiligenlegenden (Periyapurāṇa und*

Tiruvātavūrar-Purāṇa) (Eugen Diederichs, Jena, 1925), p. 71). Mention must be made of the view of Kulke: 'Entirely baseless is the often repeated assertion . . . that by the *Tillaivāl-antaṇar* whom Sundaramūrti praises are already meant the '3000 Brahmans'. *Tillaivāl-antaṇar* means nothing other than 'the Brahmans dwelling in Tillai', (Kulke, *Cidambaramāhātyma: Eine Untersuchung*, p. 211 fn. 162). Kulke takes the view that Kulottuṅga brought new priests to Cidambaram from his Eastern Cāḷukya homeland, noting that Kulottuṅga's capital, Veṅgi, was near the Godāvarī, and suggesting that the Gauḍa region of which the *Cidambara Māhātmya* speaks got its name from Godā, the short form of Godāvarī (*ibid.*, p. 200). 'As the memory of the king began to fade', both the new priests and the old priests, 'the whole priesthood of Cidambaram, must have found the authority of the king in the legend displeasing. Furthermore, the "3000" are likely to have become dissatisfied with their legendary history. That left no doubt that their own tradition did not reach back to the first *ānandatāṇḍava*, which in the meanwhile had moved so much into the centre of the holiness of Cidambaram, that it must have amounted to a lasting slight upon them not to have participated in this divine manifestation of Śiva. In this situation the reworking of the legends of Cidambaram may have begun.' *Ibid.*, p. 212. [My translation from the German.]

44 *Rājendrapura Māhātmya* 9. This is the prelude to his meeting with Maṟaiñāṉa Campantar, which will be discussed in detail in chapter 5.

45 Except the word *ṛtvig* in verse 24, following the *Citsabheśotsavasūtra*, but this expression has Vedic dignity.

46 Quoted above, chapter 2, p. 37.

47 *nityaṃ ṣaṭkālapūjāṃ naṭanapatimude kurvatāṃ bhūsurāṇām*
tadbhaktānāṃ dvijādipramukhatanubhṛtāṃ saukhyadātā bhrakuṃsaḥ /
svasthāne liṅgam ekaṃ sphaṭikamaṇimayaṃ majjanādīni kartuṃ
yajvabhyodattavān yas tam atisukhakaraṃ kuñcitāṅghriṃ bhaje'ham //15//

Line b. *bhrakuṃsa* – a variant of *bhrūkuṃsa*, 'speaking with the brow'.

48 *yo'dān nāijottamāṅgāmṛtakiraṇasudhāmaṇḍapiṇḍīkṛtāṅgaṃ*
tejobhagnenduvahnidyumaṇighanarucijyotiṣaṃ hīrakalpaṃ
nityaṃ dedīpyamānaṃ pratisamayam api svasya pūjāṃ vidhātuṃ
liṅgaṃ vipreṣu modād bhavabhayaharaṇaṃ kuñcitāṅghriṃ bhaje'ham //276//

49 Trans. B. Natarajan, *Tirumantiram* (Madras: Sri Ramakrishna Math, 1991), pp. 270f.

50 The repeated use of 'where' (*kva*) is a standard Sanskrit idiom, signifying a great difference between, usually, two persons or things; and thus here, 'There is a great difference between my humble self and the Cit Sabhā, the casket, and you . . .' But there is also the basic significance of *kva*, 'I do not know where the casket is' and further perhaps the implication that there is no difference in anything in Umāpati's state of *samādhi*, Umāpati whom they have just called 'the knower of the Great Self'.

51 *antarvedyāṃ mahatyāṃ śatadhṛtir akarod abdasāhasrasādhyaṃ*
yajñaṃ tasmin munīndrāḥ sadasi samabhavan vyāghrapādoktibhir ye /
tatpūjārthaṃ śikhīndraprabhavamaṇinaṭaḥ preṣito yena modāt
tanmūrter mūlabhūtaṃ navamaṇimakuṭaṃ kuñcitāṅghriṃ bhaje'ham //16//

52 *nityaṃ puṇyāham ādau guruvaranamanaṃ śoṣaṇāditrayaṃ ca*
bhautiṃ śuddhiṃ karāṅgapraṇavasuramukhanyāsajātaṃ ca kṛtvā /
japtvā mantrān samastāñ chivamayatanavaś cāntar ārādhya yam prāg
viprā bāhye yajanti prabhuvaram api taṃ kuñcitāṅghriṃ bhaje'ham //17//

53 It is also the case that Āgamic temples introduce Vedic mantras. See
W. Surdam, 'The Vedicization of Śaiva ritual', in S. S. Janaki (ed.) *Śiva*
Temple and Temple Rituals (Madras: Kuppuswami Sastri Research Institute,
1988), pp. 52–63.

54 *Patañjalipūjāsūtra*, p. 8.

55 The *Umāpatiśivacaritrasaṃgraha* composed by Śrīmad Śrīcidambarabrah-
mayativarya, Paramahaṃsaparivrājaka, born in a Brahman family of the
Blessed Three Thousand – a brief life of Umāpati prefixed to the published
Kuñcitāṅghristava, Preface pp. 3–6.

56 *Patañjalipūjāsūtra*, pp. 10–11.

57 *sthānādi prokṣya pādyācamanam api sumair arcayitvātha śaṃkhaṃ*
gavyārcyāṃ kumbhapūjāṃ jalayajanavṛṣābhyarcane dvārapūjāṃ /
kṛtvā vighnādipūjāṃ sphaṭikajanimaratneśayor majjanādyair
yanmūrtiṃ pūjayanti pratidinam anaghāḥ kuñcitāṅghriṃ bhaje'ham //18//

58 *gavyais tailaiḥ payobhir dadhighṛtamadhubhiḥ śarkarābhiś ca śuddhaiḥ*
paścāt pañcāmṛtādyair likucaphalarasaiḥ kairapāthobhir annaiḥ /
gandhair gaṅgādbhir anyair anudinam anaghā yasya liṅgaṃ munīndrāḥ
ṣaṭkālaṃ pūjayanti prabhum api tam ajaṃ kuñcitāṅghriṃ bhaje'ham //19//

59 *bhittau śrīcakrasaṃsthāṃ tadanu naṭapatiṃ śaivacakrāntarasthaṃ*
tadvāme yugmahastām api ca śukakaraṃ jñānaśaktiñ ca yaṣṭvā /
gobrahmādīn atheṣṭvā sakalavidhacarūn arpayitvā balīṃs tān
homaṃ kṛtvā yajanti pratidinam api yam kuñcitāṅghriṃ bhaje'ham //20//

Note the rare gerund of *yaj, yaṣṭvā* for the proper *iṣṭvā*.

60 *Patañjalipūjāsūtra* p. 99.

61 *Ibid..* The verse is incomplete. The Goddess today also holds a lotus, and
Rājagaṇeśa Dīkṣita omits mention of the parrot in his Tamil translation of
Kuñcitāṅghristava 20; he also quotes a verse from the *Cidambarakalpa* on
Śivakāmasundarī in her separate shrine which describes that form of the
Goddess as holding a Mynah bird (*śārikā*).

62 See *Patañjalipūjāsūtra*, pp. 97f.

63 *dhūpair dīpair athākhyaiḥ phaṇipuruṣavṛṣaiḥ kumbhapañcāgnihotrair*
ṛkṣaiḥ karpūrabhasmavyajanavarasitacchatrakaiś cāmaraiś ca /
ādarśair mantrapuṣpair uparitalasukarpūrakaiḥ prārcya yan drāk
tyaktvā'vidyāṃ prapaśyanty anudinam anaghāḥ kuñcitāṅghriṃ bhaje'ham //21//

64 *yadgehaprāntabāhye daśavṛṣabhasahitāny abjapīṭhāni nityaṃ*
śakrādīnāṃ trikāleṣv api baliharaṇe pīṭham uttuṅgam anyat /
yadbāhye dikṣu cāgre navaśikharisamā bhānti daṇḍā dhvajānāṃ
tadgehāntaḥ sabhāyāṃ anavaratanaṭaṃ kuñcitāṅghriṃ bhaje'ham //22//

It is not clear what the nine flagpoles were. See below, note 67.

65 *ṣaṭkālārcāsu nityaṃ sphaṭikamaṇimaye liṅganṛtteśamūrtī*
śuddhais tīrthaiḥ kadācit svam api naṭapatiṃ cābhiṣektuṃ samantram /
mūrdhālaṅkārabhūtā pravahati paramānandakūpe yaduktyā
gaṅgā taṃ citsabheśaṃ suravaravinutaṃ kuñcitāṅghriṃ bhaje'ham //74//

66 *yadvarṣaṃ mānuṣāṇāṃ tad api ca divasaṃ devatānāṃ prasiddhaṃ*
proktaṃ taccāpakumbhaprathamayugaharistrīṣu māseṣu ṣaṭsu /
āsan yannṛttamūrter udayamukhavarābhyarcanās te tam indrā-
dyaṣṭāśāpālapūrvākhilasuravinutaṃ kuñcitāṅghriṃ bhaje'ham //202//

Hindu months correspond to the zodiacal constellations of Western astronomy. The equivalent Tamil names of the months are *mārkaḻi*, *māci*, *cittirai*, *āṉi*, *āvaṇi*, and *puraṭṭāci*.

67 *pratyabdaṃ jyeṣṭhamāse navavṛṣasahitāḥ ketavo bhānti māghe*
māse pañcadhvajāḥ syur mṛgaśirasi tathā ketur ekaḥ pradhānaḥ /
yasya brahmotsavānāṃ navaśaraśikhinaś caikavahniḥ pradhānaḥ
taṃ devaṃ citsabheśaṃ navanidhinilayaṃ kuñcitāṅghriṃ bhaje'ham //23//

Lunar months (*jyeṣṭha*, Tam. *jeṣṭa*; *māgha*. Tam. *mākam*; *mṛgaśiras*, Tam. *mārkkaciram*) are here referred to, which only approximately correspond to the zodiacal constellations given in the translation.

It is not clear what is meant by the nine flagpoles. Several of the shrines within the temple have their own flagpoles, but they consequently have their own rituals. Only the Naṭarāja shrine is in question. S. S. Janaki cites the *Uttarakāmika Āgama* (6.62–3) to the effect that there can be one, five or nine *dhvajastambha*s in a temple: 'The chief *dhvajastambha* should be at the outer *prākāra* in front of the Śiva *liṅga* and in line with Bali *pīṭha* and Nandi. In case of five *dhvajastambha*s the other four should be allocated in the four directions, East, West, South and North, presided over respectively by Tatpuruṣa, Sadyojāta, Aghora and Vāmadeva. If there are nine of them in a temple, they should be placed in all eight directions and associated with the eight Vidyeśvaras, namely, Ananta, Sūkṣma, Śivottama, Ekanetra, Ekarudra, Trimūrti, Śrīkaṇṭha and Śikhaṇḍin.' S. S. Janaki, '*Dhvaja-stambha*: Critical Account of its Structural and Ritualistic Details', in S. S. Janaki (ed.), *Śiva Temple and Temple Rituals* (Madras: Kuppuswami Sastri Research Institute, 1988), pp. 122–93, p. 130. Janaki also cites Aghora Śivācārya, who 'in his *Mahotsavavidhi* [ed. K. Shanmugasundara Mudaliar, p. 97] points out that it is best (*uttama*) to have nine *dhvaja*s for the conduct of *dhvajārohaṇa*; with eight it will be middling (*madhyama*) and with a single *dhvaja* it will be the least desirable (*adhama*)' (*ibid.*). She concludes her discussion of the number of *dhvajastambha*s by quoting *Kuñcitāṅghristava* 22 and 23.

At present two flags fly from the South Cidambaram *gopura* throughout the year. Perhaps in the past two flags were raised from each of the *gopuras* for festivals? The Festival text describes the worshipping of a flag (*dhvaja*) and a banner (*patāka*) in each of the eight directions (pp. 119–22).

68 *yasyādye saptaviṃśaty amaladinamahe ṛtvigagryā nava syur*
māghe pañca rtvigagryā mṛgaśirasi śivarkṣotsave caika eva /
nityārcāsv eka eko yajanakṛta ime yajvavaryeṣu śuddhāḥ
taṃ devaṃ citsabheśaṃ nirupamitatanuṃ kuñcitāṅghriṃ bhaje'ham //24//

Line b. June–July, *māghe*. Tamil, *āṉi*.
Line c. February–March, *mṛgaśirasi*. Tamil, *māci*.
Line c. December–January, *śivarkṣa*. Tamil, *mārkaḻi*.

69 *ādau kṛtvāgnihotraṃ vapanapavanamantrācamānāni paścāt*
kūśmāṇḍair dehaśuddhiṃ padayajanamukhaṃ vāstuparyagnikarma /
nāndī mṛtsvaṃkurāṇi pratisaram ṛṣabhaprokṣaṇaṃ yanmaheṣv apy
ārād ārohayanti dhvajapaṭam anaghāḥ kuñcitāṅghriṃ bhaje'ham //25//

ācamānāni, incorrectly for *ācamanāni*, to fit the metre.

70 *Citsabheśotsavasūtra*, p. 1.

71 *yad devā devaheḍanam* etc. (*Vāj.S.* 20.14–16; *Tait.Ā.*II.3.1).

72 Somasetu Dīkṣita, in the Tamil introduction to his edition of the *Citsabheśotsavasūtra*, pp. 4f.

73 See Janaki, '*Dhvaja-stambha*', pp. 134f.

74 *mamce candrārkabhūteṣv api vṛṣagajarāḍrājatādriṣv athāśve*
somāskandasvarūpaḥ svayam urunayane gorathe mārgaṇo yaḥ /
sthitvā brahmotsaveṣu triṣu ca naṭapatiḥ pratyahaṃ vīthiyātrāṃ
kṛtvā snātvā sadas svaṃ praviśati śivayā kuñcitāṅghriṃ bhaje'ham //26//

Line b. *urunayane* 'its eyes open wide'. Note that the Festival Ritual text, the *Citsabheśotsavasūtra*, refers to the opening of the eye (*unmīlana*) of Bhikṣāṭana's chariot, p. 214.

75 The guardian of the temple or, more particularly, the guardian of the functioning of the temple, who is found in all South Indian Śiva temples. The role of Caṇḍeśvara is clearly set out by Davis: 'Like Śiva's own power of reabsorption, the fierce Caṇḍa removes and absorbs a host of things: the afflictions of his devotees, mistakes made in worshipping Śiva, and Śiva's too-pure leftovers.' R. Davis, *Ritual in an Oscillating Universe* (Princeton University Press, 1991), p. 157. The Hymn to the Deities of the Naṭarāja Temple, the *Devatāstotra*, says that it is by Caṇḍeśvara's grace that worship of Śiva bears fruit (verse 120, *Patañjalipūjāsūtra*, p. 213). For Caṇḍeśvara as a Nāyaṉār, see chapter 9, p. 209f.

4 THE HALL OF CONSCIOUSNESS, THE HEART OF THE UNIVERSE

1 '*Citsabhānāthadehamayacitsabhāmandiram*', *Citsabheśotsavasūtra*, p. 86.

2 David Dean Shulman, *Songs of the Harsh Devotee: The Tēvāram of Cuntaramūr-*

ttināyaṉār translated and annotated (Department of South Asia Regional Studies, University of Philadelphia, 1990), p. 567–72. The 'refrain' varies slightly from verse to verse.

3 Since there is no evidence to suggest that Cidambaram was seen as the heart of the world in Pallava times, why the hall was first given the Tamil name 'Little' (*ciṟ*) is not apparent. Inscriptions at Cidambaram speak of a *pērambalam*, a great hall 'opposite' to the Cit Sabhā, and Graefe suggested that Śiva's hall was small in contrast to the great hall of Kālī, the original goddess of the site ('Legends as Mile-Stones', p. 139). But there is no evidence of any such temple; and the provision of a separate shrine for the Goddess within the precincts of a Śiva temple began only in the late Cōḻa period. Perhaps the Cit Sabhā was seen as small in comparison with a regular shrine with *vimāna* over a *garbhagṛha* and an *ardhamaṇḍapa*?

4 Trans. by Robert Ernest Hume, *The Thirteen Principal Upanishads* 2nd edn (Oxford University Press, 1931), pp. 262f.

5 And other Cidambaram texts, most notably the *Daharavidyākhaṇḍa* of the *Cidambararahasya*.

6 *Sūta Saṃhitā, Jñānayoga khaṇḍa* 11.50b–52, 62.

7 Trans. John Loud, with slight alteration by me.

8 *Citsabheśotsavasūtra*, pp. 302–3.

9 *mūlādhārādiṣaṭke'py anavaratanaṭaṃ yaṃ virājo hṛdabje*
sarpendravyāghrapādapramukhamuninutaṃ ṣaṭsu kāleṣu vedaiḥ /
ārādhyābhīṣṭasiddhi[ṃ] dvijakulatilakāḥ prāpnuvanti prabhuṃ taṃ
cicchaktyāyuktam ādyaṃ kanakagirikaraṃ kuñcitāṅghriṃ bhaje'ham //65//

In the light of the passage in the Festival Ritual text just referred to, it might be that the *ṣaṭsu kāleṣu* referred to here is six times a year rather than six times a day, each of the *cakra*s once a year.

10 Somesethu Dikshitar in his introduction to the Festival Ritual text says that there are five *yantra*s in the Rahasya (p. 3 of unnumbered sequence).

11 S. Meyyapan, *Chidambaram Golden Temple* (Madras, 1992), p. 22.

12 Sivaramamurti, *Naṭarāja*, p. 383.

13 Harle, *Temple Gateways in South India*, p. 29. Again, Kane, in his long list of pilgrimage sites (very weak on South India) in his authoritative study of Dharmaśāstra, says that the Cidambaram temple 'contains the "air *liṅga*" i.e. no *liṅga* is actually visible but a curtain is hung before a wall and when visitors enter the curtain is withdrawn and the wall is exhibited' (P. V. Kane, *History of Dharmaśāstra* (Pune: Bhandarkar Oriental Research Institute, 1958), vol. IV, p. 743).

14 *tilvavanyāṃ triśikharamakuṭe saṃsthām ākāśaliṅgam* . . . //100//

15 According to Somasekhara Dikshitendra, the *ākāśa liṅga* is situated above the bedroom of the Divine Couple (*paḷḷi-y-aṟai*) in the north-west corner of the inner courtyard. Somasethu Dikshitar (ed.), *The History of Chidambaram: Sri Nataraja's Temple* (*A Guide to Sri Nataraja Temple*), Part I *Legends, History and Architecture* by T. Satyamurthy; Part II *Descriptions of Shrines* by Somasekharendra

Dikshitendra (translated by R. Sasikala) (Chidambaram: S. Somaraja Dikshitar, 1987), Part II, p. 36.

16 B. G. L. Swamy, *Chidambaram and Naṭarāja: Problems and Rationalization* (Mysore: Geetha Book House, 1979), p. 76.

17 T. Ramalinga Dikshitar, 'A Study of Chidambaram and its Shrine as Recorded in Sanskrit Literature', unpublished MLitt thesis, Annamalai University, 1963, p. 94.

18 The threefold division has a natural logic, and is commonly found; only the identification of the Candramaulīśvara is worthy of remark, though that identification also is entirely to be expected. An instance of the division into formless, with form, and both together is Umāpati's statement in his *Śataratnasaṃgraha* that Śiva while his Śakti is inert is formless (*niṣkala*), when he is about to act he is both formless and with form (*sakalaniṣkala*) as Sadāśiva, and when he is acting he has gross form (*sthūla*) as Īśvara (Tanjavur edn., p. 88).

19 The Tanjavur painting of Naṭarāja within the Cit Sabhā has already been considered in chapter 1. The circumambulatory is formed by the gap between the double set of walls around the *garbhagṛha*. The width of this ambulatory or vestibule is a little over 1.5 m. The buttressing of both sets of walls every 3 m or so provides boundaries to the paintings. These paintings were discovered only in the 1930s, for they had been painted over in the eighteenth century. According to Sivaramamurti there is a second painting portraying the Cit Sabhā: 'One of the paintings shows the temple at Chidambaram, Naṭarāja dancing in the *ānandatāṇḍava* pose, in the *sabhā* of the temple, represented with the front porch approached by steps' (*Naṭarāja*, p. 223). Sivaramamurti is followed by B. G. L. Swamy, who gives a rough sketch of part of the structure. However, both authors ignore what is clearly visible on the French Institute of Pondicherry/École Française d'Extrême-Orient photograph of the painting (neg. no. 10393–7), namely a high *vimāna* rising from the left half of the structure. In my opinion, this is a representation of the Tanjavur temple itself, with Naṭarāja in the *maṇḍapa* facing South. The alternative is that it is a visualization of the Cit Sabhā provided with a *vimāna*, with Śiva dancing in the front, lesser, structure. The staircase closely matches the staircase at Tanjavur.

B. G. L. Swamy attempts to argue that the Kanaka Sabhā was built by Kulōttuṅga III (1178–1216), on the grounds that it is the *mukhamaṇḍapa* (front porch) for Sabhāpati that the king mentions in an inscription in his temple at Tribhuvanam enumerating his victories and temple-building activities (190 of 1907). But Swamy perversely makes no mention of the painting there that clearly shows both Sabhās. Swamy, *Chidambaram and Naṭarāja*, p. 36.

20 Sivaramamurti, *Naṭarāja*, p. 223.

21 Chamber no. 9 in the ground plan given by B. Venkataraman, *Rajarajesvaram*, p. 15.

22 Stella Kramrisch, *The Hindu Temple* 2 vols. (University of Calcutta, 1946), vol. 1, p. 163. Cf. Michael W. Meister, 'The Hindu temple constructs *ākāśa*', 'The Hindu Temple: Axis of Access' in Kapila Vatsyayan (ed.), *Concepts of Space*

Ancient and Modern (New Delhi: Indira Gandhi National Centre for the Arts /Abhinav Publications, 1991), pp. 268–80, p. 268. And Stella Kramrisch, 'the edifice of the temple . . . is a reiteration in its own terms, a re-construction of the all-filling *ākāśa* and of the waves of the flood prior to creation', 'Space in Indian Cosmogony and in Architecture', *ibid.*, pp. 101–4, p. 103.

23 The opening verse of the poem is an obvious choice, stating as it does that Śiva dances in the heart of the world; the second verse is this:

> By the grace of His Śakti
> great Ādiśeṣa incarnated on earth
> as the lord of yogis
> to remove from embodied selves
> the extensive sin
> in mind, speech and body
> and to tell them how to worship Him
> according to the correct procedures.
> As Patañjali he wrote those books named after him
> on yoga, grammar, medicine and ritual.
> Him Whose foot is curved
> I worship.

śakter yasya prasādād adhidharaṇi mahān ādiśeṣāvatāro
yogīndro dehabhājām agham ativipulaṃ cittavākkāyasaṃstham /
dūrīkartuṃ ca yaṣṭuṃ yam akṛtakapathā yogaśabdauṣadhārcā-
granthān pātañjalākhyān svayam api kṛtavān kuñcitāṅghriṃ bhaje'ham //278//

24 There are all told more than fifty verses which refer to the Cit Sabhā, distributed throughout the poem, though with a large gap between verses 159 and 219. Śiva is often referred to as Citsabheśa, 'Lord of the Cit Sabhā'.

25 *yasminn āmūlapīṭhāvadhikanakaśilāmātṛkāvarṇaklpte*
brahmaśrīnātharudreśvaraśaramukhabhāksāmbasādākhyamūrdhni /
bhūtaiḥ śāstraiś ca vedaiḥ stutabahucaritaṃ stambharūpaiś ca kudye
nṛtyantaṃ citsabheśaṃ niravadhisukhadaṃ kuñcitāṅghriṃ bhaje'ham //3//

26 '*akārādyekapañcāśadvarṇamukhasarvamantrasvarūpādhiṣṭhāna*', *Citsabheśvarotsvasūtra*, p. 86.

27 V. Sudanthiran analyses the *adhiṣṭhāna* of the *gopura*s and the shrines of Cidambaram; the Nṛtta Sabhā seems to be the oldest ('*Adhiṣṭhāna*s of the various structures of the Naṭarāja Temple at Chidambaram', *Tamil Civilization*, 6/1–2, 1988, pp. 53–70); however, more detailed analysis of Cidambaram and other temples is necessary before any firm conclusions can be reached as to date.

28 *sṛṣṭyai brahmāṇam ādau harim atha jagatāṃ rakṣaṇāyātmarūpaḥ*
saṃhṛtyai rudramūrtiṃ tv atha nikhilatirodhānahetor maheśam /
tallokānugrahārthaṃ himagiritanayāsaktasādākhyamūrtiṃ
yaḥ sṛṣṭvānandanṛttaṃ sadasi vitanute kuñcitāṅghriṃ bhaje'ham //102//

Umāpati always refers to Sadāśiva as Sādākhya. This verse was also cited in chapter 1, p. 18.

29 *andhaḥkośe vidhātā garuḍavararathaḥ prāṇakośe ca rudraś*
cetaḥkośe maheśas tadanu ca varavijñānakośe sadākhyaḥ /
ānandābhikhyakośe lasati ca satataṃ yasya śambhor nideśāt
taṃ devaṃ rājarājeśvaravarasuhṛdaṃ kuñcitāṅghriṃ bhaje'ham //105//

Line b. Sādākhya: here Sadākhya for the metre.

30 The relation of these thrones to the actual building is not apparent. The clearest exposition is that provided by Ramalinga Dikshitar ('Study of Chidambaram'), but he is at times at odds with his one cited source, the *Tilvavana Māhātmya*, which itself is by no means clear. On occasion, even where the Sanskrit is clear, as in the case of Rudra's five pillars, Ramalinga Dikshitar differs, here assigning the pillars to Viṣṇu's *pīṭha*. Somasekhara Dikshitendra, in his description of shrines in *The History of Chidambaram*, ed. Somasethu Dikshitar, p. 42, assigns them to Rudra. Another order of complication is that the *Tilvavana Māhātyma* locates Brahmā's throne (*āsana*) in the Cit Sabhā, comprised of the twenty-eight pillars that are the Āgamas (5.52), and also in the Kanaka Sabhā (*brahmāsanamayīṃ vediṃ*) (7.31) comprised of the eighteen Purāṇas. The Festival Ritual text mentions the sets of pillars without associating them with particular forms of Śiva (p. 86).

31 *yatsaṃsatpūrvabhāge diśi diśi vilasatpūrvabhāgā nitāntaṃ*
svāntargūḍhottarāṃśāḥ śivamukhabhavanāś cāgamāḥ kāmikādyāḥ /
aṣṭāviṃśānusaṃkhyā dhṛtakanakamayastambharūpāḥ stuvanti
stutyaṃ taṃ nṛttamūrtiṃ śrutiśatavinutaṃ kuñcitāṅghriṃ bhaje'ham //4//

32 The mutual relations of these two types of revealed texts will be considered in the following chapter. Naṭarāja being praised by *śruti* is also mentioned in verses 67 and 78. In verse 36 Śiva is said to have created Brahmā and then to have given him the whole collection of *śruti* (*śrutigaṇam akhilaṃ*).

33 *yadgoṣṭhyāṃ dvārabāhye rajatagirinibhaṃ pañcavarṇasvarūpaṃ*
sopānaṃ dvārabhāgaṃ jayavijayamukhai rakṣitaṃ dvārapālaiḥ /
tattvānāṃ ṣaṇṇavatyā saha vidhimukharāḥ pañcadevāś ca nityam
yasyāntar bhānti tasminn aviratanaṭanaṃ kuñcitāṅghriṃ bhaje'ham //5//

34 For Appar, see R. Nagaswamy, *Śiva-Bhakti* (New Delhi: Navrang, 1989), p. 94. Tirumūlar refers to the 96 *tattvas* several times (154, 1155, 2027, 2146, 2438). The most commonly cited source of information on these *tattvas* is the *Tattuva-k-kaṭṭaḷai*, trans. by Henry R. Hoisington, '*Tattuva-kaṭṭalei*. A Synopsis of the Mystical Philosophy of the Hindus', (*Journal of the American Oriental Society* 1, 1853–4, pp. 3–30) but the list given in the *Tilvavana Māhātmya*, 5.35–51 differs considerably.

35 *Neñcuviṭutūtu*, trans. T. N. Ramachandran, '*Neñju Vidu Thoothu* (Message through the Heart)', *Śaiva Siddhānta*, XI/3 and 4 (1976), pp. 101–6; 131–5, p. 132.

36 *yatstūpyaḥ śaktirūpās tadadharavilasadromarūpāś ca kīlā*
ucchvāsāḥ svarṇapaṭṭās taduranihitā daṇḍarūpāś ca nāḍyaḥ /
nāḍyantaḥ sarvalokāḥ phalakatanugatā hastarūpāḥ kalāś ca
tasyāṃ yo nṛtyatīśas tam anupamatanuṃ kuñcitāṅghriṃ bhaje'ham //6//

Line b. *taduranihitā* ? One short syllable is missing here.

37 They are Vāmā, Jyeṣṭhā, Raudrī, Kālī, Kalavikarṇī, Balī, Balavikarṇī, Balapramathanī, and Manonmanī, according to the *Tilvavanamāhātmya* 7.25–27, which adds, as another possibility, the seven *svaras* along with short and long stress.

38 *vighneśaskandalakṣmīvidhimukhaśararāṭpādukāvajraliṅga-*
jyotinṛttasvarūpair varuṇamukhajuṣā hāṭakākarṣamūrtyā /
svāgre dakṣe ca vāme parivṛtasadasi śrīśivānāyako yo
madhye nṛttaṃ karoti prabhuvaram anaghaṃ kuñcitāṅghriṃ bhaje'ham //7//

39 *stambhākāraiḥ purāṇair dhṛtakanakasabhā bhāti yasyāgrabhāge*
yasyāṃ dharmasvarūpo vṛṣabhapatir udagvaktrapadmo vibhāti /
yasyāṃ īśasya devyāḥ sphaṭikavaṭukayo ratnamūrter munīndrāḥ
kurvanty adbhiḥ prapūjāṃ tam api naṭavaraṃ kuñcitāṅghriṃ bhaje'ham //75//

40 Nagaswamy, perhaps unnecessarily, is concerned to separate the bull from the 'human figure' (*Śiva-Bhakti*, p. 200). He also stresses the importance of Nandikeśvara, 'a tremendous personality': 'In the fields of philosophy, literature, music, dance, medicine, Kāmaśāstra and other fields, he is claimed to be the very originator of these *śāstras*' (*ibid.*).

41 *adrākṣīn nandikeśaḥ kanakasadasi yaṃ hy ardhanārīsvarūpaṃ*
paścān nārāyaṇārdhaṃ punar api girijārūpam ākārahīnam /
tāraṃ tanmaṇḍalāntarjvalanam anupamaṃ saccidānandamūrtiṃ
nṛtteśānaṃ muhurtaṃ tam aparasugamaṃ kuñcitāṅghriṃ bhaje'ham //246//

42 *oṃkārasvarṇasaṃsatprasṛtaparaśivajyotir ānandanṛttā-*
lokād uttīrṇam ugraṃ bhavam ativipulaṃ vārdhikalpaṃ munīndraiḥ /
ūhāpohādihīnasvatanugatajagadvṛndam adhyātmavidyā-
bodhācāryaṃ purāṇaṃ praśamitatamasaṃ kuñcitāṅghriṃ bhaje'ham //222//

43 *yadbhāsā bhāti nityaṃ sakalam api jagat tatparaṃjyotir eva*
vairāje hṛtsaroje kanakasadasi vai sāmbanṛtteśamūrtiḥ /
bhūtvā nṛttaṃ karoti prabhur api jagatāṃ rakṣaṇe jāgarūkaḥ
taṃ devaṃ citsabheśaṃ vidhṛtasumasṛmiṃ kuñcitāṅghriṃ bhaje'ham //85//

44 *brahmāṇḍaṃ yasya dehaṃ ravijadiśi pado vaktrabṛndāny udīcyāṃ*
tadvairājāntaraṅge vilasati hṛdayāmbhoruhe dakṣiṇāgre /
madhye sammelanākhye munivaramanasā bhāvite yantrarāje
yaḥ śaktyā nṛtyatīśas tam api naṭapatiṃ kuñcitāṅghriṃ bhaje'ham //1//

45 *pañcāśatkoṭisaṃkhyāparimitadharaṇiśrīvirāḍākhyadhātor*
ekasvāntābjabhittisthitakanakamahāyantrarāṭkarṇikāyāṃ /
nṛtyantaṃ citsabheśaṃ trisṛbhir api sadā śaktibhiḥ sevitāṅghriṃ
nādānte bhāsamānaṃ navavidhanaṭanaṃ kuñcitāṅghriṃ bhaje'ham //2//

46 I have seen a coloured drawing of this *cakra* by Rājagaṇeśa Dīkṣita, now in the possession of G. Parameśvara Dīkṣita. A different version, without Śivakāmasundarī, is given on the frontispiece of S. V. Chamu's *The Divine Dancer* (Mysore: Astanga Yoga Vijnana Mandiram, 1982), representing the Sammelanacakra as understood by his deceased guru, Shri Ranga Guru, with the form of Naṭarāja within the Śrīcakra, his head and limbs circumscribed by apexes of the enclosure of fourteen triangles.

47 *śrīcakrādiviśeṣayantraghaṭitaṃ bhittisvarūpaṃ sadā-*
nandajñānamayaṃ naṭeśaśivayoḥ saṃmelanaṃ bodhayat /
śrījāmbunadabilvapatraracitair mālāgaṇair lakṣitaṃ
kastūrīmasṛṇaṃ cidambaram idaṃ sthānaṃ rahasyaṃ numaḥ //111//
lokātiśāyivibhavaṃ mahad āseve cidambararahasyam /
pañcākṣarī yadīyā jīvātuḥ sarvalokaśubhadātrī /
śaktīḥ samagrāḥ grasate dinānte yasmiṃś ca gauryāvalate kapardī /
yasmāt prage viśvam upaiti śaktiṃ cakāsti tatcetasi me cakāstu //112//

48 Cf. Ramalinga Dikshitar, 'A Study of Chidambaram and its Shrine', p. 72.
49 Rao, *Hindu Iconography*, 2.1, p. 233.
50 Coomaraswamy, *The Dance of Śiva*, p. 68 and p. 70.
51 M. A. Dorai Rangaswamy, *The Religion and Philosophy of Tēvāram*, 4 vols (University of Madras, 1958), vol. 1, pp. 493f.
52 Shulman, *Songs of the Harsh Devotee*, pp. 532f.
53 Trans. Shulman, *ibid.*, p. 536.
54 Trans. Natarajan (slightly altered).
55 There is a variety of possibilities. 'The Śaivāgamas state that Śiva danced in a hundred and eight modes but content themselves with the description of nine modes only as it is very difficult to describe all' (Rao, *Hindu Iconography*, vol. II/1, p. 224). The Āgamas Rao refers to distinguish first the standard form of Naṭarāja in the Ānanda Tāṇḍava. The second, third, and fourth are variations of this. The fifth, sixth, seventh, and eighth are varieties of Ūrdhvatāṇḍava, where Śiva has his right leg raised vertically. The ninth has both feet on the ground. The *Vyāghrapura Māhātmya* (17.70–2) mentions nine dances, as Ramalinga Dikshitar notes ('A Study of Chidambaram and its Shrine', p. 130), but they are all said to be performed in Śvetāraṇyam (Tiruvengadu); the same *Māhātmya* also mentions Cidambaram as one of nine sites of Śiva's dance (17.73–5). The nine Tāṇḍavas of Śvetāraṇya are shown in modern paintings in the temple's Nava-tāṇḍava *maṇḍapa*. A different nine are sculpted in stone in the Uttarapatisvaram temple, Tichchengattangudi (S. R. Balasubrahmanyam, *Middle Chola Temples: Rajaraja I to Kulottunga I* (Faridabad: Thomson Press (India) Limited, 1975), p. 101). Mention should also be made of the *Saundaryalaharī*, verse 41, where Śiva's *tāṇḍava* is said to be the embodiment of the nine *rasas*. This famous poem attributed to Śaṅkara is discussed in relation to the *Kuñcitāṅghristava* in chapter 8; see also chapter 6.

56 *sūkṣmāt sūkṣmāntaraṅge daharakuharacitpuṇḍarīkākhyaveśmany*
antaś cinmātrarūpaṃ racayati naṭanaṃ kuñcitāṅghriṃ bhaje'ham //273//

The rest of this verse is discussed in chapter 5, pp. 106f.

5 ŚAIVA SIDDHĀNTA AND VEDĀNTA

1 My understanding of the doctrines, philosophy and history of the Sanskrit Śaiva Siddhānta is based almost entirely on the authoritative work of H. Brunner.

2 Śakti and her forms in the *Kuñcitāṅghristava* are considered in chapter 6.

3 This is the second *sūtra*, the first being exhortatory. It is a *mūlasūtra*, its importance signalled by its first word, *atha*, 'now'. Umāpati says it is from the *Raurava Āgama*, but it is not in the published edition. It is found in the *Svāyambhuva Āgama*, in the part published as the *Svāyambhuvasūtrasaṃgraha* (ed. and trans. P.-S. Filliozat, *Le Tantra Svayaṃbhū, Vidyāpāda, avec le commentaire de Sadyojyoti*, (Geneva: Droz, 1991), 1.2).

4 *Śataratnasaṃgraha* (all references are to the Tanjavur edn), p. 15.

5 *svāmin saṃsāravārdhāv adhikabhayakare dustare pāśanakra-*
cchanne magnāntaraṃ mām anadhigatasadācāravṛttiṃ śaṭhāgryam /
dīnaṃ tvatpādapūjāvimukham aghayutaṃ rakṣa rakṣety ajasraṃ
sarve lokāḥ śrayante yam api sadasi taṃ kuñcitāṅghriṃ bhaje'ham //300//

6 *bhojaṃ bhojaṃ yadarcājanitam anupamaṃ bhogam adhyātmayogāt*
tāraṃ tāraṃ bhavābdhiṃ vipulabhayakaraṃ yasya bhāvāt sudhīndrāḥ /
dāhaṃ dāhaṃ hṛdantargatam atijaraṭhaṃ pāśavargaṃ yadarṇaṃ
jāpaṃ jāpaṃ ramante paramahasipade kuñcitāṅghriṃ bhaje'ham //308//

7 T. N. Ramachandran, '*Neñju Vidu Thoothu* (Message through the Heart)', *Śaiva Siddhānta*, XI/3 and 4, 1976, pp. 101–6; 131–5, p. 106.

8 *Sūtra* 73, from the *Mataṅgapārameśvara Āgama*.

9 *Śataratnasaṃgraha*, ad *sūtra* 73, p. 304.

10 *bhogāt prārabdhakarmāpy adhikabhayakare sañcitāgāmike dve*
jñānān nāśaṃ prayāte iti nigamavacāṃsy āhur etat prasiddham /
tāny apy ālokamātrān nijanaṭanatanoḥ prāṇināṃ jātu diṣṭyā
nighnan yacchan sukhaṃ yaḥ sadasi vijayate kuñcitāṅghriṃ bhaje'ham //268//

Nigama elsewhere in the *Kuñcitāṅghristava* is used in respect of the Vedas. The first two *pāda*s could of course apply to Advaita, e.g. *Śaṅkarabhāṣya ad* 4.1.15, but the doctrine is not found in the Vedas and Upaniṣads.

11 This famous verse (*Kiraṇa Āgama vp* 6.13b–14a) is quoted by Hélène Brunner-Lachaux, *Somaśambhupaddhati*, Text, Translation and Notes, 3 vols. (Pondicherry: Institut Français d'Indologie, 1963, 1968, 1977), vol. III, p. xxiii, where the topic is fully discussed. Note also Sanderson's comment that the fact *dīkṣā* does not deal with *prārabdhakarman* 'explains . . . why individuals continue to live after initiation and indeed why the survivors generally appear no wiser or better for having gone through it' ('The Doctrine of the

Mālinīvijayottaratantra' in *Ritual and Speculation in Early Tantrism*, ed. T. Goudriaan (Albany: State University of New York Press, 1992), pp. 286f.)

12 *vidyām agnau pratiṣṭhāṃ payasi ca dharaṇau yo nivṛttiṃ samīre*
śāntyākhyāṃ śāntyatītāṃ nabhasi nijakalāṃ yojayan hy aprameyaḥ /
sūkṣmāc chūkṣmāntaraṅge daharakuharacitpuṇḍarīkākhyaveśmany
antaś cinmātrarūpaṃ racayati naṭanaṃ kuñcitāṅghriṃ bhaje'ham //273//

13 Verse 17, chapter 3, p. 70.
14 Verse 111, p. 12.
15 *Śataratnasaṃgraha*, *sūtra* 54, p. 263.
16 *Śataratnasaṃgraha*, p. 267.
17 *Civapirakācam*, trans. Henry R. Hoisington, '*Siva-pirakāsam.* Light of Sivam. A Metaphysical and Theological Treatise', *Journal of the American Oriental Society*, IV/2 (1854), pp. 127–244, pp. 133f.
18 Nor is there opening praise of Gaṇeśa, unlike in his other major works. However, it is now generally accepted to be the work of Umāpati.
19 *Śataratnasaṃgraha*, p. 4. The claim in both the Sanskrit lives of Umāpati that he was an incarnation of Trilocana Śivācārya, presumably the author of the *Siddhāntasārāvali*, is a tribute to Umāpati's mastery of Sanskrit sources, including the principal *Paddhatis*.
20 *Ibid.*
21 The fivefold *mala* comprises *mala, karman, mahāmāyā* , the universe that arises from *māyā*, and the Śakti that obscures, according to a verse cited by Umāpati in the *Śataratnasaṃgraha*, p. 222; and the same in verse 33 of the *Civapirakācam*.
22 See chapter 4, p. 94 and note 34.
23 Trans. T. N. Ramachandran.
24 *Pōṟṟippahroṭai*, trans. T. N. Ramachandran, '*Poorip Phahrotai* (Multiple Hymn of Praise'), *Śaiva Siddhānta*, XII/3 (1977), pp. 100–8.
25 *Irupāvirupatu* of Aruḷnanti and *Uṉmaiviḷakkam* of Maṉavācakam Kaṭantār.
26 *divāndha eṣa yūyaṃ manāk paśyata samyag eti* /.
27 Cf. Aruḷnanti's description of the worthless rich: 'With spices smeared and with garlands adorned, wearing cloths of gold and followed by attendants, men of prosperity, speechless and devoid of understanding, lounging proudly in the palanquin born by carriers, on either side fans swinging, amidst the harmonious music of the instruments and the wild sound of the clarion, are but corpses.' *Civañāṉa Cittiyār* 3.2.95, trans. J. M. Nallaswami Pillai, *Sivajñāna Siddhiyar of Aruḷnandi Sivāchārya* translated into English (Madras, 1913), p. 192.
28 The *Pārthavana Māhātmya* gives circumstantial details of the physical process of initiation. When Maṟaiñāṉa sees Umāpati, his body shakes and he is tormented by hunger. It seems to be this hunger that leads him to drink a weaver's rice gruel. The same hunger leads Umāpati to do the same, careless of his purity.

29 Cf. Brunner's remark, apropos the pupil's right to worship Śiva on his own account after the second, *viśeṣa, dīkṣā,* 'it is logically at the end of this second *dīkṣā* that he receives fom the hands of his *guru* a personal *liṅga* in the form of a pebble (*bāṇaliṅga*)', *Somaśambhupaddhati*, vol. III, p. 143 n. 45. [My translation from the French.]

30 See Brunner, *ibid.*, pp. 477f. She concludes, 'Such a din (*tintamarre*) has for its avowed aim to block out all other noise and to proclaim to the neighbourhood the highly important event that is taking place at that moment' [My translation from the French]. That in the case of Umāpati's story the celebrations continue beyond the lustration is not surprising, given the excitement of the event and the numerous personnel assembled.

31 Our befuddled *citta* He clarified
By his divine presence, but not content
With this, He did initiate us in th'path
Supreme of Śaiva wisdom infinite
Beginning with Samaya and ending
In *abhiṣeka*; by his divine look. (*Pōṟṟippahroṭai* 64)

Trans. T. N. Ramachandran, '*Poorip Phahrotai* (Multiple Hymn of Praise)', p. 106.

32 The *Cidambara Māhātmya* does once mention *dīkṣā*. When Śeṣa is practising asceticism in order to see the dance, Śiva tells him in a passage that looks like an insertion, 'One form of mine is shown in the Ācārya who alone in his compassion can cut the mass of bonds for men whose *mala* is ripe through the *viśeṣa dīkṣā*' (15.15–16). The *Kōyil Purāṇam* omits this. The title Dīkṣita, it may be mentioned, refers to the Vedic rather than Āgamic tradition, referring to the *dīkṣā* of the *yajamāna* in the Soma Sacrifice. For the use of Dīkṣita as a title and then a name, see C. G. Kashikar and Asko Parpola, 'Śrauta Traditions in Recent Times', in F. Staal (ed.), *Agni* (Berkeley: Asian Humanities Press, 1983), pp. 199–251.

33 *Tiruvarutpayaṉ* II. 8, trans. J. M. Nallaswami Pillai, *Tiruvarutpayaṉ: Commentary and English Translation*, 2nd edn. (Dharmapuram: Dharmapuram Adhinam, 1958), p. 14.

34 *Śataratnasaṃgraha, sūtra* 76 (misprinted 75), p. 309.

35 *yaḥ śambhur nṛttarāṅ me prabalataramahāmantrasiddhiṃ pradattvā*
gurvīṃ yogasya siddhiṃ jananamṛtaharaṃ cātmabodhaṃ mahāntam /
sūtādināṃ vimuktipradam api mahitagauravaṃ patramūlaṃ
svaṃ nṛttaṃ darśayitvā sukhayati nitarāṃ kuñcitāṅghriṃ bhaje'ham //305//

36 The Tamil text of this chit is given in T. B. Siddalingaiah, *Origin and Development of Śaiva Siddhānta up to 14th Century* (Madurai Kamaraj University, 1979), p. 126, with the remark, 'This poem is quoted in almost all Śaiva works.' A small shrine to Sūta was being built in the grounds of the *maṭha* in 1992.

37 Lee Siegel, *Net of Magic: Wonders and Deceptions in India* (University of Chicago Press, 1991).

38 *Śataratnasaṃgraha*, p. 339.
39 *Pārthavana Mahātmya*, 113–15.
40 The actions said to have been performed by Umāpati are the province of an Ācārya, not a *sādhaka*, the latter not being able to confer *dīkṣā*.
41 For a full discussion of this claim, see H. Brunner, 'Le Śaiva-siddhāntam "Essence" du Veda', *Indologica Taurinensia* 8 (1980–1), pp. 51–66.
42 *Mataṅgapārameśvara Vṛtti*, p. 1; but see also Sanderson, 'Meaning in Tantric Ritual', unpublished essay, p. 23. An instance of the strength of opposition to the Vedas among some Siddhāntins is Aghora Śivācārya's claim in his *Dīpikā* to Bhaṭṭa Nārāyaṇakaṇṭha's *Vṛtti* on the *Mṛgendra Āgama ad* 11.11, that the Vedas had an author, namely Hiraṇyagarbha, and further an author who, as Prajāpati/Brahmā, was not omniscient. Claims for Vedic credibility were not of course limited to Śaivas. Thus the *Bhāgavata Purāṇa* declares itself to be 'equal to the spiritual essence of the Vedas' (*brahmasammitam*, 1.3.40; 2.1.8; 2.8.28), the 'quintessence extracted from all the Vedas and the epics' (*sarvavedetihāsānāṃ sāraṃ sāraṃ samuddhṛtam*, 1.3.42), 'the essence of the Upaniṣads' (*sarvavedāntasāram*, 12.13.12, 15).
43 The verse is quoted and translated by Nallaswami Pillai, *Śivajñāna Siddhiyār*, p. li. The attribution to Umāpati is mentioned by J. Jaswant Raj, *Grace in the Śaiva Siddhāntam and in St. Paul* (Madras: South Indian Salesian Society, 1989), p. 497, citing the anthology *Sivaneṟiccheyyut tirattu* edited by P. Rāmanātha Piḷḷai (Kaḻagam, 1969), p. 4; Jaswant Raj points out the pun on *veṇṇey*, butter.
44 *Civañāṉa Cittiyār* 3.11.13, trans. J. M. Nallaswami Pillai, *Sivajñāna Siddhiyar*, p. 229.
45 On the term *iṟaivaṉṉūl*, 'revelations of God', see S. Arulsami, *Śaivism: A Perspective of Grace* (New Delhi: Sterling, 1987), p. 15 and p. 152.
46 '*Catvāro'pi vedā atha srotorūpā eva*', *Śataratnasaṃgraha*, p. 31
47 *Ibid.*, p. 29.
48 *Ibid.*, p. 33.
49 *Pauṣkarāgama* (*Jñānapāda*) with the *Bhāṣya* of Umāpati Śivācārya, ed. Ambalavana Navalar (Cidambaram, 1925), p. 10. In verse 177 Umāpati refers to an important Śaiva philosopher, Haradatta, who took a position similar to that of Nīlakaṇṭha on the Vedic authenticity of Śaivism. Haradatta's date is uncertain. Umāpati quotes from Haradatta's *Śrutisūktimālā* in the *Pauṣkarabhāṣya*. In the *Kuñcitāṅghristava* Umāpati does not mention Haradatta's name, referring only to his demonstration of his faith in Śiva by sitting on a red-hot plate, while at the same time 'explaining that Supreme Śiva is made known in the Upaniṣads' (*śrutyantavedyaṃ śivam api paramaṃ bodhayan svāṃ ca bhūtim*). It was in this uncomfortable postion that he is said to have composed his *Śrutisūktimālā*; see. S. Swaminathan, 'Haradattar', *Śaiva Siddhānta* vol. xv, 1980, pp. 17–25, p. 18. S. S. Suryanarayana Sastri lists 'doctrinal affinities' between Śrīkaṇṭha's *Bhāṣya* and Haradatta's *Śrutisūktimālā* (*The Śivādvaita of Śrīkaṇṭha* (University of Madras, 1972, first published 1930), pp. 285f.).
50 *Pauṣkarabhāṣya*, p. 10.

51 *śiṣyāṇāṃ vedabāhyasthitim adhijuṣatāṃ bodhanārthaṃ paṭhantaś*
caryāyogāṅghribhedaprakaṭitavibhavān kāmikādyāgamāṃs tān /
bhūdevā vājapeyakratugatanṛpatiproddhṛtoddāmaśukla-
cchatrā yaṃ pūjayanti śrutipathavidhinā kuñcitāṅghriṃ bhaje'ham //107//

52 *yeṣāṃ vedoktakarmasv anadhikṛtir abhūd adrijātā pṛthivyāṃ*
teṣāṃ dharmādim āptyai paraśivaracitaṃ kāmikādiprabhedam /
sāṅgaṃ siddhāntatantraprakaram api catuṣṣaṣṭisaṃkhyāḥ kalāś ca
yasyādeśāt prakāśaṃ tv anayad aganutaṃ kuñcitāṅghriṃ bhaje'ham //146//

Puzzling is the mention of the sixty-four arts in this connection; in Umāpati's *Civapirakācam* they are found in similar contexts. In his invocation to Subrāhmaṇya he says that that god taught the true meaning of the limitless arts, *aṅgas* and the Vedas (*āraṇaṅkaḷ*), and in verse 14 of the same work he says that 'the leading object of the many arts, the Āgamas, and the Vedas (*palakalai ākamavētam*) is to explain the three eternal entities, Pati, Paśu and Pāśa'. A parallel may be found in the *Tilvavana Māhātmya* 4.17:

This holy place Cidambaram,
situated in the heart of Virāj
is the cause of the three Vedas,
the Siddhānta and the sixty-four arts.
catuḥṣaṣṭikalānāṃ ca trayīsiddhāntakāraṇam /
cidambaram idaṃ kṣetraṃ virāḍdhṛdayasaṃsthitam //4.17//

In verse 146 the *aṅgas* pertain to the Vedas; and the sense is probably 'the Siddhānta as well as the Vedas with their constituent parts'.

53 *sadyojātādimānāṃ vadanajalabhuvāṃ pañcākād yasya jātān*
mantrāṃs trailokyavaśyapramukhavaramahāsiddhidān saptakoṭīn /
śrutvā gaurī yaduktyā jagadupakṛtaye saprayogān sakalpān
tān lokān ānināya svayam atulakṛtiṃ kuñcitāṅghriṃ bhaje'ham //245//

54 *prakaṭaysvedaṃ jñānaṃ madbhaktānāṃ varānane /*
rakṣaṇīyaṃ prayatnena taskarebhyo dhanaṃ yatha //90//

This verse is from the *Niśvāsakārikā,* an Upāgama, quoted in the *Śataratnasaṃgraha*, p. 343.

55 *Śiva Purāṇa*, *Vāyu Saṃhitā*, VII.2.7.38. Umāpati wrote a commentary on the *Vāyu Saṃhitā*, according to the *Rājendrapura Māhātmya*, verse 46. Appar also refers to the teaching of the Āgamas given by Śiva to the Goddess (*Tēvāram* 5.15.4.)

56 *kalpārambhe yadīyād varagalavivarād om atheti dviśabdau*
siddhāntārthaprabodhṛpravaraśivakarāv āvirāstāṃ purastāt /
paścād vedādividyā vidhiharimukharā devatāḥ sarvalokā
jātās taṃ dakṣiṇāsyaṃ dyutikaranilayaṃ kuñcitāṅghriṃ bhaje'ham //251//

57 *Vṛtti* on the first *śloka* of the *Mṛgendra*, *vidyāpāda*, Dēvakōṭṭa edn. pp. 8–9, cited

by N. R. Bhatt, *Mṛgendrāgama* (*Kriyāpāda et Caryāpāda*) (Pondicherry: Institut Français d'Indologie, 1962), Introduction, p. ii.

58 Brunner-Lachaux, introduction to *Mṛgendrāgama: Section des rites et section du comportement* (Pondicherry: Institut Français d'Indologie, 1985), p. vii.

59 *sṛṣṭvā brahmāṇam ādau śrutigaṇam akhilaṃ dattavān yo maheśas*
tasmai nirmālyabhuktvaṃ svasadasi vilasatpañcapīṭhādharatvam /
sūtatvaṃ svasya mūrdhasthitamakuṭavaraprekṣaṇe haṃsabhāvaṃ
taṃ devaṃ citsabhāyāṃ sthitijuṣam amalaṃ kuñcitāṅghriṃ bhaje'ham //36//

60 *yadbrahmocchvāsarūpā śrutir api sakalā tatsamānā smṛtiś ca*
kalpā gāthāḥ purāṇaṃ vividhamanuvarāḥ setihāsāś ca vidyāḥ /
sarvatrādyāpi bhānti svayam api kṛpayā yatsabhāyāṃ naṭeśo
bhūtvā lokān samastān avati tam asamaṃ kuñcitāṅghriṃ bhaje'ham //87//

Line b. *gādhāḥ* emended to *gāthāḥ*.

61 The Sanskrit seems to say 'Their's is a release higher than *sārūpya*' (*sārūpyād adhikā muktis teṣām*), but this is against the logic of the passage, which demands the meaning 'as high as *sārūpya*.'

62 *Kōyil Purāṇam, Iraṇiyavaṉmaccarukkam* 2, trans. John Loud.

63 *Kōyil Purāṇam, Iraṇiyavaṉmaccarukkam* 5, trans. John Loud.

64 *lokeṣv advaitavidyāṃ prakaṭayitumanā yaḥ svayaṃ kṛttivāsā*
modāt sarvajñapīṭhasthitijuṣam amalaṃ śaṅkarākhyaṃ yatīndram /
svāṃśān naijāṅghripūjāpraśamitatamasāṃ bhūsurāṇāṃ kulābdhāv
utpādyānvagrahīt taṃ śukamunivinutaṃ kuñcitāṅghriṃ bhaje'ham //295//

65 *vedānte vākyarūpā upaniṣada imā brahmasāmīpyabhājas*
tāsāṃ mukhyā daśa syur yativiracitamahābhāṣyayuktā mahatyaḥ /
stambhākārāḥ stuvanti svaviditanaṭanaṃ sarvadā brahmarūpaṃ
taṃ devaṃ citsabheśaṃ param atimahasaṃ kuñcitāṅghriṃ bhaje'ham //88//

66 *vedānte vyāsarūpair . . .*
taiś śrutiṣu vidhisamaiḥ . . . munīndraiḥ
. . . //89//

This verse is quoted in full in chapter 3, pp. 62f.

67 My discussion of this text is based on N. Murugesa Mudaliar, '*Sankarpa-Nirakaranam*, Translation and Commentary', *Śaiva Siddhānta* 3 (1968), and subsequent issues.

68 *dikkālādyair vicintyaṃ svamanumananakṛnmānyam advaitasāraṃ*
madhyādyantādihīnaṃ sakalajanamanovṛttidṛṣṭāram ādyam /
māyātītaṃ praśāntaṃ dyutikaram akhilajyotiṣāṃ īśvarākhyā-
vācyaṃ tejomayaṃ taṃ param aparanaṭaṃ kuñcitāṅghriṃ bhaje'ham //267//

69 *satyaṃ brahmaiva nānyaj jagad idam akhilaṃ ceti mīmāṃsayitvā*
trayyantoktyā budhendrā hṛdi ca yam aniśaṃ cidghanaṃ durnirīkṣyam /
dīpajvālāśikhāvat satataparicayānandanṛttaṃ vimāyaṃ
śubhraṃ paśyanti tatsatpadaviṣayamaraṃ kuñcitāṅghriṃ bhaje'ham //272//

70 *Tāḷ*, 'foot', is Śiva's foot which communicates Śiva's grace to the devotees who bow beneath it.

71 Gordon Matthews, *Śiva-ñāna-bōdham, A Manual of Śaiva Religious Doctrine*, trans. from the Tamil, (London: Oxford University Press, 1948), p. 10. I have substituted 'grace' for 'foot'.

72 Trans. Hume, *The Thirteen Principal Upanishads*, p. 151.

73 *Chāndogya Upaniṣad* 3.14.1, trans. Hume, *ibid.*, p. 209.

74 *tyaktasvasvādhikārāḥ sarasijanayanāś cāgataṃ devasaukhya-*
prāptyai govindam uktvā kuśalam api karāśleṣapūrvaṃ pramodāt /
vatsa tvaṃ brahmatattvaṃ hṛdi na vikalayan prārthyase duḥkhahetuṃ
karmetyudbodhayanto yam api girivare kuñcitāṅghriṃ bhaje'ham //215//

75 For the phraseology here, cf. Śaṅkara on *Brahmasūtra* 3.2.21: *brahmasvabhāvo hi prapañco na prapañcasvabhāvaṃ brahma tena nāmarūpaprapañcapravilāpanena brahmatattvāvabodho bhavati.* (*Brahmasūtraśāṅkarabhāṣya*, ed. J. L. Shastri (Delhi: Motilal Banarsidass, 1980), p. 648.

76 *bho bho brahmarṣimugdhāḥ sadayam api mayā śikṣitāś cāpy ajasraṃ*
vedānte tattvabodhe na bhavata vibudhā yattato 'dyāpi yūyam /
medhāprāptyai sabheśaṃ vrajata śaraṇam ity ādarād bodhayitvā
dhātā yatkṣetrarājaṃ munigaṇam anayat kuñcitāṅghriṃ bhaje'ham //216//

77 *gīrvāṇādriṃ kadācid vipularadanayor antare svarṇarambhā*
bhrāntyā saṃdhāya vegād rajatagirivare krīḍayantaṃ gaṇeśam /
dṛṣṭvā premṇādrijātā yam api ca tarasāhūya nirdiśya sūnor
vṛttaṃ tuṣṭābhavat taṃ diviṣadadhipatiṃ kuñcitāṅghriṃ bhaje'ham //217//

78 *ekānte jātu yasya pramuditamanasā proktavedāntatattvo-*
pekṣāruṣṭasya vākyād dhimagiritanayā dhīvarādhīśavaṃśe /
āvirbhūyāmbudhisthaprabalaśapharasaṃgrāhiṇaṃ yaṃ vareṇyaṃ
vṛtvā tadvāmabhāge vasatim api gatā kuñcitāṅghriṃ bhaje'ham //157//

79 *sarveśaṃ sarvasattvaprakṛtim avikṛtiṃ sarvadaṃ sarvabhūṣaṃ*
sarvātītaṃ sadākhyaṃ sakaruṇanayanaṃ sarvavedāntasāram /
satyaṃ sad vyomasaṃsthaṃ sanakamunimukhair arcitaṃ sāmagītyām
utsāhaṃ saṃsadīśaṃ sakalakavinutaṃ kuñcitāṅghriṃ bhaje'ham //284//

80 *vedāntodgītarūpaṃ jvalanaḍamarukau dhārayantaṃ karābhyāṃ*
. . . //108//

81 *vedāntoktātmarūpaṃ vidhiharitanujaṃ viśvanāthaṃ sadasthaṃ*
. . . //66//

82 *yasmāc candrārdhacūḍān mṛduhasitamukhān nīlakaṇṭhāt triṇetrād*
vedāntodgītavṛttād vidhiharijanakād viśvamāyāvilāsāt /
vāmāvāmāṅgabhāgāt . . . //302//

83 *dhāvaṃ dhāvaṃ sadā yatpriyakaranilayaṃ bhūtirudrākṣavargair*
bhūṣaṃ bhūṣaṃ svakīyāṃ tanum api caritaṃ yasya vedāntagītaṃ /

karṇaṃ karṇaṃ nitāntaṃ triṣavaṇayajanaṃ brahmaniṣṭhā yatīndrāḥ
kāraṃ kāraṃ labhante bhavapadam abhavaṃ kuñcitāṅghriṃ bhaje'ham //311//

84 Trans. J. M. Nallaswami Pillai, *Uṇmaiviḷakkam* (Dharmapuram Adhinam, 1946).
85 *Tiruvaruṭpayaṉ* 83, trans. G. U. Pope, *The Tiruvaçagam*, p. xl.
86 Trans. Matthews, *Śiva-ñāna-bōdham*, pp. 22f.
87 Trans. Matthews, *ibid.*, p. 24.
88 *Tiruvaruṭpayaṉ* IX.1, trans. J. M. Nallaswami Pillai.
89 C. N. Singaravelu, *Unmai Vilakkam (The Exposition of Truth)* (Tellipazhi, 1981), p. 72.
90 See above, chapter 4, p. 93.
91 'In my view, the majority of Āgamas, especially those dealing with the temple cult, consisted originally of a continuous series of *paṭalas*, arranged according to a logical sequence, but not distributed into four sections' – thus Brunner summarizes the evidence she presents in 'Four *pādas* of Śivāgamas', *Journal of Oriental Research*, Dr. S. S. Janaki Felicitation volume, LVI-LXII (1986–92), pp. 260–78, p. 275. Note also her statement, 'in the vast majority of cases, it is the eminent position of the *kriyāpāda* which is striking: all other teachings converge to make the ritual effective' ('The place of Yoga in Śaivāgamas', in P.-S. Filliozat *et al.*, *Pandit N. R. Bhatt Felicitation Volume* (Delhi: Motilal Banarsidass, 1994), pp. 425–61, p. 444).
92 I refer to Brunner's article, 'The Place of Yoga in Śaivāgamas'. She states, 'the Śaiva ritual is through and through penetrated by *yoga*' (p. 452); and later says, 'From the statement, by several Āgamas, that the practice of *yoga* is the sole affair of the *sādhaka*, we can easily infer the existence, in their time, of a different kind of cult for the other Śaivas. Such is the situation which has probably prevailed for a rather long period. Then at a certain time and for reasons that we may only guess, the *yoga*-oriented cult of the *sādhaka* must have been adopted by other kinds of private worshippers, whose motivations and attitude were different, but who preserved the inherited model. Finally, the same model was integrated into the common temple ritual, where it was associated, not always harmoniously, with elements coming from the other direction' (p. 456). [My translation from the French.]

93 *yogān nirbījasaṃjñāt samuditaparamānandakāṣṭāsamādhi*
. . . *nityaniḥsaṅgavidyo*
'py ādyaḥ siddho yam antaḥ kalayati nitarāṃ kuñcitāṅghriṃ bhaje'ham //185//

94 *pratyāhārādiyogair hṛdayakamalato brahmarandhraṃ svakīyaṃ*
prāṇān ānīya divyaṃ gaṇam api śaradāṃ vāhayanto mahāntaḥ /
yogīndrāḥ siddhavidyauṣadhimaṇigulikāsevayā vajradehāḥ
svātmānaṃ yaṃ bhajanti jvalanavaradṛśaṃ kuñcitāṅghriṃ bhaje'ham //226//

95 *yadrūpaṃ yogivaryā hṛdayasarasije cintayanty anvahaṃ* . . .
. . . . . //73//

96 *sarveṣāṃ prāṇināṃ yaḥ svapadasarasijaṃ pūjituṃ pāṇiyugmaṃ*
svaṃ draṣṭuṃ locane dve svacaritam akhilaṃ vaktum īśaḥ suvācam /
svasya prādakṣiṇārthaṃ caraṇayugam api dhyānayogāya cittaṃ
dattvā rakṣatyajasraṃ tam udakamakuṭaṃ kuñcitāṅghriṃ bhaje'ham //94//

97 *lebhe yasya prasādād anitarasulabhaṃ mṛtyubhīter abhāvam /*
kalpe kalpe . . .
'py āste yaddhyānayogāt kanakagirivare . . . //168//

6 THE GODDESS

1 For some details of contemporary practice, see Douglas Renfrew Brooks, *Auspicious Wisdom: the Texts and Traditions of Śrīvidyā Śākta Tantrism in South India* (Albany: State University of New York Press, 1992).
2 R. Nagaswamy, 'Chidambaram Bronzes', *Lalit Kalā* 9 (1979), pp. 9–16, p. 16.
3 Cf. Ramalinga Dikshitar, 'A Study of Chidambaram and its Shrine', p. 72.
4 Trans. T. N. Ramachandran, '*Sivaprakasam* of Saint Umapathi Devanayanar', *Śaiva Siddhānta* 12 (1977), p. 155, slightly altered. Cf. *Tirumantiram* 1225.

5 *gaṅgātīrasya paścād vilasati sadane saccidānandarūpā*
devī yā sarvavidyālayamukhakamalā bhāsate vedahastā /
yā yasya jñānaśaktiḥ śivapadasahitā kāmasundaryabhikhyā
taddevyā dṛṣṭanṛttaṃ śrutinihitapadaṃ kuñcitāṅghriṃ bhaje'ham //77//

Line d. *śrutinihitapadaṃ*: *pada* here is both Śiva's foot, and the state of being Śiva.
6 It may not be by chance that the Hundred-pillared Hall adjoins the shrine. The power of the Goddess would have been adjacent to the place of coronation; such considerations might have had less force by the time of the building of the Thousand-pillared Hall on the other side of the tank.
7 *Kuñcitāṅghristava*, p. 33.

8 *ābālyād dravyam etat sumukhi tava mude yan mayāttaṃ tad adya*
svīkurvāṇā nitāntaṃ madanaśarahataṃ gāḍham āliṅgya dorbhyāṃ /
atraivāśvāsayeti tvaritagatim umām ālibhir vārito'pi
śrīmān yo hy anvagacchann agataṭabhuvi taṃ kuñcitāṅghriṃ bhaje'ham //256//

Line a. Please, it's for you, *tava mude*. Literally, 'to please you'.

9 *hemādriprāntabhāgasthalakamalavanākrīḍanodyogahaṃsa-*
vrātālokāpadeśāt savidhagataśivāhastagāḍhopagūḍham /
nānākārānubhūtānupamaratisamutkūjitāryākucāgra-
sparśonmṛṣṭālikāntasthalasitabhasitaṃ kuñcitāṅghriṃ bhaje'ham //200//

10 *kelyām autsukyabhājā tuhinagirijayā saspṛhaṃ dattavīṭī-*
sevāraktādharoṣṭhadyutijitadinakṛdbālabimbāṃśucakram /
gītiprāvīṇyaśailīprakaṭanakutukād dhastavāstavyalolāṃ
vīṇāṃ saṃvādayantaṃ prathamarasamayaṃ kuñcitāṅghriṃ bhaje'ham //212//

11 Kalhaṇa, *Rājataraṅgiṇī* IV, 427.

12 *krīḍāsaṃsaktagaurīkanakaghaṭanibhottuṅgavakṣojaśaila-*
prodyatśṛṅgāramādhvīmadhurarasadhunīlolabhṛṅgāyatākṣam /
bhūṣānāgoktasaukhyapravacanaghaṭajastabdhagarvābdhitārksya
vrīḍākṛtśvāsavaktrapramathapatinutaṃ kuñcitāṅghriṃ bhaje'ham //149//

13 *kastūrīpaṅkalepaṃ mṛgamadatilakaṃ puṣpamālāṃ ca nūtnāṃ*
dṛṣṭvā jātv ambujākṣī dharaṇidharasutāpy anyathā tarkayantī /
nāthedaṃ lakṣma satyāṃ mayi tava samabhūd brūhi kasyā mude cety
āyāntaṃ nirbabandhādhikaśapathamaraṃ kuñcitāṅghriṃ bhaje'ham //261//

The last line of this verse is not clear to me.

14 *jñānecchābhyāṃ sakhibhyāṃ saha rahasi mudā naktam aśrāntalīlo*
bhūtvā prātaḥ sabhāyām iha kim u bhavataḥ sāhasaṃ nandanīyam /
yātu svargāpagāyā nikaṭataṭam ayaṃ nārthanīyo janaś cety
uktvā sācīkṛtām anvanayad agasutāṃ kuñcitāṅghriṃ bhaje'ham //235//

15 *āli tvaṃ sāntvayāryāṃ mayi kupitadhiyaṃ dārukāraṇyavāsi-*
strīṇāṃ kelīvilāsair haridhṛtasutanoḥ sāhasāt parvatendre /
saṅgād divyāpagāyā madanadahanataś ceti sākūtam uktvā
kāntāgāre jayāṃ yo'gamayad asulabhaṃ kuñcitāṅghriṃ bhaje'ham //257//

16 *paśyedaṃ svarṇaśṛṅgaṃ mama sadanavaraṃ gauri kedārasaṃjñaṃ /*
kāśīṃ kāñcīpurīṃ apy aruṇagirivaraṃ śvetakāntāradeśyam /
vedāraṇyaṃ ca setuṃ muhur api vṛṣabhaṃ yo 'dhitiṣṭhan priyāyai /
nirdiśyāpnoti naijaṃ nilayam anudinaṃ kuñcitāṅghriṃ bhaje'ham //231//

17 *kātyāyanyāḥ karābjaṃ dinakaravadanādhītavedārthabodhāl*
labdhānandāntaraṅgapraśamitatamasas tāpasasyāśrame yaḥ /
gṛhṇan saṃsāravārdhāv adhikabhayakare magnasatvaprapañcaṃ
nityaṃ rakṣann ajasraṃ jayati śivapure kuñcitāṅghriṃ bhaje'ham //180//

18 It has been suggested that this is the *Edirambalam* or 'shrine opposite [the Cit Sabhā]' ascribed in inscription No. 119 of 1888 to the time of Kulottuṅga I. Built perhaps in the reign of Cōḻa Kulottuṅga III (1178–1216), it is similar to the *ratha maṇḍapa*s of Tribhuvanam, Paḻaiyāṟai, and elsewhere. The most notable example of such stone chariots is in the Sun temple at Konārak, which would seem chronologically to be due to Southern influence, though the chariot is an integral feature of the Sun and more obviously appropriate for him than for Śiva. L'Hernault remarks that the stone chariot 'must have served as the statue of the god's procession to symbolize his excursions (*pour ses sorties symboliques*)', F. L'Hernault, *et al.*, *Darasuram*, vol. 1, p. 7. [My translation from the French.]

19 Harle, *Temple Gateways*, figs. 132, 133. Neither figure is dancing; the erect hair gives the identification.

20 *kālyā sākaṃ purā yaḥ suramunisadasi svāṅghrim udyama cordhvaṃ*
nṛttaṃ kṛtvātha kālīṃ paśupatir ajayat tadbahiṣkārapūrvam /
sarve devā munīndrāḥ prabhur iti ca vadanty ūrdhvanṛtteśamūrtiṃ
yaṃ devaṃ pūjayanti pratidinam anaghāḥ kuñcitāṅghriṃ bhaje'ham //46//

21 K. A. Nilakantha Sastri, *A History of South India from Prehistoric Times to the Fall of Vijayanagar*, 3rd edn (London: Oxford University Press, 1966), p. 213.

22 *kālīṃ caṇḍordhvanṛttāvanatamukhagaṇāṃ brahmacāmuṇḍikākhyāṃ*
gaurī kopāgnijātāṃ ditisutabhayadāṃ aṃśayuktāṃ vidhātuḥ /
svāgaḥ śāntyai nitāntaṃ savidhakṛtanutiṃ yaḥ kṛpāpūrṇadṛṣṭyā
rakṣan svakṣetrapālāṃ akuruta paramaṃ kuñcitāṅghriṃ bhaje'ham //283//

23 *kṛtvā pādaṃ rasāyāṃ punar api tathā pādam ekaṃ nabhaḥsthaṃ*, 14.22.

24 *bhuktvā hālāhalāṃśaṃ yudhi nihatatanuṃ dārukākhyaṃ surāriṃ*
kṛtvā ghorasvakṛtyapracalitabhuvanāṃ bhadrakālīṃ śivo yaḥ /
pratyetyānandanṛttaṃ pitṛpatibhuvane darśayitvā tayāṇḍān
sarvān saṃrakṣatīśas tam inavidhunutaṃ kuñcitāṅghriṃ bhaje'ham //192//

25 *Liṅga Purāṇa* 1.106.
26 *Ibid.*, 1.106.25.
27 R. C. Hazra, *Studies in the Purāṇic Records* (Delhi: Motilal Banarsidass, 1973), p. 95.
28 Harle, *Temple Gateways in South India*, p. 111.
29 R. Nagaswamy, *Tantric Cult of South India* (Delhi: Navrang, 1982), p. 179.
30 *Ibid.*, p. 175. This identification was first suggested by J. M. Somasundaram, *Cōḻar Kōyil Paṇikal*, p. 6, according to P. R. Srinivasan ('Important Works of Art of the Early Chōḷa Period from near Tanjore', *Transactions of the Archaeological Society of South India*, 1956–7, pp. 36–52, p. 38; Srinivasan himself however, argues that this is a Pallava sculpture, and on p. 41 suggests as Vijayalāya's Niśumbhasūdanī the Niśumbhasūdanī sculpture in the Ugramākāḷi temple in Tanjavur; so also S. R. Balasubrahmanyam, *Early Chola Art* (New York: Asia Publishing House, 1966), p. 43 and plate 8.
31 Nagaswamy, *Tantric Cult*, p. 175.
32 It should be noted that Srinivasan describes the sculpture in the Vaḍabhadrakāḷi temple as 'seated and trampling on five male figures', 'Important Works of Art of the Early Chōḷa Period', p. 37.

33 *dakṣe yaṣṭuṃ pravṛtte paramaśivam anādṛtya tatkanyakāyāṃ*
gatvā tatra svatātaṃ natavadanam upekṣyaindram agniṃ viśantyām /
gauryāṃ kopād ya īśo daśaśatavadanaṃ vīram utpādya kālīṃ
tābhyāṃ dakṣādināśaṃ vyaracayad atulaṃ kuñcitāṅghriṃ bhaje'ham //52//

34 Another possible explanation for the form of Vīrabhadra is provided by David Knipe's account of the Vīrabhadra cult in Andhra. Writing of the East Godavari District, Knipe says, 'it is clear that in this part of coastal Andhra, the wrathful Vīrabhadra, antithesis of establishment sacrifice and its circulation of cosmic energies, is alive and well. He is one Vīrabhadra, Śiva's rage personified, and many *vīrabhadras*, all the children of rage who, even if they died after taking their mother's milk for a single day, are said to be, like Vīrabhadra, the children of Śiva.' David M. Knipe, 'Night of the Growing Dead', in Alf Hiltebeitel (ed.), *Criminal Gods and Demon Devotees* (Albany: State University of New York Press, 1989) pp. 123–56, p. 139. There

is no reason to doubt that some such cult underlies the formation of the iconography of Vīrabhadra, though it may be not be precisely this. Could such a cult explain the boyish form of Vīrabhadra on the West *gopura* image? Knipe's chapter is considered further in chapter 8, p. 200.

35 *Kantapurāṇam*, 6.20.38–49 as summarized in R. Dessigane and P. Z. Pattabiramin *La Légende de Skanda* (Pondicherry: Institut Français d'Indologie, 1967), p. 211.

36 *yuddhe bhagnorukāyaṃ naraharivapuṣaṃ gaṇḍabheraṇḍarūpī*
bhūtvā garjantam agre śarabhakhagapatir yaḥ svaphālākṣikuṇḍāt /
ugrapratyaṅgirākhyāṃ śataśatavadanāṃ kālikām āśu sṛṣṭvā
tasyājihvāgravahniṃ sucaruvad anayat kuñcitāṅghriṃ bhaje'ham //126//

37 *kālinṛttapramuditahṛdayaṃ kuñcitāṅghriṃ bhaje'ham* //262//
Kāli for *kālī* for the metre. The Tamil form of Kālī is Kāḷi.

38 Pope, *The Tiruvaçagam*, p. 16.

39 *kācin nālāyanīti prathitamunisatī bhartur iṣṭānukūlā*
māṇḍavyaproktaśāpajvalanaśamanakṛddurdinaśrīvilāsā /
yanmantradhyānayogād anitarasulabhān pañcakāntān narendrān
lebhe janmādihīnaṃ śivapadam api taṃ kuñcitāṅghriṃ bhaje'ham //224//

Line d. *janmādihīnāṃ* 'free from birth and the other [ills of life]'.

40 *Citsabheśvarotsavasūtra*, p. 3 of unnumbered sequence.

41 *āmanvaśraṃ sudīptāṃ nijatanum abhitaḥ satyarūpaprabhāntar*
vāme yuktaṃ svaśaktyā vasudalakamalasvārṇakiñjalkaśobham /
yāptaṃ sāhasrakoṣṭhasthitaśivamanubhir mohanādyair yadīyaṃ
cakraṃ sampūjayanti pratidinam anaghāḥ kuñcitāṅghrim bhaje'ham //109//

42 Verses 18, 19, 21, 25, 46. Umāpati speaks several times of the *kuñcitāṅghri* as *anaghaṃ*, reinforcing the intimate connection of the Dīkṣitas with the God they worship.

43 *traicatvāriṃśadaśre vasunṛpakamale vṛttabhūcakramadhye*
bindau santānakalpadrumanikarayute ratnasaudhe manojñe /
brahmādyākārapāde śivamayaphalake svarṇamañce niṣaṇṇo
devyā yaḥ pūjyate taṃ harimukhavibudhaiḥ kuñcitāṅghriṃ bhaje'ham //110//

vṛttabhūcakramadhye is difficult. Clearly the verse moves from the outer to the inner, though in the first line the constraints of metre prevent the linear expression of this order. *bhūcakra* must be the *bhūpura* or *bhūgṛha*, the 'city' or 'house' 'of the earth', and there is no problem about the use of the word *cakra* in respect of the square, since the several enclosures, including the polygons, are often called *cakra*s (e.g., Bhāskara writes of 'the eight *cakra*s beginning with the *bhūpura*' (p. 109) but why *vṛtta* 'round', unless we have *avṛtta*, meaning 'not-round', 'square'?

44 For other parallels, see Madhu Khanna, 'The Concept and Liturgy of the Śrīcakra based on Śivānanda's Trilogy' (unpublished DPhil thesis, University of Oxford, 1986), p. 98.

45 *sudhāsindhor madhye suraviṭapivāṭīparivṛte*
maṇidvīpe nīpopavanavati cintāmaṇigṛhe /
śivākāre mañce paramaśivaparyaṅkanilayāṃ
bhajanti tvāṃ dhanyāḥ katicana cidānandalaharīm//

Śiva here is, of course, Sadāśiva. *Saundaryalaharī* 94 mentions that Īśvara, Rudra, Viṣṇu, and Brahmā are also present as the four supports of the couch.

46 *śrīnāthavīrair gurubhir api nutāṃ*. Rājagaṇeśa Dīkṣita offers no assistance, repeating the Sanskrit, and not translating *gurubhir*: *śrī nātavīrarkaḷināl tutikkappaṭṭavaḷum*.

47 *yo yasya jñānaśaktiṃ daharakuharaṇīṃ śrīmahāṣoḍaśārṇāṃ*
vidyāṃ śrīnāthavīrair gurubhir api nutāṃ yoginīdūtisevyām /
ātmābhinnāṃ śivāṃ tāṃ hṛdi paricinute sa svayaṃ nirvikalpo
bhūtvā yogīndrapūjyo bhavati tam aguṇam kuñcitāṅghriṃ bhaje'ham //207//

48 The way temple paintings are taken for granted and not subjected to critical attention is illustrated by the comment on the paintings in question by S. Meyyapan, a university professor and long resident in Cidambaram, 'As they ['Devi Mahatmiyam' paintings] were drawn long time ago they are in decayed stage', *Chidambaram Golden Temple* (Chidambaram: Manivasagar Pathippakam, 1987), p. 67. Painted in fact in 1972 these central panels faded rapidly, and were severely damaged by fire in 1989. According to Job Thomas, earlier paintings of the 'Devīmāhātmīya' were scraped off in 1972 (Isaac Job Thomas, 'Painting in Tamil Nadu A.D. 1350–1650', unpublished PhD thesis (University of Michigan, 1979), p. 311). However, it is worth noting that the central portion of the ceiling is visible in James Fergusson's drawing of the *maṇḍapa* (woodcut no. 221) in his *History of Architecture Indian and Eastern Architecture*, 2 vols. (vol. I, London: John Murray, 1876; vol. II, New York: Dodd, Mead and Co., 1891), and that section of the ceiling looks blank.

49 *śrīcakrasyandanasthāṃ gajaturagasamārūḍhaśaktyagrabhāgāṃ*
nityāvārāhimantriṇyanucarasahitāṃ dṛṣṭabālāstravidyām /
sarvāstrāśliṣṭahastāṃ raṇabhuvi vilasadyuddhaveṣāṃ bhavānīṃ
dṛṣṭvātuṣṭo'bhavat taṃ dhanapatisuhṛdaṃ kuñcitāṅghriṃ bhaje'ham //128//

50 *Lalitāsahasranāma* with the *Saubhāgyabhāskara* commentary of Bhāskararāya (Bombay: Nirnaya-sagar Press, 1914), p. 46.

51 *Nityāparākramāṭopanirīkṣaṇasamutsukā*, *Lalitāsahasranāma* p. 47.

52 *viṣṇor aṃśāvatārān daśakaranakharair yuddharaṅge sṛjantī*
kāmeśālokanodyadgajavadanakaradhvastavighneśayantrā /
yasyāstreṇāśu bhaṇḍaṃ sasutagaṇapuraṃ nāśayām āsa daityam
devīśrīcakrasaṃsthā tam api śivakaraṃ kuñcitāṅghriṃ bhaje'ham //129//

53 *śrīhīrāl labdhacintāmaṇimanum anusandhāya nirjīvadehe*
mātur māmalladevyā niśi vigatabhayo harṣaṇāmopaviśya /
vipraḥ śrīrudrabhūmau yad adhikakṛpayā mātaraṃ sarvavidyāṃ
siddhīr anyāś ca lebhe karadhṛtaḍamaruṃ kuñcitāṅghriṃ bhaje'ham //114//

Harṣa, or Śrīharṣa, was one of the greatest Sanskrit poets, author of the *Naiṣadhacarita*. The identification is beyond doubt, for he refers to his father and mother at the conclusion of every canto of his poem. He also refers to a Cintāmaṇi mantra, which with meditation on Sarasvatī gives poetic inspiration (14.88–90); and which he claims as the cause of his own poem (1.145). At the conclusion of the twelfth canto he describes his head as a bee attending the lotus feet of his mother, *mātṛcaraṇāmbhojālimauler*. But other than what is stated here, nothing is known with regard to the events described in this verse of Umāpati's. (There is a passing reference, by no means unusual, to bringing the dead to life: *kiṃ yoginīyaṃ rajanī ratīśaṃ yājīvat padmam amūmuhac ca* / 22.22 'Is not this night a Yoginī, for she has brought Love back to life and rendered unconscious the lotus.') In the *Naiṣadhacarita*, Sarasvatī concludes the gods' boon-giving to Nala with the gift which was the armature of the poem itself: 'King, reflect inwardly and meditate always on my pure mystic formula, which, without any form, embodies Śiva, and is accompanied by the moon [HRĪM], and represents the form that goes by the name Pārvatī and Parameśvara, universal, but twofold owing to the union of two shapes, male in one half and female in the other. May this formula prove effective to thee.' *Naiṣadhacarita* 14.88, trans. K. K. Handiqui, *Naiṣadhacarita of Śrīharṣa* (Poona: Deccan College, 1965), p. 214.

avāmāvāmārdhe sakalam ubhayākāraghaṭanā-
dvidhābhūtaṃ rūpaṃ bhagavadabhidheyaṃ bhavati yat /
tadantarmantraṃ me smaraharamayaṃ sendum amalaṃ
nirākāraṃ śaśvaj japa narapate sidhyatu sa te   //14.88//

54 *yasyāhur nṛttamūrteḥ śrutihṛdayavidaḥ śaktim ekām apīdyāṃ
kālīṃ kope ca durgāṃ yudhi jagadavane viṣṇurūpāṃ bhavānīṃ /
bhoge jñānakriyecchāmayavividhatanuṃ sarvasaṃhārakāle
svāntarlīnāṃ prasannāṃ tam ibhamukhasutaṃ kuñcitāṅghriṃ bhaje'ham*   //113//

7 BHIKṢĀṬANA

1 On the second tier, on each side of the gateway are four niches. The grandest of these is always the second from the gateway. It is the widest, it has a pillared portico immediately above it, and its outermost pilasters are the farthest apart. It is the centre part of each side, with two figures on the outer edge, one figure on the inner edge; but the innermost figure is powerfully supplemented by the gateway, so that the balance is equal. (On the first tier, the largest niche is not so clearly dominant, having four niches beyond it to the outer edge, and two to the inner edge.)

2 Dorai Rangaswamy, *Religion and Philosophy of the Tēvāram*, p. 387.

3 *Tēvāram* VII 72, trans. Shulman, *Songs of the Harsh Devotee*, pp. 465f.

4 *Tēvāram* VII 45.5, trans. Shulman, *ibid.*, p. 284.

5 *Tēvāram* VI 58.7., trans. Nagaswamy, *Śiva-Bhakti*, p. 236 (slightly altered).

6 Nagaswamy, *ibid.*, p. 236.

7 Shulman, *Songs of the Harsh Devotee*, p. li.

8 *Tevāram* VI 36 1, trans. Shulman, *ibid.*, p. 218.

9 *svāmin bhikṣo bhaved kva nu tava nagare parvate vā vane vā*
vāsaḥ kasmād iha tvaṃ carasi vada vibho kutra gantāsi bhikṣām /
kurvann atraiva tiṣṭhan viracayatu bhavān kelim asmābhir evaṃ
straiṇaṃ yaṃ cābhyadhāvad vanabhuvi vivaśaṃ kuñcitāṅghriṃbhaje'ham //232//

10 *dvātriṃśadrāgabodhacyutamakuṭaśaśisvacchapiyūṣadhārā*
saṃgāvāptasvajīvāmbujabhavavadanoddāmagītābhirāmam /
stabdhībhūtarṣinārīgaṇam adhivipinaṃ sarvaśṛṅgārarūpaṃ
yaṃ dṛṣṭvā viṣṇumāyā patimatim atanot kuñcitāṅghriṃ bhaje'ham //130//

11 *dārukāraṇyavāsistrīṇāṃ kelīvilāsair haridhṛtasutanoḥ sāhasāt parvatendre /*

12 A version of the legend is given in the *Kanta Purāṇam*, 'which presents the major myths of Śiva in their authoritative Tamil version', Peterson, *Poems to Śiva*, p. 343. Dessigane and Pattibiramam (*La Légende de Skanda*, Pondicherry: Institut Français d'Indologie, 1967, p. 1.) date this text to the twelfth century, but its account of the Pine Forest is clearly later than what we find in the Cidambaram versions. Not only does Śiva explicitly copulate with the wives, the wives at once give birth to 84,000 boys who immediately undertake asceticism, on Śiva's advice. The sages recognize the divinity of the intruders before commencing their magical assault. The products of their magic are more numerous, and include two items essential to the persona of Śiva as Bhikṣāṭana, his trident and drum. Lacking these, how could he have made a proper entrance? The Sanskrit version of this text also includes the instantaneous birth of sons to the *ṛṣis*' wives (*Dakṣakhaṇḍa* 14.4), and it is therefore highly improbable that it is, as Kulke thought (*Cidambaramahātmya: Eine Untersuchung*, p. 151), earlier than the *Cidambara Māhātmya*. I am most grateful to Kulke for sending me a copy of T. Ramalinga Dikshitar's transcript of this text.

13 *mohinyā śambhur ādāv atiniviḍavane dārukākhye caranyaḥ*
saundaryād vipradārān munigaṇam api taṃ māyayā mohayitvā /
vyarthīkṛtyābhicāraṃ dvijakulavihitaṃ saṃpradarśyātmanṛttaṃ
viprāṃś cānvagrahīd yas tam api giriśayaṃ kuñcitāṅghriṃ bhaje'ham //40//

14 'Bringing about rebirth for themselves', translates the brief *janmano hetum*; a pun may be intended on birth, in the sense of 'attempting to impregnate'.

8 BHAIRAVA THE TERRIBLE AND OTHER FORMS OF ŚIVA

1 *Śivapurāṇa* 3.8.2 speaks of Bhairava as the *pūrṇarūpa* of Śaṅkara the supreme self; Kramrisch paraphrases this as 'Bhairava is the total, complete Śiva.' Stella Kramrisch, *The Presence of Śiva* (Princeton University Press, 1981), p. 265.

2 *Śataratnasaṃgraha*, p. 30.

3 *yaḥ śambhulīlayā svaṃ janima sukhakaraṃ tāpasānāṃ vacobhir*
hastād utpātya devaiḥ kim idam iti bhayād vīkṣito 'ranyadeśe /
cikṣepa brahmaviṣṇustutibhir api punas tān munīn jñātatattvān
kṛtvāpy antardadhe taṃ praṇataphaladharaṃ kuñcitāṅghriṃ bhaje'ham //258//

4 *Kāñcipura Māhātmyam* 34 as summarized by Dessigane *et al.*, *Les Légendes Çivaïtes de Kāñcipuram*, pp. 44f. [My translation from the French.]

5 *āhṛtya brahmaśīrṣaṃ sakalajanimatāṃ darśanāya svadakṣe*
pārśve saṃsthāpya pūrvaṃ śrutivadanavidhiṃ vāmato'sthāpayad yaḥ /
adyārabhyātmayone madupahṛtahaviḥśeṣabhuk tvaṃ bhaveti
svājñāpyākāśarūpas tam api naṭapatiṃ kuñcitāṅghriṃ bhaje'ham //30//

Lines a and b. on His right side, *svadakṣe pārśve.* That is, the Mukhaliṅga, referred to in verse 7.
Line b. on His left, *vāmato.* That is, in the shrine Brahmā shares with Caṇḍeśvara, to the left of the Cit Sabhā.

6 *yasya kṣetre mṛtānāṃ sakalajanibhṛtāṃ sañcitādīni pāpāny*
abdānekaprabhoḥyāny api ca nimiṣato bhairavaḥ śūlaghātāt /
bhasmīkṛtyāśu bhūyo jananamṛtiharaṃ tārakaṃ yannideśāt
tattvaṃ sambodhayan yatsadasi vasati taṃ kuñcitāṅghriṃ bhaje'ham //159//

Rājagaṇeśa Dīkṣita quotes the *Puṇḍarīkapura Māhātmya* 4.49–53 to the effect that worshipping Śiva in Cidambaram means that Kṣetrapāla will destroy all one's sins with his trident, *Kuñcitāṅghristava*, p. 79.

7 In the Cit Sabhā to the left of Śivakāmasundarī and facing West. There is also a Bhairava shrine in the first enclosure to the east of the Cit Sabhā. The shrines of Brahmā Caṇḍeśvara and Bhairava receive worship after Śiva, in the form of his sandals, has been placed in the bed-chamber.

8 (*Cidambareśvaraśrīnaṭarājadevālayastha*) *devatāstotra* in *Cidambarakṣetrasarvasva*, ed. Somasetu Dīkṣita (Kadavasal: Sri Meenakshi Press, 1977), p. 212.

9 Somasethu Dikshitar (ed.), *The History of Chidambaram*, p. 49.

10 'A Study of Chidambaram', p. 29. He also quotes the statement of the *Tilvavana Māhātmya* that the Rahasya is worshipped by Svarṇākarṣaṇabhairava along with the Eight Lakṣmīs (3.45). However this is that Māhātmya's sole reference to those deities, and it is difficult to comment. Cf. Rao, *Hindu Iconography*, vol. I. 1, p. 398: 'An explanation of the worship of Jyeṣṭhādevī is found in the *Śaivāgamas*. The *Siddhāntasārāvali* of Trilocana Śivācārya and the commentary on it give what follows: Parā Śakti, in the form of Vāmā, is the author of the *pañcakṛtyas*, or the five acts called *sṛṣṭi*, *sthiti*, *saṃhāra*, *tirodhāna* and *anugraha*. She, therefore, assumes the eight forms representing the eight *tattvas*.'

11 *Mahārthamañjarī* of Maheśvarānanda, with his commentary *Parimala*, ed. V. Dviveda, Yogatantra-Granthamālā 5 (Varanasi: Varanaseya Sanskrit Vishvavidyalaya, 1972), p. 188.

12 Alexis Sanderson, 'The Visualization of the Deities of the Trika', in André Padoux (ed.), *L'Image Divine: Culte et Méditation dans l'Hindouisme* (Paris: Centre National de la Recherche Scientifique, 1990), pp. 31–88, p. 55.

13 *Mahārthamañjarīparimala*, p. 194.

14 *Ibid.*, p. 195.

15 *Mahārthamañjarī*, p. 160:
vayaṃ tv imāṃ viśvatayāvabhānaṃ bahirmukhasyāsya tavonmukhasya /
svasaṃhitaṃ viśvavilāpanodyatsvatantratānandamayīṃ namāmaḥ //

My translation is only an approximation: the verse is not fully understandable in isolation.

16 *Mahārthamañjarī*, p. 163.

17 *kalpānte vṛddhibhājāṃ kabalitajagatāṃ saptavārān nidhīnāṃ*
madhye pālāśaśāyī harir iha puruṣo nāsti matto 'paro 'nyaḥ /
evaṃ darpāvalīḍho 'py anupadam uditaṃ śūlinaṃ bhairavaṃ yaṃ
dṛṣṭvā bhītyā nanāma stutibhir abhinavaiḥ kuñcitāṅghriṃ bhaje'ham //236//

18 *yasyeśasyāṃśabhūtāḥ śarabhavaṭukarāḍvīrabhadrādidevāḥ*
kalpe kalpe'mbujākṣadruhiṇamukhadhṛtakrūrasattvograkṛtyam /
nighnantaḥ sārvakālaṃ jagad api sakalaṃ pālayanto'ntaraṅge
dhyāyanto yaṃ jayanti prasṛmaramahasaṃ kuñcitāṅghriṃ bhaje'ham //203//

19 This is supposed to have happened at Tiruvaiyaru. I could find no representation of the event in the temple, though there is a shrine to Saṭṭanātha.

20 *bhītyā santrāsamāne naraharivapuṣo devatānāṃ samūhe*
dhātrā saṃstūyamānaḥ śarabhavaratanuḥ sāluvaḥ pakṣirājaḥ /
vegāt taṃ chedayitvā svapadanakhamukhais tattvacālaṅkṛto'bhūd
daṃṣṭrāsaṃdīptalokas tam akhilavaradaṃ kuñcitāṅghriṃ bhaje'ham //125//

21 L'Hernault *et al.*, *Darasuram*, vol. 1, p. 88 [my translation from the French]. For Śarabheśa, plate 41.

22 In the *Kuñcitāṅghristava*, Umāpati refers in passing to Śiva destroying the [Triple] Cities with a smile (*smita*) (90); and as epithet alone in 62, 103, 230.

23 For Śaṭṭanātha at other sites, and for an interesting discussion of Bhairava in Pallava and Cōḻa art, see L'Hernault *et al.*, *Darasuram*, vol. 1, p. 90.

24 *yācñākharvīkṛtāṅgaṃ balimakhasadasi svāṃ tanūṃ vardhayitvā*
dyāv ābhūmisurārer makuṭam api padām ānayitvā trilokīm /
huṅkārād bhīṣayantaṃ suragaṇavinuto vāmanaṃ yo vinighnan
kaṅkālaṃ tasya dehatvacam api hṛtavān kuñcitāṅghriṃ bhaje'ham //127//

25 *viṣṇau nirjvālacakre bhramitahṛdi vidhau bhāskare dantahīne*
śakre nirbhinnagaṇḍe hutabhuji viśikhe tyaktajīve 'khile'nye /
cchitvā dakṣottamāṅgaṃ makhabhuvi sagaṇaṃ vīrabhadraṃ carantaṃ
dṛṣṭvā yo 'toṣayat taṃ pramuditahṛdayaṃ kuñcitāṅghriṃ bhaje'ham //240//

Line b. *anye* for *anyasmin*.

26 *viṣṇor lalāṭadeśacyutarudhirajharīsaṅgamenāpy apūrṇaṃ*
brāhmaṃ haste kapālaṃ ḍamarum api vahan viśvakadrūn svapārśve /
daṃṣṭrāgrābhāpiśaṅgīkṛtavipulajaṭo bhairavaḥ kṣetrapālo
viśvaṃ rakṣann upādher yam api bhajati taṃ kuñcitāṅghriṃ bhaje'ham //183//

Line d. *upādhi* is here used in the sense of the Tamil *upāti*, 'torment'.

27 *godāvaryās taṭastho'nṛtavacanaparo duṣṭakārtāntiko yat-*

kṣetre gaulyāṃ janitvā nijasukṛtalavāt svīyapātoktidoṣam /
bhasmīkartuṃ ciraṃ yaṃ stutibhir abhinaman sundarāṅgo yaduktyā
jāto yatkṣetrapālo jayati tam asamaṃ kuñcitāṅghriṃ bhaje'ham //191//

28 M. Biardeau, *Hinduism: The Anthropology of a Civilization* (Delhi: Oxford University Press, 1989), p. 135.
29 Dessigane *et al.*, *Les Légendes Çivaïtes de Kāñcipuram*, p. 50, st. 28–9; p. 63, st. 1–2.
30 Cf. Alf Hiltebeitel, 'Draupadī's Two Guardians: The Buffalo King and the Muslim Devotee', in Alf Hiltebeitel (ed.), *Criminal Gods and Demon Devotees* (Albany: State University of New York Press, 1989) pp. 339–71, p. 366.
31 Viṣṇu 'the towering tall one, suggesting the Trivikrama form measuring the world, often represented in the sculptures of this age'. Dorai Rangaswamy, *The Religion and Philosophy of Tēvāram*, vol. I, p. 357.
32 *Tēvāram* VI. 9. 2, trans. Shulman.
33 *Tēvāram* VI. 16. 2, trans. Shulman.

34 *yaḥ śambhuḥ kālahantā jaladharam asuraṃ svāṅghricakreṇa hatvā*
tadduṣkṛtyāstraśastrair vinihatavapuṣaḥ sarvalokān arakṣat /
yaṃ svakrodhasvarūpaṃ jaladharam asuraṃ nāśayantaṃ vareṇyaṃ
sarve lokā vadanti pramathapatinutaṃ kuñcitāṅghriṃ bhaje'ham //48//

Lines a. and c. *jaladharam*. The usual form of this name is Jalandhara (Calantaraṉ in Tamil), here changed for the metre. The most important part of the story in the South is not mentioned here, though it is in verse 56, namely that to win the *cakra* Viṣṇu offered a thousand lotuses to Śiva, and finding one missing offered one of his eyes in its place. One of Viṣṇu's names is Lotus-eyed.
35 This is an abbreviation of the summary of *Kanta Purāṇam* 6.13.198–270 given by R. Dessigane and P. Z. Pattabiramin, *La Légende de Skanda*, pp. 195f.
36 The same apotropaic face adorns the waist-bands of elegant bronzes.

37 *kailāsādrau kadācit paśupatinayanāny adrijātā pidhāya*
krīḍāṃ cakre 'ndhakārāt suraripur udabhūd andhakākhyo'tiduṣṭaḥ /
tadduṣkṛtyaṃ jagatyāṃ prasṛmaram asahaiḥ sarvalokaiḥ stuto yaḥ
taṃ hatvārakṣad etāṃs tam ajaharinutaṃ kuñcitāṅghriṃ bhaje'ham //49//

38 Dorai Rangaswamy, *Religion and Philosophy of Tēvāram*, vol. I, p. 369. The list of the eight heroic actions (*aṣṭavīrasthāna)* gives Tirukkōvalūr (Tirukkoliyur) in South Arcot District as the place where this deed took place. (Cf. Balasubrahmanyam, *Early Chola Temples*, p. 85.) There is a bronze said to be Andhakāsurasaṃhāramūrti (Pl. XXIII, fig. 2 from the Viraṭṭeśvarar temple in that place), but the downward directed trident is not the characteristic Andhakāsurasaṃhāra blow. Note that Cuntarar mentions Kōvalūr as one of the places where Śiva 'sprang at Death with his feet and knocked him down' (*Tēvāram* VII.12.1; Shulman, *Songs of the Harsh Devotee,* p. 74.). It is not mentioned in the *Kanta Purāṇam*, 'which presents the major myths of Śiva in their authoritative Tamil version' (Peterson, *Poems to Śiva*, p. 343).

39 See note 34 to chapter 6, above, p. 272.

40 *maulau gaṅgā galāntargaralam ahitateḥ kaṅkaṇaṃ doṣi phāle*
candraṃ tārtīyanetraṃ jvalanasamaśikhaṃ śūlam ājaṃ kapālaṃ /
bhūtapretādisenā nigamamayaśuno yasya līlākirāta-
syāgre dṛṣṭvā kirīṭī bhramitamatir abhūt kuñcitāṅghriṃ bhaje'ham //260//

41 *pārthāya svāstradānaṃ paśupatir akarod yaḥ purā rājatādrau*
yuddhaṃ tenaiva kṛtvā vanacaratanubhāg bhinnaśīrṣas tathāsīt /

42 *mārkaṇḍeye purā śrīrajatagiripater liṅgapūjāpravṛtte*
pāśaiḥ karṣaty athārkau bhayakaravadane liṅgamadhyān maheśaḥ /
āgaty ārakṣad etaṃ munim atha śamanaṃ mārayām āsa devo
yas taṃ nityaṃ naṭeśaṃ nikhilanṛpanutaṃ kuñcitāṅghriṃ bhaje'ham //35//

43 Kulke follows P. R. Srinivāsa in claiming that a Naṭarāja is to be seen on the northern face of the Dharmarāja Ratha at Mahābalipuram. Śivarāmamūrti also takes that view, but I would follow K. R. Srinivasin who does not hesitate to say that this figure is Kālāri, Śiva as the 'Foe of Death'. Kulke, *Cidambara-Māhātmya: Eine Untersuchung*, p. 115; K. R. Srinivasin, *The Dharmarāja Ratha and its Sculptures* (New Delhi: Abhinav Publications, 1975), p. 28.
44 *Cidambara Māhātmya* 23.32–7.

45 *kailāsodyānadeśaṃ saha girisutayāptvaikadā candracūḍaḥ*
sadyas tatrendirāgādharabhuvi nivasan yaḥ kapīśārcito'bhūt /
yas tasmai sārvabhaumatvapadam api dadāv astraśastrāvalīñ ca
taṃ devaṃ pārijātādyakhilasumadhuraṃ kuñcitāṅghriṃ bhaje'ham //57//

46 *svargādhīśaḥ kadācit kapivadananṛpān nāśayitvā svaśatrūn*
dattvāsmai tyāgarājaṃ ṣaḍ api taditarān preṣayām āsa rājñe /
so'py ādhārādisaptasthalavarasadaneṣv agrajair arcate sma
tanmūrtīnāṃ ca mūlaṃ munigaṇavinutaṃ kuñcitāṅghriṃ bhaje'ham //58//

47 There are two other indirect references to Tiruvārūr in the *Kuñcitāṅghristava*: the story of the Nāyaṉār Cōmācimāṟar, the main subject of verse 170 (see chapter 9), is generally held to have taken place in Tiruvārūr. Verse 270 refers to the original myth of Tiruvārūr, concerning the Vālmīkinātha *liṅga* /anthill, wherein Indra in the form of an ant cuts through the bowstring that cuts off Viṣṇu's head. Ramalinga Dikshitar cites *Kuñcitāṅghristava* 97 apropos Somāskanda ('A Study of Chidambaram and its Shrine', p. 54). In this verse Śiva is said to be worshipped by the Pāṇḍavas, but is said to have five heads, which does not fit Somāskanda.
48 R. Nagaswamy, 'Ādavallān and Dakṣiṇameruviṭaṅkar of the Tanjore Temple', *Lalit Kalā*, 12 (1962), pp. 36–8, p. 38.

49 *maṃce candrārkabhūteṣv api vṛṣagajarāḍrājatādriṣv athāśve*
somāskandasvarūpaḥ svayam urunayane gorathe mārgaṇo yaḥ /
sthitvā brahmotsaveṣu triṣu ca naṭapatiḥ pratyahaṃ vīdhiyātrāṃ
kṛtvā snātvā sadaḥ svaṃ praviśati śivayā kuñcitāṅghriṃ bhaje'ham //26//

50 *kañjākṣyā svasya śaktyā sahakṛtanaṭanaṃ kasya śīrṣacchidantaṃ*
kālaṃ kāmaṃ purāṇi svapadasarasijāt phālanetrāt smitāc ca /
hatvā brahmarṣisūnuṃ sakaladiviṣadaś cāpi rakṣantam īśaṃ
devedyaṃ citsabheśaṃ daśaśatavadanaṃ kuñcitāṅghriṃ bhaje'ham //90//

9 SAINTS, DANCING GIRLS, *GAṆAS* – AND APASMĀRA

1 Marie-Louise Reiniche, *La Configuration du Temple Hindou*, vol. IV of *Tiruvannamalai: un lieu saint śivaïte du sud de l'inde* (Paris: École Française d'Extrême-Orient, 1989), p. 116.

2 For Nāyaṉārs, some write Nāyaṉmār, using the Tamil plural; others add the English plural *s* to the Tamil plural, Nāyaṉmārs. The singular, *Nāyaṉār*, is an honorific plural.

3 The exceptions are precisely the poets: Ñāṉacampantar, Appar, Cuntarar, Kāraikāl Ammaiyār, Māṇikkavācakar, and Tirumūlar, all of whom sing the praises of Dancing Śiva. However, their descriptions of the God predate the canonical Naṭarāja.

4 Cēkkiḻār refers to the fact that his poem *Tirumantiram* has three thousand verses, and it is likely that he was earlier than Cēkkiḻār.

5 *bālo viprasya goṣṭhasthitapaśunikaraṃ dohayitvā payobhir*
nadyās tīre yadīyaṃ janimasukhakaraṃ pārthivañ cābhiṣiñcan /
dhyāyan krodhāt svapūjāvikṛtikarapituś chedayitvā padaṃ yaṃ
stutvā yatpārṣadānām adhipatir abhavat kuñcitāṅghriṃ bhaje'ham //145//

6 David Dean Shulman, *Tamil Temple Myths: Sacrifice and Divine Marriage in the South Indian Śaiva Tradition* (Princeton University Press, 1980), p. 134.

7 See G. Vanmikanathan, *Periya Purāṇam by Sekkizhar*, Condensed English Version (Madras: Sri Ramakrishna Math, 1985), p. 487.

8 *kaś cil lubdho girīndre mṛganibiḍavane liṅgam aiśaṃ yadīyaṃ*
dṛṣṭvā gaṇḍūṣatoyaiḥ svakacadhṛtasumair bhuktaśeṣaiś ca māṃsaiḥ /
pūjāṃ kurvan kadācin nijanayanavaraṃ cārpayitvātibhaktyā
netre yasyānurūpaṃ padavaram abhajat kuñcitāṅghriṃ bhaje'ham //144//

9 *jāyādānaprakupyatsvajanakṛtaraṇā veśakāle prasannaṃ*
yaṃ dṛṣṭvā netravārisnapitatanulatābhogasātaṅkakampaḥ /
yasyāṅghridhyānabhānuprakaṭitavibhavo vaiśyajo bhaktavaryo
'pyadhyārūḍho vṛṣendraṃ rajatagirim agāt kuñcitāṅghriṃ bhaje'ham //214//

10 *jyotiṣṭhomākhyasomakratusavanahaviḥpuñjam atyantabhaktyā*
gūḍhākāraṃ yam īśaṃ sagaṇam api śivaṃ yajñavāṭapraviṣṭam /
heramboktyā prabudhvā svayam api mudito yājyayā yatkarābje
datvā mārābhidhogryaḥ śivanagaram agāt kuñcitāṅghriṃ bhaje'ham //170//

11 *kalpe kalpe svakīyaprabhavalayabhayaṃ tyaktum ādye parārdhe*
vedā yaṃ kālakālaṃ bahuvidhatapasā toṣayitvā yaduktyā /
traisāhasraṃ dvijatvaṃ diviṣadasulabhaṃ labdhavantaḥ krameṇa
nityaṃ yaṃ pūjayanti svasaraṇividhinā kuñcitāṅghriṃ bhaje'ham //176//

12 Shulman, *Songs of the Harsh Devotee*, p. 239.

13 *nirmātṝṇām ghaṭānāṃ kulajaladhimaṇir nīlakaṇṭhābhidho'yaṃ*
paśyan nityaṃ munīnāṃ nayavacanagaṇair yogirātpratyayārtham /
svastrīdaṇḍāgrahastaḥ sarasi saśapathaṃ gāhamānaḥ prapede
tāruṇyaṃ yatprasādāt tam anaṇum aguruṃ kuñcitāṅghriṃ bhaje'ham //298//

14 Vanmikanathan, *Periya Puranam*, p. 379.

15 *bhaktās traiṣaṣṭisaṃkhyā dvijamukhakulajā yatsaparyāviśeṣaiḥ*
sārūpyaṃ yasya nāmnāṃ muhur api paṭhanād yasya sāmīpyasiddhim /
sālokyaṃ yasya bhaktiprakaraṇajanatāsaṅgasambhāṣaṇādyaiḥ
sāyujyaṃ yasya bhāvād anupamam abhajan kuñcitāṅghriṃ bhaje'ham //292//

16 H. W. Schomerus, *Śivaitische Heiligenlegenden*, p. xxx.

17 *Civapirakācam*, verses 83 and 84, ed. and trans. K. Subramania Pillai (Dharmapuram: Dharmapuram Adhinam, 1949), p. 130.

18 *kaś cid vipro riṭākhyaḥ svapatiniyamavidhvaṃsakampātaraṅgāṃ*
nārīṃ dagdhvā satīṃ taccitigatabhasitair lepayan sāmbamūrtim /
naivedyaṃ kartum icchann iha naya carum ity āhvayan yatprasādāt
kāntāṃ bheje nijānte śivapadam api taṃ kuñcitāṅghriṃ bhaje'ham //155//

19 *Skanda Purāṇa, Brahmottara Kāṇḍa* 17.

20 *yogān nirbījasaṃjñāt samuditaparamānandakāṣṭāsamādhi* –
sthityā valmīkagūḍhāṃ tanum avanigatāṃ nītakalpāṃ dharan svām /
śrīmāñ chrīmūlasaṃjño nṛpanutacarito nityaniḥsaṅgavidyo
'py ādyaḥ siddho yam antaḥ kalayati nitarāṃ kuñcitāṅghriṃ bhaje'ham //185//

21 *Śataratnasaṃgraha*, p. 4.

22 Śiva wrote a letter to Umāpati telling him to give final release to the wood-cutter who served his *āśrama*. See chapter 5, n. 33.

23 *yaś śambhur nṛttarān me prabalataramahāmantrasiddhiṃ pradattvā*
gurvīṃ yogasya siddhiṃ jananamṛtaharaṃ cātmabodhaṃ mahāntam /
sūtādināṃ vimuktipradam api mahitagauravaṃ patramūla[ṃ]
svaṃ nṛttaṃ darśayitvā sukhayati nitarāṃ kuñcitāṅghriṃ bhaje'ham //305//

24 Kāraikāl Ammaiyār is, moreover, based in Tiruvalangadu, earlier a rival site to Cidambaram; see below.

25 *Arputa Tiruvantāti* 20, trans. by Kārāvēlane (*Kāraikkālammaiyār Chants dévotionnels tamouls*. Edition and translation by Kārāvēlane. Publication No. 1 of L'Institut Français d'Indologie. New edition. Pondicherry, 1982), p. 26 [my translation from the French].

26 *Arputa Tiruvantāti* 70, trans. by Kārāvēlane, *ibid.*, p.38 [my translation from the French].

27 In verses 15 and 219 Śiva is referred to as *bhrakuṃsa*. Difficult to determine is the extent to which dancing is intrinsically a woman's art. Were it to be seen as essentially feminine in the Indian context, this would link with Śiva's incorporation of Pārvatī within himself.

28 Gaston, *Śiva in Dance, Myth and Iconography*, plate 115, p. 200 ('This female dancer is on the base of the fifty-six pillared hall' i.e. the Nṛtta Sabhā.)

29 Marco Polo, *The Description of the World*, ed. A. C. Moule and Paul Pelliot, 3 vols. (London: George Routledge and Sons, 1938), vol. I, pp. 393f. Is it purely chance that this pose is associated with a quarrel between the God and Goddess?

30 *yatsaṃsatsvarṇabhittiṃ paritar anupamāḥ svarganāryaḥ karābjair*
ādarśādyaṣṭabhadraṃ kanakamaṇimayaṃ yasya tuṣṭyai vahantyaḥ /
sevāṃ kurvanti pañcāvaraṇam adhigatair brahmavidyeśapūrvaiḥ
stutyaṃ taṃ citrakūṭasthitibhir atha suraiḥ kuñcitāṅghriṃ bhaje'ham //291//

The eight auspicious objects are a metal mirror, a full pot, a bull, a pair of chowries, a *śrīvatsam* (here a name for an image of Lakṣmī), a svastika, a conch, and a lamp. The Festival Ritual text describing the ritual for a fire-offering pavilion states that the priest should imagine each of these being held by a particular *apsaras* (pp. 115–19). Thus he must imagine that the mirror is held by Ūrvaśī, the full pot by Menakā and so on. See also Brunner, *Somaśambhupaddhati*, vol. II, p. 331.

Citrakūṭa is the name used by Vaiṣṇavas for Cidambaram.

31 François Gros, *Tēvāram: Hymnes Śivaïtes du Pays Tamoul*, ed. T. V. Gopal Iyer under the direction of François Gros, 2 vols (Pondicherry: Institut Français d'Indologie, 1984, 1985), vol. i, p. xxvii.

32 M. A. Dhaky, 'Bhūtas and Bhūtanāyakas: Elementals and Their Captains' in Michael W. Meister (ed.), *Discourses on Śiva: Proceedings of a Symposium on the Nature of Religious Imagery* (Bombay: Vakils, Feffer & Simons Ltd, 1984), pp. 240–56, p. 252.

33 Dhaky, 'Bhūtas and Bhūtanāyakas', *ibid.*, p. 253.

34 *sṛṣṭyartham brahmaṇā yaḥ stutanijavibhavas tasya lālāṭadeśād*
āvirbhūya svatantro vikṛtatanuvarān rudravargān gaṇendrān /
sṛṣṭvā tān prerayitvā jagadavanavidhau sarvadā sa tv asaṃstho
'rakṣad viśvādhikaṃ taṃ natajanasukhadaṃ kuñcitāṅghriṃ bhaje'ham //228//

35 Dhaky, 'Bhūtas and Bhūtanāyakas', p. 243.

36 Kramrisch, *The Hindu Temple*, p. 344.

37 There is a parallel instance in the *Sūta Saṃhitā*. When the sage Saunaka has seen the dance of Śiva in the Dabhra Sabhā, 'exceedingly happy, he sang hymns with all his might. Through his devotion the great sage was for a period of time in a state of ecstatic possession (*paravaśo bhūtvā*); and again seeing the lord of the Gods, the leader of the Gods, dancing, in his joy, O Brahmans, performed himself the stick-dance (*daṇḍanartana*)' (*Sūta Saṃhitā* 3.9.21–2). Mādhava in his commentary on the *Sūta Saṃhitā* glosses this as *daṇḍapraṇāma*. In the light of the passage from the *Cidambara Māhātmya*, it is likely that Saunaka also dances holding his staff. In this case also, the real sequence of dance followed by trance is inverted.

38 Tiruñāṉacampantar cures a girl afflicted with epilepsy: *maṉṉu perumpiṇiyākum muyalakaṉ vantaṇaivuṟ* (*Periyap. Tiruñāṉ.* 311).

39 Dorai Rangaswamy, *Religion and Philosophy of Tēvāram*, p. 530.

40 *Tēvāram* VII.2.3, trans. Shulman, *Songs of the Harsh Devotee*, p. 8.

41 *Tēvāram*, VI 310, Peterson, *Poems to Śiva*, pp. 131f.

42 A complete list of Cuntarar's references to Rāvaṇa is given by Dorai Rangaswamy, *The Religion and Philosophy of Tēvāram*, pp. 300–3.

43 For the conception of a controlled dancer (Naṭarāja) on top of an uncontrolled, sprawling figure (Apasmāra), compare the up and down in social hierarchy noticed by Gombrich and Obeyesekere apropos the body's temporary takeover by another spirit. 'This kind of ecstasy and enstasis do seem prima facie polar opposites. In possession awareness of the self is obliterated and there is complete dissociation from normal experience, so that the person is afterwards not aware of what has been going on. Enstasis, on the other hand, is supposed to be a condition of control . . . Cultural prestige attaches to enstasis, and . . . traditionally ecstasy, since it is an extreme form of loss of self-control, was condemned and indeed not allowed except for certain practical purposes. Our data show a strong tendency for the lower classes to practice ecstasy, the middle classes to strive for enstasis. But these two forms of escape from normal experience are not easy to differentiate.' Richard Gombrich and Gananath Obeyesekere, *Buddhism Transformed: Religious Change in Sri Lanka* (Princeton University Press, 1988), p. 453.

10 LAST WORDS

1 Coomaraswamy, *Dance of Śiva*, p. 78.

2 *Civapirakācam* verses 83 and 84, trans. K. Subramania Pillai, p. 13.

3 *Mālavikāgnimitra* of Kālidāsa, ed. and trans. R. D. Karmakar (Poona: R. D. Karmarkar, 1937), 1.2, p. 2 [my translation].

4 *Neñcuviṭutu*, verse 25.

5 The kings of Umāpati's own time were Pāṇḍyas, from Madurai, and it was one of them who built the small shrine to the Madurai forms of Śiva and Pārvatī, Sundara and Mīṇākṣī, to the south of the Hundred-pillared Hall.

6 In his *Tirukkōvaiyār* Māṇikkavācakar refers twice to a Pandyan king called Varaguṇa who is probably one of two of that name who lived in the ninth century. For a discussion of the poet's date, see Glenn E. Yocum, *Hymns to the Dancing Śiva: A Study of Māṇikkavācakar's Tiruvācakam* (New Delhi: Heritage, 1982), p. 47.

7 *Tiruviḷaiyāṭaṟpurāṇam* of Parañcōtimuṉivar 61.60–6.

8 *pūrvaṃ jñānopadeśaṃ maṇimayavacase kundavṛkṣasya mūle*
kṛtvā sāditvam āptvā nṛpatikaralasatsvarṇavetraprahāram /
labdhvā tenoktagānair madhurasabharitais tṛptim āptvātha tasmai
muktiṃ prādād ya īśas tam akhilasuhṛdaṃ kuñcitāṅghriṃ bhaje'ham //28//

9 Pope, *The Tiruvaçagam*, p. xxxiii. The *Tirukkōvaiyār* 'is ostensibly an erotic poem, although it has traditionally been interpreted as an allegory of god's love for the soul'. Yocum, *Hymns to the Dancing Śiva*, p. 10. The *Tirukkōvaiyār* was extensively commented on by Pērāciriyar in the thirteenth century, whereas other, more important, parts of the Śaiva canon were not commented upon until modern times.

In the final chapter of the *Tiruvātavūrar Purāṇam*, a biography of Māṇikkavācakar by Kaṭavuḷ Māmuṉivar, probably of the fifteenth century, as summarised by Yocum (*ibid.*, p. 50), Śiva himself is said to have sung, and transcribed, Māṇikkavācakar's poems:

One day, the god himself took the form of a guru and visited him, requesting him to sing all of the hymns which he had composed. This the poet did, while the guru wrote down the entire *Tiruvācakam* and *Tirukkōvaiyār*, disappearing as soon as he had finished. Śiva now assembled the gods and sang Māṇikkavācakar's hymns to them. Then, he took the copy of the hymns, which he had made with his own hands, and placed it at the entrance of the Ampalam so that the whole world would know how Māṇikkavācakar gained salvation. When the text was discovered and the contents read, the devotees went to Māṇikkavācakar and asked him to explain the hymns. There, pointing to the god, he said, 'This One alone is the meaning of this garland of Tamil songs', and at that he disappeared, having united with Śiva.

10 *sambandhaḥ sundaraḥ śrīmaṇimayavacano jihvikārājanāmā*
catvāro 'py ātmagānair vividharasabharaiḥ stotrarūpair yam īśam /
stutvā tattatsthalāntaḥ sthitijuṣam api yaṃ caikam advaitamūrtiṃ
prāpur muktiṃ tam ādyaṃ kṛtavidhumakuṭaṃ kuñcitāṅghriṃ bhaje'ham //43//

11 George W. Spencer, 'The Sacred Geography of the Tamil Shaivite Hymns', *Numen* 17 (1970), pp. 232–44, p. 235.

12 Appar seems to be Umāpati's favourite among the three, for he chooses 64 verses from Appar, as against 23 from Campantar, and 12 from Cuntarar.

13 *āsīn meruḥ śarāso dharaṇir api ratho jyābhavat sarparājo*
'py āstāṃ cakre 'rkasomau sarasijanilayaḥ sārathir yasya śambhoḥ /
āsannāśvāś ca vedā jalanidhiśaradhes traipuraṃ hantum icchor
hetuṃ taṃ lokasṛṣṭisthitilayakaraṇe kuñcitāṅghriṃ bhaje'ham //32//

14 Shulman, *Songs of the Harsh Devotee*, p. 324.

15 *Tēvāram* 7.51.6, trans. Shulman, *ibid.*, p. 321.

16 Appar, *Tēvāram* 6.54.5, trans. by V. A. Devasenapathi, *Tiruarutpayan & Aruṇmuraittiraṭṭi*, with an English rendering (Thanjavur: Tamil University, 1987), p. 50; translation slightly altered.

17 *ekaṃ brahmādvitīyaṃ trividham api caturvāṅmayaṃ pañcabāṇa-*
bhrātṛvyaṃ ṣaḍvipakṣadviṣadabhivinutaṃ saptajihvālikākṣam /
aṣṭamyeṇāṅkacūḍaṃ navarasanaṭanālolavāsodaśāśaṃ
rudraiḥ sādityavargaiḥ satatanatapadaṃ kuñcitāṅghriṃ bhaje'ham //182//

18 *krīḍāsaṃsaktagaurīkanakaghaṭanibhottuṅgavakṣojaśaila-*
prodyacchṛṅgāramādhvīmadhurarasadhunīlolabhṛṅgāyatākṣam /
bhūṣānāgoktasaukhyapravacanaghaṭajastabdhagarvābdhitārkṣya-
vrīḍākṛcchvāsavaktrapramathapatinutaṃ kuñcitāṅghriṃ bhaje'ham //149//

19 *kelyām autsukyabhājā tuhinagirijayā saspṛhaṃ dattavīṭī-*
sevāraktādharoṣṭhadyutijitadinakṛdbālabimbāṃśucakram /
gītīprāvīṇyaśailīprakaṭanakutukād dhastavāstavyalolāṃ
vīṇāṃ saṃvādayantaṃ prathamarasamayaṃ kuñcitāṅghriṃ bhaje'ham //212//

20 *sadvṛttāṃ sragdharāṅgāṃ vipulaguṇavarālaṅkṛtiṃ mañjupāka-*
sthāyīśayyārasādyair vibudhaparibṛḍhāhlādirītiṃ suvṛttim /
vedāntārthaprabodḍhrīṃ suguṇapadagatiṃ yo 'smadīyāṃ stutiṃ tāṃ
aṅgīkurvan sukhaṃ me pradiśati guru taṃ kuñcitāṅghriṃ bhaje'ham //304//

Line b. *sthāyī* for *sthāyi*. Should we read *śayyāsthāyīrasādyair*?

21 *Tantrāloka* 3.262–4. My translation is based on that of Paul Eduardo Muller-Ortega, *The Triadic Heart of Śiva* (Albany: State University of New York Press, 1989), p. 195.

22 *Tantrāloka* 26.63–5, trans. Muller-Ortega, *ibid.*, p. 194.

23 *dhūpair dīpair athākhyaiḥ phaṇipuruṣavṛṣaiḥ kumbhapañcāgnihotrair*
ṛkṣaiḥ karpūrabhasmavyajanavarasitacchatrakaiś cāmaraiś ca /
ādarśair mantrapuṣpair uparitalasukarpūrakaiḥ prārcya yan drāk
tyaktvā'vidyāṃ prapaśyanty anudinam anaghāḥ kuñcitāṅghriṃ bhaje'ham //21//

24 *gavyais tailaiḥ payobhir dadhighṛtamadhubhiḥ śarkarābhiś ca śuddhaiḥ*
paścāt pañcāmṛtādyair likucaphalarasaiḥ kairapāthobhir annaiḥ /
gandhair gaṅgādbhir anyair anudinam anaghā yasya liṅgaṃ munīndrāḥ
ṣaṭkālaṃ pūjayanti prabhum api tam ajaṃ kuñcitāṅghriṃ bhaje'ham //19//

25 *śrāvaṃ śrāvaṃ śrutibhyāṃ yad amalacaritaṃ yatpadāmbhojamādhvīṃ*
pāyaṃ pāyaṃ sabhāyāṃ mama ca rasanayā yaṃ prabhuṃ mānasena /
smāraṃ smāraṃ prasannaṃ śrutiśikharagataṃ bhuktimuktipradaṃ yaṃ
darśaṃ darśaṃ prabuddho 'smy atanubudhadṛśā kuñcitāṅghriṃ bhaje'ham //313//

26 *etat stotraṃ paṭhanti pratidinam asakṛd ye mamomāpater vāg-*
udbhūtaṃ citsabhāyāṃ viracitaparamānandanṛttasya śambhoḥ /
agre labdhvākhileṣṭān iha tanayakalatrādimān ātmayajñād
ante kaivalyasaṃjñaṃ padam api manujāḥ saṃlabhantāṃ nitāntam //

27 *umāpatir nāma vanāśramo 'haṃ trayodaśādhikyaśatatrayānvitam* /
śrīkuñcitāṅghristavarājam uktvā sākṣād apaśyaṃ naṭanaṃ sabhāpateḥ //

Bibliography

Texts in Sanskrit and Tamil are listed under title.

Arulsamy, S., *Saivism: A Perspective of Grace*, New Delhi: Sterling, 1987.

Balasubrahmanyam, S. R., *Early Chola Art*, New York: Asia Publishing House, 1966.

Later Chola Temples: Kulottunga I to Rajendra III, Madras: Mudgala Trust, 1979.

Middle Chola Temples: Rajaraja I to Kulottunga I, Faridabad: Thomson Press (India) Limited, 1975.

'The Oldest Chidambaram Inscriptions', *Journal of Annamalai University* XII/2 & 3 (1943).

Barrett, Douglas, 'The "Chidambaram" Naṭarāja', in *Chhavi 2*, ed. Anand Krishna, Varanasi: Bharat Kalā Bhavan, 1981, pp. 5–20.

Biardeau, M., *Hinduism: The Anthropology of a Civilization*, Delhi: Oxford University Press, 1989.

Brahmāṇḍa Purāṇa (*Brahmāṇḍamahāpurāṇa*), ed. K. V. Sarma (reprint of Bombay Sri Venkateshwar Steam Press edn.), 1983.

Brahmasūtraśāṅkarabhāṣya, ed. J. L. Shastri, Delhi: Motilal Banarsidass, 1980.

Brooks, Douglas Renfrew, *Auspicious Wisdom: The Texts and Traditions of Śrīvidyā Śākta Tantrism in South India*, Albany: State University of New York Press, 1992.

Brunner, Hélène, 'Le *sādhaka*, personnage oublié du Śivaisme du sud', *Journal Asiatique* 263 (1975), pp. 411–43.

'Le Śaiva-siddhāntam, "Essence" du Veda', *Indologica Taurinensia* 8 (1980–1), pp. 51–66.

'The Four Pādas of Śaivāgamas', *Journal of Oriental Research*, Dr S. S. Janaki Felicitation Volume, LVI–LXII (1986–92), pp. 260–78.

'The Place of Yoga in Śaivāgamas' in P.-S. Filliozat *et al.*, *Pandit N. R. Bhatt Felicitation Volume*, Delhi: Motilal Banarsidass, 1994, pp. 425–61.

Brunner-Lachaux, Hélène, *Mṛgendrāgama: Section des rites et section du comportement, avec le Vṛtti de Bhaṭṭanārāyaṇakaṇṭha*, translation, introduction and notes, Pondicherry: Institut Français d'Indologie, 1985.

Capra, Fritjof, *The Tao of Physics:An Exploration of the Parallels between Modern Physics and Eastern Mysticism*, London: Fontana, 1976.

Chamu, S. V., *The Divine Dancer*, Mysore: Astanga Yoga Vijnana Mandiram, 1982.

Cidambarakṣetrasarvasva: Patañjalipūjāsūtra, Cidambareśvaraśrīnaṭarāja-devālayasthadevatā-

stotra, *Sūtasaṃhitāsaṃgraha*, *Patañjalipūjāsūtravivaraṇa*, *Patañjalyaṣṭottaraśatanāma*, ed. Somasetu Dīkṣita, Kadavasal: Sri Meenakshi Press, 1977.

Cidambara Māhātmya, ed. Somasekhara Dikshitar, Kadavasal: Sri Meenakshi Press, 1971.

Citsabheśotsavasūtra, *Cidambarakṣetrasarvasva*, vol. II, ed. Somasetu Dīkṣita, Chidambaram: M. S. Trust, 1982.

Civapirakācam (*Sivaprakasam*), ed. and trans. K. Subramania Pillai, Dharmapuram: Dharmapuram Adhinam, 1949.

Coomaraswamy, A. K., *The Dance of Śiva*, New York: The Noonday Press, 1957.

Dakṣa Khaṇḍa of the *Śaṅkarasaṃhitā*, *adhyāya*s 13 and 14, transcript by Ramalinga Dikshitar.

Davis, Richard H., *Ritual in an Oscillating Universe*, Princeton University Press, 1991.

Dessigane, R., Pattabiramin, P. Z, and Filliozat, Jean, *Les Légendes Çivaïtes de Kāñcipuram*, Pondicherry: Institut Français d'Indologie, 1964.

Dessigane, R. and Pattabiramin, P. Z., *La Légende de Skanda*, Pondicherry: Institut Français d'Indologie, 1967.

De Zoete, Beryl, *The Other Mind*, London: Victor Gollancz, 1953.

Dhaky, M. A., 'Bhūtas and Bhūtanāyakas: Elementals and Their Captains' in Michael W. Meister (ed.), *Discourses on Śiva: Proceedings of a Symposium on the Nature of Religious Imagery* (Bombay: Vakils, Feffer & Simons Ltd., 1984), pp. 240–56.

Dhavamony, Mariasusai, *Love of God According to Śaiva Siddhānta*, Oxford: Clarendon Press, 1971.

Diehl, Carl Gustav, *Instrument and Purpose*, Lund: CWK Gleerup, 1956.

Dorai Rangaswamy, M. A., *The Religion and Philosophy of Tēvāram*, 4 vols., University of Madras, 1958.

Fergusson, James, *History of Architecture: Indian and Eastern Architecture*, 2 vols., vol. I London: John Murray, 1876; vol. II, New York: Dodd, Mead and Co., 1891.

Ganesh, K., *Boundary Walls: Caste and Women in a Tamil Community*, Delhi: Hindusthan, 1993.

Gaston, Anne-Marie, *Śiva in Dance, Myth and Iconography*, Delhi: Oxford University Press, 1982.

Gombrich, Richard and Obeyesekere, Gananath, *Buddhism Transformed: Religious Change in Sri Lanka*, Princeton University Press, 1988.

Gonda, Jan, *Medieval Religious Literature in Sanskrit*, A History of Indian Literature, vol. II, Wiesbaden, 1977.

Graefe, W., 'Legends as Mile-Stones in the History of Tamil Literature'. *P. K. Gode Commemoration Volume*, Poona, 1960, vol. II, pp. 129–46.

Handiqui, K. K., *Naiṣadhacarita of Śrīharṣa*, Poona: Deccan College, 1965.

Hardy, F., *Viraha-Bhakti: The Early History of Kṛṣṇa Devotion in South India*, Delhi: Oxford University Press, 1983.

Harle, J. C., *Temple Gateways in South India: The Architecture and Iconography of the Cidambaram Gopuras*, Oxford: Bruno Cassirer, 1963.

The Art and Architecture of the Indian Subcontinent, Harmondsworth: Penguin, 1986.

Hazra, R. C., *Studies in the Purāṇic Records*, Delhi: Motilal Banarsidass, 1973.

Hemasabhānātha Māhātmya, Adyar Library MS TR775. G2020.

Hiltebeitel, Alf, 'Draupadī's Two Guardians: The Buffalo King and the Muslim Devotee', in Alf Hiltebeitel (ed.), *Criminal Gods and Demon Devotees*, Albany: State University of New York Press, 1989, pp. 339–71.

Hoisington, Henry R., '*Siva-pirakāsam*. Light of Sivam. A Metaphysical and Theological Treatise', *Journal of the American Oriental Society*, IV/2 (1854), pp. 127–244.

'*Tattuva-kaṭṭaḷei*. A Synopsis of the Mystical Philosophy of the Hindus', *Journal of the American Oriental Society* IV, (1853–4), pp. 3–30.

Hume, Robert Ernest, *The Thirteen Principal Upanishads*, London: Oxford University Press, 2nd ed. 1931.

Huntington, Susan L., *The Art of Ancient India*, New York/Tokyo: Weatherhill, 1985.

Ingalls, D. H. H., *An Anthology of Sanskrit Court Poetry*, Harvard Oriental Series vol. 44, Cambridge, Mass.: Harvard University Press, 1965.

Janaki, S. S., '*Dhvaja-stambha*: Critical account of its Structural and Ritualistic details', in S. S. Janaki (ed.), *Śiva Temple and Temple Rituals*, Madras: Kuppuswami Sastri Research Institute, 1988, pp. 122–93.

Jaswant Raj, J., *Grace in the Śaiva Siddhāntam and in St. Paul*, Madras: South Indian Salesian Society, 1989.

Kane, P. V., *History of Dharmaśāstra*, 5 vols., Pune: Bhandarkar Oriental Research Institute, 1958.

Kāraikkālammaiyār Chants dévotionnels tamouls. Edition and translation by Kārāvēlane. Publication No. 1 of Institut Français d'Indologie. New edition. Pondicherry, 1982.

Kashikar, C. G. and Parpola, Asko, 'Śrauta Traditions in Recent Times', in F. Staal (ed.), *Agni*, Berkeley: Asian Humanities Press, 1983.

Khanna, Madhu, 'The Concept and Liturgy of the Śrīcakra based on Śivānanda's Trilogy', unpublished DPhil thesis, University of Oxford, 1986.

Knipe, David M., 'Night of the Growing Dead', in Alf Hiltebeitel (ed.), *Criminal Gods and Demon Devotees*, Albany: State University of New York Press, 1989, pp. 123–56.

Kōyil Purāṇam of Umāpaticivācāriyar, ed. Kāñcipuram Capāpati Mutaliyār, Madras, 1867.

Kramrisch, Stella, *The Hindu Temple*, 2 vols., University of Calcutta, 1946.

The Presence of Śiva, Princeton University Press, 1981.

'Space in Indian Cosmogony and in Architecture' in Kapila Vatsyayan (ed.), *Concepts of Space Ancient and Modern*, New Delhi: Indira Gandhi National Centre for the Arts/Abhinav Publications, 1991, pp. 101–4.

Krishna, Anand, (ed.), *Chhavi–2*, Rai Krishna Dasa Felicitation Volume, Varanasi: Bharat Kalā Bhavan, 1981.

Kriyākramadyotikā of Aghoraśiva with the commentary of Nirmalamaṇi, ed. Karunkulam Krishna Sastri and Polagam Srirama Sastri, Cidambaram: Jñānasambandham Press, 1927.

Kulke, Hermann, *Cidambaramāhātmya: Eine Untersuchung der religionsgeschichtlichen und historischen Hintergründe für die Entstehung der Tradition einer südindischen Tempelstadt* (Freiburger Beiträge zur Indologie vol. 3), Wiesbaden: Otto Harrassowitz, 1970.

Kuñcitāṅghristava of Umāpati Śivācārya, ed. with a Tamil translation and notes by K. M. Rājagaṇeśa Dīkṣita (K. Mī. Rājakaṇēca Tīkṣitar), Cidambaram: Kirāsvēṭu Piras, 1958.

Kūrma Purāṇa ed. Rāmaśaṃkarabhaṭṭācārya, Varanasi: Indological Book House, 1967.

Lalitāsahasranāma with the *Saubhāgyabhāskara* commentary of Bhāskararāya Bombay, Nirnaya-sagar Press, 1914.

L'Hernault, F., *et al.*, *Darasuram*, 2 vols., Paris: École Française d'Extrême-Orient, (Mémoire Archéologique XVI), 1987.

Liṅga Purāṇa with *Śivatoṣiṇīṭīkā* of Gaṇeśa Nātu, ed. J. L. Shastri, Delhi: Motilal Banarsidass, n.d.

Lorenzen, David N., *The Kāpālikas and Kālāmukhas*, New Delhi, 1972.

Loud, John Alden, 'The Diksitars of Chidambaram: A Community of Ritual Specialists in a South Indian Temple (India)', unpublished PhD thesis, University of Wisconsin, Madison, 1990.

with A. Anandanataraja Dikshitar and K. Paramasivam, 'A Translation of *Koyil Puranam* of Umapati Civacariyar', unpublished typescript. n.d.

Mahārthamañjarī of Maheśvarānanda, with his commentary *Parimala*, ed. V. Dviveda, Yogatantra-Granthamālā 5, Varanasi: Varanaseya Sanskrit Vishvavidyalaya, 1972.

Mālavikāgnimitra of Kālidāsa, ed. and trans. R. D. Karmakar, Poona: R. D. Karmarkar, 1937.

Mataṅgapārameśvarāgama (Vidyāpāda) with the commentary of Bhaṭṭa Rāmakaṇṭha, ed. N. R. Bhatt, Publ. IFI No. 56, Pondicherry, 1977.

Matthews, Gordon, *Śiva-Ñāna-Bōdham*, A Manual of Śaiva Religious Doctrine. Trans. from the Tamil, London: Oxford University Press, 1948.

Meister, Michael W., 'The Hindu Temple: Axis of Access' in Kapila Vatsyayan (ed.), *Concepts of Space Ancient and Modern*, New Delhi: Indira Gandhi National Centre for the Arts/Abhinav Publications, 1991, pp. 268–80.

Meyyapan, S. *Chidambaram Golden Temple* trans. S. Leela, Chidambaram: Manivasagar Pathippakam, 1987; 2nd edn., Madras, 1992.

Mṛgendrāgama (*Kriyāpāda et Caryāpāda*), ed. N. R. Bhatt, Pondicherry: Institut Français d'Indologie, 1962.

Muller-Ortega, Paul Eduardo, *The Triadic Heart of Śiva*, Albany: State University of New York Press, 1989.

Murugesa Mudaliar, N., '*Sankarpa-Nirakaranam*, Translation and Commentary', *Śaiva Siddhānta* 3 (1968), and subsequent issues.

Nagaswamy, R., 'Ādavallān and Dakṣiṇameruviṭaṅkar of the Tanjore Temple', *Lalit Kalā*, 12 (1962), pp. 36–8.

'Chidambaram Bronzes', *Lalit Kalā* 9 (1979), pp. 9–16.

Śiva-Bhakti, New Delhi: Navrang, 1989.

Tantric Cult of South India, Delhi: Navrang, 1982.

Naidu, B. V. N. *et al.*, *Tāṇḍava Lakṣaṇam or The Fundamentals of Ancient Indian Dancing*, Madras, 1936.

Nallaswami Pillai, J. M., *Sivajñāna Siddhiyar of Aruḷnandi Sivāchārya* translated into English, Madras, 1913.

Tiruvarutpayaṉ: Commentary and English Translation, 2nd edn, Dharmapuram: Dharmapuram Adhinam, 1958.

Natarajan, B., *The City of the Cosmic Dance: Chidambaram*, New Delhi: Orient Longman, 1974.

Tillai and Nataraja, Madras: Mudgala Trust, 1994

Nilakanta Sastri, K. A., *A History of South India from Prehistoric Times to the Fall of Vijayanagar*, 3rd edn., London: Oxford University Press, 1966.

The Cōḷas, 2nd edn., 2 vols. Madras University Historical Series. University of Madras, 1955.

Pandya, Shveni, *A Study of the Technique of Abhinaya in Relation to Sanskrit Drama* Bombay: Somaiya Publications, 1988.

Pārthavana Māhātmya (from the *Cidambarasāra*), in *Pauṣkarāgama* (*Jñānapāda*) with the *Bhāṣya* of Umāpati Śivācārya, Tamil introduction by Ambalavana Navalar, Cidambaram, 1925, pp.9–16.

Patañjalipūjāsūtra see *Cidambarakṣetrasarvasva.*

Pattabiramin, P. Z., 'Notes d'iconographie dravidienne', *Arts Asiatiques* VI (1959), pp. 13–22.

Pauṣkarāgama (*Jñānapāda*) with the *Bhāṣya* of Umāpati Śivācārya, Tamil introduction by Ambalavana Navalar, Cidambaram, 1925.

Peterson, Indira Viswanathan, *Poems to Śiva: the Hymns of the Tamil Saints,* Princeton University Press, 1989.

Polo, Marco, *The Description of the World*, ed. A. C. Moule and Paul Pelliot, 3 vols. London: George Routledge and Sons, 1938.

Pope, G. U., *The Tiruvaçagam*, Oxford: Clarendon Press, 1900.

Pressler, Franklin A., *Religion under Bureaucracy: Policy and Administration for Hindu Temples in South India,* Cambridge University Press, 1987.

Puṇḍarīkapura Māhātmya, Adyar Library MS 75253.

Purchas, Samuel, *Hakluytus Posthumus or Purchas His Pilgrimes*, vol. x, Glasgow: James MacLehose, 1905.

Raghavan, V., 'The *Sūta Saṃhitā*', *Annals of the Bhandarkar Oriental Research Institute,* XXII (1941), pp. 236–53.

Rājendrapura Māhātmya of Śivānandanātha Dīkṣita, in *Pauṣkarāgama* (*Jñānapāda*) with the *Bhāṣya* of Umāpati Śivācārya, Tamil introduction by Ambalavana Navalar, Cidambaram, 1925, pp. 17–28.

Ramachandran, T. N., '*Neñju Vidu Thoothu* (Message through the Heart)', *Śaiva Siddhānta*, XI/3 and 4 (1976), pp. 101–6; 131–5.

Periya Puranam Part I, Tanjavur: Tamil University, 1990.

'*Poorip Phahrotai* (Multiple Hymn of Praise)', *Śaiva Siddhānta*, XII/3 (1977), pp. 100–8.

'*Sivaprakasam* of Saint Umapathi Devanayanar', *Śaiva Siddhānta* 12 (1977) and subsequent issues.

Ramalinga Dikshitar, T., 'A Study of Chidambaram and its Shrine as Recorded in Sanskrit Literature', unpublished MLitt thesis, Annamalai University, 1963.

Raman, K. V., 'Gopura Sculptures from Vriddhagirisvara Temple', in *Śrīnidhiḥ: Shri K. R. Srinivasan Festschrift*, ed. K. V. Raman *et al.*, Madras: New Era Publications, 1983, pp. 203–12.

Rao, T. A. Gopinath, *Elements of Hindu Iconography*, Madras: Law Printing House, 2 vols. in 4, 1914–16.

Reiniche, Marie-Louise, *La Configuration du Temple Hindou*, vol. IV of *Tiruvannamalai: un lieu saint śivaïte du sud de l'inde*, Paris: École Française d'Extrême-Orient, 1989.

Sanderson, A. 'The Doctrine of the *Mālinīvijayottaratantra*' in *Ritual and Speculation in Early Tantrism: Studies in Honor of André Padoux*, ed. T. Goudriaan, Albany: State University of New York Press, 1992, pp. 283–312.

'Meaning in Tantric Ritual', unpublished typescript.

'The Visualization of the Deities of the Trika', in André Padoux (ed.), *L'Image Divine: Culte et Méditation dans l'Hindouisme*, Paris: Centre National de la Recherche Scientifique, 1990, pp. 31–88.

Sastri, H. Krishna, *South Indian Images of Gods and Goddesses*, Madras Government Press, 1916.

Śataratnasaṃgraha, ed. A. Sundareśa Śivācārya, Tanjore Sarasvatimahal Library Publication no. 257, Tanjavur: Tanjore Sarasvatimahal Library, 1976.

Satyamurti, T., *The Nataraja Temple: History, Art and Architecture*, New Delhi: Classical Publications, 1978.

Schomerus, H. W., *Der Śaiva-Siddhānta: Eine Mystik Indiens*, Leipzig, 1912.

Śivaistische Heiligenlegende (Periyapurāṇa und Tiruvātavūrar-Purāṇa), Jena: Eugen Diederichs, 1925.

Shulman, David Dean, 'The Mythology of the Tamil Talapuranam', unpublished PhD thesis, London University, 1976.

Songs of the Harsh Devotee: The Tēvāram of Cuntaramūrttināyaṉār, translated and annotated, Philadelphia: Department of South Asia Regional Studies, University of Philadelphia, 1990.

Tamil Temple Myths: Sacrifice and Divine Marriage in the South Indian Śaiva Tradition, Princeton University Press, 1980.

Siddalingaiah, T. B., *Origin and Development of Saiva Siddhanta up to 14th Century*, Madurai Kamaraj University, 1979.

Siegel, Lee, *Net of Magic: Wonders and Deceptions in India*, University of Chicago Press, 1991.

Śiva Purāṇa (*Śivamahāpurāṇa*), Delhi: Nag Publishers, 1986.

Sivaramamurti, C., *Kalugumalai and Early Pandyan Rock-Cut Shrines* (Heritage of Indian Art Series, no. 3), Bombay: N. M. Tripathi Private Ltd, 1961.

Naṭarāja in Art, Thought, and Literature, New Delhi: National Museum, 1974.

Sivaraman, K., *Śaivism in Philosophical Perspective*, Delhi: Motilal Banarsidass, 1973.

Skanda Purāṇa (*Skandamahāpurāṇa*), Delhi: Nag Publishers, 1986–9.

Smith, David, 'The Dance of Śiva', in *Perspectives on Indian Religion*, ed. P. Connolly, Delhi: Sri Satguru Publications, 1986, pp. 87–98.

Ratnākara's Haravijaya: An Introduction to the Sanskrit Court Epic, Delhi: Oxford University Press, 1985.

Somaśambhupaddhati, text, translation and notes by Hélène Brunner-Lachaux, 3 vols., Pondicherry: Institut Français d'Indologie, 1963, 1968, 1977.

Somasethu Dikshitar (ed.), *The History of Chidambaram: Sri Nataraja's Temple* (*A Guide to Sri Nataraja Temple*), Part I, Legends, History and Architecture by T. Satyamurthy; Part II, Descriptions of Shrines by Somasekhara Dikshitendra (translated by R. Sasikala), Chidambaram: S. Somaraja Dikshitar, 1987.

Somasundaram Pillai, J. M., *Siva-Nataraja – the Cosmic Dance in Chid-Ambaram*, Annamalainagar: Annamalai University, 1970.

The University's Environs: Cultural and Historical (A Silver Jubilee Souvenir of the Annamalai University), 4th impr., Annamalainagar: Annamalai University, 1963.

Spencer, George W., 'The Sacred Geography of the Tamil Shaivite Hymns', *Numen* 17 (1970), pp. 232–44.

Srinivasin, K. R., *The Dharmarāja Ratha and its Sculptures*, New Delhi: Abhinav Publications, 1975.

Srinivasan, P. R., 'Important Works of Art of the Early Chōḷa Period from Near Tanjore', *Transactions of the Archaeological Society of South India*, (1956–7), pp. 36–52.

Sudanthiran, V.,'*Adhiṣṭhānas* of the Various Structures of the Naṭarāja Temple at Chidambaram', *Tamil Civilization*, 6/1–2, 1988, pp. 53–70.

Surdam, W. 'The Vedicization of Śaiva Ritual', in S. S. Janaki (ed.), *Śiva Temple and Temple Rituals*, Madras: Kuppuswami Sastri Research Institute, 1988, pp. 52–63.

Sūtasaṃhitā with commentary of Mādhava, ed. S. Ramachandra Sastri and K. Kuppuswamy Sastri, Madras: Sarada Mandiram, 1916.

Svāyambhuvasūtrasaṃgraha, *Le Tantra Svayaṃbhū*, *Vidyāpāda*, *avec le commentaire de Sadyojyoti*, ed. and trans. P. -S. Filliozat, Geneva: Droz, 1991.

Suryanarayana Sastri, S. S., *The Śivādvaita of Śrīkaṇṭha*, University of Madras, 1972, first published 1930.

Swaminathan, S. 'Haradattar', *Śaiva Siddhānta* xv (1980), pp. 17–25.

Swamy, B. G. L., *Chidambaram and Naṭarāja: Problems and Rationalization*, Mysore: Geetha Book House, 1979.

Tantrāloka of Abhinavagupta, ed. Mukunda Rāma and Madhusūdana Kaul, Srinagar: Research Department, Jammu and Kashmir Government, 1918–38.

Tēvāram: Hymnes Śivaïtes du Pays Tamoul, ed. T. V. Gopal Iyer under the direction of François Gros, 2 vols., Pondicherry: Institut Français d'Indologie, 1984, 1985.

Tēvāra Aruḷmuṟaittiraṭṭu of Umāpati Śivam, see *Tiruarutpayan & Aruṇmuraittiraṭṭi*.

Thomas, Isaac Job, 'Painting in Tamil Nadu A. D. 1350–1650', unpublished PhD thesis, University of Michigan, 1979.

Tilvāranya Māhātmya, Adyar Library MS no. 73804.

Tiruarutpayan & Aruṇmuraittiraṭṭi, ed. with an English rendering by V. A. Devasenapathi, Thanjavur: Tamil University, 1987.

Tirumantiram of Tirumūlar, Tamil text with English translation and notes by B. Natarajan, Madras: Sri Ramakrishna Math, 1991.

Umāpatiśivācāryacaritrasaṃgraha of Cidambarabrahmayativarya, in *Kuñcitāṅghristava* of Umāpati Śivācārya, ed. with a Tamil translation and notes by K. M. Rājagaṇeśa Dīkṣita (K. Mī. Rājakaṇēca Tīkṣitar), Cidambaram: Kirāsvēṭu Piras, 1958, preface pp. 3–6.

Uṇmaiviḷakkam, Tamil text, and trans. by J. M. Nallaswami Pillai, Dharmapuram, 1946.

Uṇmai Vilakkam: The Exposition of Truth, Tamil text, trans. with notes and index by C. N. Singaravelu, Tellipazhi, 1981.

Vanmikanathan, G., *Pathway to God through the Thiruvaachakam* (Sri Kasi Mutt Publication New Series, no. 4), Thiruppanandal: Sri Kasi Mutt, 1980.

Periya Puranam by Sekkizhar, condensed English version, Madras: Sri Ramakrishna Math, 1985.

Van Troy, J., 'The Social Structure of the Śaiva-siddhāntika Ascetics (700–1300 A.D.)', *Indica* 11 (1974), pp. 77–86.

Vatsyayan, Kapila, *Classical Indian Dance in Literature and the Arts*, New Delhi: Sangeet Natak Akademi, 1968.

Venkataraman, R. *Rājarājeśvaram, The Pinnacle of Chola Art*, Madras: Mudgala Trust, 1985.

Vyāghrapura Māhātmya, Adyar Library MS 771.

Yocum, Glenn E., *Hymns to the Dancing Śiva: A Study of Māṇikkavācakar's Tiruvācakam*, New Delhi: Heritage, 1982.

Index and glossary

Abhinavagupta, 236–7
abhiṣeka ('consecration by anointing or inundating'), 35, 73, 75–6
ācāryābhiṣeka ('initiation as *ācārya*'), 113
Acyutadeva Rāya, 44, 57
adhiṣṭhāna ('base of a temple'), 91, 258 n. 27
adhyātmayoga ('spiritual' – yoga), 106
Ādiśaṅkara, *see* Śaṅkarācārya
Ādiśaiva caste, 58
Ādiśeṣa, *see* Śeṣa
Advaita, 103, 121–4, 132
Āgamas, 58, 62, 64, 93, 106, 109, 116–20, 131, 215
Agastya, 215
Aghora Śivācārya, 109, 112–13
agnihotra ('fire-oblation'), 70, 77
ākāśa ('ether', 'space'), 81, 84, 233
ākāśa liṅga, Liṅga of Space, 84, 241 n. 8
Akṣapāda, 62
Ambā, 44, 97
Anāhata *cakra*, 83
ānandatāṇḍava, Ānanda Tāṇḍava, *see* Dance of Bliss
Ānandatāṇḍavavilāsastotra, 190
āṇavamala, Āṇava Mala, 110, 113, 122
Andhaka, 198, 200
Āndhra Bhāratamu, 41
añjali (gesture of respect and salutation, with the two palms joined and raised), 13, 86, 112, 209
anklet, 18, 171, 182, 226
Antaka, 198
Antarvedi, 34–6, 69
anugraha ('grace'), 17
Apasmāra, 8, 15, 23, 25, 30, 177, 223, 225–6
Appar, 94, 100, 164, 201, 215, 226, 231, 233, 234
ardhamaṇḍapa ('a hall adjoining a shrine'), 56
Arjuna, 121, 134, 200
Arputa Tiruvantāti, 217
artha ('material advantage'), 17
Ārudra Darśana, 76
Aruḷnanti, 116, 122
Aruṇa, 51
Aruṇācala, 83
Aruṇagiri, 143
āśrama ('hermitage'), 8, 171
Astradeva, 95
aṭiyāṉ ('slave', 'devotee'), 15
ātman, 107–8, 122
Ātmārthapūjā, ('worship for oneself'), 18
aṭṭavīraṭṭāṉam (shrines of Śiva's eight heroic deeds), 186
avatāra, 7, 126, 158, 192

bali ('offering of grain or rice'), 74–5
Balināyaka, 89
balipīṭha ('pedestal for offerings'), 74–5, 132
Bāṇa, 19, 223
bāṇaliṅga ('pebble' *liṅga*), 113
Barrett, Douglas 12, 14
Baṭukarāja, 191
betel, 140, 213, 235
Bhaṇḍa, 158
Bhadrakālī, 145, 148–51
Bhaga, 146, 187
Bhāgavata Purāṇa, 265 n. 42
Bhairava, 7, 54, 186, 188–91, 195–7, 237
Bhairava tantras, 186
Bhānukampa, 20
Bhāskararāya, 158
Bhaṭṭa Rāmakaṇṭha, 116
Bhaṭṭa Nārāyaṇakaṭha, 119
Bhava, Śiva, 128, 146, 187
Bhavānī, Pārvatī, 146, 158, 160
Bhikṣāṭana, 43, 79, 139, 161, 163–4, 166, 175, 186, 190, 197
bhoga ('enjoyment'), 191, 234
Bhṛṅgin, 22–4, 244 n. 34
Bhūmi, 33
Bhuṣuṇḍa, 133
bhūta ('creature'), 15, 23, 25, 30, 54, 78, 107, 170, 177, 183